Palgrave Insights into Apocalypse Economics

Series Editor
Richard Westra
Centre for Macau Studies
University of Macau
Macau, China

This series is set to become the lodestone for critical Marxist and related Left scholarship on the raft of apocalyptic tendencies enveloping the global economy and society. Its working premise is that neoliberal policies from the 1980s not only failed to rejuvenate capitalist prosperity lost with the demise of the post-Second World War 'golden age' economy but in fact have generated a widening spectrum of pathologies that threaten humanity itself. At the most fundamental level the series cultivates state of the art critical political economic analysis of the crises, recessionary, deflationary and austerity conditions that have beset the world economy since the global meltdown of 2008–2009. However, though centered on work that critically explores global propensities for devastating financial convulsions, ever-widening inequalities and economic marginalisation due to information technologies, robotised production and low wage outsourcing, it seeks to draw on exacerbating factors such as climate change and global environmental despoliation, corrupted food systems and land-grabbing, rampant militarism, cyber crime and terrorism, all together which defy mainstream economics and conventional political policy solutions.

For critical Marxist and related Left scholars the series offers a non-sectarian outlet for academic work that is hard-hitting, inter/trans-disciplinary and multiperspectival. Its readership draws in academics, researchers, students, progressive governmental and non-governmental actors and the academically-informed public.

More information about this series at
http://www.palgrave.com/gp/series/15867

Birsen Filip

The Rise of Neo-liberalism and the Decline of Freedom

palgrave
macmillan

Birsen Filip
Ottawa, ON, Canada

ISSN 2523-8108 ISSN 2523-8116 (electronic)
Palgrave Insights into Apocalypse Economics
ISBN 978-3-030-61622-9 ISBN 978-3-030-61623-6 (eBook)
https://doi.org/10.1007/978-3-030-61623-6

Cover illustration: Dina Belenko / Alamy Stock Photo

This Palgrave Macmillan imprint is published by the registered company Springer Nature Switzerland AG.
The registered company address is: Gewerbestrasse 11, 6330 Cham, Switzerland

Contents

CHAPTER 1

Introduction

Over the last four decades, the neo-liberal[1] school of economic thought rose in prominence en route to achieving its current status of dominance. During that time, the world has effectively become the sum of many neo-liberal societies that have adopted single systems of beliefs, reasoning, thinking, lifestyles, practices, goals, technologies, institutions, etc. Throughout human history, no other ideology, school of thought, political, religious or military institution, kingdom, or empire has ever experienced such success in terms of shaping people's ideals, goals, and values on a global scale. However, this acceptance of a single belief system and uniform ways of thinking and behaving in a vast number of domains and activities, even when there is no monetary and material gain involved, is dangerous, because it neglects the importance of alternative beliefs, ideas, values, and goals. It also diminishes the roles of the particular historical development of societies, critical thinking, and moral and ethical reasoning.

The dominant position of neo-liberalism as the leading program of economic research has led to its theorists and adherents ignoring its limitations, while also being unaware of, or disinterested in, other economic schools of thought that existed throughout the history of economics.

[1] The following terms are used interchangeably: neo-liberalism, the neo-liberal school of economic thought, the neo-liberal economic program of research, neo-liberal paradigm, free-market system, and free-market capitalism.

B. Filip, *The Rise of Neo-liberalism and the Decline of Freedom*,
Palgrave Insights into Apocalypse Economics,
https://doi.org/10.1007/978-3-030-61623-6_1

Accordingly, they have advocated for treating different areas of life as though they are business transactions, meaning that choices are to be made based on the economic efficiency and economic benefits they generate, instead of factors like traditions, customs, habits, ethical and moral values, compassion, sympathy, convictions, etc. The application of the neo-liberal economic approach, or economic reasoning in a narrower sense, to different aspects of human life has drastically impacted societies by transforming the nature of relationships between individuals, as well as the ways in which people interact with their surroundings, including other species. Consequently, societies around the world have been faced with an increasing number of similar problems and issues, including social and economic inequality, the unprecedented exploitation of people and natural resources, a biodiversity crisis, the destruction of rainforests and oceans, threats of electromagnetic radiation, corruption, climate change, etc. This combination of factors, among others, has led many scientists to speculate whether humanity, and many of the species it shares the planet with, have any future at all.

Neo-liberalism first began to noticeably thrive in the 1970s, when the Vietnam War and the 1973 oil crisis led to stagnation (i.e. inflation, rising unemployment, deep recession, etc.) in Western economies, to the extent that questions were raised about the reliability of Keynesian economics. Up to that point, Keynesian economics was the leading program of research within the discipline of economics and in the development of state policies, a status that it attained immediately following the Great Depression. Subsequently, neo-liberal economic views began to gain prominence with a focus on restructuring the economic system and implementing new reforms and policies. The implementation of neo-liberal reforms and policies reached its first peak in the 1980s, during the Reagan-Thatcher Era. Technological, institutional, social, political, economic and cultural practices started to change considerably during that time, and have continued to do so ever since.

Since the 1980s, elite economists at leading universities, academic journals, major graduate research institutions, important international and local organizations, and democratically elected governments have focused their efforts on the study, application and promotion of neo-liberal economic principles, approach, models, reforms and policies. However, the official triumph of neo-liberal economics over all other systems was not solidified until the sudden collapse of the Soviet Union in 1991. Subsequently, the world experienced radical changes in terms of the understanding and definition of man, the goals and nature of society and its institutions, and the role of the state. In other words, neo-liberal economics has very subtly and systematically influenced virtually every aspect of society by transforming everything into something calculable and exchangeable, much like a commodity or service in the market place. In fact, since the 1980s, all areas of social and political life, enterprises, governments, interest groups, associations, universities, institutions, technology, the arts, scientific research, and modern systems of justice and administration, have been implementing the principles of neo-liberal economics within their fields. However, this widespread adoption of neo-liberal values, principles and views in every aspect of life, to the point of domination, could be described as an era of intellectual and moral bankruptcy. Consequently, people have been unable to lead free, meaningful, and autonomous lives based on their own will, thoughts, reasoning, values, convictions and conscience; instead, they determine their goals and ends according to the prescriptions and values of neo-liberal economics, which were originally developed for the marketplace.

Despite the fact that neo-liberal economists frequently claim that economics is a branch of the natural sciences, their sophisticated and abstract mathematical models did not allow them to recognize the warning signs of the impending financial crisis and global recession in 2008, nor did it enable them to provide effective solutions in their aftermath. Consequently, a number of studies have been published that not only emphasized the severity of the economic crisis, but also accentuated the role that neo-liberal economics played in facilitating its onset. In particular, heterodox economists believe that neo-liberal economics is fundamentally flawed in its present form and, as such, advocate for significant changes or the emergence of a new paradigm. Most of the critiques put forth by this segment of economists revolve around the fundamental assumptions and methodological monism within the discipline of economics. Additionally, some of them focused their criticisms on the extensive application of highly sophisticated mathematical models on the part of neo-liberal economists. Unfortunately, this important body of work did not receive the respect and attention it warranted, because neo-liberal economists generally exhibit a hostile attitude towards any work criticizing their fundamental assumptions, methodology, and models. This is a consequence of neo-liberal economists having a monistic approach[2] to the discipline of economics, whereby they view their paradigm as infallible and rigorous, much like a paradigm of the natural sciences. Actually, this represents a clear point of contrast between economic and the natural sciences. Unlike neo-liberals who are intolerant of dissent, similar to defenders of dominant ideologies or ruling elite classes, practitioners of the natural sciences are welcoming of alternative views and new ideas, and do not consider existing paradigms to be infallible. Scientists are perfectly willing to abandon old paradigms when the evidence proves that a new one has emerged.

Therefore, neo-liberal economists represent the main obstacle to the emergence of alternative programs of research within the discipline of economics.

Since they do not envisage any defects within their program of research, neo-liberal economists are able to systematically dismiss the critiques put forth by their heterodox counterparts, reject the necessity of a paradigm change,[3] and ignore warning signs that neo-liberal economics is the origin of many disastrous global problems. They simply glorify the positive outcomes associated with their models, while disregarding any destructive results. That means neo-liberal economists are generally more focused on sustaining the status quo as opposed to addressing negative outcomes in order to improve their program of research. Furthermore, even on the rare occasions that they do acknowledge that negative outcomes may have emerged following the implementation of their models and policies, they

[2] Neo-classical economists reject the notion that there is a methodological monism in the discipline of economics. Instead, they hold the belief that there are important changes and variety in their domain and that their ideas are evolving. For example, they argue that one of the important recent evolutions in the discipline of economics was plurality in orthodox economics. They consider the existence of game theory, experimental economics, evolutionary economics, and behavioural economics as testimony for plurality in orthodox economics. In fact, they believe that the existence of those theories has meant that the difference between terms 'orthodox' and 'heterodox' economics became unimportant.

While it is true that some changes have taken place within the neo-classical economics, neo-liberal economists' claims of plurality are based on the acceptance of different forms of rationality and different techniques, rather than different methodologies in the discipline of economics. Furthermore, their arguments for the existence of plurality in orthodox economics have nothing to do with plurality in the methodology of economics. Game theory, experimental economics, evolutionary economics, and behavioural economics all use similar or the same methodology in addition to the same formal mathematical and econometric modelling.

[3] In some rare instances, a few mainstream economists did recognise the post-Keynesian research programme, but only during periods of recession, high inflation, and economic crises, like the 2008 economic crisis.

typically attribute the blame elsewhere. That means neo-liberal economists represent the main barrier to finding solutions to incessantly growing global problems caused by their paradigm. Despite the growing body of evidence that neo-liberal economics played a significant role in producing disastrous global outcomes, it remains the leading program of research in the economics departments of most universities, and according to major economic journals and textbooks. Politicians also continue to rely on neoliberalism to interpret the economic world and implement new policies.

Unlike many of the books, papers and studies published by heterodox economists, this book does not propose an alternative paradigm or immediate solutions to the 'special anomalies' that continue to persist within neo-liberal economics. Instead, it closely examines the concept of freedom[4] that continues to be promoted by neo-liberals, mainly focusing on the views of a select group of influential neo-liberal theorists. In particular, it refers to the concepts of freedom put forth by the Austrian School of Economics (ASE) and the Chicago School of Economics, which played prominent roles in the development of neo-liberalism. More specifically, the main focus of this book is on the works and views of Milton Friedman (1912–2006) of the Chicago School of Economics, and Friedrich August von Hayek (1899–1992) of the ASE, two prominent neo-liberal economists whose respective versions of freedom shared many similarities.

There are also numerous references to the works of a number of other influential economists and theorists who were among the leading proponents of neo-liberalism, including: Ludwig von Mises (1881–1973), one of the main contributors to the ASE and a founding member of the Mont *Pèlerin* Society; James McGill Buchanan (1919–2013), an economist, professor at George Mason University, and member of the Mont *Pèlerin* Society, who made major contributions to political science, social philosophy and public policy economics, and was awarded the Nobel Prize in economics in 1986 for 'his development of the contractual and constitutional bases for the theory of economic and political decision-making';[5] Gordon Tullock (1922–2014), an economist, professor at the George Mason University, and member of the Mont *Pèlerin* Society; George Stigler (1911–1991), a leading professor at the Chicago School of Economics and a founding member of the Mont *Pèlerin* Society, who was

[4] The terms freedom and liberty are used interchangeably in this book.

[5] The Nobel Prize. 'James M. Buchanan Jr. Facts.' https://www.nobelprize.org/prizes/economic-sciences/1986/buchanan/facts/.

awarded the Nobel Prize in economics in 1982 'for his seminal studies of industrial structures, functioning of markets and causes and effects of public regulation';[6] and, and Gary S. Becker (1930–2014), a very influential economist at the University of Chicago and a member of the Mont *Pèlerin* Society, who received the 1992 Nobel Memorial Prize in Economic Sciences for 'for having extended the domain of microeconomic analysis to a wide range of human behavior and interaction, including non-market behavior.'[7] Additionally, in order to evaluate some of the views put forth by these influential advocates of neo-liberalism, there are a number of references to the works of Frank Hyneman Knight (1885–1972) (1922, 454), an economist and moral philosopher, who was among the founders of the Chicago School of Economics and a founding member of the Mont *Pèlerin* Society. In fact, Knight taught Friedman, Stigler and Buchanan when he was a professor at the University of Chicago.

With the exception of Knight, all of these prominent neo-liberal economists, attributed a minimal role to the state and its institutions, as mere guarantors and promoters of the conditions of freedom. They also valued and defended freedom for its instrumental value, as it could be deployed as an effective tool to promote free-market economies around the world. Specifically, these proponents of neo-liberalism argued that the free-market economy not only generates economic prosperity, efficiency, and growth, but that it also guarantees a higher level of freedom. This particular conception of freedom has been a very important and useful instrument in the development of liberal thought and the implementation of neo-liberal reforms around the world.

Given the wide influence that neo-liberal economists exert globally when it comes to spreading similar values, beliefs, views, and practices, even among the most conservative and isolated communities, it is important to comprehend and analyze the concept of freedom that they promote. In fact, applying the fundamental principles and values of neo-liberal economics in different areas of life has created an 'iron cage,' where freedom is poorly understood and practiced in a destructive manner. For example, the spread and acceptance of the concept of freedom derived

[6] The Nobel Prize. 'George J. Stigler. Facts.' https://www.nobelprize.org/prizes/economic-sciences/1982/stigler/facts/.

[7] University Chicago News. 'Gary S. Becker, Nobel-winning scholar of economics and sociology, 1930–2014.' https://news.uchicago.edu/story/gary-s-becker-nobel-winning-scholar-economics-and-sociology-1930–2014.

from neo-liberal economics has played a major role in engendering devastating financial crises, global, social and economic inequality, mass production and consumption, the over-exploitation of natural resources, immense pollution, obsessions with technological innovation and artificial intelligence, climate change, widespread militarisation, increased terrorism, etc.

This book claims that the neo-liberal concept of freedom is detrimental for civilization, and the future of the earth. This is due in part to the fact that theorists of neo-liberal economics formulated a minimal form of concept of freedom, because they worshiped freedom for its instrumental value, and primarily used it to promote the global implementation of free-market economics over centrally-planned economies. They have used this conception of freedom to defend the spontaneous order against artificial order, negative freedom against positive freedom, and a limited state role against a paternalistic state. Advocates of neo-liberalism do not particularly care about the spread of genuine freedom or the conditions needed to achieve it. In actuality, the conception of freedom formulated and defended by neo-liberals represents a regression in the development and practice of freedom, because it only supports freedom for the few, treats freedom as a private matter, and downplays the importance of the state in the achieving the of conditions of freedom.

This book is divided into thirteen chapters. The introduction is followed by a chapter that describes how Hayek and Friedman became influential figures in the discipline of economics, as both played significant roles in developing some of the fundamental ideas of free-market capitalism in the twentieth century. It also explains that both of them made key contributions to the widespread adoption of a concept of freedom that was largely derived from neo-liberal economics.

Chapter 3 focuses on the two main components of the neo-liberal concept of freedom: economic freedom and negative freedom (or 'freedom from'). It also discusses positive freedom (or 'freedom to'), which the neo-liberal concept of freedom completely excludes among its components. Furthermore, the distinction that Isaiah Berlin made between positive and negative freedom in his book *Four Essays on Liberty* (1969) is described, in order to better comprehend the limitations of the neo-liberal concept of freedom.

It is important to understand the main components and limitations of the neo-liberal concept of freedom, which has been highly promoted by many theorists, institutions, organisations and democratically elected governments. It has also been unquestionably accepted by the masses, as the definition and components of the neo-liberal concept of freedom include some ideas, views and features that are very attractive and desirable for many people. More precisely, Chap. 3 explains that by limiting the definition of liberty to the freedom to choose, and consistently claiming that only the free-market system can ensure and maintain the conditions of freedom, neo-liberals have been able to gain the support of the masses in spreading their ideology around the world. However, a close examination of the arguments put forth by neo-liberal economists reveals that they have been using the concept of freedom as a tool to further the implementation of free-market economic principles to all aspects of life. Consequently, many government activities aimed at achieving the common good, social justice, and distributive justice were curtailed or eliminated altogether, as neo-liberals argued that the achievement of these moral and ethical ends did not justify the violation of freedom in a free-market society. In fact, they claimed that any state program or policy intended to achieve social or distributive justice was antithetical to freedom. This chapter concludes that a genuine conception of freedom needs to take a number of important values and issues into consideration, including self-determination, equality, justice, fairness, happiness, security, diversity, and the protection of the environment.

The subject of Chap. 4 is the neo-liberal understanding of the relationship between freedom and the role of state. As such, it presents neo-liberal arguments against central deliberate planning (artificial order or the command economy), primarily in socialist, communist and welfare states. This chapter largely focuses on the arguments against central planning put forth by Friedman, Hayek and Mises, all of whom dedicated much of their work to demonstrating the superiority of the free-market economy (spontaneous order of open society) over all other systems of governance in terms of ensuring the conditions of freedom. In fact, all three treated many economic issues and problems as matters of conflict between the voluntary organization of society for the purpose of achieving individual ends, and the artificial organization of society to attain collective ends. In doing so, their goal was to expose the weaknesses and flaws of centrally planned systems.

This chapter also discusses contradictions of the neo-liberal state. In particular, it explains that even though neo-liberals strongly advocate for limited state action and the elimination of many publicly-funded services and programs, they are actually quite tolerant of increases in government expenditures and employment provided that they help establish and sustain the condition of a free-market system. To provide an example, the chapter briefly describes one of most well-known cases of neo-liberals supporting state intervention, that being the violent, coercive and oppressive regime of General Augusto Pinochet (1915–2006) in Chile. Both Friedman and Hayek supported the overthrow of the democratically-elected Allende government, because they believed that it threatened to weaken and destabilize the free-market economy and inhibit the profit maximizing potential of corporations. Hayek and Friedman's defense of the 'Chilean Miracle' demonstrates how little regard they actually had for freedom and the achievement of its conditions. Furthermore, it clearly illustrates that neither of them particularly cared about whether a political system was democratic, or fascist, as long as it secured the conditions of a free-market economy.

Chapter 5 explains that the rise of neo-liberalism coincided with the expansion of freedom for corporations and the simultaneous decrease in the role of the state in achieving the collective good. It begins by pointing out that the policies and regulations implemented by the New Deal directly targeted the growing power of corporations. Subsequently, however, the Reagan-Thatcher Era enabled large corporations to amass unprecedented freedom, power and influence over many aspects of society. At the same time, many states became quasi-powerless in terms of their ability to ensure the interests of their citizen, which allowed corporations to take full advantage of their newfound power and freedom. Even though corporations have been playing an increasingly important role in terms of governing society since the Reagan-Thatcher Era, they have not been overly concerned with issues pertaining to social responsibility, justice, equality or the collective good. This is not particularly surprising given that a corporation is defined as a free, independent, impersonal and amoral entity with a mandate to maximize the profits of its shareholders; in fact, any actions taken with the intent to achieve ethical ends, such as social responsibility, justice, equality or the collective good, would be considered unethical according to its mandate. Consequently, corporations operate in a manner that maximizes the interests of their shareholders at the expense of the freedom, health, and rights of ordinary people, the safety of their workers, and the purity of the environment.

Part of the problem is that governments tend to prioritize the freedoms, rights and interests of corporations over those of their citizens, often through deregulation. This is partly attributable to large corporations and industry associations using their vast financial and economic resources to engage in significant lobbying efforts to eliminate what little regulatory powers governments have managed to retain. Even though neo-liberals strongly oppose state programs and social services designed to protect the interests of citizens and achieve social justice on the basis that they violate freedom, they fully endorse the partnership that has emerged between corporations and governments, which overwhelmingly serves the private interests of the former at the expenses of the masses. At the end of this chapter, it becomes evident that the neo-liberal concept of freedom has been an effective mechanism for extending the freedom of powerful corporations to the detriment of the masses, who have gotten weaker and poorer, with little hope of ever being free.

Chapter 6 emphasizes that mass consumption is playing a major role in the approaching environmental apocalypse. Since the rise of neo-liberalism, mass consumption has become accepted as the normal pattern of behaviour in developed countries, as people obtain some sort of satisfaction from the acquisition of goods and services. Furthermore, people feel an urgent compulsion to purchase and consume the latest products as soon as they are made available, while paying little attention to the destructive outcomes of their wasteful behaviour. This type of consumption has been consistently promoted by neo-liberals, on the basis that it improves economic growth. Meanwhile, since corporations are continuously striving to earn ever greater profits, they aim not only to provide consumers with products and services that will satisfy their immediate demands, they also expend great efforts to convince people what they should want. In fact, it is not uncommon for corporations to develop sophisticated marketing campaigns to manipulate consumers into buying their products and services in order to satisfy artificial needs and desires that the very same corporation helped create in the first place via advertising.

Neo-liberals have used the concept of freedom to defend the rapid creation of new products to meet the ever-expanding demands of consumers in societies that are characterized by mass consumption. More specifically, they contend that the freedom of consumers would be violated by any state interference that limits their ability to access the widest range of goods that producers are capable of providing. They further claim that if an individual's freedom to choose their own consumption is abolished, then all freedoms have essentially been taken away from them. The widespread acceptance of the neo-liberal concept of freedom (or 'free to choose') has also played a significant role in facilitating mass production, because it is required to satisfy the demands emerging from a mass consumption society. At the end of this chapter, it will become very clear that the growth strategy of neo-liberalism, which is highly supportive of mass production and mass consumption, bears a great deal of responsible for many global environmental, social, economic and political problems.

For decades, scientists have been warning that, if people do not change the direction of their social and economic lives, there will be no avoiding an ecological apocalypse in the foreseeable future. Neo-liberals are adamantly opposed to placing significant limitations on business activities on the basis that doing so would represent a threat to the preservation of a free society, as well as the freedom to choose. In fact, the notion of having the freedom to choose has played an important role in the design and development of market-oriented environmental regulations which, in practice, have been unable to confer even a modest degree of protection on the environment against the destructive business practices of enterprises and the wasteful consumption patterns of people.

Environmental policies are designed in extremely politicized settings, where influential parties will attempt to steer decisions in a way that serves to benefit their interests at the expense of others. Accordingly, Chap. 7 discusses the advance of market-oriented neo-liberal environmental regulations during the Reagan Era, which prioritize economic efficiency while doing very little in the way of genuinely remedying environmental problems. It also illustrates the extent to which neo-liberal environmental regulations have failed by detailing the considerable environmental damage caused by the business practices and activities of some major polluters among industries, including mining, agriculture, livestock farming, and clothing.

Over the last four decades, technological innovation has accelerated to unprecedented levels, as technologies have assumed much more prominent roles in many aspects of people's lives, including work, shopping, entertainment, communication, family and relationships, information and knowledge acquisition, goals, and nature. However, many technological innovations were motivated by capitalist gains as opposed to a desire to make tangible contributions to the progress of science and knowledge. In many cases, the innovations amounted to little more than slight upgrades or improvements to distinguish certain consumption goods from previous versions or models, with the intention of enticing consumers to purchase them.

Chapter 8 focuses on role that neo-liberalism has been playing in directing the course and objectives of scientific research and technological innovation and progress. It explains that even though neo-liberal economists lack a formal education and training when it comes to areas like the natural sciences, political science, environmental issues, social relationships, ethics, and philosophy, they are adamant that the ultimate goal of science should be innovation for the purpose of achieving economic growth, productivity and efficiency. This is not particularly surprising given that proponents of free-market economies have been suggesting that economic growth, productivity, and living standards are positively correlated with technological innovation for decades. They have also consistently argued that the private sector was much better suited for accelerating technological innovation than the public sector. Accordingly, neo-liberal reforms have helped the private sector gain considerable control over the direction and objectives of science and technological innovation since the 1980s, while limiting the role of governments in these areas. Given that contemporary technological innovation is largely driven by deliberate efforts to produce commodities at a lower cost, faster pace, and larger capacity, business-oriented scientific research projects are unlikely to stimulate the imaginations, creativity, and intellectual freedom of scientists. That means the significantly expanded role of the private sector in modern scientific research and technological innovation has resulted in scientists essentially losing their freedom to choose when it comes to the subjects and types of projects they can work on. For example, instead of finding solutions for the various issues and problems facing nature, science in the era of neo-liberalism was primarily used to challenge the earth in search of monetary gains, which ultimately contributed to accelerating pace of the impending environmental apocalypse that is threatening humanity.

Chapter 9 examines neo-liberal opposition to labour unions. Historically, labour unions have maintained close relationships with left-wing groups and social democratic political parties which, according to neo-liberals, threatened the success of the free-market system. During the rise of neo-liberalism, prominent economists consistently targeted labour unions with selective arguments with the intention of creating a hostile environment towards them. Foremost among them were Friedman, Hayek and Mises, all of whom criticized unions for violating economic and individual freedom, relying on coercive powers to achieve their objectives, and causing unemployment and inflation. In reality, however, neo-liberals were determined to oppose unions and weaken their ability to collectively bargain in order to prevent them from further advancing their goals of achieving social and economic justice.

Union membership in the US expanded rapidly from the early decades of the twentieth century until the beginning of the Cold War Era (1947–1991). However, that trend began to change in the 1950s, as business classes and republicans managed to successfully spread their long-held anti-communist sentiments among much of the general population. Subsequently, union membership began to gradually decrease. However, a much more dramatic decline was to come with the rise of neo-liberalism, which was committed to diminishing the strength and influence of unions in labour markets and society in general. In particular, unions were weakened considerably during the Reagan presidency, as employers were emboldened to oppose them more forcefully, while the public was also less supportive. Neo-liberals contributed to the downfall of unions by promoting the notion that they violated the individual and economic freedom of their own members, because the act of joining a union did not involve a voluntary decision, and the payment of union dues was mandatory. They also claimed that unions had incomparable privileges when it came to violence and coercion, arguing that every strike was an act of coercion that involved violence directed against employers. They further suggested that the various types of coercion that were available to unions put capitalist enterprises at a considerable disadvantage against them. In reality, labor movements and their battles should be associated with the struggles for freedom and equality, as they sought to eliminate all class privileges and establish social justice and freedom for society.

Following the collapse of the Soviet Union, many neo-liberal theorists and political scientists declared capitalism to be the winner of the final ideological battle against communism, and without a valid rival. Some went so far as to suggest that this marked the end of history, meaning that there would be no fighting over large ideological issues going forward. Subsequently, free-market capitalism has ruled over the global economy. However, while the global spread of free-market capitalism may have contributed to significant improvements in economic growth, productivity, technological progress, and efficiency, it also brought unprecedented economic and social inequality and injustice to the world.

Chapter 10 explains that the global implementation of neo-liberal economic reforms has resulted in unfair economic outcomes, as some have profited disproportionately at the expense of others. In particular, people in western countries have seen their living standards rise markedly, while a very small proportion of the global population controls most of the world's wealth and live in extravagance. On the other hand, the widespread adoption of neo-liberal principles has resulted in countless people around the world, but primarily in developing countries, being faced with landlessness, homelessness, joblessness, hopelessness, and unfreedom. This chapter largely focuses on the nature of the inequalities that have emerged with the implementation of neo-liberal economic reforms, the relationship between freedom and equality, and some of the views expressed by prominent neo-liberal economists on the subject of inequality.

Neo-liberal economists accept the premise that a free-market system would eventually produce inequality. Nonetheless, they are opposed to state interventions intended to achieve equality in the name of distributive justice or social justice. They believe that the principles of distributive justice, which are based on ethical and moral frameworks, require the state authority to intentionally impose particular and discriminatory sets of values on society. That said, they maintain that, in all likelihood, more harm than good would come from a state imposing moral and ethical values on society, because doing so would violate people's freedom by indoctrinating them with a definite set of values.

Neo-liberals argue that economics is a discipline of physical science, which would make it a value-free science. In other words, economic decisions, actions and policies are immune from any moral and ethical judgements. This position is not particularly surprising, given how rarely neo-liberal economists actually criticize the free-market system for producing outcomes that are unjust, unfair, immoral, unethical, etc. As such, Chap. 11 outlines neo-liberal arguments against the use of moral and ethical judgements in determining economic decisions and actions. Neo-liberal economists consistently advocate for people to adopt self-interested, rational, impersonal, and individualistic behaviors when making choices in their daily lives, which is supposed to make them feel as though they are free to choose. That means neo-liberals have not only managed to make economics into a discipline of the natural sciences, they also elevated themselves to the status of ideologues, whose principles have effectively replaced religion and moral philosophy as the main sources of people's core beliefs, views, practices, and values. To be more precise, freedom and happiness were no longer sought out through virtue in the Ancient Greek or Aristotelian sense, nor were they granted by the heavens, as advocated by Aquinas and Augustine; rather, they were to be found through individual self-interest maximization, an unrestrained desire for power, and acquisitiveness.

Very few countries and societies have been immune to the penetration of the standards and principles prescribed by neo-liberalism. Consequently, neo-liberalism has led to the emergence and spread of societal diseases on a global scale, particularly moral failure, which is one of the main causes of social and economic inequality, and environmental apocalypse. This chapter mainly focuses on the rise of neo-liberalism and simultaneous the decline of moral and ethical values in people's lives. Furthermore, it presents neo-liberal arguments against ethical and moral philosophy, while also explaining the views of some prominent philosophers throughout human history with respect to the importance of moral and ethical values, from Aristotle to Hegel. This chapter also briefly discusses Adam Smith (1723–1790), who is widely considered to be the founding father of modern economics, as his *Theory of Moral Sentiments* (1759) revealed that did not consider economics to be a 'value neutral' science, a fact that has been largely ignored by contemporary neo-liberals economists. Unlike most contemporary neo-liberal economists, Smith was very familiar with works of Ancient Greek philosophers, and his work was largely influenced by Stoicism.

Neo-liberal economists are committed to the misguided notion that economics should be treated as a branch of the natural sciences, which led them to take measures to eliminate moral and ethical judgements from their discipline. As a result, studying and conducting research in the field of economics now requires a strong understanding of mathematics. In fact, a proficiency with mathematical formulas and modeling is far more valuable for contemporary economists than understanding economic issues and realities. Conversely, an inability to master mathematical tools is regarded as a sign of weakness and incompetence within the discipline.

Chapter 12 investigates the efforts taken in order to make economics into a branch of the natural sciences, which has significantly contributed to the mathematization of the discipline; it also briefly discusses the downfall of the history of economic thought since the post war era. In doing so, this chapter presents the dissenting views of some prominent neo-liberal economists who did not share the enthusiasm of many of their counterparts when it came to the extensive application of sophisticated mathematics within economics, and openly questioned whether that much stood to be gained from doing so. For the most part, neo-liberal economics embraced this approach to conducting economic research, while largely ignoring the concerns and criticisms expressed by detractors. However, this outright rejections of alternative viewpoints on this subject is indicative of the methodological monism that is prevalent among neo-liberal economists when it comes to their discipline. This approach of dealing with dissent is detrimental to the discipline of economic as a whole, because discourages alternative viewpoints, independent thinking, and freedom in research and analysis, which ultimately obstructs the development and progress of economics. This book is concluded at Chap. 13.

CHAPTER 2

The Importance of Hayek and Friedman to the Neo-Liberal Concept of Freedom

Although many neo-liberal economists made important contributions to the development of the idea of freedom, Friedman and Hayek's respective concepts of freedom were among the most influential tools used to promote free-market economics around the world. This chapter explains why Friedman and Hayek played such key roles in spreading a concept of freedom that was largely derived from neo-liberal economics.

2.1 Why Friedman's Concept of Freedom?

Milton Friedman was one of the leading economists and political thinkers of the twentieth century. He considered himself a 'freedom fighter,' and was widely regarded as a threat to people who feared freedom (Pacific Institute 1984, 13). He was also viewed as an authority when it came to the definition and interpretation of the concept of freedom, and as an articulate and influential advocate of individual freedom. He dedicated a significant part of his work to influencing public opinion, and was personally involved in the formulation of government economic policy. He was awarded the 1976 Nobel Prize in Economics for his work on monetary theory, which further enhanced his reputation and influence among respected economists. His reputation was also boosted by his time at the University of Chicago Economics Department, widely regarded as the 'Mecca and Rome' of the discipline of economics, where he worked from

B. Filip, *The Rise of Neo-liberalism and the Decline of Freedom*,
Palgrave Insights into Apocalypse Economics,
https://doi.org/10.1007/978-3-030-61623-6_2

1946 until 1976. Many economists viewed Friedman as the 'intellectual leader' and 'primary architect of the Chicago School,' because of his strong belief in economics as 'a true science,' his defense of laissez-faire capitalism, his vigorous opposition to state intervention, and his defense of freedom (Van Overtveldt 2007, 8).

It is well-known that, in the twentieth century, the University of Chicago Economics Department played a major role in the evolution of mainstream economics (or capitalism), the development of the American economics profession, and the formulation of US economic policy. Friedman believed that the University of Chicago, which opened its doors in 1892, was more important than other universities and institutions on account of its 'strong, cohesive, and intellectually respectable group of defenders of a free society' (Friedman 1961, 11). More specifically, he explained that in the 1930s and 40s, the University of Chicago had 'a strong liberal tradition, conveyed and maintained by eminent and respected members of the academic community like Frank H. Knight, Jacob Viner, Henry Calvert Simons, and others' (Friedman 1961, 11). Then, in the early 1960s, it was 'almost surely the only' university at which the majority of students highly valued 'a free society,' vigorously studied the historical and the intellectual foundations of a free society, and seriously discussed real problems (Friedman 1961, 11). Friedman greatly influenced his students during his time at the University of Chicago, providing them with 'numerous illustrations and applications,' which led many of them to integrate Friedman's economic theories into their own views and work (Ebenstein 2007, 89). In fact, it was often claimed that 'the Chicago school of economics is largely the Friedman school of economics; his positions and views are those associated with the school' (Ebenstein 2007, 132). At the 54th annual Board of Trustees dinner for the faculty of the University of Chicago held on January 9, 1974, Friedman stated that:

> "Chicago" designates not a city, not even a University, but a "school." The term is used sometimes as an epithet, sometimes as an accolade, but always with a fairly definite—though by no means single-valued—meaning. In discussions of economic policy, "Chicago" stands for belief in the efficacy of the free market as a means of organizing resources, for skepticism about government intervention into economic affairs, and for emphasis on the quantity of money as a key factor in producing inflation. In discussions of economic science, "Chicago" stands for an approach that takes seriously the

use of economic theory as a tool for analyzing a startlingly wide range of concrete problems. (Ebenstein 2007, 133)

The University of Chicago is now among the world's leading universities. Since 1969, many of the economists that became Nobel laureates in their field were directly or indirectly associated with the economics department at the University of Chicago (i.e., professors, students, researchers, etc.). Furthermore, many of its former students became involved with 'governmental organizations,' as well as national and international institutions based in the United States[1] and other countries around the world (Van Overtveldt 2007, 323–324).

In addition to the prominent role that he played at the economics department of the University of Chicago, Friedman is also well-known for being a dominant figure in American economic and intellectual life. He was considered 'a political activist with a right-wing agenda,' and 'an ideologue of the right' (Van Overtveldt 2007, 91). Many also regarded him as the 'greatest champion of liberty.'[2] Friedman's lifetime goal was to convince Americans that his idea of freedom and his views on the role of the state were the right ones. To achieve this mission, 'he devoted great energy, in writing Newsweek[3] columns, appearing on television shows [or public television series, *Free to Choose,*[4] as well as influential TV advertisement], writing popular books and other efforts to publicize his views' (Van Overtveldt 2007, 238). In particular, his public television series, *Free*

[1] Michael Mussa, who received his master's degree and PhD in economics at the University of Chicago, 'joined President Reagan's Council of economic Advisers' between 1986 and 1988 (Van Overtveldt 2007, 194). Furthermore, George Shultz, who was a professor at the Chicago School, became President Reagan's Secretary of State for 7 years; he was also 'a shadow president in the Nixon administration, and this was probably even more evident during the Reagan administration' (Van Overtveldt 2007, 327). Two other people from the University of Chicago also played key roles in the Reagan administration: Allen Wallis was given 'the post of Undersecretary for Economic Affairs' and Kenneth Dam became 'Deputy Secretary of State' (Van Overtveldt 2007, 327–329). Together they 'played a pivotal role in keeping the Reagan administration on the free-trade track' and their work during that period 'confirmed their Chicago beliefs' (Van Overtveldt 2007, 328–329). 'Many others who knew, were influenced by, or were students of Friedman participated in the Reagan administration as well as elsewhere in government, academia, and business' (Ebenstein 2007, 208).

[2] Cato Institute. 'The Milton Friedman Prize for Advancing Liberty.' https://www.cato.org/friedman-prize

[3] Friedman regularly wrote for Newsweek between 1966 and 1984.

[4] Friedman's 'widely acclaimed' TV show, Free to Choose, was the basis for 'his national best seller Free to Choose' (Rayack 1987, 6).

to Choose,[5] was watched by many Americans and was 'regarded as being a major factor in shifting American public opinion toward appreciating the need to dismantle government largess' (Pacific Institute 1984, 6). This series also allowed Friedman to introduce many of his neo-liberal views to general audiences around the world, including in 'England, Japan, Australia, Canada, and other countries' (Pacific Institute 1984, 6).

Friedman's notoriety helped him become an important figure within 'the U.S. Treasury' and in 'the Hoover Institution' (Pacific Institute 1984, 19). It also aided him in becoming the economic advisor to many 'presidents and premiers and cabinets,' including the administrations of Richard Nixon, Gerald Ford and Margaret Thatcher (Pacific Institute 1984, 6, 13). For example, President Nixon appointed Friedman to 'the Advisory Commission on an All-Volunteer Armed Force, adopted his negative income tax idea, and appointed him to the Commission on White House Fellows, a group that selects fifteen to twenty young people each year to serve as assistants to the president and cabinet level officials' (Ebenstein 2007, 187). Although Friedman did not hold an official post in the Reagan administration when it was in power from 1981 to 1989, Ronald Reagan considered him to be his 'most trusted' advisor on economic and foreign policy matters (Rayack 1987, 2, 7). In fact, 'Reagan sometimes referred to Friedman in his regular radio addresses' prior to becoming president, indicating that he was familiar with Friedman's ideas before entering the White House (Ebenstein 2007, 205). Moreover, Friedman was part of a 'committee prior to Reagan's election that prepared policy papers for implementation if Reagan were elected' (Ebenstein 2007, 207). According to Friedman, Reagan 'acted very much along the lines' the committee suggested after being elected president in 1980 (Ebenstein 2007, 207). Friedman (2004) had a very high opinion of president Reagan, even going so far as to contend that '[f]ew people in human history have contributed more to the achievement of human freedom than Ronald Wilson Reagan.'

An examination of many of President Reagan's speeches and policies reveals the extent to which his administration was influence by the views of Friedman. In particular, President Reagan's speeches emphasized the importance of individual freedom, reducing the role of government, and cutting expenditures at a time when Friedman was advocating the same measures in his columns. President Reagan also described Friedman as

[5] Friedman's television series, Free to Choose, was 'financed' by a number of 'large corporations' (Rayack 1987, 6).

'one of the greatest thinkers in modern history,' and claimed that, 'not since the time of Adam Smith has such a finely focused mind concentrated on the intellectual underpinnings of a free society' (Pacific Institute 1984, 19). He also characterized him as 'inflexible and single-minded in his devotion to the cause of freedom' (Pacific Institute 1984, 13, 19). President Reagan also believed that Friedman had 'a major role in disseminating the philosophy of freedom' within the US and in many other countries around the world (Pacific Institute 1984, 20). In other words, Friedman's economic views and emphasis on the importance of freedom, which he frequently expressed in his public television series, books, articles, speeches, and interviews, not only influenced the Reagan administration, but also other world leaders and the vision of the mass majority.

Friedman's work has been translated into more than twenty languages. Thus, he was not only able to convince the citizens, politicians and presidents of his own country that a strong correlation existed between a free-market economy and freedom, but also their peers in many other countries. Due to his widespread global influence, it is vital to study, understand and analyze the idea of freedom that Friedman sought to develop in his two influential books *Capitalism and Freedom* (1962)[6] and *Free to Choose* (1980), where he claimed that, based on liberal thought, freedom is the ultimate goal and the individual is the ultimate agent in society. According to him, the achievement of the greatest freedom requires denationalization, privatization, free trade, deregulation, a limited state role, lower taxes, etc. Friedman's devotion to and promotion of the free-market, combined with his ability to understand the difference between addressing the academic community and popular audiences, essentially made him into an effective salesman of free-market economics to the general public, academics, and democratically elected politicians.

2.2 Why Hayek's Concept of Freedom?

Friedrich August von Hayek was well known for his contributions to the Austrian School of Economics. Although Friedman belonged to the Chicago School, a separate school of thought, in the end they were both neo-classical economists. They both played major roles in developing some of the fundamental ideas of free-market capitalism in the twentieth century. In particular, Hayek was recognized for his attempt to develop a

[6] *Capitalism and Freedom* became a bestseller in 1962.

theory against artificial order/central deliberate planning during his career, which resulted in an extended defense of spontaneous order. However, his intellectual contributions were not limited to the field of economics; his work also contributed to a variety of other disciplines including psychology, sociology, the history of ideas, the philosophy of law, the philosophy of science, and political philosophy. In fact, Friedman (1976, XXI) not only acknowledged that Hayek's views on free-societies were very influential in his own work, but he also underlined Hayek's importance in many disciplines when he stated:

> Hayek's influence has been tremendous. His work is incorporated in the body of technical economic theory; has had a major influence on economic history, political philosophy and political science; has affected students of the law, of scientific methodology, and even of psychology…all of these are secondary to Hayek's influence in strengthening the moral and intellectual support for a free society.

Hayek worked at the London School of Economics (LSE) from 1932[7] to 1950. He was highly regarded for his contributions to the LSE, along with his colleague Lionel Robbins (1898–1984). These two economists were credited with initiating the 'resistance' that developed against John Maynard Keynes (1883–1946) at LSE in the 1930s (Hacohen 2000, 317). Hayek (2005, 77) explained that shortly after taking his position at the LSE in 1932, he got 'engaged into a controversy with J.M. Keynes.' In fact, Hayek earned a reputation for being 'the only intellectual opponent' of Keynes during his time at LSE (Van Overtveldt 2007, 341). Hayek (2005, 90) was fully aware of his status, as evidenced by his statement that:

> In the middle 1940s—I suppose I sound very conceited—I think I was known as one of the two main disputing economists: there was Keynes and there was I.

In addition to being an influential figure at LSE, Hayek also worked at a number of other prestigious universities, including the University of Chicago and the University of Freiburg (Germany). Interestingly, his candidature was rejected when he initially applied to work at the University of

[7] Hayek had a one year visiting post at the LSE in 1931.

Chicago's economics department. As it turned out, economists in the department were opposed to 'his appointment,' because they considered *The Road to Serfdom* 'too popular' for 'a respectable scholar to perpetrate' (Mirowski and Plehwe 2009, 165). Consequently, Hayek ended up obtaining a post at the University of Chicago's Committee on Social Thought (Hayek 2005, 113, 114). Nonetheless, he often interacted with well-known economists like Aaron Director, George Stigler, and Friedman during his time at the University of Chicago. Meanwhile, Friedman regularly participated in Hayek's seminars on political philosophy. It is obvious that many of the ideas that Friedman put forth in *Capitalism and Freedom* were similar to views expressed in Hayek's work on a number of subjects, including freedom, the limited role of the state, and free-market capitalism. Friedman acknowledged that, since he first read Hayek's works, and over the course of their many interactions over the years, Hayek's 'powerful mind, his moral courage, his lucid and always principled exposition have helped to broaden and deepen' his own 'understanding of the meaning and the requisites of a free society' (Friedman 1976, X). Friedman (1976, X) never hesitated to emphasize Hayek's importance to the development and spread of the free-market system, as he stated:

> Over the years, I have again and again asked fellow believers in a free society how they managed to escape the contagion of their collectivist intellectual environment. No name has been mentioned more often as the source of enlightenment and understanding than Friedrich Hayek's. I cannot say that for myself, since I was influenced in this direction by my teachers at the University of Chicago before I had come to know Hayek or his work. But I, like the others, owe him a great debt.

Hayek is also well-known for inspiring the foundation of the Mont Pèlerin Society (MPS) in 1947, as well as the many the contributions that he subsequently made to it. His motivation was 'to create a space where like-minded people who shared philosophical ideas and political ideals could mingle and engage in a process of further education and collective learning dedicated to advancing a common neoliberal cause,' which resulted in the establishment of the MPS (Plehwe 2009, 5). In fact, Hayek was the long-serving president of the MPS, holding this position from its founding until 1960 ('honorary president thereafter'). The goal of the MPS was clearly stated in 1947:

> The central values of civilization are in danger. Over large stretches of the earth's surface the essential conditions of human dignity and freedom have already disappeared. In others they are under constant menace from the development of current tendencies of policy. The position of the individual and the voluntary group are progressively undermined by extensions of arbitrary power.[8]

Basically, the MPS was worried about the growing role of the state in society. Its members were particularly concerned that the increasing regulatory powers of the state were resulting in a decline of faith and confidence in the effectiveness of private property ownership and the benefits of competitive markets. Consequently, they wanted to redefine the role of 'the state so as to distinguish more clearly between the totalitarian and the liberal order.'[9] They also cared about 'the problem of the creation of an international order conducive to the safeguarding of peace and liberty and permitting the establishment of harmonious international economic relations.'[10] In other words, they basically wanted to establish and maintain the conditions of the free-market system on a global scale. Today, the membership of the MPS includes 'high governmental officials, Nobel prize recipients, men of affairs, journalists, and scholars,' who 'see the dangers to civilized society.'[11]

In addition to Hayek, other founding members of the MPS included Raymond Aron, Aaron Director, Milton Friedman, Albert Hunold, Frank H. Knight, Ludwing von Mises, Karl Popper, Micheal Polanyi, and George Stigler. Friedman (1976, XXI) recognized that, like many other specialists, he too owed 'a great indirect debt to Hayek for the role he played in establishing the Mont Pelerin Society,' as he stated:

> I was fortunate enough to be in at the birth, at the founding meeting held in 1947 at Mont Pelerin, Switzerland. It was a great occasion, the bringing together on that mountaintop of a goodly company from all of the world, differing in many details, but all aware of the threat to freedom and all

[8] Mont Pèlerin Society n.d. 'Short History and Statement of Aims.' https://www.montpelerin.org/statement-of-aims/

[9] Mont Pelerin Society n.d. 'Short History and Statement of Aims.' https://www.montpelerin.org/statement-of-aims/

[10] Mont Pelerin Society n.d. 'Short History and Statement of Aims.' https://www.montpelerin.org/statement-of-aims/

[11] Mont Pelerin Society n.d. 'Short History and Statement of Aims.' https://www.montpelerin.org/statement-of-aims/

> determined to do what they could, as intellectuals and as citizens, to stem and reverse the tide.

Members of the MPS have always been specialized in a variety of different disciplines, including economics, philosophy, law, history, and political science. They used their expertise to collaborate on the development of liberalism, with each individual member playing a significant role in promoting and protecting liberal thought in their work. They believed that freedom was under threat from supporters of artificial order, and that Europe had to be protected from the threat of collectivism. In the ideological battle of ideas, the MPS could be described as a collection of 'the opponents of socialism in the intellectual, political, and business worlds' (Boettke 2006, 51). Since being founded, the MPS has consistently defended free-market economies, limited governments, free-trade, economic freedom, and individual freedom. As such, it has played a significant role in the spread of liberal thought across the world. In fact, Hayek (1992) expressed how pleased he was with the 'progress' of the MPS when he stated that:

> its main purpose has been wholly achieved. I became very much aware that each of us was discovering the functioning of real freedom only in a very small field and accepting the conventional doctrines almost everywhere else. So I brought people together from different interests. Any time one of us said, 'Oh yes—but in the field of cartels you need government regulation,' someone else would say, 'Oh no! I've studied that.' That was how we developed a consistent doctrine and some international circles of communication.

Despite his important contributions to the development of liberal thought at the MPS, as well as at a number of prestigious universities, Hayek was almost forgotten as an economist from the time of the Keynesian revolution right up until 1970s. At one time, Hayek (2005, 127) believed that he would become 'probably the best-known economist living' in the immediate after of Keynes' death in 1946. However, he conceded that 'ten days later [after Keynes's death] it was probably no longer true. At that very moment, Keynes became the great figure' (Hayek 2005, 127). Subsequently, he gradually gained prominence in the discipline of economics with the decline of Keynesian economics, culminating with being awarded the Nobel Memorial Prize in Economics, along with Karl Gunnar

Myrdal, in 1974. In 1991, he was awarded the Presidential Medal of Freedom. In the end, Hayek did manage to become one of the most influential economists in the history of economic thought.

Although Hayek never held an official post in the political arena, he was a very influential figure and source of inspiration for a number of prominent politicians, including Margaret Thatcher and Ronald Reagan (Backhouse 2006, 34). Despite the fact that *The Road to Serfdom* (1994 [1944]) was not taken seriously by economists, it was accepted as 'a key text of the emerging New Right, a movement whose influence ultimately made possible the elections of Margaret Thatcher, Ronald Reagan, and George W. Bush' (Feser 2006, 1). Furthermore, it is well documented that Thatcher publicly endorsed the contents of *The Constitution of Liberty* (1960) as the basis for her Conservative party's platform and 'famously tried once to end debate on Conservative Party policy by slamming a copy of Hayek's more dryly academic tome *The Constitution of Liberty* (1960) down on the table and exclaiming, "This is what we believe!"' (Feser 2006, 1). Meanwhile, Reagan claimed that 'his thinking on economics was directly influenced by Hayek's writings' during his presidency (Feser 2006, 1).

In addition to being a popular book, *The Road to Serfdom* also played an important role in spreading free-market capitalism among the intellectual community of Eastern Europe, as well as those of many Western European and South American countries (Kukathas 2006, 182). That is to say, Hayek's criticisms of central deliberate planning and praise for free-market processes have been read and taken into consideration worldwide. He was regarded as the successor to the classical liberals, namely John Locke and Adam Smith. Although he was not actually a libertarian and 'distanced himself from the sort of free market utopianism,' a number of prominent libertarian philosophers regarded him as an important figure in the development of their own theories (Feser 2006, 2, 6). For example, Robert Nozick (1938–2002) referred to 'Hayek's Individualism and Economic Order, along with Mises's Socialism, as the works which converted him away from socialism while he was in graduate school' (Feser 2006, 11, n.5).

Hayek became an important public intellectual and 'a philosopher of freedom' with the publication of *The Road to Serfdom* in 1944 (Backhouse 2006, 34). His role in the development of neo-liberal economics, his influence in the realms of public policy, and his work in an array of disciplines, including sociology, psychology, biology, philosophy, law, and political science, were important factors in communicating his concept of freedom to a wider public. In addition to being an influential economist, a source of inspiration for a number of well-known politicians, and an important figure for neo-liberal and libertarian philosophers, Hayek's economic views and his emphasis on the importance of individual freedom played crucial roles in the global triumph of free-market capitalism. His work merits the attention of anybody seeking to understand the concept of freedom supported by the defenders of free-market capitalism, and the worldwide spread and success of neo-liberalism and its destructive global outcomes.

References

Backhouse, Roger E. 2006. Hayek on Money and the Business Cycle. In *The Cambridge Companion to Hayek*, ed. Edward Feser, 34–50. Cambridge: Cambridge University Press.

Boettke, Peter J. 2006. Hayek and Market Socialism. In *The Cambridge Companion to Hayek*, ed. Edward Feser, 51–66. Cambridge: Cambridge University Press.

Ebenstein, Lanny. 2007. *Milton Friedman: A Biography*. New York: Palgrave Macmillan Ltd.

Feser, Edward. 2006. *The Cambridge Companion to Hayek*. Cambridge: Cambridge University Press.

Friedman, Milton. 1961. Introduction. In *New Individualist Review*. 1(1). Ed. Ralph Raico. (Indianapolis: Liberty Fund, 1981). https://oll.libertyfund.org/titles/2136. 8–13. Accessed June 6 2020.

———. 1976. Foreword. In *Essays on Hayek*, ed. Fritz Machlup, XXI–XXIV. Hillsdale: Hillsdale College Press.

———. 2004, June 11. Freedom's Friend. *Wall Street Journal*.

Hacohen, M.H. 2000. *Karl Popper: The Formative Years, 1902-1945*. Cambridge: Cambridge University Press.

Hayek, F.A. 1960. *The Constitution of Liberty*. Chicago: University of Chicago Press.

———. 1992 [1977]. The Road from Serfdom. *Reason*. http://reason.com/archives/1992/07/01/the-road-from-serfdom/5.

———. 1994 [1944]. *The Road to Serfdom*. Chicago: The University of Chicago Press.

———. 2005 [1994]. In *Hayek on Hayek: An Autobiographical Dialogue*, ed. Stephen Kresge and Leif Wenar. London: Routledge.

Kukathas, Chandran. 2006. Hayek and Liberalism. In *The Cambridge Companion to Hayek*, ed. Feser Edward, 182–207. Cambridge: Cambridge University Press.

Mirowski, P., and P. Plehwe. 2009. *The Road from Mont Pèlerin: The Marketing of The Neoliberal Thought Collective*. Cambridge: Harvard University Press.

Mont Pelerin Society. n.d. Short History and Statement of Aims. https://www.montpelerin.org/statement-of-aims/.

Pacific Institute for Public Policy Research. 1984. *Politics and Tyranny: Lessons in Pursuit of Freedom by Milton Friedman*. California: Pacific Institute for Public Policy Research.

Plehwe, Dieter. 2009. 'Introduction.' In *The Road from Mont Pèlerin: The Marketing of The Neoliberal Thought Collective*, eds. Mirowski, P., and Plehwe, P., 1–42. Cambridge: Harvard University Press.

Rayack, Elton. 1987. *Not so Free to Choose: The Political Economy of Milton Friedman and Ronald Reagan*. New York: Praeger Publishers.

Van Overtveltd, J. 2007. *The Chicago School: How the University of Chicago Assembled the Thinkers Who Revolutionized Economics and Business*. Chicago: Agate.

CHAPTER 3

The Neo-Liberal Concept of Freedom: Economic and Negative Freedom

Throughout human history, people have cherished freedom and made great sacrifices to achieve it. As such, philosophers, political thinkers and theorists have examined the concept of freedom and attempted to define its meaning and components since the times of the Ancient Greeks. They also tried to establish a system of rules and conditions that need to be satisfied in order to attain freedom. The result has been the formulation of a number of contrasting versions of freedom, often influenced by the social, political, economic and ideological realities of their respective times. The concept of freedom promoted by neo-liberalism is very distinct from various other conceptions that were conceived throughout the histories of philosophy and political thought. This is on account of the fact that the primary intellectual sources of the neo-liberal definition of freedom are found in the fundamental assumptions and principles of neo-liberal economics, which has consistently advocated for the supremacy of economic freedom over equality, voluntary choices of actions over imposed centrally-planned actions, individuals over communities, and rationality over moral and ethical principles.

Neo-liberals have rejected the natural freedom that Thomas Hobbes (1588–1679) described in *Leviathan* (1651), as a component of their concept of freedom. Their opposition to natural freedom is largely premised on the fact that it exists in the absence of civil society, where there is no law and people have unrestricted rights to freely pursue their desires,

B. Filip, *The Rise of Neo-liberalism and the Decline of Freedom*,
Palgrave Insights into Apocalypse Economics,
https://doi.org/10.1007/978-3-030-61623-6_3

emotions, impulses, and compulsions. According to Hobbes (1998, 86), freedom is the 'liberty each man hath, to use his own power, as he will himself, for the preservation of his own nature; that is to say, of his own life; and consequently, of doing any thing, which in his own judgment, and reason, he shall conceive to be the aptest means thereunto.' There is a complete absence of coercion by the law under natural freedom, meaning that individuals can do whatever they please. This type of freedom would inevitably lead to social chaos. Neo-liberal theorists could not support the premise of people being absolutely free; instead, they would insist that people need to give up some of their freedom, by adhering to a legal framework, in order to prevent the onset of chaos.

Neo-liberals also distinguished their conception of freedom from political freedom, despite the fact that Friedman (1982, 15) claimed that 'economic freedom is also an indispensable means toward the achievement of political freedom.' That would suggest that political freedom can only survive within a free-market economy. It appears that whenever Friedman was discussing political freedom, he was actually referring to individual freedom. In other words, he seemed to confuse the concept of individual/personal freedom with political freedom. Meanwhile, Hayek's (2011, 61) account of freedom emphasized the differences between individual freedom and political freedom, whereby the latter strictly refers to citizens voting or otherwise participating politically 'in the choice of their government, in the process of legislation and in the control of administration.' He did not believe that political participation could ensure the conditions of freedom, pointing out that 'there were a number of instances in the twentieth century when democratic elections led to millions of individuals voting to elect a tyrant, who would subsequently eliminate individual freedom' (Filip 2018, 110). Hayek further argued that it was entirely possible for people to be free without participating in the choice of their government via democratic elections.

Neo-liberal economists also strongly opposed positive freedom (*'freedom to'*), which has been defended by a number of prominent philosophers including Rousseau, Hegel, Marx, Mill, Fichte, Kant, and Humboldt. Based on positive freedom, the essence of human beings is that they are self-determined and strive to achieve their highest self-development, or the highest development of their individuality. Positive freedom 'derives from the wish on the part of the individual to be his own master. I wish my life and decisions to depend on myself, not on external forces of whatever kind' (Berlin 2002, 178). According to the concept of positive freedom, there is nothing worse than treating people as though they are not self-directed or self-determined entities. In order to achieve development of individuality, a positive action is required on the part of the government, usually in the form of investing in individuals, communities, or some combination of both. In defending free-market capitalism against centrally planned systems, Hayek and Friedman argued that positive freedom has historically produced many horrible and destructive outcomes. In fact, they associated any state aiming to achieve conditions that would support the development of individuality with totalitarian regimes, believing that a system of serfdom would eventually emerge.

The concept of freedom promoted by neo-liberals has two key elements: economic freedom and negative freedom (‘*freedom from*’), which finds its origins in the writings of Hobbes, Locke, Hume, Bentham, etc. Economic freedom is the liberty to consume, produce and exchange voluntarily in the marketplace. More specifically, achieving economic freedom requires that individuals choose their own courses of action with regards to their wealth, income and work since they are the ones that have to bear ‘the consequences of their decisions’ (Friedman and Friedman 1990, 138). Meanwhile, negative freedom entails ‘the absence of coercion of a man by his fellow men’ (Friedman 1982, 15). In fact, Friedman repeatedly emphasised the interdependence that exists between negative freedom (though he did not referred to it by name) and economic freedom, claiming that a societal organization based on economic freedom will usually guarantee general freedom, which includes civil liberties, freedom of speech, freedom of expression, freedom of religion, freedom of assembly, freedom of the press, and intellectual freedom. Therefore, applying any restrictions or forms of coercion to economic freedom would represent a threat to freedom in general. Hayek and Friedman shared the same view with respect to the role of coercion on economic freedom and freedom in general. In particular, they believed that some frontiers of freedom needed to be established where no one would be permitted to intervene. On this basis, they associated protecting the private spheres of individuals from coercion with a higher level of civilisation and development on the part of both individuals and communities.

This chapter explains the two main components of the neo-liberal idea of freedom, namely negative freedom and economic freedom. Based on negative freedom, any attempt to realize equality or justice via state authority or intervention would end up jeopardizing freedom, as neo-liberals believe that state intervention is associated with coercion. Gaining a proper understanding of the neo-liberal concept of freedom requires a brief examination of the distinction that Isaiah Berlin made between positive and negative freedom in his book *Four Essays on Liberty* (1969). These differences will be investigated in order to better comprehend the limitations of the neo-liberal concept of freedom, which completely excludes the concept of positive freedom.

3.1 Economic Freedom

Economic freedom and unfreedom are outcomes of the economic arrangements that prevail in a particular society. In neo-liberal societies, according to Friedman and Hayek, the economic arrangement is based on a free-market system, which is a necessary condition for economic freedom. Neo-liberal economists claim that free-market systems protect and promote economic freedom, as well as freedom in general. This is because, in a free-market economy, 'no external force, no coercion, no violation of freedom is necessary to produce cooperation among individuals all of whom can benefit' (Friedman and Friedman 1990, 2).

Friedman and Friedman (1990, 65) explained that 'an essential part of economic freedom is freedom to choose how to use our income; how much to spend on ourselves and on what items; how much to save and in what form; how much to give away and to whom.' Moreover, economic freedom also involves the 'freedom to enter any occupation, engage in any business enterprise, buy from and sell to anyone else' through voluntary cooperation (Friedman and Friedman 1990, 66). Basically, individuals will choose to voluntarily cooperate with each other by pursuing their self-interests. In fact, voluntary cooperation between people for the purpose of satisfying their individual wants and desires is the central principle of free-market capitalism (Friedman 1981a, 7–8). According to Friedman, employees, employers, consumers, and producers are all sovereign actors in a free-market system, and no restraints or regulations are required on the part of the state to facilitate the conditions of voluntary exchange. The relationships that emerged between employees, employers, consumers and producers are purely voluntary, and cooperation is dictated by self-interests on either side of any transaction. According to Friedman (1982, 112), this unrestrained voluntary cooperation between economic agents without state intervention should produce maximum benefits for society as a whole because, by pursuing their own individual interests, each person promotes the interests of society 'more effectually than when he really intends to promote it.'

Economic freedom also requires that all individuals in society are committed to the mutual recognition of their basic rights. Neo-liberals believe that one of the most important basic individual rights in a free-market economic system is private property ownership. Meanwhile, they perceived public ownership to be among the greatest threats to private property. Accordingly, it was necessary to establish a legal system that would safeguard private property rights against the coercive powers of the state, including its ability to nationalize, expropriate or collectivize property ownership. All privately-owned properties should be controlled by either an individual or a group of individuals, whose rights are protected by the courts and police services. Hayek (2011, 207) claimed that establishing private property rights was 'clearly the first step in the delimitation of the private sphere which protects us against coercion.' In other words, private property rights are one of the main components of the private spheres that protect people against coercion. According to Hayek, private property ownership is considered to be the foundation of voluntary exchange in a free society, and its mutual recognition is mandatory in order to have economic transactions. The recognition of private property rights permits individuals to bargain voluntarily. Therefore, in a free-market system, the voluntary coordination of activities on the part of individuals is an outcome of people pursuing their own interests within the framework of private property ownership.

Once property rights and individual rights are well-defined by the legal system, voluntary cooperation between individuals can determine the price, quantity, and quality of commodities and services. Accordingly, no interference is required on the part of governments in terms of establishing or manipulating prices and wages in a free-market system, since the prices of goods, services, and labour are subject to bargaining between economic agents. Neo-liberals believe that fixing the prices of goods via state authority for the purpose of making them more accessible to poor people was inefficient and destructive to economic freedom. They often pointed out that centrally planned systems were unsuccessful in their attempts to coordinate the actions of consumers and producers through price controls, which condemned them to economic inefficiency and large misallocations of resources. Neo-liberals explain that if the state were to fix the price of a good at a level that was too low for whatever reason in a free society, then sellers would not earn a profit from the sale of that particular product. Accordingly, producers might reduce or completely cease production of that product if they end up making a loss at the fixed price, which might lead to shortages and workers being laid off. In this case, the state authority's decision to fix prices has affected employment and the quantity of goods available in a way that has made both consumers and producers worse off. Consequently, neo-liberals contend that if the state fixes the prices of all goods and services, while also forcing 'people to continue producing and working at these prices and wage rates, it eliminates the market altogether' (von Mises 1949, 759). Friedman (2002, 135) associated price controls with economic unfreedom, arguing that 'price controls, whether legal or voluntary, if effectively enforced would eventually lead to the destruction of the free-enterprise system and its replacement by a centrally controlled system.'

According to Friedman and Friedman (1990, 16), the free price mechanism transmits all of the information needed to make a free and rational decision, from 'buyers to retailers, wholesalers, manufacturers, and owners of resources.' Friedman (1981b, 4) elaborated that 'prices transmit information about tastes, about resource availability, about productive possibilities.' The demands of consumers determine the prices of goods, which in turn tell the producers what to produce, how to produce it, and in what quantity and quality. Consequently, the quantity of demand coincides with the quantity of supply. Friedman and Friedman (1990, 17) emphasized that 'anything that prevents prices from expressing freely the conditions of demand or supply interferes with the transmission of accurate information' (Friedman and Friedman 1990, 17). That is to say, the free price mechanism in the market place transmits information and helps people achieve voluntary cooperation, while simultaneously preventing one person from interfering with the decisions and actions of others. Friedman and Friedman (1990, 13) further argued that 'the prices that emerged from voluntary transactions between buyers and sellers … could coordinate the activity of million people … in such a way as to make everyone better off.'

Neo-liberals have also argued that any spontaneous changes in the costs of production or the prices of goods in the free-market system affect technological innovation, the quantity of production, and quantity of exchange. As such, they believe that the free adjustment of prices is absolutely essential in order to have improvements in productivity and technological innovation. Conversely, fixing prices would prevent any further advancement in these areas. Therefore, according to neo-liberals, the flexibility of commodity prices and wage rates, as well as the voluntarily adjustment of individual actions in response to spontaneously changing conditions, serve as the engines of improvement and progress in a free-market economy.

Neo-liberals have asserted that economic freedom has nothing to do with the practice of good habits and virtuous actions, as each individual is free to voluntarily 'determine to whom he wants to render services and on what terms' without any consideration for moral and ethical values (Hayek 2011, 203). For example, Hayek (2011, 20) explained that individuals are 'independent of the will of those whose services' they require, since people engage in exchange for 'their own purposes' and are not particularly interested in how their counterparts make use of the goods or services that were exchanged after the transaction has been completed. Buchanan (1975) agreed with Hayek about the indifference of economic actors when it comes to how their partners make use of the goods and/or money exchanged in an economic transaction. Buchanan (1975, 25) also pointed out that economic agents exchange with each other without any 'knowledge of the political persuasions, sexual attitudes, or economic statuses of their actual trading partners.' Each agent in the free-market place is 'treated strictly as he is, and presumably as he wants to be, in such a relationship' (Buchanan 1975, 25). For example, Buchanan (1975, 25) suggested that 'the fruit stand operator may beat his horse, shoot dogs, and eat rats. But none of these qualities need affect my strictly economic trade with him.' In other words, economic transactions under free-market capitalism are impersonal and value-free.

Neo-liberal economists clearly believe that the voluntary organization of activities in the market place does not require any kind of personal, moral or ethical relationships between buyers and sellers. All relationships in the free-market economic system are individualistic, formal, rational, instrumental, neutral, and impersonal. Friedman (2002, 21) explained that 'an impersonal market separates economic activities from political views and protects men from being discriminated against in their economic activities for reasons that are irrelevant to their productivity—whether these reasons are associated with their views or their color.' For him, buyers have no interest in knowing where, how and under what conditions sellers obtained their goods and brought them to market and, similarly, sellers are not concerned with where and how buyers made their money. They do not know, nor do they need to know, the origins of each other's economic status. Furthermore, sellers, producers, distributers and consumers have no particular interest in each other's well-being (Buchanan 1975, 24). There is a complete absence of concern about anyone else's social and economic situations, or their moral and ethical values, under free-market capitalism, because such issues are wholly irrelevant to economic freedom. Similarly, Mises (1949, 270) argued that consumers:

> are merciless egoistic bosses, full-of whims and fancies, changeable and unpredictable. For them nothing counts other than their own satisfaction. They do not care a whit for past merit and vested interests. If something is offered to them that they like better or that is cheaper, they desert their old purveyors. In their capacity as buyers and consumers they are hard-hearted and callous, without consideration for other people.

Mises (1949, 270) also claimed that the 'hard-hearted and callous' behaviours of consumers meant that enterprises had 'their hands tied; they are bound to comply in their operations with the orders' of their customers. Despite the selfish, egotistical and insensitive behaviours of consumers described by Mises, Friedman not only claimed that compliance with free-market economic principles was the best and most efficient way of organizing economic life, but also that these principles had to be adhered to in different areas of social and political life. He was adamant that the neoliberal economic approach could be applied to every action, relationship and interaction between individuals. In other words, people should be able to calculate every action rationally, based on their own self-interests, in order to distinguish between profitable and unprofitable choices.

Buchanan (1975) appears to have agreed with Friedman, as he treated rationality, instrumentalism and the pursuit of self-interests as values that should be adopted in all aspects of life. That means everything can essentially be transformed into a good or service, with an exchange value and an associated opportunity cost, that can be voluntarily bought or sold in the marketplace. According to Friedman (1982, 24), the broader the number of 'activities' that are organized based on the principles of voluntary cooperation, 'the fewer are the issues on which explicitly political decisions are required.' Friedman (1982, 16) argued that people are not free to choose if they are prevented from voluntarily cooperating with each other.

Furthermore, Friedman and Friedman (1990, 25, 27) promoted the notion that people in any discipline could cooperate based on voluntary interactions, including music, language, common law, 'physics, chemistry, meteorology, philosophy, humanities, economics.' Friedman (1967, 90) also maintained that 'the whole wondrous body of modern scientific knowledge has been built up by free exchange in the market place for ideas.' Additionally, Friedman and Friedman (1990, 26) attributed the development of social and cultural practices, conventions and values to voluntary exchange. They even suggested that the trading of 'information' and 'gossip' functioned in much the same way as the exchange of 'goods and commodities' in the free marketplace (Friedman and Friedman 1990, 25). In fact, they believed that relations between billions of individuals were organized as though they are in a free marketplace, where individuals do not need to follow commands and orders in order to realize their separate plans, or particular goals and ends.

Becker was highly influenced by Friedman's application of economics to disciplines of the social sciences and other areas of social life.[1] Friedman described Becker as 'the greatest social scientist who has lived and worked' in the second half of the twentieth century.[2] It is widely accepted that Becker 'made historic changes to the study of economics and the social sciences, combining disciplines to understand decisions in everyday life, while spawning rich new questions for scholars in diverse fields to pursue.'[3] Much like Friedman, Becker (1968, 1973, 1976) is well-known for arguing that the neo-liberal economic approach was applicable to areas of human behaviour and social life that are not considered parts of traditional economic analysis, such as daily activities, education, the use of time, family, hobbies, crime, marriage, fertility, politics, law, criminology, healthcare, illness, pollution, etc. According to him, families are accepted as households, a marriage will happen if it is mutually beneficial for both parties, and procreation only takes place if children are going to provide a higher level of utility (Becker 1973, 1976). Based on the views of Friedman and Becker (1976), treating different areas of life as though they are business transactions means choices are made according to their economic

[1] Other prominent neo-liberal economists also did extensive work on the application of the economic approach to different aspects of human life, including Aaron Director, Ronald Coase, and George Stigler.

[2] University Chicago News. 'Gary S. Becker, Nobel-winning scholar of economics and sociology, 1930–2014.' https://news.uchicago.edu/story/gary-s-becker-nobel-winning-scholar-economics-and-sociology-1930-2014.

[3] University Chicago News. 'Gary S. Becker, Nobel-winning scholar of economics and sociology, 1930–2014.' https://news.uchicago.edu/story/gary-s-becker-nobel-winning-scholar-economics-and-sociology-1930-2014.

efficiency and the economic benefits they generate instead of factors like traditions, customs, habits, ethical and moral values, compassion, sympathy, convictions, etc. In reality, however, the application of the economic approach, or economic reasoning in a narrower sense, to different aspects of human life has drastically impacted societies by significantly transforming the nature of relationships between individuals, as well as the ways in which people interact with their surroundings, including other organisms.

Knight (1972, 9) was among the few neo-liberal economists who was critical of the concepts of individual freedom and economic freedom defended by the free-market capitalist system. He was of the opinion that, taken together, these two concepts 'logically and necessarily means that the individual is to be left free to use power in his possession in practically any way he pleases-including its use to acquire more power' (Knight 1972, 9). He further argued that the concept of freedom defended by neo-liberals, 'as expressed through a social order based on free exchange,' does not provide any help in terms of finding 'the solution of the problem of economic justice' (Knight 1929, 139).

Neo-liberals define freedom as the ability to engage in voluntary exchange or cooperation in the free-market place without being subjected to coercion. In reality, however, the actions and options available to individuals can still be limited by a variety of factors, such as income, work, property ownership, education, training, etc. These kinds of limitations clearly restrict the economic freedom of people. Even though economic freedom is an important part of the neo-liberal concept of freedom, neo-liberals oppose recognizing certain economic rights as components of economic freedom, including the right to work, the right to property, the right to education, the right to professional training, and the right to income.

Contrary to the neo-liberal concept of economic freedom, which is limited to the principles of free-market capitalism, a genuine definition of economic freedom should mean 'freedom to use means to achieve ends; the means include one's own personal capacities and external materials and instruments, which one owns or controls—either is useless without the other … Freedom is empty without power, and its effective content depends both on the possession of power (in all these forms) and on what the individual actually wants to do with power' (Knight 1948, 52, 53). That means the neo-liberal concept of economic freedom is rendered largely useless and meaningless when people do not have jobs, training, education, properties or income. In reality, for someone to be truly free economically, they must feel secure in their employment and income, which includes having opportunities available to seek employment elsewhere if so desired, in addition to having the capability to own a home, increase their savings, obtain necessary goods etc. For example, a low-skilled employee working at a sweatshop in an underdeveloped country is not free to choose, because all aspects of his working conditions are imposed on him by the employers. He has no choice other than to accept working under coercive conditions due to fear and distress, as losing his job would mean being faced with the prospects of starvation and homelessness. Free-market capitalism has not provided this worker, and billions of others like him, with the ability to live his life according to his own will; rather, most aspects of his life are determined and directed by the wills of others. Under such a scenario, not only is the economic freedom of the worker violated, but also his positive freedom. Essentially, the limits of economic freedom are determined by economic power. Ultimately, the economic freedom defined by neo-liberals could 'become slavery for the person who has little power at his disposal, since life itself requires practically continuous control of a certain minimum of economic power' (Knight 2007, 184). Consequently, the widespread adherence to free-market capitalism around the world has resulted in unpresented levels of economic unfreedom for the masses, whose lives have essentially been turned into a form of slavery. This is not surprising as 'poverty and exploitation' have always been 'products of economic freedom; time and again, people were liberated all over the globe by their lords and masters, and their new liberty turned out to be submission, not to the rule of law but to the rule of the law of the others. What started as subjection by force soon became "voluntary servitude"' (Marcuse 1998 [1956], XIII).

The concept of economic freedom has become a subtle instrument used by neo-liberals to facilitate the domination of their ideas over society by applying the principles and goals of the free-market system to every aspect of life. Therefore, economic freedom, as defined by neo-liberals, has essentially transformed common individuals into defenders of the free-market economy, which they have come to regard as a promotor and protector of freedom. In the minds of the masses, an abundance of choice in the free-market system has become so important that it essentially defines their freedom. This has led to the creation of mediocre, weak, and narrow-minded people who think and act according to the capitalist spirit, which has led to wars, many forms of social and economic inequality, and the real risk of an environmental apocalypse.

3.2 Negative Freedom

Whenever neo-liberal economists speak about freedom, they are always referring to liberty from some constraint or coercion, which is defined as the negative concept of freedom ('freedom from'). Negative freedom is often associated with libertarian political philosophers. Historically, the concept was embraced by Locke, Constant, Tocqueville, Hobbes and Bentham, all of whom were reacting against despotism. Meanwhile, in the twentieth century, Sir Isaiah Berlin (1969) is renowned for outlining the differences between negative and positive freedom. Although neo-liberal economists did not specifically refer to Berlin's work, an examination of their own concept of freedom reveals that it includes the negative concept of freedom, while excluding the positive concept of freedom, both of which corresponded to the definitions outlined by Berlin.

Negative freedom does not concern itself with conditions that are necessary for the development of individuality. Instead, it is preoccupied with answering one question: 'How much am I to be governed?' (Berlin 2002, 39). Defenders of negative freedom are adamant that there should be always a frontier between public and private spheres, and that individuals should always be free to do as they please and live as they like when they are in their private spheres (Berlin 2002, 283). In other words, individuals are not deprived of their freedom in their private spheres, because they can govern themselves as opposed to being governed or controlled by someone else. Hayek (2011, 315) explained that, in a free society, 'each individual has a recognized private sphere clearly distinct from the public sphere, and the private individual cannot be ordered about but is expected to obey only the rules which are equally applicable to all.' He also stated that, within a private sphere, 'there is some set of circumstances' in an individual's 'environment with which others cannot interfere' (Hayek 2011, 61). That is to say, when individuals are in their private spheres, they have a degree of authority and control that allows them to make the best use of their knowledge, ideas, expectations, and foresight, without any intervention on the part of the state or any other institutions. Therefore, individuals are protected from any kind of coercion, political intervention or interference by actors of the free-market system when they are in their private spheres. Hayek (2011, 206) was convinced that coercion would 'be much more common' if protected private spheres did not exist.

Based on negative concept of freedom, nobody interferes with the activities of individuals when they are in their private spheres, nor does anyone impose obstacles, deliberately or otherwise, to the achievement of their goals. People are free to choose as long as they are left alone to make their own decisions and choices. That is to say, the wider the area of non-interference, the wider one's freedom. Accordingly, interference on the part of an external authority (e.g., government, institutions, organisations, other individuals, group of individuals, etc.) represents a real threat to freedom, as it prevents people from making their own decisions and choices.

Hayek (1991, 63) believed that the best way to ensure freedom was to avoid coercion by limiting the coercive actions of individuals and the coercive power of the state. In *The Constitution of Liberty* (1960), he made it clear that freedom is a product of law, because people are not subject to the will of another man when they obey the law.[4] That means the premise that a free society is regulated by laws lies at the very heart of neo-liberal views on freedom. Similar to Hayek, Knight (1929, 140) also emphasized the point that people do not feel coerced when the rule of law has been established. He further elaborated that, 'as long as every thing is assumed to be in accordance with accepted standards of fairness, there is no feeling that freedom is interfered with' (Knight 1929, 140). Therefore, based on the negative concept of freedom, some restrictions need to be placed on the freedom of all citizens, as well as the state, via a legal system to ensure that individuals can pursue their personal ends while being free from interference or coercion. In other words, coercion has to be used in order to prevent coercion. However, Hayek (2011, 323) also made it clear that 'coercion is to be used only in accordance with general rules, the justification of every particular act of coercion must derive from such a rule.'

In fact, neo-liberals regarded the relationship between freedom and the rule of law as an important factor in the achievement of freedom. In particular, the legal system needs to protect private property rights, individual freedom, and individuals against violence, malice, and fraud. Hayek (2011, 312) conceded that, under the legal system, the state has the authority to

[4] Neo-liberals are opposed to legal positivism, which is based on the conscious and intentional construction and development of a legal system. The development and progress of laws is a slow process based on piecemeal evolution as opposed to rapid central planning and design. Laws are not outcomes of the particular will of an individual, monarch or a dictator. Rather, they are outcomes of a cumulative development, having been adjusted over many generations.

'infringe a person's protected private sphere only as punishment for breaking an announced general rule.' In other words, even though individuals do not have to obey any orders from a superior authority in their private spheres, they are expected to obey the rules that are known in advance and equally applicable to all. To maintain the complex social order that exists in a society, people have to obey the laws and bear the consequences if they violate them. Accordingly, Mises (1949, 285) explained that, in the free-market system, 'direct compulsion and coercion are practiced only for the sake of preventing acts detrimental to social cooperation. For the rest individuals are not molested by the police power.' In other words, people are free from interference as long as they respect the law. Similarly, Hayek (2011, 221) stated that:

> when we obey laws, in the sense of general abstract rules laid down irrespective of their application to us, we are not subject to another man's will and are therefore free.

That means individuals are free so long as they act in accordance with the law. Hayek opposed any kind of coercion that violated any of the freedoms that the general rules are intended to protect. In fact, he defined freedom as the absence of coercion. He explained that coercion implies the deliberate interference of one man within the scope of activities of another man, whereby the former prevents the latter from attaining a particular goal or objective. Consequently, freedom requires restricting the power of all individuals, so that they cannot force others to do something against their will. The rule of law[5] also imposes restrictions on the government, so that state coercion is only accepted in cases where 'the enforcement of general abstract rules equally applicable to all' (Hayek 2011, 404). That is to say, laws are not assigned to particular individuals, cases, actions and goals. They do not discriminate and are equally applicable to all citizens. Furthermore, the rule of law does not allow the state 'to achieve particular aims' such as 'distributive or 'social justice' (Hayek 2011, 340). To the contrary, the rule of law restricts the coercive powers and activities of the government in order to prevent state authorities from possessing

[5] The rule of law is the governance of society under a set of rules. Hayek (2011, 311) explained that the rule of law is 'a rule concerning what the law ought to be.' It is 'a limitation upon all legislation' (Hayek 2011, 310).

unlimited powers to act as they please. According to Hayek, the government should embody the rule of law in order to safeguard freedom.

Friedman (2002, 15) also defined freedom as non-interference, specifically stating that freedom means 'the absence of coercion of a man by his fellow men. The fundamental threat to freedom is power to coerce, be it in the hands of a monarch, a dictator, an oligarchy, or a momentary majority.' He explained that coercion is deliberate interference, on the part of an individual or a group of individuals, that prevents someone from attaining their goals. Much like Berlin and Hayek, Friedman believed that the primary danger to freedom was any form of strong central power that intervenes in the private spheres of individuals and implements policies and reforms to achieve a predetermined end. He associated the extent of one's freedom with the limits of government coercive activities. In his arguments against coercion, Friedman (2002, 39) stated that:

> A liberal is fundamentally fearful of concentrated power. His objective is to preserve the maximum degree of freedom for each individual separately that is compatible with one man's freedom not interfering with other men's freedom. He believes that this objective requires that power be dispersed. He is suspicious of assigning to government any functions that can be performed through the market, both because this substitutes coercion for voluntary co-operation in the area in question and because, by giving government an increased role, it threatens freedom in other areas.

Friedman supported limiting state power and interference. For him, the wider the area of non-interference, the broader the range of choices available to individuals, which corresponds to a greater degree of freedom. Knight (1929, 132) agreed with Friedman, as he suggested that people had more choices available to them and were 'free to choose' when interference on the part of an external authority was kept to a minimum. Similarly, Buchanan also defended negative liberty, as he essentially defined freedom as the absence of coercion. According to Buchanan, coercion occurs whenever an individual: forces one of his peers to perform an act against their will; or, is prevented from performing his choice of action, based on his own individual will, by one of his peers.

Neo-liberals have purposefully chosen to use the concepts of negative freedom and economic freedom to convince the general public that the free-market system was superior to any other form of societal organization in terms of securing and maintaining the conditions of freedom. By convincing the masses that the freedom to choose is of the utmost importance, neo-liberals have managed to disarm their opponents. In all likelihood, this was a far more important outcome for neo-liberal theorists than actually delivering genuine freedom to all members of society. In fact, the combination of negative freedom and economic freedom does not really provide freedom for all, as both of them are very individualistic concepts of freedom. In actuality, the concept of freedom defended by neo-liberal economists has been largely effective in extending the freedom of the powerful and elite classes, thereby making them stronger, whereas the masses have gotten weaker and poorer, with little hope of ever being free. The free-market system has armed the powerful, rich and elite classes with coercive powers that they can exercise over the unfree majority.

Contrary to the arguments put forth by neo-liberals, Berlin associated the free-market system with coercion, as he believed that unrestrained economic freedom and individual self-interest maximization leads to the oppression and weakening of the masses. Berlin (2002, 37–38) actually went so far as to use terms like 'brutal' and 'bloodstained,' to describe the coercive power of the powerful and rich classes over the poor masses, which he labeled 'wolves' and 'sheep,' respectively. He suggested that proponents of the free-market system supported 'politically and socially destructive policies which armed the strong, the brutal and the unscrupulous against the humane and the weak, the able and ruthless against the less gifted and the less fortunate. Freedom for the wolves has often meant death to the sheep' (Berlin 2002, 38).

3.3 Positive Freedom

According to neo-liberals, the definition of freedom includes economic and negative freedom, which essentially means that individuals must be free in their private spheres and in the marketplace. For them, negative freedom is not concerned with the achievement of equality, social justice, ethical practices, etc. Berlin believed that this was no coincidence, as defenders of negative freedom are aware that positive freedom can 'easily destroy too many of the "negative" liberties that they held sacred' (Berlin 2002, 208). It should also come as no surprise that any advocate of positive freedom would not be satisfied with the neo-liberal definition of freedom.

In *Four Essays on Liberty* (1969), Berlin defined positive freedom as personal autonomy, 'self-mastery,' and 'self-direction;' in other words, positive freedom is 'the wish on the part of the individual to be his own master' (Berlin 2002, 178). Positive freedom is also referred to as self-realisation, self-determination, self-development, the development of individuality, and the highest achievement of individuality. According to the concept of positive freedom, individuals act based on personal will and reason, as opposed to the will and reason of others. Freedom is attributed to the wills of individuals, as 'it is the will that is free' (Marcuse 1968 185). Based on their own free wills, individuals have a particular way of thinking, deliberating, and reasoning. Essentially, freedom as self-determination means that people are 'free to play' with their 'faculties and potentialities and with those of nature, and only by "playing" with' them they are free to achieve their highest development (Marcuse 1998, 188). That means freedom is realized through a free 'self-determining will.' Berlin (2002, 181, 182) explained that, based on positive freedom:

> I am the possessor of reason and will; I conceive ends and I desire to pursue them; but if I am prevented from attaining them, I no longer feel master of the situation.

Even though different philosophers defended the concept of positive freedom as self-determination throughout the history of philosophy, they did not hold identical views about the relationship between self-determining will and universal will. For example, Rousseau argued that each individual's free self-determining will identifies with the universal will. However, Hegel believed that an individual could realize 'the universal will' by freely following his or her own self-determining will or 'particular will' ('individual will'), which could be done by simply obeying the laws of the state and rationally participating in the life of the community without the state's predetermination of universal will (Neuhouser 2000, 88, 89). Through rational participation in the life of the community, individuals could achieve the universal will via the 'suppression of all unmediated and inhuman relations with nature' (Weil 1998, 32, 33). Although there is no consensus among philosophers as to the extent to which the state should be involved in achieving of universal will and particular will, they do agree that some level of state participation will be needed in order to achieve the conditions of freedom.

Based on the positive concept of freedom, the development of the natural abilities and physical and mental capacities of individuals is necessary in order to achieve self-mastery and self-realization. Self-realisation also includes the achievement of different goals, the possession of ethical values, and aspirations for the enhancement of human life. That means there is a direct connection between freedom and the development of individuality. Individuals need to have the opportunities and conditions necessary for the development of their individualities if they are to achieve their own particular goals and ideals. Consequently, if such opportunities and conditions were lacking in a society, then it would be necessary for the state to intervene, with the objective of facilitating the conditions of positive freedom. For example, if people are too poor to afford necessary goods such as housing, food, education, and health care services, then their freedom is restricted. Defenders of positive freedom contend that these kinds of cases prevent people from making use of their freedom for the purpose of achieving the highest development of their individualities. Accordingly, they believe that freedom is strongly linked to the protection of social rights under the law, so as to ensure that everyone has access to the resources and services that are necessary for self-development. Since access to resources and opportunities are important aspects of freedom, any interference or obstacles to this access would represent a restriction of freedom. Conversely, if a state were to establish a legal system with the intention of helping its citizens gain better access to resources and opportunities, then, according to positive freedom, it has provided the conditions of the self-development of all individuals, thereby allowing them to be free.

In addition to individual autonomy and self-determination, the concept of positive freedom also involves moral or ethical judgements. Defenders of positive freedom stress the importance of collective responsibility, which refers to the positive obligation to help others achieve justice and equality. For example, Mill (1991 [1859]) and von Humboldt (1969) both underscored the importance of harmonious relationships within the community and social cooperation as important factors in the development of individuality. They both believed that self-development included a social dimension, meaning that it could not be achieved without the existence of social relationships. Furthermore, they were of the view that the state should eliminate all of the obstacles that would prevent citizens from achieving the highest development of individuality. However, they were also concerned that state intervention could represent a threat to freedom, diversity, and the incentives for individual self-development. As a result, they suggested that it was necessary to limit the state's authority. In fact, Humboldt (1969, 85) went so far as to deny the state 'all positive solicitude for the citizen's welfare.' However, this view was not shared by Mill, who was not opposed to a state that provided the conditions for the welfare of its citizens. He believed that state intervention aimed at establishing the conditions for individual self-development could be justified if individuals are unable to achieve individual improvement on their own. For example, Mill defended state intervention in reforming its institutions so as to counteract some of the destructive aspects of industrial capitalism and free trade. In other words, a state that aims to achieve distributive or social justice in order to rectify injustices is permitted on ethical grounds. This type of state can intervene by imposing positive obligations on people, who will in turn comply, because they believe that the state knows what is best for society as a whole. Such forms of state intervention can improve the conditions of less fortunate people to the point that they can achieve the development of individuality. Once people attain the development of their own individuality, they will feel free and understand that the imposition of positive obligations by the state is necessary in order to have freedom.

The negative freedom defended by neo-liberals requires the state to abstain from coercive action, meaning that the state does not have the right to interfere in the private spheres of individuals. To the contrary, positive freedom can involve applying state intervention to restrain and coerce individual actions, because unrestrained freedom is not considered to be freedom. In other words, governments are able to restraint freedom while still acting in the common interests of society. Individuals are allowed to make choices based on their own thoughts, views, ideas and wills while simultaneously respecting restraints, which do not hinder the development of their individualities.

Neo-liberals have always opposed self-development as a component of freedom. For example, Hayek never acknowledged that there was any connection between freedom and the development of individuality, despite the fact that he was very familiar with the works of prominent defenders of positive freedom such as John Stuart Mill's (1806–1873) *On Liberty* (1991 [1859]) and Wilhelm von Humboldt's (1767–1835) *The Limits of State Action* (1792). This is because he was well aware that including self-development, or the development of capacities and abilities, as a component of freedom would justify positive state intervention for the purpose of achieving the conditions of distributive justice. For Hayek, these are the types of arguments often used by tyrants or despots to justify their oppressive regimes. In other words, according to him, tyrants or despots uses positive freedom to justify their oppressive rule and actions. When addressing the subject of self-development, Hayek (1958, 26) stated that:

> This cult of the distinct and different individuality has, of course, deep roots in the German intellectual tradition and, through the influence of some of its greatest exponents, especially Goethe and Wilhelm von Humboldt, has made itself felt far beyond Germany and is clearly seen in J. S. Mill's Liberty. This sort of "individualism" not only has nothing to do with true individualism but may indeed prove a grave obstacle to the smooth working of an individualist system.

Like Hayek, many neo-liberal economists do not accept the capacity and ability to achieve self-development, or self-realization, as a component of their concept of freedom. In fact, they believe that state interventions designed to achieve the conditions of positive freedom by promoting equality, peace, fairness, welfare, justice, and happiness have nothing to do with freedom. According to them, while a lack of income, education, and other resources could be interpreted as signs of incapacity, they are not obstacles to the actualisation of freedom. Friedman was very explicit that state regulations mandating the redistribution of wealth and income for the purpose of achieving equality, fairness, welfare and justice, constituted real threats to freedom. For him, defenders of state interventions aimed at attaining social and distributive justice confused the lack of freedom with social and economic inequality. He was of the opinion that economics should not be concerned with just and unjust decisions, choices or actions, as every society includes some people who enjoy greater economic success relative to others. People who are better off do not coerce the poor or less economically successful people in a manner that prevents them from attaining economic prosperity or vice versa. Similarly, Hayek maintained that poverty had nothing to do with freedom, understood as the absence of coercion. According to him, coercion has to be intentional, and poverty is generally not the outcome of specific intentions. That means poverty and a lack of income are not forms of coercion, since they are not caused by the deliberate intentions of one individual to prevent someone else from doing something.

Hayek was of the opinion that a person or entity acting in a manner that deliberately deprives others of goods required for human survival represented a clear form of coercion and a violation of freedom. That means he was simultaneously opposed to the government provision of certain services and goods that are important for the survival of its citizens, and to an individual, or a group of individuals, exploiting these necessary goods by intentionally preventing others from accessing them. He explained that since coercion is strongly related to the intention of the economic agent, there is a case to be made in favour of state intervention when a monopoly deliberately exercises its coercive powers over others. As an example, Hayek put forth the scenario of a proprietor of the only 'spring in an oasis,' who demanded that people pay an exorbitant price to buy water from him. He stated that this would represent 'a clear case of coercion,' given that water is a necessary good or 'an essential commodity' for survival (Hayek 2011, 203). This example suggests that the ability to access to goods that are necessary for survival is an important aspect of Hayek's concept of freedom. It should be noted that Hayek did not consider monopolies to be coercive in and of themselves despite the fact that they could restrict supply in order to sell their products and services at higher prices. However, it seems that he acknowledged that any company that intentionally controls the supply of a good that is necessary for survival does indeed exercise coercion (Hayek 2011, 203). Therefore, the case of a large transnational corporation gaining monopoly control over a poor country's water utility via privatization and then raising prices to the extent that access is significantly curtailed for a large segment of the population would satisfy Hayek's definition of coercion. It seems that there was a relationship between freedom and the possession of necessary goods in Hayek's political thoughts. His acknowledgement that people had the right to access and obtain necessary goods implies some level of support for social justice, positive rights to resources, and positive freedom. However, he still maintained that freedom had nothing to do with justice, equality, and fairness, a view he shared with many other neo-liberals. Knight (1929, 140) held similar opinions to those of Hayek, as he explained that a poor person is not coerced when he is not able to buy a commodity that 'he does not have money enough to pay for (unless, again, the fact is due to some "unfair" manipulation).' According to him, it is a 'misuse of words to describe' a lack of money as a 'deprivation of freedom' (Knight 1929, 140). In this case, the societal organization or public policy might be 'criticized' for having an 'inequitable distribution of power rather than unethical coercion or interference with the use of power' (Knight 1929, 140). That means an unequal distribution of wealth and income resulting from the free-market system did not constitute an obstacle to the achievement of freedom. According to neo-liberals, freedom justifies disparities in incomes, which can affect the quality and variety of goods and services that an individual is able to consume. However, unlike Hayek, Knight (1929, 137) recognized that these kinds of 'inequalities tend overwhelmingly to reduce and not to increase "total satisfactions"' of society as a whole.

Contrary to Hayek, advocates of positive freedom would argue that the definition of coercion should not be limited to one individual intentionally forcing someone to perform an act against their will, or preventing someone from performing their own choice of action. According to them, individuals are also coerced if they lack the necessary capacity, ability, money, training, education, or health to achieve self-development, as they would not be free to choose. It does not matter how many choices are available to people if they lack the means to take advantage of them, which would mean they are not free. Nevertheless, Hayek maintained that individuals could still be free or 'feel free' if many options were not available to them due to a lack of certain qualities, capacities and abilities, provided that they are still free to choose. This view was also held by most neo-liberals, who generally believe that freedom has nothing to do with equality, fairness, justice, happiness, self-development, or moral and ethical values. Consequently, it should come as no surprise that neo-liberals reject positive freedom, where one's freedom is measured by the extension of their ability and capacity to achieve their highest development.

The critiques put forth by neo-liberal economists with respect to the achievement of social justice via governmental intervention are important for understanding the foundations of the modern state. They believe that state intervention for the purpose of achieving the conditions of positive freedom violates economic and negative freedom. According to them, since positive freedom aims for the achievement of conditions of self-development, it requires the unequal treatment of citizens on the part of the state in the form of reallocating resources. Neo-liberals have argued that reallocating resources necessitates deliberate central planning, which involves interventions by the state that constrain the free direction of individuals in their own affairs by imposing patterns and norms that dictate their actions and activities. In other words, by interfering in order to achieve the conditions of positive freedom, the state intentionally makes people serve a particular goal by inhibiting their free actions. Essentially, neo-liberals believe that the ability of individuals to make their own choices would be eliminated. They claim that the state does the greatest harm to people by deciding what is best for them, because it destroys individual freedom. Generally, neo-liberals are of the view that, even if individuals are not able to fully utilize their freedom on account of inadequate social and economic conditions, it is best to leave all choices up to them to decide. They maintain that, in a free society, nobody should have anything to say about what any individual does with their freedom. According to them, the state has a duty to secure the conditions of a free-market economy, but it has no responsibility to provide certain services and goods that are necessary for the achievement of self-development and the development of individual abilities.

Based on the concept of positive freedom, negative freedom alone does not provide people with all of the resources and conditions necessary to allow them to make the fullest possible use of their physical and mental capacities. Proponents of positive freedom argue that when individuals lack certain necessary goods and services, such as adequate education, training, health, housing, income, food, and information, they are not able to achieve self-development. Therefore, they are not free. Presently, billions of people around the world lack certain necessary goods and services due to the intentional and coercive actions of large and powerful corporations, which would be considered unjust based on the concept of positive freedom, and coercive based on the concept of negative freedom. That means free-market capitalism is directly responsible violating the freedom of a large segment of the global population. For instance, having to work in order to obtain necessities of life required for survival is a form of true unfreedom, because 'the human existence in this realm is determined by objectives and functions that are not its own and that do not allow the free play of human faculties and desires' (Marcuse 1998, 195). That is to say, when people are treated as though they are merely mechanical means of production in the workplace, they are stripped of their potentialities for the highest self-development. Furthermore, people have no freedom when they are struggling to obtain their basic needs (such as food and shelter), because freedom as self-determination lies beyond the realm of necessity. In other words, if individuals dedicate their entire lives to working to obtain their basic needs, they would not be able to achieve their highest self-development, as it is 'the sphere outside labor which defines freedom' (Marcuse 1998, 156). Possessing and obtaining 'procurement of the necessities of life are the prerequisite, rather than the content, of a free society' (Marcuse 1998, 195). In fact, the notion of freedom is meaningless when individuals do not live based on their own values, faculties and desires, but rather according to the requirements of an unjust economic system. In this situation, individuals themselves become instruments of repression. If individuals are freed from the enslavement of providing for their basic needs, then 'productivity loses its repressive power and impels the free development of individual needs' (Marcuse 1998, 156).

Positive freedom has motivated many powerful and ethical movements in the twentieth century, including socialist regimes and left-wing movements around the world. However, the last four decades have been a complete failure in terms of understanding these movements that were motivated by the achievement of positive freedom. Since the rise of neo-liberalism, freedom has been declining with the increasing focus on individual interests. Individuals now measure their freedom according to cost-benefit analyses, with the objective of possessing as much as possible. In reality, however, they have lost their ability to dissent and no longer control their own destinies. Presently, freedom as self-determination can only be realized if the masses are 'liberated from all propaganda, indoctrination, and manipulation, capable of knowing and comprehending the facts and of evaluating the alternatives' (Marcuse 2007, 256).

3.4 Conclusion

Friedman acted as though he was a salesman of free-market capitalism and its conception of freedom, which often led him to over-simplify philosophical and political terms, theories and concepts, so that his ideas would resonate with popular audiences. One of the reasons why the neo-liberal definition of freedom is unquestionably accepted by the masses is because they have been inundated by its constant use and presentation in the mass media, public speeches, articles, books and other modes of communications for decades. People feel reassured that they know what freedom is when they see, hear and read about prominent figures and personalities, including scholars, professors, democratically-elected leaders, members of the military, actors, and athletes using the term in a uniform way that corresponds with their understanding of the concept. Furthermore, by limiting the definition of freedom to the freedom to choose, and consistently claiming that only the free-market system can ensure and maintain the conditions of freedom, neo-liberals have been able to gain the support of the masses in spreading their ideology around the world. Additionally, the definition and components of the neo-liberal concept of freedom also includes some ideas, views and features that are very attractive and desirable for the masses. In particular, it promotes the idea that individuals should focus on advancing their own self-interests without feeling remorse for any destructive outcomes of their behaviours based on moral and ethical considerations.

Applying neo-liberal economic principles and reasoning to every aspect of life has resulted in external forces shaping the majority of people's choices, including when it comes to their education, jobs, spending patterns, savings, investments, daily habits, and ephemeral and long term goals. That is because all aspects of people's lives are essentially being determined by powerful actors within neo-liberalism, particularly those that exercise coercive power over lifestyle choices made by the mass majority of the population. Those powerful actors are then free to satisfy new and limitless wants and desires that they often played a role in creating, which is misinterpreted as an expansion of freedom in neo-liberal societies, where people have been conditioned to associate freedom with number of choices available to them in the marketplace.

It could be argued that, after four decades of being exposed to the neo-liberal concept of freedom, the masses understand and see the world through a framework that has been provided to them by neo-liberal economists. More specifically, all aspects of people's physical, spiritual and emotional lives are viewed through this framework. However, a close examination of this framework reveals that neo-liberals have been using the concept of freedom as a tool to further the implementation of free-market economic principles and approach to all aspects of life, as opposed to delivering genuine freedom to the masses.

Another reason why the neo-liberal concept of freedom was able to triumph over other versions is because its advocates have been able to mask its limitations by providing incomplete and inaccurate information about positive freedom. If a majority of the world population were able to distinguish between positive and negative freedom, and understand freedom as self-realisation and the development of individuality, then they would realize that they have not been free. That is to say, they would understand that 'being free' is completely different than 'feeling free.' Moreover, if freedom was understood in the sense of self-realization, then people would realize that the neo-liberal defense of freedom as being 'free to choose' is an illusion. Once people are freed from the neo-liberal concept of freedom, they will be liberated from the entire system that supports the maximization of self-interests, productivity, economic growth, and mass consumption, which are propelling them towards an environmental apocalypse.

References

Becker, Garry S. 1968. Crime and Punishment: An Economic Approach. *The Journal of Political Economy* 76 (2): 169–217.

———. 1973. A Theory of Marriage: Part I. *The Journal of Political Economy* 81 (4): 813–846.

———. 1976. *The Economic Approach to Human Behaviour*. Chicago: The University of Chicago Press.

Berlin, Isaiah. 2002 [1969]. *Incorporating Four Essays on Liberty*. Ed. Henry Hardy. Oxford: Oxford University Press.

Buchanan, James. 1975. *The Limits of Liberty*. Chicago: University of Chicago Press.

Friedman, Milton. 1967. Value Judgments in Economics. Ed. Sidney Hook. *Human Values and Economic Policy, A Symposium*, 85–93. New York: New York University Press.

———. 1981a. *The Invisible Hand in Economics and Politics*. Singapore: Institute of Southeast Asian Studies. https://miltonfriedman.hoover.org/friedman_images/Collections/2016c21/InvHan1980.pdf.

———. 1981b. Market Mechanisms and Central Economic Planning. From *The Collected Works of Milton Friedman*. Ed. Robert Leeson and Charles G. Palm. Washington, DC: American Enterprise Institute.

———. 1982 [1962]. *Capitalism and Freedom*. Chicago. The University of Chicago Press.

———. 2002 [1962]. *Capitalism and Freedom*. Chicago. The University of Chicago Press.

Filip, Birsen. 2018. 'Hayek and Humboldt on Freedom and the Role of the State.' Ed. Robert Leeson. Hayek: A Collaborative Biography: Part XIV: Liberalism in the Classical Tradition: Orwell, Popper, Humboldt and Polanyi, 105–152. Cham: Palgrave Macmillan.

Friedman, Milton, and Friedman, R.D. 1990 [1980]. *Free to Choose: A Personal Statement*. New York: Harcourt Brace Jovanovich.

Hayek, F.A. 1958 [1948]. *Individualism and Economic Order*. Chicago: University of Chicago Press.

———. 1991. *The Trend of Economic Thinking: Essays on Political Economists and Economic History*. Ed. William Warren Bartley and Stephen Kresge. Abingdon: Routledge.

———. 2011 [1960]. *The Constitution of Liberty*. Chicago: The University of Chicago Press.

Hobbes, Thomas. 1998 [1996]. *Leviathan*. Ed. J. C. A. Gaskin. Oxford: Oxford University Press.

Humboldt, Wilhelm von. 1969 [1854]. *The Limits of State Action*. Cambridge: Cambridge University Press.

Knight, Frank H. 1929. Freedom as Fact and Criterion. *International Journal of Ethics* 39 (2): 129–147. Chicago: The University of Chicago Press. https://www.jstor.org/stable/2377742.

———. 1948. Free Society: Its Basic Nature and Problem. *The Philosophical Review* 57 (1): 39–58.

———. 1972. Social Science. *Ethics* 83 (1): 1–12.

———. 2007 [1935]. *The Ethics of Competition*. New York: Routledge.

Marcuse, Herbert. 1968. *Reason and Revolution*. London: Routledge & Kegan Paul Ltd.

———. 1998 [1956]. Eros and Civilisation: A Philosophical Inquiry into Freud. Abingdon: Routledge.

———. 2007. *The One-Dimensional Man: Studies in the ideology of advanced industrial society*. London: Routledge.

Mill, John Stuart. 1991 [1859]. *On Liberty and Other Essays*. Oxford: Oxford University Press.

Mises, Ludwig von. 1998 [1949]. *Human Action: A Treatise on Economics*. Auburn: The Ludwig von Mises Institute.

Neuhouser, F. 2000. *Foundations of Hegel's Social Theory. Actualizing Freedom*. Cambridge: Harvard University Press.

Weil, E. 1998. *Hegel and The State*. London: The John Hopkins University Press.

CHAPTER 4

Spheres of Government in Totalitarian, Welfare and Neo-Liberal States

According to Hayek, economic activities can be organized in two ways: voluntary cooperation (spontaneous order) or central deliberate planning (artificial order or the command economy). That said, neo-liberals worship voluntary cooperation, where decentralized planning is performed by many separate individuals, and the state governs least. Meanwhile, they explain that welfare, socialist, fascist and communist states, all of which are variations of centrally planned systems, are directed by a social engineer (or engineers) who enacts policies intended to achieve predetermined collective goals and perennial justice. They argue that central deliberate planning engenders harmful economic and social consequences, because achieving a predetermined common end requires regular intervention on the part of the state. Neo-liberal economists claim that this type of state intervention is highly inefficient, eventually leading to high inflation, more unemployment, lower productivity, and slower economic growth. They further allege that central deliberate planning aimed at achieving the common good results in corruption, mismanagement, unfreedom. Consequently, they support the notion of dismantling of centrally planned economies.

Before the end of the Cold War Era (1947–1991), liberals and neo-liberals closely examined the power and authority of the state in the Soviet Union. In doing so, they tried to demonstrate that the tenets of communism were false, because they were unable to deliver the collective good

B. Filip, *The Rise of Neo-liberalism and the Decline of Freedom*,
Palgrave Insights into Apocalypse Economics,
https://doi.org/10.1007/978-3-030-61623-6_4

that they promised. They pointed to the collapse of the Soviet Union as official confirmation of their view that centrally planned systems decisively failed to realize their objective of attaining social justice. They also believed communism no longer posed a legitimate threat to capitalism after the Soviet Union disintegrated, because communism lost its intellectual base and popular appeal around the world. Subsequently, free-market capitalism consolidated its grip on the social, political and economic arenas throughout the world, unopposed by a true ideological rival. Still, neo-liberal economists were not satisfied that all the enemies of open societies had entirely vanished.

In the early decades of the twentieth century, welfare states were considered to be the most prominent opponents of free-market economies, from the time the New Deal was being implemented in the United States until the onset of the Cold War Era, when communism assumed the mantle of main rival. With communism out of the way following the collapse of the Soviet Union, the paternalism of the welfare state once again came under focused attack by proponents of neo-liberalism. As a result, they were regarded as legitimate threats to economic freedom, freedom in general, and open societies, along with socialist, communist and fascist regimes.

This chapter focuses on the neo-liberal understanding of the relationship between freedom and the role of government. As such, it presents neo-liberal arguments against state interventions via central deliberate planning, mainly in socialist, communist and welfare states, while also explaining the types of state interventions that they would support. However, there will be no discussion of the role of the state under fascism and Nazism. This chapter relies on various arguments against central planning put forth by Friedman, Hayek and Mises in an effort to promote the superiority of the free-market economy over all other systems of governance. More specifically, Mises and Hayek discussed their strong opposition to central economic planning for eliminating freedom in their respective books *Socialism* (1922) and *The Road to Serfdom* (1944). Meanwhile, Friedman dedicated a significant portion of his work to demonstrating the superiority of capitalism over centrally planned systems when it came to ensuring the conditions of freedom. All three treated many economic issues and problems as matters of conflict between the voluntary organization of society for the purpose of achieving individual ends, and the artificial organization of society to attain collective ends. In doing so, their goal was to expose weaknesses and flaws in centrally planned systems. This chapter also discusses contradictions of the neo-liberal state. In particular, it explains that even though neo-liberals strongly advocate for limited state action and the elimination of many publicly-funded services and programs, they are actually quite tolerant of increases in government expenditures and employment provided that they help establish and sustain the condition of a free-market system.

4.1 Totalitarian Regimes and the State

In a number of countries, socialist and communist revolutionary movements succeeded in abolishing many of the conditions of capitalism in an effort to correct social, political and economic inequality and injustices, which may have prevailed for centuries due to colonialism, imperialism, hegemony, military occupation, etc. Among the specific features of a capitalist economy targeted for abolishment or change were the free adjustment of wages and prices charged for goods and services in the market, private control of the factors of production, private property ownership, voluntary exchange, etc. Accordingly, the governments of some of these countries nationalized enterprises, factories, and utilities, and confiscated vast properties owned by very rich entrepreneurs and landlords, which were often redistributed in line with newly-implemented land and agrarian reforms. Basically, these countries aimed to achieve 'the improvement of the position of the propertyless classes of society by a redistribute on of income derived from property. This implies collective ownership of the material means of production and collectivist direction and control of their use' (Hayek 1958, 129).

Since the means of production were no longer privately owned, the state was now the sole employer and responsible for organizing all production and distribution activities via central planning, to the extent that it would run all of the factories, plants and farms in the country. That means the state was responsible for answering 'the major economic questions through its ownership of resources and its power to enforce decisions' (Samuelson and Nordhaus 2010, 8). For example, the state authority will determine what types of factories are in operation, and work out precise details like their exact locations, their methods of operation, the machines and equipment they use, how many workers they employ, and the physical and chemical qualities of various materials used at all stages of production. However, all decisions concerning production and distribution were aimed at achieving the predetermined ends of the centrally planned and designed system, which are intended to increase the well-being of the nation as opposed to being guided by selfish profit-seeking behaviour and competition. The centrally planned state also decides 'who is to be allowed to provide different services or commodities, at what prices or in what quantities—in other words, measures designed to control the access to different trades and occupations, the terms of sale, and the amounts to be produced or sold' (Hayek 2011, 336). Friedman (1981, 5) also stated that, in centrally planned systems, the state authority decides 'who should sweep the streets and who manage the factory, who should be the policeman and who the physician.' That means the central authority instructs citizens as to where they should work, how much they should earn, and how much they are allowed to consume. In effect, production and consumption become compulsory, because people have to accept what the central authority decides for them.

Neo-liberals were highly critical of centrally planned states for allowing a central authority to direct all details of economic matters and control all aspects of people's lives based on carefully constructed and elaborate plans. In particular, they argued that individuals were no longer entrepreneurs that could freely sell their labour at a negotiated price; they were reduced to little more than instruments of the state authority to be used for the attainment of a predetermined collective end. Neo-liberals have claimed that such strict state control over all economic matters makes it very difficult to channel resources to innovate modes of production so as to increase productivity, achieve efficiency, and elevate economic growth. Furthermore, they have frequently argued that centrally planned systems were inefficient and constituted a burden on the state treasury. According to them, centrally planned systems infringed upon private enterprise and private property, which are essentially swept away by expropriation and nationalisation. Subsequently, nationalized enterprises would sell their products or services at prices fixed by the state that were often lower than the cost of producing or providing them, thereby contributing to inefficiency and fiscal deficits. Neo-liberals also contended that corruption, bribery, black-markets, and long lines to purchase scarce products were rampant in countries with centrally planned economies. Therefore, state intervention in a centrally planned system is incapable of making people feel free and satisfied with their economic activities; it only has the power to make them feel unfree, unsatisfied and coerced.

When comparing capitalist and centrally planned systems, Friedman focused on contrasting material well-being, competition, the variety of stores and goods available for consumption, the effective use of time, factors of production, the quality of housing, entertainment, and the freedom of expression. In doing so, he glorified capitalism for providing economic prosperity, and offering a variety of stores, goods and services, while disregarding any of its deficiencies. According to Friedman, a state cannot achieve the common good by engaging in some of the practices that are typically associated with centrally planned economies, including fixing prices and wages, redistributing incomes and wealth, preventing citizens from buying, producing and selling certain products, or discouraging individuals from striving for self-interest maximization. Those 'ordinary citizens are in political fetters, have a low standard of living, and have little power to control their own destiny' (Friedman and Friedman 1990, 55). In fact, neo-liberal economists were adamant that every person living under a centrally planned economy would be worse off than even the poorest individual in a capitalist system. This is because they believed that a centrally planned system did not have the appropriate tools needed to make the large scale calculations required to achieve the common good. For example, Mises (1949, 698) stated that:

> The paradox of "planning" is that it cannot plan, because of the absence of economic calculation. What is called a planned economy is no economy at all. It is just a system of groping about in the dark. There is no question of a rational choice of means for the best possible attainment of the ultimate ends sought. What is called conscious planning is precisely the elimination of conscious purposive action.

Neo-liberals contend that the absence of appropriate economic calculations means that central planning does not even attempt to be economical. In fact, they point out that, on many occasions, it will choose the costliest measure available instead of the best one, because of its fixation with achieving the common good. Hayek (2011) maintained that centrally planned systems would require a great variety of specialized, reliable and relevant information in order to plan efficiently. That said, he was certain that it was not possible for any individual or entity to possess perfect knowledge, which would be required to achieve such an efficient degree of planning, because knowledge is dispersed and fragmented among all the people. Individuals, including social engineers, can only possess a tiny fraction of the whole base of knowledge. Given the vast amounts of knowledge present in complex modern societies, Hayek (1958, 131) was convinced that a central authority could not determine best allocation of resources 'with a reasonable degree of accuracy, with a degree of success equaling or approaching the results of competitive capitalism.' Accordingly, he claimed that the lack of perfect knowledge combined with the complex and spontaneous nature of societies limites 'the ambitions of the engineer' (Hayek 1958, 124). He further argued that 'it is not possible for a conscious central planning authority to spontaneously adjust and change the patterns, values, rules, goals, and ends of a society when a new situation emerges. To the contrary, he believed that such an authority would end up producing negative outcomes if such an undertaking was ever attempted' (Filip 2018a, 117).

Neo-liberal economists believe that, unlike centrally planned economies, the free-market system does not suffer from an absence of appropriate economic calculations. In fact, all of its agents employ them and, as a result, everyone enjoys higher levels of supply and consumption, as well as better quality goods and services, compared to their counterparts living under systems based on central deliberate planning. They explain that the pursuit of individual goals in a free-market system leads to voluntary cooperation between economic agents, which in turn determines the price, quality and quantity of the goods and services sold in the marketplace, as well as the wage rate paid to workers. Consequently, each person achieves efficiency in various areas of economic life without the need for intervention on the part of the state.

One of the defining characteristics that distinguishes free-market systems from centrally planned systems is their respective positions on the achievement of social justice. In centrally planned systems, the state should ensure the conditions of greater security and equality, because they considered freedom, equality, social justice, the role of the state and ethical values to be inseparably intertwined. Consequently, centrally planned governments sought to achieve the collective good by redistributing economic power and implementing policies and programs that would improve the lifestyles of the masses by addressing a variety of social problems, including poverty, unemployment, homelessness, and illiteracy. Specific government measures included providing universal healthcare, free education, full employment, land reforms, access to affordable housing, food security, etc. By doing so, these governments managed to attain a number of notable achievements in a number of social development indicators, such as raising life expectancy, lowering child mortality, and reducing poverty rates, thereby improving the living standards of hundreds of millions of people who had previously endured oppression for centuries.

Wassily Leontief (1906–1999) (1985, 225), a Russian-American economist, who was awarded the Nobel Prize in 1973 in economics 'for the development of the input-output method and for its application to important economic problems,'[1] explained that, in the Soviet Union, 'the Communist leaders were engaged in the unprecedented task of transforming literally at breakneck speed a technologically backward, predominantly peasant country into an industrialized military power dedicated to the pursuit of further economic growth. They were their own economists.' He maintained that the 'technique of economic planning' developed by the communist regime of the Soviet Union was highly advanced, and as such, garnered a great deal of interest on the part of capitalist countries during the Cold War Era. However, while 'Western economists have often tried to discover "the principle" of the Soviet technique of planning. They never succeeded' (Leontief 1985, 225). Furthermore, Tariq Ali (1988, 71), a British political activist, writer, and journalist, as well as a leading figure in the international left, stated that, despites its flaws and defects, central deliberate planning in the Soviet Union achieved some 'remarkable results,' stating that:

> it was not perfect, of course, not economically optimal, but very remarkable if one compares it to economies at a similar level of development as the Soviet economy in the Twenties, Thirties, Forties and Fifties.

The state-run economies of Cuba, Eastern Europe and the former Soviet Union faced considerable difficulties due to the poverty and underdevelopment they inherited from the oppressive and exploitive regimes that previously governed them. These nations were also forced to endure the constant efforts of capitalist countries to destroy their collectivist regimes, such as being subjected to destructive embargos and sanctions, intimidation, and destabilization. Nevertheless, they still managed to transform 'impoverished semi-feudal countries into relatively advanced societies. Whatever their mistakes and crimes, they achieved' (Parenti 2015, 144). Regardless of their achievements, supporters of free-market capitalism have never recognized any of positives outcomes attained by current and

[1] The Nobel Prize. 'Wassily Leontief.' https://www.nobelprize.org/prizes/economic-sciences/1973/leontief/facts/.

former communist regimes. That is to say, they consistently emphasized the many evils that they associated with totalitarian regimes without fully acknowledging any of their remarkable achievements. In particular, they condemned 'the Soviet Union as a Stalinist monstrosity and a Leninist moral aberration' (Parenti 1997, 46).

According to liberals and neo-liberals, all centrally planned systems have at least one social engineer who acts as a single planning authority that directs the economic activities of the nation, while also frequently regulating people's choices and actions, all in the name of achieving a predetermined collective end. They further claim that, since this often involves relying on oppressive and violent measures, the social engineer will justify the conduct of the state with moral and ethical arguments, similar to those put forth by dictators, inquisitors and tyrants. In other words, liberals and neo-liberals associated centrally planned systems with dictatorships and tyrannies, where the state uses its police and military forces to grant privileges to a minority of people who comprise the ruling classes, while oppressing the mass majority via terror. Hayek argued that the central deliberate planning authority does not seek out approval for their predetermined collective ends prior to implementing policies and programs, because they believe that citizens do not know what is best for themselves. In fact, Friedman (1961, 4) stated that a centrally planned system resembles the structure of 'an army' in a communist state, as it essentially involves having a commander in place who chooses, decides, and acts for all. Similarly, Hayek suggested that the social engineer represented a commander, giving orders at every stage of the production and distribution processes, while ordinary citizens act as soldiers and obey their dictates.

Furthermore, Mises (1949, 849) stated that defenders of central planning 'become more and more entangled in contradictions and absurdities,' to the point where they are willing to accept the idea of a 'superhuman dictator,' because that is what would be required to achieve the many diverse objectives of a state. According to him, it makes no difference 'whether the absolute ruler bases his claims on the divine rights of anointed kings or on the historical mission of the vanguard of the proletariat or whether the supreme being is called Geist (Hegel) or Humanité (Auguste Comte),' under central planning, the social order is designed by a social engineer, who plans and controls of all the activities of individuals (Mises 1949, 151).

Based on the arguments put forth by Friedman, Hayek and Mises, citizens living under centrally planned systems are bound to unconditionally obey all orders issued by the state authority. In the event of widespread disobedience with respect to the commands, prohibitions, and orders issued by the state, the government will eventually transform itself into a coercive power and use violent means against its own people. The state has a variety of mechanisms at its disposal to enforce its rule, including coercion on the part of police services, the military, prisons, and intelligence agencies. Under such circumstances, the centrally planned state ignores individual will and choices, and violates the private spheres of individuals in the name of the collective good. In other words, the state uses coercive means and violent measures to prevent individuals from living their lives in accordance with their own goals, wills and reason.

According to Mises (1949, 282, 283), even though achieving freedom through centrally planned systems has 'become the most popular slogan of the champions of totalitarian government and the Russification of all nations,' it is a delusion to believe that central deliberative planning can achieve freedom by imposing restrictions on the private spheres and economic activities of individuals. Since individuals are bound to unconditionally obey the orders and instructions issued by the state authority in a centrally planned system, they are deprived of the opportunity to make their own decisions based on their own values and goals. In fact, he argued that, in a centrally planned system, 'there is nothing to which the attribute "free" could be attached but the unlimited arbitrariness of the dictator' (Mises 1949, 281).

Mises was of the opinion that it did not matter whether the central planning authority was called a dictator, despot, tyrant, 'superhuman dictator' or social engineer, they all violate freedom by imposing rules of individual conduct and intervening in the private spheres of people. He explained that when the state controls all means of production, in addition to 'all the other rights of men,' people cannot shape their lives freely according to their own wills and plans (Mises 1949, 285). Hayek (2011, 341) also emphasized the point that centrally planned systems require that 'people be told what to do and what ends to serve,' meaning that there is no room for individual judgments and decisions. That means they are unconditionally subject to authoritarian control because, ultimately, only the ideas, values, goals, decisions and actions of the government count for anything. Consequently, individual freedom has been purged, and citizens are powerless against the oppressive and coercive actions of their central authorities, which essentially had 'full power to relegate every citizen it dislikes to the arctic or to a desert and to assign him "hard labor" for life'

(Mises 1949, 284). Friedman (2002 [1962]) believed that centrally planned economic systems represented the single greatest threat to freedom, even going so far as to claim that this type system would destroy all freedoms. That is to say, he was of the opinion that as soon as economic freedom was eliminated, political freedom and freedom in general would soon follow. Mises (1949, 285) concurred, stating that when people's 'fate is determined by the plans of a superior authority, in which the exclusive power to plan is vested,' they are not free.

Neo-liberals, much like any ideologue, devoted much of their analysis to demonstrating that capitalism was absolutely superior to centrally planned systems, because it ensured the conditions of a free-market economy, which in turn facilitated economic growth, productivity gains, higher efficiency, technological innovation, and freedom. It also increases the quantity, variety and quality of goods available to consumers. Conversely, they claim that the inefficient and oppressive economic planning implemented by a central authority via coercion would eventually drive the nation to impoverishment, unfreedom, un-productivity, and economic crisis. Friedman, Hayek and Mises emphasized that the methods and instruments used to achieve one unified plan in a centrally planned system violated freedom in general, as well as the economic freedom of individuals. Furthermore, they maintained that placing any restrictions or limitations on freedom would inevitably threaten and inhibit progress. That means centrally planned societies do not inspire progress to the extent that a free-market society does, because the former suspends the free-market mechanism and exercises total authority over all development. According to Friedman, Hayek and Mises, centrally deliberative states cannot survive, because they cannot prevent the eventual onset of an economic collapse, regardless of how wise and effective the control is. In other words, they believed that centrally planned systems were destined to fail and disappear.

A majority of the arguments put forth by neo-liberals criticizing state interference for the purpose of achieving the common good were developed during the battle of ideologies between communism and capitalism. Since then, they have kept associating state interference designed to achieve the common good with the errors and failures of totalitarian regimes in the past. Unfortunately, neo-liberal economists have not been able to fully understand the importance of state interference in attaining social justice, which facilitates the establishment and maintenance of the conditions of freedom. They have also conveniently ignored the fact that centrally planned countries were able to improve the lives of hundreds of millions of people. Despite the flaws and weaknesses of communist and socialist regimes, centrally planned and designed systems have shown that some level of state intervention in the economic and social lives of citizens can make positive contributions to their welfare.

4.1.1 *Methodological Individualism and Methodological Collectivism*

Many well-known political and philosophical theorists contributed to the development of the neo-liberal concept of individualism, including John Locke, Bernard Mandeville, David Hume, Adam Smith, Josiah Tucker, Adam Ferguson, Edmund Burke, Lord Acton just to name a few. All of them attempted to find the forces that determined the complex social and economic lives of individuals. However, methodological individualism was actually rejected from the early 1930s up until the 1950s, when Keynesian economics was the leading program of research within the discipline of economics and in the development of state policies (Friedman 1961). To be more precise, much of the world supported Keynesian ideas during World War II, the postwar era, and the 1960s and 1970s.

Friedman (1982, 134) argued that one of the main factors behind 'the development of a collectivist sentiment' in the twentieth century, primarily in Western countries, was 'a belief in equality of income as a social goal and a willingness to use the arm of the state to promote it.' He further explained that during the 1920s and 1930s, American intellectuals were convinced that 'capitalism was a defective system inhibiting economic well-being and thereby freedom' (Friedman 1982, 162). Consequently, they regarded central deliberate control by the state over economic affairs as the only solution to achieve economic well-being and freedom. In other words, American intellectuals in the 1920s and 1930s were basically supporters of methodological collectivism who attributed all evils to free-market capitalism. In this atmosphere of demand for central deliberate control by the state, the proponents of limited state action and free-market capitalism were largely quiet.

However, the late 1950s saw the gradual growth of support for individual freedom, free enterprise, and individualism among the new generation in the United States, even as a majority of Americans continued to support New Deal ideals, such as the protection of individuals against abuses and exploitation on the part of corporations, and the achievement of the common good for the masses via expanded government regulations targeting large corporations and banks. Friedman (1961, 11) claimed that there was a 'resurgence of belief in individualism' in the early 1960s, as the ideals associated with the New Deal were no longer appealing. During that time, there was an expansion in the number of academics, intellectuals and students who supported libertarian[2] and conservative ideologies, which favour individualistic approaches over collective approaches. Once neo-liberal economics became the leading program of research, support for collectivist approach was considered unsuitable and inappropriate for any free society.

According to Hayek (1952, 38) methodological individualism is 'closely connected with the subjectivism of the social sciences.' Meanwhile, methodological collectivism is 'closely connected with "objectivism" of the scientistic approach,' but not connected with subjectivism (Hayek 1952, 53). Hayek (1952, 53) explained that methodological collectivism treats '"society" or the "economy," "capitalism" (as a given historical "phase") or a particular "industry" or "class" or "country" as definitely given objects about which we can discover laws by observing their behavior as wholes." More precisely, it considers 'social phenomena not as something of which the human mind is a part and the principles of whose organization we can reconstruct from the familiar parts, but as if they were objects directly perceived by us as wholes' (Hayek 1952, 53). The collectivist approach gathers information about different aspects of society in order to discover patterns of development and progress via the identification of empirical regularities. Once these patterns are discovered, the social engineer will attempt to obtain conscious control over all forces of society. Hayek explained that fascism, socialism and communism all used collectivist methods.

Methodological individualism reduces the behavior of a collective entity into the behaviours of the individuals that comprise it. Since society consists of a many small independent atoms, or entities, the individual is the starting point of any social analysis. Neo-liberals first began to use the concept of methodological individualism in order to derive the principles of action for isolated individuals. Subsequently, it was applied to groups and complex social relationships and organisations. Basically, methodological individualism is associated with individualistic and selfish behaviours, meaning that economic systems, society and its institutions function according to the individualistic tradition. Consequently, social phenomena

[2] The libertarian resurgence was still at an early stage at that point.

are determined by the actions of independent atoms that are directed towards other people.

Many of the arguments put forth by neo-classical economists in defense of methodological individualism actually consisted of criticisms directed against methodological collectivism. This was the case with Carl Menger (1841–1921) (1985), founding father of the Austrian School of Economics, who was highly critical of the methodological collectivism in formulating his arguments in support of methodological individualism. The most important debate on methodology in the history of economic thought occurred between Menger and Gustav von Schmoller (1838–1917), who was leader of the younger German Historical School of Economics (GHSE). One of the main disputes in the methodological battle between Schmoller and Menger pertained to Schmoller's defence of methodological collectivism and his opposition to Menger's methodological individualism (Filip 2018d, 108). Menger (1985) regarded methodological collectivism as one of the main obstacles to finding solutions to a number of economic problems. He explained that, contrary to methodological collectivism, methodological individualism does not have any commitment to the common good, which he supported, given that he did not regard individuals as parts of a collective entity such as a state, nation, or social group. Based on methodological individualism, people respond to specific circumstances in their own manner, using their own particular knowledge and views, meaning that different people could produce vastly different outcomes under the same conditions. Because there is no social engineer to prevent individuals from making mistakes, producing failures, or engaging in wasteful and unjust activities under methodological individualism, it is up to each individual to achieve progress, success or failure on their own. Since the rise of neo-liberalism, methodological individualism has become an important analytical tool for neo-liberal economists in their attempts to explain economic phenomena, predict the future economic outcomes of actions undertaken by economic agents, and justify the implementation of state policies.

Buchanan (1975, 11) was highly supportive of methodological individualism, explaining that people live together in a society 'because social organization provides the efficient means of achieving' their individualistic ends. According to him, individuals contribute to the achievement of the best possible outcome for the whole society in the free-market economy by simply pursuing their own individual interests and desires. In other words, there is no conflict between the pursuit of individual interests and those of society as a whole. Buchanan (1975) argued that promoting the pursuit of individual self-interests as a motivating factor behind people's choices and behaviours has served as the basis for organizing relationships between economic agents and institutions in capitalist systems. In their book, *The Calculus of Consent: Logical Foundations of a Constitutional Democracy*[3] (1962, 21), Buchanan and his colleague Tullock claimed that methodological individualism is 'the genuine contribution that economic analysis can make, and has made, toward a better understanding of organized human activity.'

Methodological individualism is also an important component of Friedman's concept of freedom, and his economic theory. According to him, the individual, as an independent and atomic decision maker, is the heart of neo-liberal economics. He viewed society in terms of separate, individualistic goals as opposed to common and universal ends. Friedman assumed that, in a free-market economy, every individual basically behaves as thought he were Robinson Crusoe, meaning that each economic agent decides what to produce and consume based on a comprehensive set of information they have gathered about the entire economy. Buchanan and Tullock (1962, 14) suggested that, in this scenario, intervention is unnecessary, because each individual, as a producer, labourer, consumer, or investor, is 'the only ultimate choice-maker,' who maximizes his own utility. In other words, no external authority is able to make decisions with respect to the actions of individuals, because each individual is the only one capable of measuring his own utility and determining what actions are needed to maximize his self-interests.

Friedman argued that, by simply pursuing their own interests, individuals contribute to the interests of society as a whole in a more efficient manner than if they had actively or intentionally attempted to do so. For him, the objective of achieving self-interest maximization lies behind every effort undertaken by individuals, whether it be taking risks, working harder, saving, cooperating, or improving their lives. The private interest in question can be monetary gains, special rewards, 'the esteem or approval of fellow scholars,' or personal pleasure and satisfaction (Friedman and Friedman 1990, 23–26). Meanwhile, Hayek (1958, 6) claimed that the only way to comprehend social phenomena is by gaining an 'understanding of individual actions directed toward other people and guided by their

[3] This book had a particularly significant impact on the field of public choice, and was much more influential than any of their other contributions to the discipline of economics.

expected behavior.' According to him, many of the social and economic achievements of civilizations, as well as the institutions they created, could be attributed to methodological individualism instead of methodological collectivism. In essence, Hayek (1958, 8) was claiming that these achievements of humanity were the 'unforeseen result of individual actions.' He argued that central deliberate design placed too much value on the power of methodological collectivism. To the contrary, 'man has achieved what he has in spite of the fact that he is only partly guided by reason, and that his individual reason is very limited and imperfect' (Hayek 1958, 8). Hayek (1958, 11) was convinced that 'if left free, men will often achieve more than individual human reason could design or foresee.' Furthermore, he suggested that since methodological individualism allows people to pursue their dissimilar and conflicting personal goals and resolve all conflicts of interest through voluntary cooperation, it also limits the coercive activities of the state. He concluded that it would be impossible to achieve the common good by fully controlling and planning all aspects of a complex society without making errors or engaging in wasteful and unjust activities.

Advocates of methodological individualism insist that methodological collectivism diminishes the importance of achieving individual interests and having the freedom to choose. They further claim that, since large-scale planning aims to achieve common ends and national goals, it strengthens the role of the state at the expense of individual freedom and individual interests. In fact, Mises believed that defenders of methodological collectivism wanted to destroy freedom and free-market capitalism. He maintained that the application of collectivist ideas to society would lead to 'social disintegration and the perpetuation of armed conflict' (Mises 1949, 152). In other words, he was of the opinion that any attempts at the 'substitution of collectivism for liberalism would result in endless bloody fighting' (Mises 1949, 152). In that case, the majority of people would be 'dehumanized in order to make one man their godlike master' or dictator (Mises 1949, 152).

While methodological collectivism is undoubtedly a shift from the individual to the group, there is a strong interdependence between individuals and community life. Basically, an individual is always the product and member of some kind of a community or collective organization, such as a nation, state, political party, religious organisation, cultural identity, and family. All individuals are born into a collectively organized environment, which their lives and actions are dependent upon. That would suggest that each individual is part of a social organism, meaning they are connected with all of the other people that comprise that same social organism in some way. Furthermore, they aim for the achievement of common ends as a part of the social organism they belong to. Accordingly, the actions of individuals are related to the collective, whereas the individual will and spirit are subordinated to the public will and mind. As such, all individuals are supposed to be interested in the problems and issues affecting the whole society. For example, as members of a society, they would likely be inclined to work together in order to provide security and achieve common ends. However, that would require overcoming the selfish tendencies of individuals and compelling them to sacrifice their egoistical goals. In other words, individuals need to renounce their egoistic ends for the benefit of society, meaning that the interests of the individual would be subordinated to those of society as a whole (Milford 1995, 40). Therefore, based on methodological collectivism, economic systems and society (including its institutions) did not function based on individualistic traditions, but rather, according to the public spirit of the people, which aims to achieve the collective good.

Neo-liberals insisted that the main principle of methodological individualism was that nobody should have the power to determine the status and situation of other individuals. They considered this to be an essential condition of freedom that must not be sacrificed for the achievement of distributive justice or the public good. Additionally, neo-liberals highly value methodological individualism on account of its capacity to analyse complex social and economic phenomena. In particular, they have used the imaginary Robinson Crusoe analogy to justify individualistic thinking and actions. This model is extremely important for their interpretation of interpersonal relations and analysis of human actions. In reality, however, people cannot be completely detached from all others and live their lives according to the imaginary Robinson Crusoe scenario. Individuals are not isolated atoms; who they are is mainly determined by what they feel and think, which, in turn, are largely determined within the society they belong to.

The individualist approach has convinced people that individualism serves the interests of each person, as well as society as a whole. In their defense of the individualist approach, neo-liberals have argued that individualism objects to conformism and motivates diversity. In reality, individualism promotes a single way of being, as it is mainly concerned with the maximization of individual interests, which is generally related to the acquisitiveness of material and experiencing maximum pleasure. In fact, neo-liberalism has relied heavily on marketing and propaganda to convince people that life is all about individual self-interest maximization from an early age. In doing so, the goal of its practitioners was to mold people into their own conception of what it means to be human: an individualistic atomic entity free from collective values. By promoting individual agents as selfish, and lacking in compassion and empathy for others, neo-liberal economists have managed to create a society of individuals that are completely disconnected from one another, and isolated from community life. The global implementation of free-market capitalism has contributed to a rise in individualism, even in the most traditional societies and least developed regions of the world. Consequently, people no longer participate in activities and events as members of their respective communities and states. This situation has led to an increase in isolation and a lack of personal interaction, which has resulted in an 'abandonment of being by beings' (Heidegger 1993, 242).

4.1.2 Centrally Planned Systems and Diversity

Neo-liberal opposition to central deliberately planned and designed systems also stemmed from their view that such systems obstructed diversity by imposing patterns of individual behaviour on society. According to them, diversity disappears from a society that is subjected to the central deliberate planning of an authoritarian state, because it leads to uniformity in the values, beliefs, choices, and preferences of individuals. Friedman (1982, 21) believed that 'the great advantage' of the free-market system was that it permitted 'wide diversity.' To the contrary, he maintained that deliberate central planning could never achieve 'diversity of individual action' by 'imposing uniform standards' and patterns of behaviour (Friedman 1982, 12). According to him, this was evidenced by the fact that state interventions aimed at achieving equality 'in the United States in the nineteenth and early twentieth century' did not promote diversity (Friedman 1982, 83).

Hayek argued that 'it was necessary to limit state action in order to allow citizens to freely choose their own beliefs, values, and thoughts, as well as to possess the ability to shape their lives and develop their own faculties, skills, intellects, characters, and, ultimately, achieve diversity' (Filip 2018a, 122). He was particularly worried that publicly-provided services and programs would contribute to eliminating diversity in society.

For example, he argued that 'a publicly funded education system, where the 'contents' of education is managed by the state, would inhibit the free development of individual minds and obstruct diversity' (Filip 2018a, 132). Accordingly, he defended a pluralistic and private education system,[4] which would not constitute a menace to diversity and freedom, because it would not mould students in an effort to make everyone exactly alike, or attempt to control people's minds. Hayek (2011, 507) maintained that 'no single authority should have the monopoly of judging how valuable a particular kind of education is and how much should be invested in more education or in which of the different kinds of education.' Furthermore, Friedman (1982, 85) also argued for the elimination of state 'assistance to private colleges and universities' to 'preserve their full independence and diversity.'

Hayek claimed that, in a free-market system, limited state action and the practice of coordinating and organizing society based on spontaneous forces have allowed western civilizations to achieve increasing levels of diversity, complexity, and flexibility in society. Similarly, Friedman (1982, 11) stressed that diversity is best achieved in free societies, specifically stating that:

> Newton and Leibnitz; Einstein and Bohr; Shakespeare, Milton, and Pasternak; Whitney, McCormick, Edison, and Ford; Jane Addams, Florence Nightingale, and Albert Schweitzer; no one of these opened new frontiers in human knowledge and understanding, in literature, in technical possibilities, or in the relief of human misery in response to governmental directives. Their achievements were the product of individual genius, of strongly held minority views, of a social climate permitting variety and diversity.

The fact that neo-liberals criticized centrally planned economies for imposing patterns of individual behaviour and eliminating diversity in thinking is interesting, given that the system they advocate has essentially done the same thing. Neo-liberalism has been able to dominate both private and public spheres with a monistic worldview. It has also been largely successful in eliminating all opposition and alternative forms of societal organization by arguing that free-market capitalism is the only system that ensures the conditions of economic and individual freedom. This type of

[4] Despite his opposition to publicly-funded education systems, Hayek also conceded that the state should have the right to intervene in instances where parents are not able to provide their children with an education on the grounds of preventing ignorance.

rationalization is aimed at limiting the imaginations and thinking of individuals. However, it has also created a totalitarian universe in which individual thoughts, wills, minds and ideas are kept in a state of permanent mobilization in support of the free-market system.

Presently, people generally conform to the principles, norms, and views of neo-liberalism. By doing so, they have effectively lost the ability to see and understand the world from different perspectives. That is to say, free-market economics has largely destroyed diversity in views, opinions, and diverse lifestyles, in addition to ethical and moral pluralism, by imposing regularities in behaviour and encouraging uniform ways of living, thinking, and acting. Such forms of diversity are typically outcomes of culture and customs, which are influenced by factors specific to the societies where they prevail, including their particular history and geographical location. Meanwhile, the viability of free-market capitalism depends on constantly weakening moral and ethical values, and hindering diverse ways of thinking and living, by imposing free-market principles on every aspects of life. That means, under a system of free-market capitalism, everyone marches towards the same direction in the absence of diversity in their individual behaviors, thoughts, ideas, goals, wills, lifestyles, etc. As long as free-market capitalism continues to flourish, neo-liberals will not genuinely care about diminishing diversity.

4.2 The Welfare State

Two major lessons that people learned coming out of the Great Depression were that: they should not trust the free-market capitalist system to maintain prosperity and stability; and, they should support an active state role in the economy in order to prevent the onset of crises and solve economic problems. However, supporters of free-market capitalism did not agree with the drastic changes in the role of the government when it came to combatting economic problems during the New Deal Era. They were particularly critical that the dominant school of economics began to be guided by humanitarian and egalitarian sentiments during that period, with an objective to achieve the collective good, much like a socialist regime. Liberals regarded the New Deal as a radical transformation in the role that the state played in the lives of Americans, whereby government power would be increased at the expense of individual freedom, thereby setting the government up to turn itself into a coercive power. The New Deal was 'reviled by many business leaders at the time and even prompted a small group of them to plot a coup to overthrow Roosevelt's administration' (Bakan 2004, 20).

Given that free-market economies were unable to self-correct during the Great Depression, the New Deal launched a number of public programs and projects between 1933 and 1939 that were designed to stabilize the economy and provide relief to those who were suffering most from the impacts of the economic collapse. More precisely, it consisted of packages of 'regulatory reforms designed to restore economic health by, among other things, curbing the powers and freedoms of corporations' (Bakan 2004, 20). The New Deal facilitated a recovery in government activity, as it supported a number of important public projects, including 'a rural electrification program,' as well as the construction of roads, 'schools, parks, playgrounds, athletic fields, and airports, along with hospitals, post offices, bridges, tunnels, and courthouses' (Parenti 2015, 125, 126). Many jobs were created in the areas of agriculture, construction, and education, which contributed to alleviating unemployment. It also created 'thousands of acres of campgrounds and improvements in firefighting, rodent control, water conservation, and prevention of soil erosion' (Parenti 2015, 126). In 1935, 'the New Deal also passed a number of key laws that strengthened the bargaining rights of labor unions,' while also establishing a national minimum wage and instituting federal limits on the number of hours worked (Parenti 2015, 126). Additionally, the New Deal addressed the rampant poverty and unemployment of the time by establishing the National Housing Act, and introducing federal programs that provided relief payments to low-income families and the unemployed. Many of the current social insurance programs in the United States were largely established by the New Deal.

In essence, the New Deal represented the foundation of the modern welfare state, as the U.S. government, as well as a number of its counterparts in Western Europe, introduced reforms and regulations aimed at achieving the collective good in an effort to boost the economy and manage the destructive outcomes of capitalism in the aftermath of the Great Depression. Hayek (1958, 136) was of the view that, with the New Deal implemented in the U.S. and similar programs adopted in a number of other countries, governments had moved 'much further in the direction of central planning of current activity than has ever been attempted before.' As such, he was concerned about governments expanding their control over the economy in order to achieve the common good via the redistribution of income. He warned that if governments continued to follow this path, they would eventually turn themselves into genuine centrally planned economies. This was based on his belief that a welfare state was destined to lead to 'socialism' via 'its coercive and essentially arbitrary methods' (Hayek 2011, 376). More specifically, Hayek (2011, 373) argued that welfare states were likely to:

> impose more and more central control over economic decisions (though private property may be preserved in name) until we get that very system of central planning which few now consciously wish to see established. Furthermore, many of the old socialists have discovered that we have already drifted so far in the direction of a redistributive state that it now appears much easier to push further in that direction than to press for the somewhat discredited socialization of the means of production.

These views are not very surprising, given that during the Cold War Era many liberals were worried that the welfare state would eventually turn itself into a totalitarian regime. For example, Mises (1949, 856) argued that 'interventionism liquidates itself and must lead to socialism of the German pattern. Most of the European countries have already reached this phase.' Meanwhile, Hayek (2011, 376) was particularly concerned that once it was accepted that the government had a legitimate role in ensuring distributive justice, 'it is then assumed that even means contrary to the principles of freedom may be legitimately employed.' On this basis, he argued that planning for the welfare of the people would eventually turn into the desire to gain more control, including control over people, which would destroy a free society. Friedman (2002, 32) also claimed that 'every act of government intervention limits the area of individual freedom directly,' including actions on the part of the welfare state. This subject was also addressed by Henry Calvert Simons (1899–1946) (1934, 1), a well-known liberal economist at the University of Chicago who was an ardent defender of the laissez-faire approach and a strong opponent of New Deal policies, when he said that, 'we have witnessed abroad the culmination of movements from constitutional government to dictatorships, from freedom back to authority.' He was concerned that New Deal policies would facilitate the expansion of state authority and a corresponding decline of freedom in the U.S., as he suggested that 'the real enemies of liberty in this country are the naïve advocates of managed economy or national planning' (Simons, 1934, 2). Simons believed that economies could only be strong if they are protected from political interference.

Hayek (1998, v2, 83) argued that, in a welfare state, 'an authority instructed to achieve particular results for the individuals must be given essentially arbitrary powers to make the individuals do what seems necessary to achieve the required result.' That means welfare states are afforded the central authority to determine the allocation of resources and incomes in a manner that ensures all citizen are able to lead lifestyles that are in accordance with distributive justice. Hayek was strongly opposed to the idea of using state power to control the distribution of income in order to achieve the collective good. Hayek (2011, 341) opposed the collective good on the basis that it necessitated 'an allocation of all resources by a central authority; it requires that people be told what to do and what ends to serve.' He believed that since state authority determines the means by which people can achieve justice, issues that should be confined to people's private spheres become matters of public concern. In other words, the achievement of social justice requires individuals to obey particular and discriminatory rules that have been imposed on them by the state, which, according to Hayek, violates the private spheres of individuals and the general and abstract feature of the laws of a free society. In fact, many neo-liberals rejected welfare states outright on account of their belief that the principles of distributive justice are based on ethical and moral frameworks, which requires the intentional imposition of particular and discriminatory sets of values on society. Accordingly, the state becomes 'a paternalistic power' that 'controls most of the income of the community and allocates it to individuals in the forms and quantities which it thinks they need or deserve' (Hayek 2011, 377). That means welfare states treat people unequally in order to achieve justice, by confiscating part of the income earned by well-off individuals and distributing it to the poorer segments of the population. According to Hayek, this is a clear case of discrimination by the state, because the law is not being applied equally to all citizens, which means the law is unable to protect individuals from injustice. He also regarded this as an obvious example of coercion, whereby the state forces individuals to accept and adhere to predetermined values, such as justice, fairness, and equality.

Hayek (2011, 374–375) suggested that defenders of the welfare state often make 'modest and innocent aims of governmental activity to show how unreasonable is any opposition to the welfare state', such as 'minimum of sustenance' for people in need, or policies to 'temporarily subsidize certain experimental developments.' To the contrary, he believed that many of the activities undertaken by the welfare state for the stated purpose of achieving the common good 'really constitute an exercise of the coercive powers of government' over citizens, meaning that they represent a genuine 'threat to freedom' (Hayek 2011, 375). Nevertheless, Hayek (2011, 428) was positive that welfare states were 'a passing phenomenon' or a 'transitional phase,' and that they would eventually vanish as 'the general growth of wealth' will make them 'unnecessary.'

Friedman and Friedman also provided a number of arguments against the distribution of wealth and resources. For example, they claimed that the achievement of distributive justice within the auspices of social security programs would weaken the family, because individuals are not contributing to old age programs out of love and 'moral responsibility,' but rather, due to 'compulsion and fear' (Friedman and Friedman 1990, 106). They also maintained that the distribution of income represented a barrier to the transmission of accurate information in the marketplace, and acted as a disincentive to working harder and being creative, productive, and efficient. Additionally, Friedman tried to make the case that, contrary to claims that the main objective of welfare state programs and policies is to help the poor segment of the population, in reality, they make the poor worse off by discouraging them from finding work. He also argued that state intervention causes some people to become dependent on government assistance, which leads to them either becoming irresponsible, losing their freedom, or some combination of the two.

Buchanan were also opposed to idea of the state redistributing income in order to satisfy the well-being of the masses on the basis that 'majority rule is at best a highly imperfect means of pursuing distributive justice' (Brennan 1999, 142). He further elaborated that 'majority rule either generates cycles (that is, is basically distributionally indeterminate) or, when appropriately restricted, generates a specific pattern of transfers that is perversely responsive to normatively relevant changes (say, to changes in the income of the poorest)' (Brennan 1999, 142). Buchanan concluded that 'faith in the capacity of ordinary majoritarian processes to generate equitable patterns of distribution is naïve' (Brennan 1999, 143).

Meanwhile, in his own opposition to welfare states, Mises (1949) argued that collecting taxes in the name of security and equality reduces the freedom of wealthy citizens, because they do not voluntarily choose to pay taxes and have their money used to finance social programs for others. Essentially, the deficits of public expenditure are transferred to the rich segment of the population, instead of being paid for by the masses that end up profiting the most from the public spending. In other words, the state is using its coercive powers to ensure that a particular group of people receive specific benefits at the expense of the rich. Mises (1949, 853) suggested that these factors explain why higher tax rates for 'the rich are very popular with interventionist dilettantes and demagogues.'

Buchanan identified high levels of taxation as the main source that discourages people from initiating creative, and innovative activities. This type of discouragement ultimately ends up lowering productivity, economic growth and innovation in the country. Accordingly, Buchanan suggested that decreasing tax rates would motivate people to work harder and be more creative, because they would be allowed to keep more of the earnings and profits generated by the products of their creation.

Friedman and Friedman (1990, 104) also emphasized the negative impacts of raising taxes on the economy and argued that social security programs are not like an 'insurance program in which individual payments purchase equivalent actuarial benefits;' rather, they are 'a combination of a particular tax and a particular program of transfer payments.' Friedman further claimed that state programs and services designed to achieve an equality of outcomes seek to realise the goal of poor people, which is to tax the wealth of the rich people for their own benefit. In other words, the government forces people to allocate their money towards financing the needs of poor people instead of using it to buy goods and services for themselves. According to Friedman and Friedman (1990), the provision of any social programs and services entails someone spending someone else's money on someone else. More precisely, they explained that 'legislators vote to spend someone else's money. The voters who elect the legislators are in one sense voting to spend their own money on themselves…the bureaucrats spend someone else's money on someone else' (Friedman and Friedman 1990, 117). They also argued that, in order to achieve an equal distribution of income, the government acts 'as a parent charged with the duty of coercing some to aid others' (Friedman and Friedman 1990, 5).

Hayek agreed with Friedman's view that welfare states exercise paternalistic power, as they determine what is in the best interests of their citizens, and then use coercion to make them comply. In other words, Hayek (2011, 164) suggested that a society organized in accordance with distributive justice is 'a society in which authority decided what the individual was to do and how he was to do it.' For that reason, the state is able to order that 'a majority takes from a minority because the latter has more' (Hayek 2011, 426). Neo-liberals argue that this type of state is irreconcilable with freedom, because it takes from one group and gives to another in the name of fairness and justice. That is to say, state authority eliminates freedom by preventing its citizens from exerting their own faculties and abilities.

Hayek (1998, v2, 85) maintained that citizens of a welfare state are not free, because they are ‘subject to specific directions by authority’ for the benefit of a particular group of people. That would suggest that individual freedom is incompatible with welfare state. He argued that if people cannot ‘exercise any choice in some of the most important matters of their lives, such as health, employment, housing, and provision for old age, but must accept the decisions made for them by appointed authority on the basis of its evaluation of their need,’ then there would be no room for freedom (Hayek 2011, 377). Hayek (2011, 378) further contended that:

> It is sheer illusion to think that when certain needs of the citizen have become the exclusive concern of a single bureaucratic machine, democratic control of that machine can then effectively guard the liberty of the citizen.

Neo-liberals have consistently argued against publicly-funded education and health care services. In the U.S., they have been particularly opposed to ‘a single scheme of state insurance,’ and ‘a free health service for all’ (Hayek 2011, 421). Hayek (2011, 421), who featured prominently among them, argued that there are two major misconceptions when it comes to publicly-funded universal health care services:

> They are, first, the belief that medical needs are usually of an objectively ascertainable character and such that they can and ought to be fully met in every case without regard to economic considerations and second, that this is economically possible because an improved medical service normally results in a restoration of economic effectiveness or earning power and so pays for itself.

He claimed that both beliefs are a ‘mistake’ (Hayek 2011, 421). He further argued that publicly-funded universal health care is too expensive, and very inefficient. For these reasons, Hayek (2011, 423) fully endorsed private health care services, specifically stating that:

> it is probably in the interest of all that under a free system those with full earning capacity should often be rapidly cured of a temporary and not dangerous disablement at the expense of some neglect of the aged and mortally ill. Where systems of state medicine operate, we generally find that those

> who could be promptly restored to full activity have to wait for long periods because all the hospital facilities are taken up by people who will never again contribute to the needs of the rest.

Based on his evaluation, Hayek concluded that, despite their 'noble' intentions, publicly-funded social programs and services are wasteful and incompetent. As such, he strongly supported their privatisation. Meanwhile, Mises was positive that welfare states would eventually break down, because they could not finance their social services and programs indefinitely. He further elaborated that 'an essential point in the social philosophy of interventionism is the existence of an inexhaustible fund which can be squeezed forever. The whole doctrine of interventionism collapses when this fountain is drained off' (Mises 1949, 854).

Friedman and Friedman (1990, 64) regarded social security programs and services inspired by the New Deal as enemies of freedom, as they claimed that the interventionist policies of the welfare state have 'greatly limited' the freedom of Americans. They subscribed to the view that social security programs and services are 'antithetical to liberty' and 'in clear conflict' with economic freedom and freedom in general (Friedman and Friedman 1990, 128, 140). Friedman also complained that state interventions for the purpose of providing public services and programs imposed heavy costs on citizens, and that the government was incapable of effectively allocating resources in the interests of society as a whole.

Neo-liberals not only opposed the distribution of income and provision of social security programs and services by the state, they were also against many of the government regulations that were applied to the economy. They considered government regulatory power to be oppressive and counter to the voluntary interactions that are supposed to drive free-market processes (Stigler 1971, 10). Stigler (1971, 3) argued that 'the state-the machinery and power of the state-is a potential resource or threat to every industry in the society. With its power to prohibit or compel, to take or give money, the state can and does selectively help or hurt a vast number of industries.' He was particularly opposed to government political decisions pertaining to taxation and the regulation of private businesses, which he described as 'coercive,' because they do not require the consent of the firms whose profits are being affected. Stigler (1971, 3) believed that state regulations designed to protect and benefit the public interest often have 'undeniably onerous' effects upon 'the regulated industry,' such as the 'heavy taxation of the industry's product.' He was also critical of the government providing certain industries with a direct 'subsidy of money', such as airlines, education, hospitals, etc. (Stigler 1971, 4). Ultimately, Stigler thought that all forms of state intervention in the economy were inefficient and ineffective; he even went so far as to describe them as primary sources of wastefulness and corruption.

Neo-liberals also oppose state regulations designed to prevent the sale of new products on the grounds that they might be damaging or hazardous to human health and the environment. Such regulations will often delay the introduction of new products into the market by forcing them to undergo lengthy approval processes or by stipulating more testing and research, which can be very costly and time consuming. Neo-liberals adamantly reject the notion that such regulations are necessary for the protection of the public interest. They simply view them as inefficient and unnecessarily obstructive.

Buchanan argued that free-market capitalism motivates innovative and productive activities, because there is no state authority to prevent or discourage people from making improvements in both their private and public spheres. That is to say, he believed that people are free to embark upon any projects and activities of their choosing in a free-market system, whereas the regulations in a welfare state discourage people from working harder and initiating creative, productive and innovative activities. Accordingly, he advocated for the elimination of such regulations, so that private businesses can introduce new products into the market as quickly as possible and start earning returns on the investments they made during the research and development phases.

Furthermore, Friedman (1982, 124) argued that state regulatory measures such as 'registration, certification, or licensure, almost inevitably becomes a tool in the hands of a special producer group to obtain a monopoly position at the expense of the rest of the public.' In fact, when addressing the subject of state regulation, Friedman (1982, 123) stated that:

> we in our capacity as voters must protect ourselves in our capacity as consumers against our own ignorance, by seeing to it that people are not served by incompetent physicians or plumbers or barbers.

Neo-liberals were frustrated that the private sector in a welfare state was forced to waste money in order to meet conditions imposed on them by costly and unproductive government regulations. If such regulations were eliminated, or did not exist in the first place, then these businesses could invest their money in other avenues that would help them become more efficient, productive and innovative, which in turn would contribute to raising the productivity, economic growth and employment of the entire country. Hayek believed that, contrary to the paternalism of welfare states, individuals are more productive, creative and innovative when they voluntarily take the initiative to maximize their own interests without being subjected to state regulations. Ultimately, more productivity, creativity and innovation benefits everyone in society, including the poorest and most vulnerable segments of the population.

Friedman believed that, much like regulations can limit the number of new products that are introduced into the market, they can also control the entry of new entrepreneurs into new occupation. For example, he explained that individuals are not free if they are unable to work in their chosen profession, because the government requires them to obtain a professional license in order to do so. More specifically, he believed that requiring occupational licences to practice certain professions or trades violated individual and economic freedom. He further maintained that 'liberal principles do not justify licensure' (Friedman 1982, 116). Similarly, Stigler (1971, 13) was also opposed to 'the licensing of occupations' on the basis that it violated economic freedom. He explained that requiring a professional license represented a real legal obstacle to entry into an occupation, as practicing a profession 'without the license is a criminal offense' (Stigler 1971, 13). Both Friedman and Stigler were of the opinion that the freedom to practice an occupation should be based on skills, competence and ability, not the possession of a licence. Furthermore, neo-liberals contend that professional licensure also violates the freedom of consumers seeking out such services, because the state has established norms to satisfy their needs while limiting their choices. That means the state treats its citizens as though they cannot distinguish a good lawyer from a fraud, or a competent doctor from an incompetent one, and so on. Friedman sought the elimination of occupational licences in order to ensure the conditions of economic freedom. He believed that abolishing this practice would bring society closer to a free-market economy, as there would no longer be a supreme authority in place to determine where particular employees should work, or interfere in the consumption patterns of the people looking to obtain their services.

In his own arguments against welfare states, Hayek (2011, 378) claimed that 'it would scarcely be an exaggeration to say that the greatest danger to liberty today comes from the men who are most needed and most powerful in modern government, namely, the efficient expert administrators exclusively concerned with what they regard as the public good.' Friedman and Friedman (1990, 106) actually went so far as to claim that an elite group of intellectuals formulated the ideas behind publicly financed social services and programs, and fooled 'the voters' into supporting these kinds of welfare states. Meanwhile, Buchanan and Tullock (1962, 59) suggested that support for a state role in collective activities was predicated on the belief that 'individuals, if left full freedom of private choice, may not educate their own children sufficiently, may not keep their residences free of fire hazards, may not free their premises of mosquito-breeding places, may not combine in sufficiently large units to purchase police protection most efficiently, etc.'

Neo-liberal economists reject the notion that factors like a lack of capacity, poor health, homelessness, poverty, and social and economic inequality could be used to justify government authority in the provision of publicly-financed social services and programs. In fact, they are adamantly opposed to the concept of a welfare state that aims to provide equality of opportunity. Instead, they were of the view that the achievement of distributive justice meant that 'people who differ greatly in strength, intelligence, skill, knowledge and perseverance' had to be treated accordingly (Filip 2018b, 346). Hayek believed that poverty and misery were common by-products of a free-market economy. Therefore, he did not regard economic inequality within a society as an outcome of 'injustice,' but rather as the product of 'misfortune' (Plant 1994, 165). Furthermore, he did not consider poverty and misery to be coercive or freedom inhibiting, because they are merely the unintended consequences of market behaviour. In fact, Hayek was convinced that the poor would be better off in a free-market society than under any form of centrally planned societal organization. He regarded distributive justice and social justice as mirages. Similarly, many neo-liberals believe that social justice is archaic.

Neo-liberal economists have expressed concerns that the achievement of social and distributive justice would result in a substantial increase in the number of public workers, given that it requires a strong role for the centrally designed government. In other words, the expansion of state-provided social services and programs would require a bigger government, which means higher public expenditures and more bureaucracy. More specifically, neo-liberals argued that state interventions designed to attain social and distributive justice entailed higher costs for private businesses and citizens, because they often required raising taxes, large numbers of highly-paid bureaucrats, diverting funds away from more productive ventures, as well as administrative and bureaucratic delays (Buchanan 1975, 40). Friedman (1982, 155) specifically claimed that the public provision of social services and programs has 'given birth to a large bureaucracy,' which raises concerns about the government extending its intervention from one area of life into another. Friedman and Friedman (1990, 247) pointed out that:

> When government pays its employees higher wages, those higher wages are at the expense of the taxpayer. But when workers get higher wages and better working conditions through the free market, when they get raises by firm competing with one another for the best workers, by workers competing with one another for the best jobs, those higher wages are at nobody's expense. They can only come from higher productivity, greater capital investment, more widely diffused skills. The whole pie is bigger—there's more for the worker, but there's also more for the employer, the investor, the consumer, and even the tax collector.

Friedman and Friedman (1990, 296) suggested that 'higher-level bureaucrats' exercised too much power over the programs, policies and laws of the state, which raised concerns about the abuse of power by favouring initiatives that would benefit them personally. They also criticized the increased bureaucratisation of the government for eliminating competition within the public sector, since civil-servants are typically payed based on a salary standard and not according to merit, which makes it almost impossible to stimulate competition between them. Similarly, Hayek expressed concerns about bureaucratic organisations eliminating competitiveness internally, due in large part to civil servants not being 'rewarded on the basis of assessable merit' (Hayek 2011, 189). Hayek (1958, 176) also believed that bureaucratic organisations were inefficient and uneconomical. He further suggested that when some services and programs are provided exclusively by the state, 'whole professions—be it medicine, education, or insurance—come to exist only as unitary bureaucratic hierarchies, it will no longer be competitive experimentation but solely the decisions of authority that will determine what men shall get' (Hayek 2011, 377).

Hayek (1958, 176) also thought that increasing the strength of bureaucratic organisations would eliminate the 'freedom of initiative.' Friedman concurred with the notion that the bureaucratic conduct of affairs was destructive to freedom, pointing out that when bureaucrats exercised their power over society, citizens were bound to obey their commands. To ensure the conditions of a free-society, he sought to eliminate any potential scenarios where economic decisions concerning the production and distribution of wealth were directed by a central authority. In other words, Friedman wanted to prevent power from being concentrated in the hands of bureaucrats of the state in the name of achieving distributive justice.

Neo-liberals often used persuasive arguments based on economic efficiency, growth, and productivity to support their opposition to welfare states. They further maintained that the social security programs and services provided by welfare states were incompetent. That is to say, the outcomes generated by welfare state policies are usually illusory and inefficient compared to the same services and programs managed by the private sector. In particular, Friedman argued that state expenditures on social services had adverse effects on productivity and economic growth. More specifically, he suggested that 'intervention has been costly in economic terms,' as excessive state spending significantly slowed economic growth in the United States (Friedman, Friedman 1990, 64). In fact, in the early 1960s, Friedman (2002, 38) explained that:

> governmental measures constitute the major impediments to economic growth in the United States. Tariffs and other restrictions on international trade, high tax burdens and a complex and inequitable tax structure, regulatory commissions, government price and wage fixing, and a host of other measures give individuals an incentive to misuse and misdirect resources, and distort the investment of new savings. What we urgently need, for both economic stability and growth, is a reduction of government intervention not an increase.

Friedman believed that if the goal of the state is to actually improve opportunities for all of its citizens and achieve productivity, prosperity and economic growth, then the private sector is the most efficient means by which to achieve those objectives. Consequently, he advocated for liberalizing trade, privatizing state-owned enterprises and other establishments, eliminating subsidies and regulations, reforming the banking and financial systems, and abolishing corporate taxes and social services (including publicly-funded health care, education, and housing). Friedman (2002,

24) argued that 'the wider the range of activities covered by the market, the fewer are the issues on which explicitly political decisions are required.'

Buchanan and Tullock (1962, 13) were convinced that individuals would generally choose to voluntary organize their actions, except in cases where 'collective action is expected to be considerably more efficient.' Accordingly, they strongly supported the notion of privatizing many areas of social and economic life, suggesting that if 'no police protection were to be provided collectively, surely voluntary arrangements would be worked out to secure some cooperation in the organization of a private police force. Towns without formally organized collective fire protection organize voluntary fire departments. Numerous other examples could be cited to illustrate the activities falling within this set for the average individual' (Buchanan and Tullock 1962, 48). Neo-liberal economists have often argued that the privatization of public goods would widen the range of choices available to people, and that competition between enterprises would play an important role in providing consumers with a variety of services and goods in a more efficient manner than a monopoly of power by the state.

Many neo-liberal economists hold the extreme view that the public sector basically acts as a parasite that feeds off of the private sector. According to them, a government should remain a 'servant' of the people and never become their 'master.' They have complete faith in the ability of self-regulating market mechanisms to ensure freedom, and are convinced that the elimination of state power would result in the emergence of more autonomous and responsible people. Furthermore, neo-liberals regarded any reductions in the size of the public sector, or any shifts of activities from the public sphere to the private sphere, as economic gains. In fact, the privatization of state-owned enterprises came with promises of material prosperity, productivity gains, and economic growth.

Developments over the last four decades suggest that the opinions expressed by Friedman, Hayek, Buchanan, Mises and many other neo-liberals with respect to the flaws and weaknesses of welfare states were taken seriously by many world leaders. In particular, the elections of Margaret Thatcher as Prime Minister of Great Britain in 1979 and Ronald Reagan as President of the US in 1980, marked the beginning of the end for many of the state policies and programs that were inspired by the New Deal. Many neo-liberals actually regarded the election of these two prominent leaders as an important step in preventing welfare states from heading down 'the road to serfdom.' Accordingly, Friedman (1982, 6) openly expressed his satisfaction that great reform programs, such as 'welfare, public housing, support of trade unions, integration of schools, federal aid to education, affirmative action were turning to ashes' since 'the overwhelming victory of Ronald Reagan in 1980' ushered in the rise of neo-liberalism.

Subsequently, beginning in the early 1980s, globally, many governments prioritised the deregulation of the private sector in order to achieve the conditions of a free-market economy, including the elimination of tariffs and quotas. Neo-liberal economic reforms also entailed the privatisation of any state-owned enterprises that could conceivably be administered independent of state power, as well as drastic cuts to publicly-funded social programs and services. Consequently, many public institutions and enterprises, natural resources and utilities were sold to rich corporations, meaning that the assent of neo-liberalism to a position of prominence essentially caused states to lose control over the commanding heights of their economies.

The rise of neo-liberalism coincided with the role of the government being reduced to a bare minimum. This is not surprising given that neo-liberals viewed every dollar spent on publicly-funded programs and services as being wasted, amounting to one less dollar in pockets of citizens. Once publicly-owned enterprises have been privatized, they function like any other private company that priorities profit maximization, makes decisions according to carefully constructed cost-benefit analyses, and only provides its products and services to those who can afford to pay for them. This is even the true in the case of services like health care and education that are regarded and quintessentially public in many countries, which has led to the emergence of private schools, hospitals and clinics that have dedicated themselves to maximizing profits and reducing costs, resulting in higher prices. For example, private hospitals and clinics in the U.S. often charge exorbitant prices for their procedures, which are out of the price range that many people can afford without going into debt or suffering financial ruin. When the public services needed to achieve the common good are privatised in line with the principles of free-market capitalism, the results can be very destructive, ineffective, and inhumane. Furthermore, when privatisation is accompanied by a limited state role in regulating the economy, then private companies enjoy excessive levels of freedom when conducting their business practices.

Certain programs and services should not be subject to exploitation by corporations for the purpose of maximize profits, because they are essential for: human survival (e.g., water, health, food, shelter, etc.); the safety and security of individuals (e.g., police force, justice systems, military, prison, etc.); the progress (technological developments); and, the development of individuality (e.g., education, training, work, cultural activities, etc.). These programs and services of the welfare state came into existence through the efforts of people who thought that society should be governed by social justice and equality, rather than the narrow-minded principle of individual profit maximization. It was only through these kinds of cumulative efforts across history that people were able to secure major social achievements like the eight-hour work day, minimum wages, public education, universal health care services, and affordable housing, all of which are important conditions for positive freedom.

4.3 Contradictions of the Neo-liberal State

In a free society, the law is abstract and general, because it does not discriminate between individuals, nor does it impose specific ends to be pursued or achieved. That means the law does not prescribe positive actions, which would lead to the freedom of some people being violated by others. Hayek argued that, contrary to centrally planned societies, where rules aim to achieve the concrete ends designed by a social engineer, rules in a free society are intended to facilitate an abstract order, meaning there are no particular ends or objectives to be achieved. More specifically, in a free society, the law cannot be used to produce specific outcomes or facilitate the conditions that satisfy the needs of a particular group of people. The achievement of specific outcomes, such as distributive justice, requires the state to arbitrarily discriminate between people, which violates the laws of a free society (Hayek 2011, 341). In other words, this type of state aims to secure the particular outcomes of some individuals at the expense of others.

Based on Hayek's conception of the rule of law, a centrally planned state that aims to provide its citizens with services and support like health care, education, housing, and work, violates the universality, equality and impartiality features of laws, because these types of goals and objectives cannot be achieved by merely enforcing general and abstract rules. That means, in a free society, the legal system cannot serve to provide social services and programs that redistribute certain resources to particular individuals. Hayek actually had more faith in the power of the legal system when it came to preventing the welfare state from violating freedom, and avoiding 'the road to serfdom.' He argued that people who strive to realize 'distributive justice will in practice find themselves obstructed at every move by the rule of law,' because the rule of law is incompatible with distributive justice (Hayek 2011, 341). Hayek (2011, 341) was very clear that by restricting the power of the state within the limits established by the rule of law, 'a great deal can be done to make the market work more effectively and smoothly; but, within these limits, what people now regard as distributive justice can never be achieved.'

Although Hayek recognized that some of the outcomes of a free-market economy might be unfortunate for some people, he believed that distributive justice was meaningless and incompatible with the universality and equality of the law. Distributive justice cares about the equality of outcomes as opposed to equality before the law. Hayek (2011, 318) argued that 'the ideal of equality of the law is aimed at equally improving the chances of yet unknown people but incompatible with benefiting or harming known persons in a predictable manner.' Furthermore, he explained that since distributive justice involves allocating 'all resources by a central authority,' people have to obey central order (Hayek 2011, 341).

According to Hayek, contrary to centrally planned systems, which resort to coercion and compulsion to attain common ends, free societies need coercion to safeguard the proper functioning of the free-market system, which is done by establishing a proper functioning legal system. However, he also emphasized that 'the observation of the rule of law is a necessary, but not yet a sufficient, condition for the satisfactory working of a free economy' (Hayek 2011, 331). Therefore, even though Hayek opposed state interference aimed at ensuring the conditions of positive freedom or achieving social justice, he was not in favour of the complete absence of state action. More specifically, he argued that economic freedom meant 'freedom under the law, not the absence of all government action' (Hayek 2011, 329). In other words, he did not believe that the government should never involve itself in economic matters.

In a free society, certain types of governmental economic measures could be deemed acceptable by neo-liberals, depending on the goal of the intervention. For example, Hayek (2011, 331) stated that a proper functioning free-market economy 'presupposes certain activities on the part of the state; there are some other such activities by which its functioning will be assisted; and it can tolerate many more, provided that they are of the kind which is compatible with a functioning market.' That means Hayek accepted that it was necessary to foresee the requirements of a free-market economy, and then attempt to manage them through the adoption of state reforms and new policies. He further explained that the rule of law provides the criteria that determine which measures, reforms and policies are compatible with a free-market system.

Buchanan and Tullock (1962) were not completely opposed to the growth of the bureaucratic apparatus of the government under a free-market system, as long as the state acted in accordance with the same motivations that drive the private sector. Based on the public choice theory, which was developed by Buchanan and Tullock (1962), the bureaucratic growth of government in a free-market system is an outcome of rational self-interest maximizing behaviour, not the desire to achieve ethical ends, as is the case in welfare states or socialist regimes. In other words, the public choice theory states that both the public and private sectors are motivated by rational self-interests in a free-market system, which basically means government bureaucrats are engaged in utility maximizing behaviour just like any other economic agent. Therefore, individual self-interest maximization has to be an important factor for every organized authority, including the government.

Buchanan and Tullock (1962, 41) believed that state intervention intended to achieve and maintain the conditions of a free-market economy was distinct from 'political action,' which is coercive in nature. Through their public choice theory, which applied the methods, presentations, and analysis of mainstream economics to the study of political processes, Buchanan and Tullock actually wanted to change the way that people thought about government. More specifically, they were convinced that they could use advanced mathematical modelling techniques to observe and quantify the effects of defined changes in political processes, like government policies. Their goal was to develop state policies and political institutions that were economically efficient. Consequently, they supported government intervention in a free-market system, provided that it was used for the rectification of market failures, or involved the application of fiscal and monetary policies to improve the economic performance of the private sector.

Buchanan and Tullock were not the only neo-liberal economists that did not completely oppose state intervention under the right circumstances, despite all of their rhetoric against governments using their authority to achieve the common good in centrally planned systems. For example, while Hayek was against using positive state intervention to achieve teleologically determined ends, which are designed by social engineers, he supported a positive state role in ensuring the proper functioning of the free-market system. In order to legitimize these types of state intervention, which Hayek considered to be compatible with the free-market system, 'he defended piecemeal engineering that allows for the state authority to intervene' in the economy 'whenever it is deemed necessary to provide' a favourable environment for the development of the private sector (Filip 2018b, 258). Friedman and Friedman (1990, 30) also defended a state role in 'facilitating voluntary exchanges by adopting general rules-the rules of the economic social game that the citizens of a free society play.' According to Friedman (2002, 15):

> The existence of a free market does not of course eliminate the need for government. On the contrary, government is essential both as a forum for determining the "rule of the game" and as an umpire to interpret and enforce the rules decided on. What the market does is to reduce greatly the range of issues that must be decided through political means, and thereby to minimize the extent to which government need participate directly in the game.

That would suggest that, contrary to the claims of neo-liberal economists, the conditions of a free-market system were consciously, deliberately and rationally planned, and a strong state role was required in order to maintain them. Neo-liberals clearly supported an active state role in establishing a legal framework that would foster competitive markets, and enforce private contracts, while simultaneously protecting property rights and individual freedom. Friedman (2002, 38) further elaborated that state intervention was required 'to provide a stable monetary framework for a free economy,' and 'a general legal and economic framework that will enable individuals to produce growth in the economy.'

According to neo-liberals, as long as state intervention stimulated productivity, economic growth and efficiency, it would be accepted as legitimate. In addition to supporting state intervention for the purpose of achieving and sustaining the conditions of a free-market economy, Friedman (2002, 33) also argued that 'paternalism is inescapable' in the case of irresponsible individuals, because it is necessary to organize 'their care through government.' That would suggest that he was of the view that 'freedom is a tenable objective only for responsible individuals,' meaning that there could be no freedom for 'madmen or children' (Friedman 2002, 33).

There were actually a number of other circumstances and cases where Friedman and Friedman (1990, 7) supported a significant role for the state, including when it came to defending 'the nation from foreign enemies, protecting each of us from coercion by our fellow citizens, adjudicating our disputes, and enabling us to agree on the rules that we shall follow.' Friedman (1981, 12) stated that 'the market cannot provide national defense. For that purpose, it is essential to depart from the market, which also involves further interference with the market through the effects of the methods used for raising funds to finance national defense.' Similarly, Hayek advocated for the state to provide national defence in cases of invasion or violence by foreign forces. He also thought the government should play a significant role in the construction and maintenance of public infrastructure including roads, highways, and bridges. Furthermore, Hayek also believed that the state should play an active role in the case of natural disasters, as the market system would be unable to supply the economy on its own at such times. It should also be noted that, even though Hayek (2011, 500–506) was adamantly opposed to publicly-funded education systems for endangering freedom, he did acknowledge that some form of public education would likely be required in instances where people did not have the ability to pay for this essential service.

Despite his opposition to welfare states, Hayek believed that it was acceptable to provide a minimum level of welfare to people who cannot earn a living in the free-market system, whether it be on a temporary or permanent basis. He supported a guaranteed minimum income, even though 'the provision of a uniform minimum for all those who cannot provide for themselves involves some redistribution of income' (Hayek 2011, 426). However, he was clear that, in a free society, the goal of a guaranteed minimum income should be to provide a minimum level of welfare for everyone, while being unconcerned with the notion of justice. That is to say, he believed that there is a significant difference between 'the provision of such a minimum for all those who cannot maintain themselves on their earnings in a normally functioning market and a redistribution aiming at a "just" remuneration' (Hayek 2011, 426). Hayek (2011, 427) also insisted that the 'assurance of an equal minimum for all in distress presupposes that this minimum is provided only on proof of need and that nothing which is not paid for by personal contribution is given without such proof.' This is because a guaranteed minimum income is intended to provide limited 'security against severe physical privation,' and is not an 'assurance of a given standard of life, which is determined by comparing the standard enjoyed by a person or a group with that of others' (Hayek 2011, 376). Since the latter form of state intervention requires that 'the coercive powers of government are to be used to insure that particular people get particular things, it requires a kind of discrimination between, and an unequal treatment of, different people which is irreconcilable with a free society' (Hayek 2011, 376). According to Hayek (2011, 376), this describes a type of welfare state that aims to achieve 'social justice,' which means it is destined 'to lead back to socialism and its coercive.'

Overall, while there may be some minor differences in the views held by neo-liberal economists when it comes to the provision of minimum social services and programs, they generally did not attribute a great deal of importance to the role of the state and its institutions in the achievement of either the collective good or the conditions of positive freedom. Although the rise of neo-liberalism has led to many publicly-funded social programs and services being privatised or eliminated altogether, the volume of state spending has not actually decreased. That is because neo-liberalism has never really been about reducing the size of the government or limiting the ability of the state to intervene in society. In fact, neo-liberals are actually quite tolerant of increases in government expenditures and employment provided that they are intended to help establish and sustain the conditions of a free-market system.

Since the rise of neo-liberalism, the role of the state and the allocation of its spending have played the major roles in shifting economic power away from the government and towards the corporate world in many countries. Accordingly, many of the public expenditures that were formerly allocated to providing public services and programs have instead been channelled to supporting corporations, often in the form of large subsidies and tax exemptions. In other words, neo-liberals have valued state interventions, provided that they supported corporate interests over those of the public. In all likelihood, the corporate world would have been unable to achieve the level of power and wealth that it currently enjoys without the various state interventions that have protected their interests, which have included deregulating the economy, providing financial support and technical assistance, safeguarding investments, and facilitating business practices that are detrimental to people and the environment (e.g., the exploitation of natural and human resources around world). Furthermore, in the event of a serious market failure, the state has shown itself to be ready and willing to step in and bail out the corporate world at great expense to public finances. Consequently, over the last four decades, states have played a central role in establishing the contemporary global economic system, where the majority of wealth and power are concentrated in a handful of powerful corporations that govern the world and its resources in a manner that best suits their interests and profits.

4.3.1 *Hayek and Friedman on the Brutal Dictatorship of Pinochet*

Even though one of the fundamental principles of neo-liberalism is limited state action, its theorists defend an active state role when it comes to ensuring the conditions of a properly functioning free-market economy. One of most well-known cases of neo-liberals supporting state intervention is the violent, coercive and oppressive regime of General Augusto Pinochet (1915–2006) in Chile. Pinochet came to power by leading a military coup that overthrew the legitimate, democratically-elected government of Salvador Allende (1908–1973) in 1973, with considerable support from the United States. Consequently, 'Chile became the focus of many human rights organizations and much of the international press because of the human rights violations that were committed during the 11 September 1973 military coup and throughout Pinochet's subsequent rule' (Filip 2018c, 424). After Pinochet seized power, the Chilean congress was dissolved and a 'State of Siege was declared,' 'the Tribunal Constitutional was dissolved,' 'all public employees were declared to be interim,' socialist political parties were liquidated, 'the universities were intervened by the Military Junta,' 'the electoral register were declared void and then incinerated,' the 'expulsion of individual from the national territory on political grounds' was legalised, etc. (Couso 2011, 402). 'These measures suspended freedom for most Chileans; while the economic freedom of multinational corporations remained largely unaffected' (Filip 2018c, 427).

Hayek visited Chile twice during the brutal dictatorship of Pinochet (1973–1990): in November 1977 and April 1981. Following his visits, he 'explained that he was surprised by the state of Chile's economic development' (Filip 2018c, 428). That is to say, he thought that 'he was going to find an 'underdeveloped' country, but now he could not use that term to describe Chile. He praised the military dictatorship for its willingness to run the country 'without being obsessed with popular commitments or political expectations of any kind,' adding that the 'painful' economic reforms they were experiencing were a 'necessary evil' that would soon be overcome' (Filip 2018c, 428). Consequently, he praised 'Pinochet's market liberalization efforts', and expressed hope that other countries around the world would view Chile as an example to be emulated (Filip 2018c, 428). Additionally, in a letter he penned to the London *Times* (3 August 1978), Hayek stated that he had 'certainly never contended that generally authoritarian governments are more likely to secure individual liberty than democratic ones, but rather the contrary. This does not mean, however, that in some historical circumstances personal liberty may not have been better protected under an authoritarian than democratic government.'[5] He even went so far as to claim that he had 'not been able to find a single person even in much maligned Chile who did not agree that personal freedom was much greater under Pinochet than it had been under Allende.'[6]

Friedman was also among the notable neo-liberals that enthusiastically defended the Pinochet regime, despite his belief that centrally planned economic systems represented a threat to freedom. In fact, Friedman's *Capitalism and Freedom* (1962) and *Free to Choose: A Personal Statement* (1980), were widely read and very influential in Chile. It is also well-documented that Friedman and some of his former students at the University of Chicago (i.e., the Chicago Boys) played a significant role in Chile's free-market miracle that followed the violent overthrow of Salvador Allende's government in 1973. Subsequently, a large number of Chicago Boys joined Pinochet's military Junta, including: Sergio de Castro, Minister of Finance (1977–1982); Jorge Cauas, Minister of Finance (1975–1977); Miguel Kast, Minister of Planning (1978–1980), Labor Minister (1980–1982), and Governor of the Central Bank of Chile, (1982–1983); Sergio de la Cuadra, President of the Central Bank of Chile (1981–1982) and Minister of Finance (1982–1983); Álvaro Bardón Muñoz, President of the Central Bank of Chile, (1977–1981) and Secretary of Economy (1982–1983); Pablo Antonio Baraona Urzúa, Minister of Economy (1976–1979); Juan Carlos Méndez, Budget Director (1975–1981); Martín Costabal, Budget Director, 1987–1989, Hernán Büchi, Minister of Finance (1985–1989) (Parmar 2014, 205). These advocates of neo-liberalism, who became 'influential policy-maker' in Chile, were convinced that they were rescuing the country from Marxist

[5] Margaret Thatcher Foundation. 1978. 'Hayek letter to The Times.' https://www.margaretthatcher.org/document/117136.

[6] Margaret Thatcher Foundation. 1978. 'Hayek letter to The Times.' https://www.margaretthatcher.org/document/117136.

ideologies (Filip 2018c, 439). It is a well-known fact that the 'National Recovery Plan' for the Chilean economy, which also labelled 'shock therapy,' was strongly supported by Friedman and the Chicago Boys (Filip 2018c, 453).

At that time, Friedman did not appear to exhibit even the slightest reservations towards the brutal, coercive, and repressive actions employed by Pinochet's military dictatorship, provided that it defended laissez-faire economics. Despite his reputation as a tireless advocate and defender of freedom, or 'freedom fighter,' it is difficult to argue that Friedman's support of the Pinochet dictatorship, which was well-known for its record of violating human rights, could be viewed as anything else but an affront to freedom. In other words, Friedman's concept of freedom rings hollow, because his support of the Pinochet regime proves that he attributed more importance to ensuring the conditions of a free-market economy than violations of human rights and the conditions of freedom; the same could be said of Hayek and the Chicago Boys.

In the end, neither Friedman nor Hayek particularly cared about whether a political system was democratic or fascist, as long as it secured the conditions of a free-market economy. Accordingly, both of them supported the overthrow of the democratically-elected Allende government, because they believed that it threatened to weaken and destabilize the free-market economy and inhibit the profit maximizing potential of corporations. Hayek and Friedman's defense of the 'Chilean Miracle' demonstrates how little regard they actually had for freedom and the achievement of its conditions. To be more precise, their defense of the Pinochet dictatorship revealed that they only valued freedom for its instrumental value in terms of contributing to the establishment and preservation of the conditions of a free-market system. The fact that the brutal regime of Augusto Pinochet was neither criticized nor condemned by Friedman and Hayek, despite their vehement opposition to state intervention aimed at achieving the collective good, shows that both of them were willing to use a very powerful philosophical concept like freedom to defend the superiority of a free-market system over any other form of societal organization at any price, even if an oppressive dictator was needed to establish and sustain its conditions.

4.4 Conclusion

Neo-liberal economists believe that the most important aspect of any system of societal organisation is how much personal, economic and political freedom it can allow. They have persistently argued against any use of state authority for the purpose of achieving the collective good, including the nationalisation of businesses, the provision of publicly-financed social programs and services, the implementation of protective trade measures, and the strengthening of trade unions. Instead, they believe that the free-market system, where people voluntarily cooperate, is not only the most efficient economic system available, but also the only one where people can have economic, individual and political freedom. Basically, they support free-market economies because they conform to their view that a government governs best when it governs least.

Since the 1980s, a number of neo-liberal theorists, intellectuals, experts and other advocates have claimed that free-market capitalism is categorically superior to centrally planned systems, because it ensures the conditions of voluntary exchange, economic freedom, and freedom in general. They have also argued that free-market capitalism has managed to achieve tremendous advances in the areas of productivity, efficiency, economic growth, technological innovation, and the expansion of private welfare. In reality, however, an absolutely free-market economy is a utopian dream. The free-market system needs state intervention to secure and maintain the conditions needed for it to thrive. In fact, neo-liberal economists do not oppose state interference designed to achieve the conditions of capitalism, as they believe that supporting the interests of the private business classes is compatible with the free-market system.

It could be argued that the last four decades serve as testimony to the fact that free-market systems are self-destructive and chronically unstable and, as such, regular state interventions are required to secure the conditions of the free-market capitalism, as well as to avert and remedy serious economic shocks and crises. In fact, the free-market system was so ill-equipped to deal with some of the unexpected events and crises that emerged during that time that governments were essentially forced to provide multi-billion dollar bailouts to save it, most of which went directly to wealthy businesses. That would suggest that the free-market economy is not all that free. In reality, a close study of history of economics reveals that free-market capitalism 'was in no way the result of the gradual and spontaneous emancipation of the economic sphere from governmental control. On the contrary, the market has been the outcome of a conscious and often violent intervention on the part of government which imposed the market organization on society for noneconomic ends' (Polanyi 2001 [1944], 258).

When it comes to the role of the state in society, the question is not whether or not government intervention is desirable, as it is essential for both centrally planned economies and the free-market system; the question is what type of government intervention is desirable. In the unfettered free-market system, state interventions are intended to ensure that the economy functions properly, without taking any consideration of moral and ethical values, which tends to produce outcomes that favour the interests of strong and powerful entities at the expense of the masses and the natural environment. In last four decades, the widespread global commitment to the free-market economic system is questionable given its tendency to engender chaos, economic crises, unprecedented social and economic inequality, misery for the mass majority of the global population, and a potential environmental apocalypse. Such outcomes are the true evils of the free-market system itself. However, while neo-liberals have always been quick to heap praise on the successes of free-market capitalism, they have remained very silent about its destructive outcomes and many flaws, while also doing everything in their power to stifle any discussion of a possible paradigm change.

There is no perfect form of societal organization, as each of them has its own defects and benefits. Furthermore, 'there are no completely pure systems; every system is something of a mixed system that, on the one hand, includes command elements and, on the other, relies predominantly on voluntary cooperation' (Friedman 1981, 12). There are certainly lessons to be learned from some of the negative outcomes associated with central planning during the twentieth century. However, it is important to recognize that many of the state policies associated with centrally planned economies, such as subsidising infant industries and strategically important economic sectors, providing universal social services and programs, and enacting restrictive and protective trade measures, are not inherently bad. In fact, these and similar measures can play important roles in addressing many of the contemporary problems that the world is facing.

References

Ali, Tariq. 1988. *Revolution from Above: Where Is the Soviet Union Going?* London: Hutchinson.

Bakan, Joel. 2004. *The Corporation: The Pathological Pursuit of Profit and Power*. New York Simon & Schuster Inc.

Brennan, Geoffrey. 1999 [1985]. *The Collected Works of James M. Buchanan, Vol. 10 (The Reason of Rules: Constitutional Political Economy)*. Foreword by Robert D. Tollison. Indianapolis: Liberty Fund. https://oll.libertyfund.org/titles/1826.

Buchanan, J.M., and G. Tullock. 1962. *The Calculus of Consent: Logical Foundations of a Constitutional Democracy*. Ann Arbor: University of Michigan Press.

Buchanan, James. 1975. *The Limits of Liberty*. Chicago: University of Chicago Press.

Couso, Javier A. 2011. Trying Democracy in the Shadow of an Authoritarian Legality: Chile's Transition to Democracy and Pinochet's Constitution of 1980. *Wisconsin International Law Journal*. 29 (2): 393–415.

Filip, Birsen. 2018a. Hayek and Humboldt on Freedom and the Role of the State. In *Hayek: A Collaborative Biography: Part XIV: Liberalism in the Classical Tradition: Orwell, Popper, Humboldt and Polanyi*, ed. Robert Leeson, 105–152. Cham: Palgrave Macmillan.

———. 2018b. Hayek and Popper on Piecemeal Engineering and Ordo-liberalism. In *Hayek: A Collaborative Biography Part XIV: Liberalism in the Classical Tradition: Orwell, Popper, Humboldt and Polanyi*, ed. Robert Leeson, 233–281. New York: Palgrave Macmillan.

———. 2018c. Friedrich Hayek and His Visits to Chile: Some Austrian Misrepresentations. In *Hayek: A Collaborative Biography – Part XIII: Fascism' and Liberalism in the (Austrian) Classical Tradition*, ed. Robert Leeson, 423–462. Cham: Palgrave Macmillan.

———. 2018d. The German Historical School of Economics and the Foundations and Development of the Austrian School of Economics. In *Hayek: A Collaborative Biography: Part XIII: 'Fascism' and Liberalism in the (Austrian) Classical Tradition*, ed. Robert Leeson, 79–128. Cham: Palgrave Macmillan.

Friedman, Milton. 1961. Introduction. Ed. Ralph Raico. *New Individualist Review*. Indianapolis: Liberty Fund. Vol. 1. No. 1: 8–13. https://oll.libertyfund.org/titles/2136.

———. 1981. Market Mechanisms and Central Economic Planning. In *The Collected Works of Milton Friedman*, ed. Robert Leeson and Charles G. Palm. Washington, DC: American Enterprise Institute.

———. 1982 [1962]. *Capitalism and Freedom*. Chicago: The University of Chicago Press.

———. 2002 [1962]. *Capitalism and Freedom*. Chicago: The University of Chicago Press.

Friedman, Milton, and Friedman, R.D. 1990 [1980]. *Free to Choose: A Personal Statement*. New York: Harcourt Brace Jovanovich.

Hayek, F.A. 1952. *The Counter-Revolution of Science: Studies on the Abuse of Reason*. London: Free Press of Glencoe.

———. 1958 [1948]. *Individualism and Economic Order*. Chicago: University of Chicago Press.

———. 1994 [1944]. *The Road to Serfdom*. Chicago: The University of Chicago Press.

———. 1998 [1976]. *Law, Legislation and Liberty Volume 2: The Mirage of Social Justice*. Chicago: University of Chicago Press.

———. 2011 [1960]. *The Constitution of Liberty*. Chicago: University of Chicago Press.

Heidegger, Martin. 1993. *Basic Writings*. New York: Harper San Francisco.

Leontief, Wassily. 1985. *Essays in Economics: Theories, Theorizing, Facts, and Policies*. New York: Routledge.

Menger, Carl. 1985. *Investigations into the Method of the Social Sciences with Special Reference to Economics*. Trans. F. J. Nock and Ed. L. Schneider. New York: New York University Press.

Milford, Karl. 1995. Roscher's Epistemological and Methodological Position Its Importance for the Methodenstreit. *Journal of Economic Studies*. 22 (3/4/5): 26–52.

Mises, Ludwig von. 1998 [1949]. *Human Action: A Treatise on Economics*. Auburn: The Ludwig von Mises Institute.

Parmar, Inderjeet. 2014. *Foundations of the American Century: The Ford, Carnegie, and Rockefeller Foundations in the Rise of American Power*. New York: Columbia University Press.

Parenti, Michael. 1997. *Blackshirts and Reds: Rational Fascism and the Overthrow of Communism*. San Francisco: City Lights Books.

———. 2015. *Profit Pathology and Other Indecencies*. New York: Routledge.

Plant, R. 1994. Hayek on Social Justice: A Critique. In *Hayek, Co-ordination and Evolution: His Legacy in Philosophy, Politics, Economics and the History of Ideas*, ed. J. Birner and R. Van Zijp, 164–177. London: Routledge.

Polanyi, K. 2001 [1944]. *The Great Transformation: The Political and Economic Origins of Our Time*. Boston: Beacon Press.

Samuelson, Paul Anthon, and William D. Nordhaus. 2010 [1948]. *Economics*. New York: The McGraw-Hill Companies, Inc.

Simons, Henry Calvert. 1934. A Positive Program for Laissez-Faire: Some proposals for a Liberal Economic Policy. In *Public Policy Pamphlet*. Chicago: The University Chicago Press. No. 15.

Stigler, George J. 1971. The Theory of Economic Regulation. *The Bell Journal of Economics and Management Science* 2 (1): 3–21.

CHAPTER 5

The Rise of Neo-liberalism and Tyranny of Corporations

In the 1930s, liberals argued that the freedom of corporations was the only type of freedom that could be extended and maintained (Simons 1934, 3). They also believed that expanding the freedom of these entities would limit the role of the state in society. However, the New Deal impeded these ambitions, as advocates of centrally planned systems stressed the irreconcilable conflict between the interests of people and those of corporations. In fact, the New Deal directly targeted the growing power of corporations, as its polices and regulations limited their freedom to operate 'through World War II, the postwar era, and the 1960s and 1970s' (Bakan 2004, 20). However, the New Deal was not able to eradicate the determination of corporations (and their backers) to gain more freedom, which they could then take advantage of in order to extend their control over governments and people. The road towards the freedom they longed for was opened by the 1973 oil crisis, when the respective roles of the state and corporations began to change. Then, during the Reagan-Thatcher Era, corporations enjoyed many victories when it came to eliminating or weakening state regulations, which led to an expansion of their coercive powers and freedom, thereby allowing them to conduct their business practices on their own terms. This is because they have invested large sums of money and expended great efforts to lobby for deregulation and undermine various state agencies tasked with monitoring and enforcing regulations pertaining to workers' rights, workplace safety, health

B. Filip, *The Rise of Neo-liberalism and the Decline of Freedom*,
Palgrave Insights into Apocalypse Economics,
https://doi.org/10.1007/978-3-030-61623-6_5

codes, environmental protections, protective trade measures, and consumer protection, among others. In other words, during the Reagan-Thatcher Era, large and powerful corporations were able to amass unprecedented freedom, power and influence over many aspect of society, which has allowed them to become leading actors in the social, political and economic lives of people, similar to the church and monarchies in the past. Presently, the global economy is driven by large corporations in a variety of economic sectors, including resource extraction (e.g., mining, oil, and gas), manufacturing, agro-industrial complexes, banking and finance, retail and wholesale trade, technology, etc. Furthermore, in some countries, corporations have even extended their influence to gain control over areas that were traditionally under the purview of governments, including education, health care, prisons, airlines, and various activities pertaining to national defense.

The vast financial and economic resources at the disposal of corporations has granted them significant influential and coercive powers, not only over regular people, but also various institutions and world leaders. Corporations and their paid lobbyists are able to gain the type of access to state bureaucrats, officials and democratically-elected politicians that the average voter could only dream of; it is also not uncommon for close relationships to be established. Now, instead of corporations being subordinated to state authority, governments will often bend to the will of corporate interests by implementing policies and regulations that are favourable to their business activities. Similarly, rather than being subordinated to the market, corporations largely control it. In fact, the immense influence of large domestic and foreign corporations has led many governments to betray the interests of their own citizens. Today, it could be argued that corporations rule over societies with more influence and authority than any democratically elected politician, despite the fact that people fought for centuries to win their freedom and 'the right to be governed by themselves or their representatives' (Berlin 2002, 207).

Even though corporations play an increasingly important role in terms of governing society, they are not concerned with issues pertaining to social responsibility, justice, equality or the collective good. This is not particularly surprising given that corporations are defined as free, independent, impersonal and amoral entities with a mandate to maximize the profits of their shareholders (Bakan 2004). Consequently, they feel no obligation to serve the interests of society, nor are they inclined to alter any of their business practices that have detrimental impacts on others.

More accurately, they are fully prepared to undertake any actions that serve to maximize the profits of their shareholders, regardless of whether they are destructive, unethical, immoral, or even illegal.

According to neo-liberals, actions on the part of corporations that are ethical, moral, and beneficial for society can be only tolerated if they, first and foremost, benefit the interests of their shareholders. For example, if implementing environmentally friendly practices under the guise of social responsibility helps a corporation generate some positive publicity at little cost, or enables it to gain some kind of competitive advantage over its competitors, then it could be accepted as a worthwhile investment. In other words, the socially responsible actions of the corporation would be deemed acceptable by neo-liberals, because they have likely generated some economic benefits. Friedman believed that any corporation that aims to achieve socially responsible and environmentally-friendly goals earns less profit for 'its stockholders,' which means it is being run immorally (Friedman 1970). In his arguments against 'social responsibilities' in the marketplace, Friedman (1970) stated:

> What does it mean to say that 'business' has responsibilities? Only people have responsibilities. A corporation is an artificial person and, in this sense, may have artificial responsibilities, but "business" as a whole cannot be said to have responsibilities, even in this vague sense. The first step toward clarity in examining the doctrine of the social responsibility of business is to ask precisely what it implies for whom.

Friedman (1970) considered the hypothetical example of a socially responsible 'corporate executive' who might allocate 'expenditures on reducing pollution beyond the amount that is in the best interests of the corporation or that is required by law in order to contribute to the social objective of improving the environment.' He attributed this kind of behaviour to 'the schizophrenic character of businessmen,' who he described as 'incredibly short-sighted and muddle-headed in matters that are outside their businesses' (Friedman 1970). In such a case, 'the corporate executive would be spending someone else's money for a general social interest. Insofar as his actions in accord with his "social responsibility" reduce returns to stockholders, he is spending their money. Insofar as his actions raise the price to customers, he is spending the customers' money. Insofar as his actions lower the wages of some employees, he is spending their money' (Friedman 1970). Instead, Friedman (1970) suggested that any of these economic agents were free to 'spend their own money on the particular action' in their private spheres if their own particular values compelled them to do so.

Friedman (1970) explained that '"social responsibility" involves the acceptance of the socialist view that political mechanisms, not market mechanisms, are the appropriate way to determine the allocation of scarce resources to alternative uses.' When it comes to a corporation, Friedman believed that morality refers to its commitment to its mandate. Consequently, any deviation from that mandate would be considered immoral. Friedman (1982, 112) maintained that this was a fundamental feature of free-market economies, where 'there is one and only one social responsibility of business to use its resources and engage in activities designed to increase its profits so long as it stays within the rules of the game, which is to say, engages in open and free competition.' He further claimed that 'the acceptance by corporate officials of a social responsibility other than to make as much money for their stockholders as possible' could 'thoroughly undermine the very foundations of our free society' (Friedman 1982, 112). That is to say, if social responsibility was taken into consideration 'seriously,' then it 'would extend the scope of the political mechanism to every human activity,' which would not be unlike the doctrine that aims to achieve the collective good under centrally planned systems (Friedman 1970).

One of the main reasons why corporations are able to get away with the destructive outcomes that their activities bestow upon people and nature is their 'unique structure,' whereby 'the corporate form generally protects the human beings who own and run corporations from legal liability, leaving the corporation, a "person" with a psychopathic contempt for legal constraints, the main target of criminal prosecution' (Bakan 2004, 79). In other words, when corporations commit crimes, the people who run them are generally not held criminally responsible, which explains why 'illegalities are endemic in the corporate world' (Bakan 2004, 79). Specifically, directors are 'protected by the fact that they have no direct involvement with decisions that may lead to a corporation's committing a crime. Executives are protected by the law's unwillingness to find them liable for their companies' illegal actions' (Bakan 2004, 79). Furthermore, shareholders cannot be held legally responsible for any crimes committed by the corporation due to limited liability. Basically, since 'courts tend to attribute conduct to the corporate "person" rather than to the actual people who run the corporations,' no actual people are held responsible for the destructive activities of corporations (Bakan 2004, 79). Hayek (1958, 116) expressed his own concerns about this situation when he stated that:

> in the field of the law of corporations we had a situation rather analogous to that in the field of the law of property...As in the law of property the rules developed for ordinary mobile property were extended uncritically and without appropriate modifications to all sorts of new rights; thus the recognition of corporations as fictitious or legal persons has had the effect that all the rights of a natural person were automatically extended to corporations. There may be valid arguments for so designing corporation law as to impede the indefinite growth of individual corporations.

Joel Bakan was also critical of the treatment of corporations under the law in his book, *The Corporation: The Pathological Pursuit of Profit and Power* (2004, 110), where he explained that:

> No one would seriously suggest that individuals should regulate themselves, that laws against murder, assault, and theft are unnecessary because people are socially responsible. Yet oddly, we are asked to believe that corporate persons-institutional psychopaths who lack any sense of moral conviction and who have the power and motivation to cause harm and devastation in the world-should be left free to govern.

Since actual people are rarely held accountable for the crimes committed by corporations, there has been little incentive for them to meaningfully change their business practices. Consequently, corporations have continued to operate in a manner that maximizes the interests of their shareholders at the expense of people's health, the rights and safety of their workers, and the environment.

State regulations that are implemented for the good of the public will usually limit the ability of corporations to operate freely, which will hinder the pursuit of their mandate to maximize shareholder profits, because the most effective methods by which to achieve this result involve exploiting the world's natural and human resources. In many instances, corporations will simply continue operating without respecting burdensome regulations, because they know that the punishment for breaching the law is negligible, often amounting to little more than a fine. In fact, it is not uncommon for corporations to factor the regular payment of fines and penalties into their cost-benefit analyses, which means that engaging in illegal activities that produce irreversible destructive outcomes for the environment, human beings and various other species is simply treated as another cost of doing business. Moreover, given the immense financial resources at the disposal of many corporations, even a very large fine might not dissuade them from engaging in banned or illegal activities that are socially and environmentally destructive, because they would still generate significant profits for their stakeholders. In rare cases where laws and regulations are properly enforced and penalties are too large to be simply brushed aside, the offending corporations will often react by finding new and innovative ways of covering up their illegal and destructive activities. In other words, even though regulations that have been designed to protect the public interests from corporate crimes have been adopted, the legal system has been unable to effectively enforce them. Part of the problem is that governments tend to prioritize the freedoms, rights and interests of corporations over those of their own citizens, which becomes readily apparent when significant deregulation is authorized and carried out.

Even though neo-liberals adamantly oppose state efforts to protect the interests of their citizens and achieve social justice through the provision social services and programs, they fully back the idea of powerful corporations using their political influence to protect and promote their own interests by corrupting politicians and other public officials. In other words, neo-liberal economists endorse the partnership that has emerged between corporations and governments, which overwhelmingly serves the private interests of the former. This is not surprising given that neo-liberals are 'the influential and invaluable ally of those whose exercise of power depends on an acquiescent public. If the state is the executive committee of the great corporation and the planning system,' it is due to the fact that neo-liberal economics is 'its instrument for neutralizing the suspicion that this is so' (Galbraith 2001, 151).

In 1961, Friedman published an article entitled 'Capitalism and Freedom' in which he underscored the importance of lobby groups and industry-backed thinktanks in influencing government policies. He claimed that 'in order to be able to advocate anything effectively it is necessary to be able to raise some money to finance meetings, propaganda, publications, writings and so on' (Friedman 1961, 25). He also argued that 'in a capitalistic society, radical movements have never been financed by small amounts from many people. They have been financed by a small number of wealthy people being willing to foot the bill' (Friedman 1961,

25). Friedman has consistently supported lobbying efforts to eliminate government involvement in regulating the activities of private enterprises.

Corporations began to organize politically in the 1970s, as they set up 'offices in Washington, D.C., and created industry organizations, lobby groups, and industry-backed think tanks to assert their collective influence' (Bakan 2004, 103). Now, all large and powerful 'corporations have offices in the nation's capital, as do the numerous industry groups, think tanks, and lobby organizations that represent their collective interests' (Bakan 2004, 103). Corporations will spend vast sums of money on lobbying political parties and making financial contributions to election campaigns, which they regard as business investments that promote the interests of their shareholders. In the United States, powerful corporations and wealthy people 'contribute 80 percent of the campaign funds for national candidates. Elections have become the multimillionaires' game to play' (Parenti 2015, 110). These campaign contributions are provided with the intent of having a say in shaping government policies down the road.

Presently, political elections are mainly about fighting over issues where the objectives of governments diverge from those of the general public. By and large, the masses tend to prefer public services and programs like state-funded housing, public transportation, free universal education and health care services, welfare, environmental protection, etc. However, once a political party has been elected, they are expected to reimburse the generous campaign contributions they received by using their state authority to implement policies that promote and protect the freedoms and interests of their corporate financial backers; this could also include limiting or eliminating existing regulations that restrict the freedoms of corporations, or preventing the introduction of new ones. Governments also have the options of reducing corporate taxes or creating (or ignoring) loopholes for tax avoidance, which is detrimental to society, because it deprives the state of funds that could be used to provide social programs or distribute income so as to achieve a more just and egalitarian society. For example, 'in any given year two of every three US companies pay no income tax' (Parenti 2015, 109). Furthermore, wealthy elite classes in many countries often manage to find 'ways, legal and illegal, to shelter much of their wealth in secret accounts. The higher one goes up the income bracket, the greater are the opportunities for enjoying tax-free income. The richest fraction of 1 percent, that is, the top one-hundredth of 1 percent super rich, enjoy seemingly boundless tax benefits' (Parenti 2015, 109).

Despite the great contradictions between the needs of corporations and those of the public, neo-liberal economists consider the partnership between corporations and governments to be an important factor in ensuring the conditions of a free-market economy, which would contribute to improving productivity, economic growth and technological progress. However, when governments intervene for the purposes of ensuring the conditions of a free-market system or deregulating the economy in the interests of corporations, freedom becomes restricted for the masses. This is because these governments are using their powers to serve the particular ends of the corporate world instead of the collective interests of their citizens. Hayek often argued that the laws and rules are abstract and general in a free society, meaning they do not discriminate between individuals or prescribe particular ends to be pursued. In reality, this is not the case under free-market capitalism, since the corporate world and rich people can use their economic power to protect and promote their own interests by corrupting politicians, or contributing to political campaigns in order to influence rules, laws and regulations. Under such circumstances, laws and rules are no longer abstract or general. Nonetheless, Hayek and other liberals never actually acknowledged that the activities of corporations violated the legal framework of free societies.

The rise of neo-liberalism has led to the emergence of large transnational corporations with an ability to exercise unparalleled power on a global scale in various areas of economy, including natural resources, and the production and distribution of goods and services. Throughout human history, defenders of positive freedom were highly suspicious of large businesses amassing too much power (Berlin 2002 [1969]). Interestingly, most neo-liberal economists have been largely uncritical of the dominant power that corporations have been able to acquire in free-market societies, which has enabled them to become coercive and tyrannical. In fact, neo-liberal economists have been largely supportive of this development, as well as the close partnership that has emerged between corporations and governments.

Neo-liberals should actually be very concerned about the tyrannical power acquired by corporations and their close partnership with governments, since similar circumstances were instrumental in the emergence of fascism in Italy. The origins of Italian fascism can be traced back to the rivalry between growing industrial monopolization and the democratic system. After WWI, Italy began to experience economic problems, primarily due to the interruption of global trade and the extensive 'network of social legislation,' which labour unions struggled to attain (Marcuse 1968, 410). Under these circumstances, the strongest 'industrial groups' generally took up 'direct political power' so as to acquire 'monopolistic production' and eliminate any 'socialist' rivals (Marcuse 1968, 410). Eventually, fascism suppressed the democratic system in Italy, thereby stripping the citizenry of their right to majority rule.

Ultimately, the wants, goals and needs of Italy's working-classes, trade unions, cooperative societies, and socialist groups and parties were destroyed by the collaboration between the Fascist Party, large corporations and the defence forces. Fascism was capable of establishing productive forces by utilizing coercion against the civil population. This coercion included 'totalitarian control' over all 'social' or 'individual' relationships and associations, the elimination of 'social and individual liberties,' and bringing the citizenry into compliance via fear and threats of violence (Marcuse 1968, 410). As a result, Italian society was essentially transformed into an 'armed camp' that served the interests of those that emerged as the dominant forces. In other words, individuals were coerced into working for only those particular 'interests of the ruling bureaucracy' (Marcuse 1968, 410). Therefore, fascism not only eliminated freedom in Italy, it also suppressed all of the individual rights that are important for the realisation of freedom.

Since the rise of neo-liberalism, the emergence of a profit-oriented mutual relationship between neo-liberal governments and corporations has led to the latter evolving into highly bureaucratic entities that centrally and deliberately plan their large scale goals and strategies. Some are even equipped with strong security forces and have military resources at their disposal to assist them in exploiting the world's resources and coercing workers. The case could be made that contemporary corporations have become more coercive, authoritarian and tyrannical than centrally planned states, monarchies, empires and even the church. Given the role of the corporate world in modern societies, countries should be cautious about the growing power and influence of corporations, so that they avoid transitioning into the type of 'corporate state' that existed in fascist Italy between World Wars I and II.

5.1 Conclusion

Since the rise of neo-liberalism, many governments have focused much of their attention on ensuring the conditions of a free-market economy through the abolition of trade restrictions, deregulation, the privatisation of public assets and enterprises, and limiting state actions, which has allowed corporations to attain unprecedented levels of freedom and power. Neo-liberals regard large corporations as important sources of economic growth, because they facilitate investment, create jobs, and spur innovation, which ultimately improves the living standards of both the worse off and the better off in every society. In reality, however, last four decades have demonstrated that many of the business practices that corporations engage in, with the intent of furthering their mandates, are very socially and environmentally destructive. The fact that corporations persist in their pursuit of power and wealth, despite the destructive outcomes of their actions, demonstrates that they fail to comprehend that, as human beings, '[w]e arrive and we depart. We are guests at a banquet continually spread, spectators and participants in an entertainment where there is room for all who come. We are passengers on an orb whirling through space. Our rights to take and possess cannot be exclusive. They must be bounded, everywhere, by the equal rights of others' (George 2006, 190–191).

Instead of trying to alter their business practices to reduce the harm that they inflict, which would likely raise their costs of production considerably, thereby violating their mandates, corporations have elected to focus their efforts on legitimizing their activities by influencing both governments and public opinion. This has led them to work closely with and support a multitude of free-market thinktanks,[1] which frequently advocate for a limited state role, the deregulation of the economy, and individual and economic freedom, all of which happen to be important components of the neo-liberal ideology that largely benefit the businesses community. Corporations also exert significant influence over various local and international organisations, institutions and agencies, many of which were

[1] Corporations have provided financial support to free-market thinktanks in about '100 nations and territories' (https://www.fraserinstitute.org/economic-freedom/our-network/member-institutes). These thinktanks claim that they are 'dedicated to improving the lives of people in their nation or territory by providing information and research on the impact of economic freedom' (https://www.fraserinstitute.org/economic-freedom/our-network/member-institutes). Free-market thinktanks publish studies and issue statements by well-trained and respected academics that support the interests of their financial backers.

originally founded to regulate their destructive business activities and practices. In other words, the rise of neo-liberalism has led to many agencies being influenced by the very companies and industries that they are supposed to be regulating.

Neo-liberal economists have argued that the concentration of power is among the greatest threats to freedom. They also have a long-standing tradition of advocating for the ability of external authorities to intervene in the private spheres of individuals to be significantly curtailed. However, since they have not objected to the coercive and controlling powers amassed by corporations, it is likely that their arguments were mainly directed at the oppressive authority of centrally planned states, such as communist, socialist and welfare states, and, to a lesser extent, the power held by monopolies. Presently, the biggest tyrants and oppressors of the people are large transnational corporations, whose ability to control and coerce has been secured and legitimized by the legal system. If freedom is to have a meaningful and constructive role in people's lives and communities, then individuals need to be protected from all forms of infringement upon their freedom, including the extensive power of large corporations. Consequently, 'the greatest' focus and concern of government social and economic policies should be 'the emancipation of the state from the control of the corporate system' (Galbraith 2001, 150).

References

Bakan, Joel. 2004. *The Corporation: The Pathological Pursuit of Profit and Power*. New York: Simon & Schuster Inc.

Berlin, Isaiah. 2002 [1969]. *Incorporating Four Essays on Liberty*. Edited by H. Hardy. Oxford: Oxford University Press.

Friedman, Milton. 1961. Capitalism and Freedom. In *New Individualist Review*, ed. Ralph Raico, vol. 1, 18–27. Liberty Fund: Indianapolis. https://oll.libertyfund.org/titles/2136.

———. 1982 [1962]. *Capitalism and Freedom*. Chicago: University of Chicago Press.

———. (September 13, 1970). The Social Responsibility of Business is to Increase its Profits. *The New York Times Magazine*. https://www.nytimes.com/1970/09/13/archives/a-friedman-doctrine-the-social-responsibility-of-business-is-to.html.

Galbraith, John Kenneth. 2001. *The Essential Galbraith*. Edited by Andrea D. Williams. Boston: Houghton Mifflin Company.

George, Henry. 2006. *Progress and Poverty: Why There are Recessions and Poverty amid Plenty—and What To Do about It!* Edited by B. Drake. New York: Robert Schalkenbach Foundation.

Hayek, F.A. 1958 [1948]. *Individualism and Economic Order*. Chicago: University of Chicago Press.

Marcuse, Herbert. 1968. *Reason and Revolution*. London: Routledge & Kegan Paul Ltd.

Parenti, Michael. 2015. *Profit Pathology and Other Indecencies*. New York: Routledge.

Simons, Henry Calvert. 1934. *A Positive Program for Laissez-Faire: Some Proposals for a Liberal Economic Policy*, Public Policy Pamphlet, No. 15. Chicago: University of Chicago Press.

CHAPTER 6

The Rise of Mass Consumption: When Irrationality Is Considered Rational

Prior to World War I, Keynes (1920, 8) observed that a majority of the population endured hardships and 'a low standard of comfort,' whereas 'the middle and upper classes' enjoyed 'comforts, and amenities beyond the compass of the richest and most powerful monarchs of other ages.' To illustrate how comfortable life was for the upper and middle classes of London at that time, he explained that these individuals could 'order by telephone, sipping his morning tea in bed, the various products of the whole earth, in such quantity as he might see fit, and reasonably expect their early delivery upon his doorstep' (Keynes 1920, 8, 9). These comforts, which Keynes observed in 1914, have been vastly expanded in contemporary capitalist countries to the extent that even poor segments of the population are able to enjoy them. There is also a stark contrast when considering the quantity, variety, and quality of goods available for consumption in the early twentieth century that Keynes was describing and those that modern consumers have access to in developed countries.

For most of human history, people were able to lead meaningful lives without resorting to mass consumption. However, the global reorientation of the world economy radically transformed this state of affairs. More specifically, the elimination of obstacles to the free movement of production and capital across borders via deregulation, delocalisation, free trade agreements, and the decentralization of complex production chains has led to corporate business practices undergoing unprecedented changes.

B. Filip, *The Rise of Neo-liberalism and the Decline of Freedom*,
Palgrave Insights into Apocalypse Economics,
https://doi.org/10.1007/978-3-030-61623-6_6

Furthermore, the intensification of technological innovation and scientific progress have led to the development of specialized machines, tools and techniques that have significantly improved the efficiency of production processes and distribution. The main outcomes of these changes have included significant increases in productivity, lower production costs and consumer prices, and faster economic growth, all of which have contributed to higher living standards and prosperity.

With globalization bringing down consumer prices, including those of many luxury products, individuals have been able to increase the quantity and variety of the goods and services that they consume. Meanwhile, corporations have deployed sophisticated psychological techniques and marketing campaigns to manipulate people into believing that the wasteful consumption of goods was necessary to achieve happiness, and that destruction of natural resources and the environment was required to achieve productivity gains and economic growth. This chapter focuses on how neo-liberal economists have consistently supported mass consumption as a sign of economic growth and productivity, while largely ignoring the destructive and irreversible environmental consequences associated with it.

6.1 Mass Consumption and the Coercive Power of Advertisements

With the advance of neo-liberalism, government authority has been extensively used to establish an environment where businesses can operate in a manner that allows them to maximise their interests. This has included taking measures and passing laws making it easier for corporations to delocalize many of their operations and activities, and then move them to more accommodating locations. The unparalleled changes in the business practices of corporations during the rise of neo-liberalism have increased their productivity and improved their distribution, thereby allowing for mass production to reach unprecedented levels. However, higher productivity and accelerated economic growth necessitate more demand. As a result, corporations have expended great efforts to continuously create the next commodity that consumers will desire, while also launching aggressive marketing campaigns to convince people to buy things that they do not really need. More precisely, with the rise in living standards that accompanied the advance of free-market capitalism, 'the economic interests of people are transferred more and more out of the sphere of fundamental needs into that of aesthetic and social gratification and pure experimentation. Thus wants become more unstable and as a result the interest of producers is centred more in the field of arousing wants or changing them to fit particular products and less in the field of studying wants and producing goods to fit them' (Knight 2007 [1935], 137). Consequently, people have experienced dramatic changes in the variety, quality and quantity of goods available for consumption. However, since corporations can earn profits 'either by producing what consumers want, or by making consumers want what one is actually producing,' they will often devote considerable resources to managing and shaping people's wants and desires, in addition to developing new and better products (Simons 1934, 32).

Mass production has not only motivated corporations to encourage people to consume more, it has also enabled them to alter the meaning of necessities and luxury goods. Presently, it is not only much easier to obtain necessary goods than at any other point in human history, but luxury goods are also more widely accessible. For example, a good that is considered a luxury item in a poor country or by a poor family can be regarded as a necessity in developed countries and by rich people. Meanwhile, in industrialized countries, many consumer goods and services that were considered luxuries only a few decades ago are now accepted as necessities by the majority of households, including cars, appliances, air-conditioners, video games, computers, cell phones, television sets, travelling/holidays etc. Accordingly, many of the homes and workplaces in western countries are filled with mass produced consumption items. Lucius Annaeus Seneca (4 BC–AD 65) (1969 [65 AD], 222), the well-known Stoic philosopher, was highly critical of luxurious consumption, as he stated that 'the whole object of luxurious living is the delight it takes in irregular ways and in not merely departing from the correct course but going to the farthest point away from it, and in eventually even taking a stand diametrically opposed to it.'

A majority of consumers in developed nations spend more money than they earn to satisfy their incessant desires to consume. Consumption appears to have become a positive experience for people, as they obtain some sort of satisfaction from the acquisition of goods and services. Furthermore, people feel an urgent compulsion to purchase and consume the latest products while they are still in fashion. However, any satisfaction they receive eventually fades, usually when companies determine that enough time has passed for a newer fashion or model to be released into the market, which will compel these same people to shop again, even if they really do not need anything. This type of unhealthy and wasteful behaviour has been accepted as normal in neo-liberal societies, because it promotes productivity and economic growth. Naturally, this aligns well with the interests of corporations, as consumers with a compulsion for the latest and most fashionable products are favourable for advancing their bottom lines and mandates.

Producers of many consumption products rely heavily on the idea of fashion in order to sell as much as possible. Fashionable products are often designed to be disposable even if they are non-perishable. Basically, when a new fashion arrives on the market, goods that are part of the previous fashion cycle are often simply discarded by their owners even if they could still be used for a significant duration of time. For example, in the case of clothing, the fashion industry no longer offers new styles according to a limited seasonal calendar, as large companies want people continuously consume their products year round. Thus, contrary to the past, when new collections might have arrived in stores every six months or so, there are now essentially 52 fashion seasons in a year, one for each week. Clearly, clothing companies are seeking to exploit the incessant impulses of many consumers to be among the first to possess the latest fashions even though the lifecycle of fashionable goods is ephemeral, meaning these items do not provide future satisfaction. In addition to clothes, it is common for people to throw away items like computers, cellphones, furniture, and appliances that are undamaged and still function properly as soon as better versions become available. In fact, many people will choose to upgrade even when: they are not fully aware of, or have little practical use for, a majority of the new features being offered by the latest model; or, their current "outdated" model is more than sufficient to meet their needs. In any given period of time, the average consumer will possess technology products, or items infused with the latest technologies, like cellphones, cameras, TVs, and vehicles that have so many sophisticated features that they will never be able fully utilize or master them. John Kenneth Galbraith (1908–2006) (2001, 149), a Canadian-American economist who was one of the most well-known critics of free-market capitalism, explained that fashion aims purely to satisfy the capitalistic tendencies of producers:

> Products are changed not to make them better but to take advantage of the belief that what is different is better. There is a high failure rate in engineering

> because its preoccupation is not with what is good but with what can be sold. So the unpersuaded or disenchanted consumer rebels. This is not a rebellion against minor matters of fraud or misinformation. It is a major reaction against a whole deployment of power by which the consumer is made the instrument of purposes that are not his own.

Corporations are continuously striving to earn ever greater profits. Since their sales are dependent upon the wants and desires of consumers, corporations aim not only to provide consumers with products and services that will satisfy their immediate demands, they also expend great efforts to convince people as to what they should want. To do so, they employ multitudes of experts and specialists to analyze vast amounts of information and produce reports on how to increase sales by persuading consumers that they have a genuine desire to continuously buy their products and services. Corporations would not make such significant investments into this kind of market research if they were not convinced of its effectiveness in terms of boosting the sales of their products and services by arousing interest and desire among potential consumers.

Advertisements are among the preferred methods used by corporations to shape the ideas, values, behaviours, desires and thoughts of individuals when it comes to choosing a store/establishment, product, or brand. However, advertisements do much more than simply guide consumers to buy products and services that they are already familiar with, or inform them about new ones that will satisfy their desires. They also assist corporations with manipulating consumer choices, including by eliciting desires that people did not previously have in order to convince them to buy things that they do not really need. Through advertising, corporations are able to shape and create consumer tastes and desires, so that they can then provide the products and services that will satisfy them. In fact, it is not uncommon for a corporation to develop sophisticated marketing campaigns to manipulate consumers into buying their products and services in order to satisfy artificial needs and desires that the very same corporation helped create in the first place. In essence corporations strive to create consumers who have been conditioned to not only want what they do not need, but also more of what they already have.

Corporations are able employ sophisticated psychological techniques and strategies in their advertisements to excite or depress people, inspire them, or paralyze their minds, bodies and actions, depending on whatever happens to suite their business interests at a given point in time.

Furthermore, corporations even have the potential to create or trigger a variety of addictions in people, including drugs, alcohol, food, cigarettes, gambling, shopping, and technological devices or gadgets. Through their advertisements, corporations basically attempt to influence and control what people eat and drink, what they watch, what they read, what they laugh at, what they wear, etc. That would suggest that individuals living in neo-liberal societies may not even know what their true needs and wants actually are.

Herbert Marcuse (1898–1979) (2007 [1964], 7), a well-known German-American philosopher, sociologist, and political theorist, and renowned member of the Frankfurt School, whose work was influential among leftist movements of the 1960s, labelled the manufactured wants and desires of people as 'false needs', such as 'needs to relax, to have fun, to behave and consume in accordance with the advertisements, to love and hate what others love and hate.' He explained that since such needs are 'determined by external powers over which the individual has no control; the development and satisfaction of these needs is heteronomous' (Marcuse 2007, 7). More precisely, people's consumption habits are formed by the will of the corporate world, which means consumers have lost their capacity to realise their own independent choices based on their wills, ideas and thoughts. In other words, consumers no longer determine their own wants, desires and needs; rather, these are imposed on them heteronomously through the marketing strategies of the dominant interests. Therefore, consumers cannot act freely, because they are incapable of resisting the domination of large corporations, which employ sophisticated advertisements, not to provide accurate or reliable information about their actual products or service, but to control people and impose artificial needs and desire on them. Presently, the ability of corporations to control and oppress the masses is immeasurably greater than at any other point in human history.

The profit-oriented activities of corporations do not appear to have any boundaries. Their insatiable desire to maximize profits means that even the practice of targeting children through highly sophisticated advertisements is not off limits. For corporations, it is important that these future consumers come to believe that the satisfaction of their self-interests and wants is a priority. As such, children are exposed to advertisements at a very early age, when the formation of their personalities is still occurring. Corporations have the resources and capacity to shape the minds, habits, choices and preferences of these future consumers by inundating them with targeted advertisements at every opportunity, whether that be at home via television and the internet, or anywhere else through various mediums including mobile devices, the radio, and billboards and posters on public transportation, in the streets, at shopping malls, theaters, sports arenas and stadiums, and various other venues. By indoctrinating and manipulating people starting at an early age, corporations bear a great deal of responsibility for facilitating the emergence of the mass consumption culture that prevails in much of the world.

In discussing the role of advertisements, von Mises (1949, 317) contended that 'advertising is shrill, noisy, coarse, puffing, because the public does not react to dignified allusions. It is the bad taste of the public that forces the advertisers to display bad taste in their publicity campaigns. The art of advertising has evolved into a branch of applied psychology, a sister discipline of pedagogy.' He further explained that advertisements 'must be obtrusive and blatant. It is its aim to attract the attention of slow people, to rouse latent wishes, to entice men to substitute innovation for inert clinging to traditional routine. In order to succeed, advertising must be adjusted to the mentality of the people courted. It must suit their tastes and speak their idiom' (von Mises 1949, 316, 317). Furthermore, he claimed that, much like many other things 'designed to suit the taste of the masses, advertising is repellent to people of delicate feeling' (von Mises 1949, 317). However, while Mises did not have a positive view of advertisements in and of themselves, he did recognize their effectiveness in terms of influencing the consumption behaviours of the masses in the free-market system. He understood that advertisements cannot be banned, as doing so would restrict 'the freedom of the consumers to spend their income according to their own wants and desires' (von Mises 1949, 317). Neo-liberals associate the banning and restriction of advertising with totalitarian regimes, where governments exercise unlimited control over individuals and society, and violate fundamental liberties.

Today, large firms that specialise in advertising, public relations, and branding are able to amass great fortunes, because corporations see the value in the creativity and skill required to repeatedly convince people to keep buying the latest versions of products that they do not need. Consequently, they have become 'an immensely powerful instrument' of free-market capitalism (Stigler 1961, 220). Simons (1934, 32) anticipated this scenario back in 1934, when he stated that 'if present tendencies continue, we may soon reach a situation where most of our resources are utilized in persuading people to buy one thing rather than another, and only a minor fraction actually employed in creating things to be bought.'

With the rise of neo-liberalism, people began to view their level of consumption as an indication of the amount of freedom they enjoyed. In other words, they regarded their freedom as a function of the satisfaction of their wants and desires, which often involved possessing the latest goods in large quantities. In fact, the rise of neo-liberalism led to people's ideas, views, and goals being motivated by the desire to attain quantitative increases in their material possessions. Furthermore, despite the fact that obtaining bigger, better, and newer commodities is not essential for survival and only provides temporary satisfaction, lacking these items can be devastating for the majority of people. The consumption patterns that have emerged in capitalist societies indicate that much of the population shares the same goal with corporations, that being the preservation of the established system of mass consumption and mass production at any price.

Mass production and mass consumption are important components of Friedman's concept of freedom. That said, he promoted mass production and consumption as if the world possessed limitless resources, and all goods would be available in the marketplace at any time and under all circumstances. In fact, Friedman and Friedman (1990, 41) stated that 'our real objective is not just jobs but productive jobs—jobs that will mean more goods and services to consume.' However, while mass consumption might be effective in terms of providing people with an abundance of goods and services, it does so by focusing on the destructive instinctual behaviours of people, which mass producers have found great success in shaping and exploiting.

Mass consumption demonstrates that the free-market system was able to transform 'the object world into an extension of man's mind and body' (Marcuse 2007, 11). In other words, the free-market system made individuals 'recognize themselves in their commodities; they find their soul in their automobile, hi-fi set, split-level home, kitchen equipment,' technological gadgets, clothing, vacations, etc. (Marcuse 2007, 11). Meanwhile, if certain people do not conform with the mass consumer culture, then 'the intellectual and emotional refusal "to go along" appears neurotic and impotent' (Marcuse 2007, 12). That means mass consumption is destructive to the free development of individual thoughts, behaviours, and faculties. In an age when the psychological techniques used by advertisements are so advanced that they can essentially control and regulate the actions, desires, and choices of most individuals, freedom is no longer a matter of protection against physical restraint and coercion, but rather, against mind control and coercive persuasion.

6.2 The Protection of Consumers

Since the rise of neo-liberalism, corporations have been able to exercise immense freedom by moving some of their activities to countries where they can take advantage of an abundance of natural resources, low wages, a lack of labour protection, low taxes, weak environmental regulation, etc. Moreover, if the conditions in these new locations are not quite ideal, corporations often find success in bribing or coercing local government officials in less developed countries into weakening or removing laws and regulations that do not suit their interests.

Even in developed countries, corporations have managed to halt or limit the activities of government agencies and organisations with mandates to enforce policies and regulations that were detrimental to their business practices and bottom lines. For example, the U.S. Environmental Protection Agency (EPA), which has mandate to maintain and enforce national standards under a number of environmental laws, had its budget significantly cut during the Reagan presidency. Neo-liberals have consistently claimed that the regulations enforced by such agencies and organisations inhibited innovation, efficiency, productivity, and economic growth. They also believed this to be true of government involvement in the marketplace aimed at protecting the interests of consumers by safeguarding them from unhealthy and unsafe products, as well as the harmful and predatory practices of producers. Neo-liberals largely dismissed these legitimate concerns, while criticizing consumer protection and environmental regulations for delaying the introduction of new and better products into the market. In their arguments against governmental regulations, Friedman and Friedman (1990, 227) stated:

> If the government has responsibility of protecting us from dangerous substances, the logic surely calls for prohibiting alcohol and tobacco. If it is appropriate for the government to protect us from using dangerous bicycles and cap guns, the logic calls for prohibiting still more dangerous activities such as hang-gliding, motorcycling, and skiing.

Friedman and Friedman (1990, 189–190) specifically criticized government intervention in the marketplace aimed at ensuring the 'safety and well-being' of consumers by safeguarding them 'from exploitation by sellers', in addition to protecting them from themselves. Accordingly, they strongly disagreed with 'economists, philosophers, reformers, and social critics' who wanted to protect consumers from sellers who, given the opportunity, might take full advantage of their 'innocence and ignorance to overcharge them and pass off on them shoddy products' (Friedman and Friedman 1990, 189). They suggested that these kinds of economists, philosophers, reformers, and social critics would likely believe that 'if you leave it to the market,' the outcomes would include pollution of 'the air we breathe, the water we drink,' and threats to 'the safety of the foods we eat' (Friedman and Friedman 1990, 1989). Neo-liberals are convinced that allowing the state to regulate products or business activities in order to protect the health of its citizens presents 'an open invitation to tomorrow's arguments about the social cost of sugar, sunbathing, saturated fat, recreational injuries, obesity, and on and on. Down this road lies not a free society but a totally regulated society with only one acceptable lifestyle as prescribed by the health paternalists' (Tollison and Wagner 1992, X).

Friedman and Friedman (1990) argued that many of the efforts taken by state agencies to protect consumers involved extensive government regulations. More specifically, they claimed that governments basically impose 'heavy costs on industry after industry to meet increasingly detailed' requirements in the name of protecting consumers (Friedman and Friedman 1990, 191). Accordingly, Friedman and Friedman (1990, 191) criticized such measures for being 'antigrowth,' and 'opposed to new developments, to industrial innovation, the increased use of natural resources.' They also contended that, by undertaking efforts to protect and monitor consumer interests, governmental agencies have delayed progress, increased the prices of goods, and restricted the choices available for consumers. Moreover, Friedman and Friedman (1990, 192) stated that the goods produced by 'government-regulated industries' were of lower quality compared to those produced by private industry without regulation, which are of 'outstanding' quality. That said, they were very disappointed that a number of 'economists, philosophers, reformers, and social critics' were convinced that 'private enterprises produce shoddy products' and that it was necessary to have 'vigilant government employees to keep business from foisting off unsafe' products on people (Friedman and Friedman 1990, 192). Friedman maintained that people could not depend on state regulations and agencies to protect their interests as consumers. In fact, he claimed that governmental agencies with mandates to protect consumers sought to discredit the products produced by private industries and mislead consumers. He also criticized such agencies for raising government expenditures and increasing the number of bureaucrats employed.

Friedman was a particularly harsh critic of the Food and Drug Administration (FDA), a federal agency of the United States Department of Health and Human Services that was formed in 1906. The FDA is responsible for the supervision and control of food and drugs in the US, and the establishment of standards in the interest of protecting and promoting public health and safety. According to Friedman, the FDA acts as an obstacle to individual freedom by limiting consumer access to a wide range of goods. In particular, he was strongly against the FDA having a role in regulating advertisements and the labelling of commodities, on the basis that it limited civil liberties and consumer choice. He also claimed that the regulatory authority of the FDA slowed innovation and the development of new products, in addition to delaying progress at all stages of the production and distribution processes for goods and services.

Similar to Friedman, Buchanan (1986, 340) believed that people who advocated for government regulations to 'impose their preferences on the behaviour of others be wary of the threat to their own liberties … their own behaviour that may also be subjected to control and regulation.' He specifically argued that state regulations based on 'scientific grounds', such as the prohibition of handguns, alcohol and smoking, were 'highly deceiving', as the state is essentially using scientific authority to impose a moral value on society (Buchanan 1986, 141). Moreover, Tollison (1986, 13) explained that Buchanan's message was 'about the wisdom of individuals respecting one another's preferences. Some may feel strongly about restricting smoking behaviour, others about open air burning of leaves, others about carrying guns … If we each seek to restrict the specific activities of others which offend us, we all end up worse of as a result.' Much like Friedman, Buchanan, and Tollison, many other neo-liberals believe that government involvement in the marketplace for the purpose of protecting consumers and the environment infringes upon the freedom of individuals. They are of the view that this kind of interference prevents individuals from spending their money and enjoying their lives according to their own desires and wants. Neo-liberals further contend that if an individual's freedom to choose their own consumption is abolished, then all freedoms are essentially taken away from them.

In reality, a community can greatly benefit from state policies that aim to improve public health and protect the environment by regulating new goods that corporations seek to launch. Today, the many destructive outcomes associated with free-market capitalism demonstrate that neoliberalism, 'along with the corporation,' have 'created the wealth' that has made it impossible to govern society with only a minimal state (Galbraith 2001, 164). To the contrary, the wealth, influence and coercive power that have been amassed by contemporary corporations would suggest that constant state interference is required to evaluate and regulate harmful corporate activities in order to safeguard the common good. In fact, a nation cannot have 'a high consumption of automobiles, alcohol, transportation, communications or even cosmetics without public rules governing their use and public facilities to rescue people from accidents and exploitation' (Galbraith 2001, 163). Galbraith (2001, 163) argued that, if private consumption increases, then:

> demand for public services—for education, health care, parks and public recreation, postal services and the infinity of other things that must be provided or are best provided by the state.

As an example, Galbraith (2001) suggested that if the consumption of cars were to significantly increase, then the government would require a larger budget for environmental regulations and health care services, because there would likely be more injuries attributable to traffic accidents, and people might get sick from the additional air pollution. The government might also need to increase its budget in order to build new roads and maintain existing ones. More indirectly, the government might also consider investing in parks and green areas so as to offsets the air pollution caused by having more cars on the roads. It might also consider regulating the polluting activities of motor vehicle and parts manufacturers, as well as the mining companies that extract materials used in the production of cars. Thus, Galbraith (2001) used the example of automobiles to illustrate how mass consumption and mass production can serve as catalysts for more state regulations and higher budgets to invest in the public good.

Karl Gunnar Myrdal (1898–1987), a Swedish left-wing socialist economist who was awarded a co–Nobel Prize in Economic Sciences in 1974, along with Hayek, often expressed strong views when it came to pollution and the environment. He recognized that rapidly increasing car ownership would generate considerable consequences in a number of areas including the environment, human health, and public infrastructure (Myrdal 1973). Like Galbraith, he believed that these issues would need to addressed by implementing policies and regulations that would mitigate such damages on society; however, he advocated for the politically unpopular approach of holding the car owners themselves accountable for covering the costs of any actions taken. (Myrdal 1973). For example, Myrdal (1973, 110) called for 'the car owners to pay the full costs, including also the heavy investment costs for roads and adjusting cities to the cramming of cars in the streets, the costs implied by all delays caused to people in the cars and on the streets, the costs of policing the traffic, and the very heavy public and private costs caused by accidents ... also for the pollution of the air' (Myrdal 1973, 110).

The ideas expressed by Galbraith (2001) and Myrdal (1973), which can be applied to any consumption goods and services, should be taken into consideration by any government seeking to achieve the common good, as well as various organizations and agencies with mandates to protect public interests. An ideal approach to dealing with the negative consequences associated with an expansion in the consumption of a particular good or services would likely involve some combination of both of their views. More specifically, the government would respond to the harmful impacts caused by an increase in the consumption of a particular good and services by implementing regulations and expanding public services; subsequently, the ensuing increase in the budget would be paid for by the direct users of those particular goods or services.

6.3 Mass Consumption: When Irrationality Is Considered Rational

During the Cold War Era, consumption levels and patterns were used to demonstrate the superiority of capitalism over communism. Since then, many neo-liberal discourses have incessantly promoted the idea of a correlation between freedom and consumption. This may may have contributed to people in free-market societies believing that they are free, because their economies are organized in a manner that allows them to satisfy their ever-expanding needs and wants Meanwhile, neo-liberalism has shaped the needs, wants and desires of the masses in such a way that they are never fully satisfied, meaning that consumers constantly have 'more, and better wants' and desires to fulfill (Knight 1922, 458).

In the free-market system, life has essentially been transformed into a process where consumers continuously try to rationally satisfy their irrational desires and wants, which, in turn, were rationally created and shaped by corporations. However, consumers are convinced that they rationally choose which goods and services they consume based on their own rational will. In reality, sophisticated advertising techniques and methods will often rationally manipulate them into consuming something that they neither need nor want. In other words, the creation of new needs and wants is accomplished by the corporations through a rational thought process.

Rationality also played a major role in corporations gaining domination and control over the world's resources, wealth and income. In fact, the rational production process is inseparably intertwined with the interests of the corporate world. While the development and utilization of all available resources for the universal satisfaction of fabricated needs and wants may be rational in in terms of maximizing the interests of producers over the short term, this approach is irrational for the masses, because it depletes the world's natural resources, degrades the environment, and engenders health problems. The irrational character of free-market capitalism is highlighted by the fact that neo-liberal economists promote wasteful consumption as a 'need,' while they regard the destruction of natural resources, ecosystems and habitats as a form of 'construction' (Marcuse 2007, 11). In fact, from the point of view of the billions of people and other species and organisms that inhabit the earth, as well as the future generations that have not yet been born, no one could objectively describe mass consumption and mass production as anything but irrational, given the extent of the damages they have caused.

The prevailing system of mass consumption and mass production is playing a main role in depleting the earth's resources, while also increasing pollution and waste. Although western consumers have become much better-informed about the unfairness of the production system, as well as the destructive environmental outcomes associated with mass production and mass consumption, they have largely chosen to ignore the global social and environmental consequences of their consumption habits. In fact, the masses may be incapable of caring about the harmful consequences of their wasteful consumption at this point for two main reason. First, people have been conditioned to view consumption as a positive experience even though it mostly provides them with only ephemeral happiness and satisfaction. Second, neo-liberalism has incessantly promoted the idea that having the freedom to choose in the market is of the utmost importance when it comes to the achievement of freedom in general. This has led to emergence of an erroneous consciousness among the masses, making them immune to the destructive results caused by their continuous consumption of artificially created wants and desires. Marcuse (1998, 100) was frustrated with the fixation on consumption in western capitalist countries; he explained that, in modern world, people have:

> innumerable choices, innumerable gadgets which are all of the same sort and keep them occupied and divert their attention from the real issue-which is the awareness that they could both work less and determine their own needs and satisfactions.

After decades of being bombarded with countless advertisements promoting consumption, people are unwilling to be inconvenienced by voluntarily reducing their wasteful consumption in order to limit their harmful societal and environmental impacts. Wasteful consumption has become part of their daily routines, often resembling an addiction or mental illness. In essence, people have been trained to live their lives without paying attention to the consequences of most of their daily habits since childhood, 'because other people behave in the same way, and because it is customary' in their environment (von Mises 1949, 47). von Mises (1949, 46) has described such people as 'common men' who do not 'speculate about the great problems.' Instead, they rely 'upon other people's authority' when it comes to great problems, and act as 'every decent fellow must behave,' like a 'sheep in the herd' (von Mises 1949, 46). These people are inescapably caged by their daily habits, ideas, and the culture of consumption, all of which were imposed upon them with the considerable help of corporations. One could argue that mass consumption has become an incurable disease, because the irreparable personal defects of the herd mentality has provided it with an ideal environment in which to grow.

Mass consumers need to understand that if humanity is to avoid an environmental apocalypse, they need to stop associating happiness and freedom with consumption, and realize that obtaining the latest fashions, or possessing more furniture, technological gadgets, and appliances will not bring meaning to their lives. Concerns about wasteful consumption might seem as though it is a fairly recent issue; however, Seneca (1969, 227–228) was already warning people about wasteful consumption about 2000 years ago, when he stated:

> Look at the number of things we buy because others have bought them or because they're in most people's houses. One of the causes of the troubles that beset us is the way our lives are guided by the example of others; instead of being set to rights by reason we're seduced by convention. There are things that we shouldn't wish to imitate if they were done by only a few, but when a lot of people have started doing them we follow along, as though a practice became more respectable by becoming more common.

Neo-liberals argue that mass consumption and mass production are rational processes from the point view of both producers and consumers. However, over-exploiting of the world's resources in accordance with wasteful business practices for the purpose of selling people goods and services that they do not really need seems highly irrational. In other words, the growth strategy of neo-liberalism, which is highly supportive of mass production and mass consumption, is responsible for many global environmental, social, economic and political problems. Moreover, the prevalence of mass production and mass consumption in contemporary societies basically means that people are willing to sacrifice environment in return for the satisfaction of their ephemeral wants and desires.

6.4 Conclusion

The acceptance of the neo-liberal concept of freedom (or 'free to choose') by the majority of people has played an important role in motivating mass consumption. Nonetheless, this concept of freedom has engendered its own issues and criticisms. For instance, it is difficult to accept the premise that the extent of one's freedom could be determined by something as superficial as the range of consumption choices available to them in the marketplace. In fact, freedom cannot be achieved under a system of mass consumption, because it does not allow people to lead free, meaningful, diverse, and autonomous lives based on their own will, thoughts, reasoning, convictions and conscience. To be more precise, individuals cannot be free when they are incapable of self-government, or self-realization, because they are constantly being indoctrinated and manipulated by the sophisticated marketing campaigns of large corporations to consume the same products, more or less, that everyone else is consuming. In other words, freedom is suppressed when individuals are subordinated to the will of the corporate world. That also means diversity of individuality and diversity of lifestyles are being suppressed by the necessities of the free-market system.

The first step to freeing oneself from this neo-liberal cage of mass consumption is to realize that '[w]e come into the material universe bringing nothing; we take nothing away when we depart. The human being, in physical terms, is just a transitory form of matter, a changing mode of motion' (George 2006, 72). This realization can help people appreciate a concept of freedom that acknowledges the importance of developing one's own individuality. Only then will people understand that their self-worth and the respect they command from others are not functions of the goods, services and brands that they consume. Similarly, they will also come to realize that consuming the same products or services does not result in the establishment of some kind of a bond between people, whether that be their peers like family members, friends, and co-workers, or people they do not personally know like the celebrities that endorse those products or people they pass in the street. However, as long as individuals continue to believe that their freedom is correlated with their ability to obtain what they want, when they want it, and in whatever quantity they desire, then it will be difficult to convince them to change their destructive behaviors and consumption patterns, which are leading us all towards a potential environmental apocalypse.

References

Buchanan, James M. 1986. Politics and Meddlesome Preferences. In *Smoking and Society*, ed. Robert D. Tollison, 335–342. Toronto: Lexington Books.

Friedman, M., and Friedman, R.D. 1990 [1980]. *Free to Choose: A Personal Statement*. New York: Harcourt Brace Jovanovich.

Galbraith, John Kenneth. 2001. *The Essential Galbraith*. Ed. Andrea D. Williams. Boston: Houghton Mifflin Company.

George, Henry. 2006. *Progress and Poverty: Why There Are Recessions and Poverty Amid Plenty—And What to Do About It!* Ed. Bob Drake. New York: Robert Schalkenbach Foundation.

Keynes, John Maynard. 1920. *The Economic Consequences of the Peace*. New York: Harcourt, Brace, and Howe. https://oll.libertyfund.org/titles/303.

Knight, Frank H. May 1922. Ethics and the Economic Interpretation. *The Quarterly Journal of Economics* 36 (3): 454–481. Oxford University Press Stable. https://www.jstor.org/stable/1886033

Knight, Frank H. 2007 [1935]. *The Ethics of Competition*. New York: Routledge.

Marcuse, Herbert. 1998 [1956]. *Eros and Civilisation: A Philosophical Inquiry Into Freud*. Abingdon: Routledge.
———. 2007 [1964]. *One-Dimensional Man: Studies in the Ideology of Advanced Industrial Society*. London: Routledge.
Mises, Ludwig von. 1998 [1949]. *Human Action: A Treatise on Economics*. Auburn: The Ludwig von Mises Institute.
Myrdal, Karl Gunnar. 1973. Economics of an Improved Environment. *World Development* 1 (1,2): 102–114. Stockholm: Institute for International Economic Studies.
Seneca. 1969 [65 AD]. *Letters from a Stoic*. London: Penguin Classics.
Simons, Henry Calvert. 1934. *A Positive Program for Laissez-Faire: Some Proposals for a Liberal Economic Policy*. Public Policy Pamphlet, No. 15. Chicago: The University Chicago Press.
Stigler, George J. 1961. The Economics of Information. *Journal of Political Economy* 69 (3): 213–225.
Tollison, Robert D. 1986. Smoking and *Society*. Ed. Robert D. Tollison. Toronto: Lexington Books.
Tollison, Robert D., and Richard E. Wagner. 1992. *The Economics of Smoking*. London: Kluwer Academic Publishers.

CHAPTER 7

The Rise of Neo-Liberalism and the Environment: Mining, Electronic Waste, Agri-business, Livestock Farming and the Clothing Industry

The idea of transforming everything into something calculable and exchangeable has encouraged specialists from various disciplines within the social and physical sciences to work against natural cycles and the natural development of all organisms. Instead of treating the earth, its resources, and all of the living organisms that it hosts as things to be respected, cultivated, cared for, and sustained, people decided to regard them as factors of production that need to be controlled, challenged, manipulated, over-exploited, and destroyed in search of material gains and profit. Under free-market capitalism, a fixation with economic growth, productivity, mass consumption, and technological innovation has played a major role in the imminent emergence of an environmental apocalypse.

The destructive activities and practices associated with free-market capitalism are causing local ecosystems, which consist of all the plants, animals, and other organisms that co-exist in a geographical area, to collapse at an accelerated pace.[1] In fact, the collapse of local ecosystems is already contributing to the destabilization of all of the earth's main systems,[2] which

[1] National Geographic. 'Ecosystem.' https://www.nationalgeographic.org/encyclopedia/ecosystem/.

[2] 'There are five main systems, or spheres, on Earth. The first system, the geosphere, consists of the interior and surface of Earth, both of which are made up of rocks. The limited part of the planet that can support living things comprises the second system; these regions are referred to as the biosphere. In the third system are the areas of Earth that are covered

B. Filip, *The Rise of Neo-liberalism and the Decline of Freedom*, Palgrave Insights into Apocalypse Economics, https://doi.org/10.1007/978-3-030-61623-6_7

threatens the existence of all life on the planet. Unfortunately, the reach of human activities appears to know no boundaries, as they have been causing irreparable damage to important ecosystems around the world, including the rapid melting of glaciers and ice sheets in the Arctic, Antarctica and Greenland, the bleaching and decline of coral[3] reefs in the South Pacific and the Caribbean, and the retreat of the Amazon rainforest, where 'thousands of acres of land are cleared for farmland, housing, and industry.'[4] In fact, '100 million hectares of tropical forest were lost from 1980 to 2000, resulting mainly from cattle ranching in Latin America (about 42 million hectares) and plantations in South-East Asia (about 7.5 million hectares, of which 80% is for palm oil, used mostly in food, cosmetics, cleaning products and fuel) among others.'[5] Meanwhile, approximately 33% of 'reef forming corals are threatened with extinction.'[6] The rapid destruction of so many diverse and important ecosystems could eventually unleash devastating results on the planet, such as rising sea levels, higher temperatures, increased flooding, the loss of biodiversity, shortages of food and freshwater, and more frequent and powerful natural disasters. According to a 2019 United Nations (UN) report, 'around 1 million animal and plant species are now threatened with extinction.'[7] More precisely, the

with enormous amounts of water, called the hydrosphere. The atmosphere is the fourth system, and it is an envelope of gas that keeps the planet warm and provides oxygen for breathing and carbon dioxide for photosynthesis. Finally, there is the fifth system, which contains huge quantities of ice at the poles and elsewhere, constituting the cryosphere' National Geographic. 'Earth's Systems.' https://www.nationalgeographic.org/encyclopedia/ecosystem/.

[3] 'Corals are a fundamental part of the marine reef system, one of the most important ecosystems in the world because of its great biodiversity and the environmental services it provides' (Vazquez-Botello et al. 2020, 25). 'Recent human impacts have changed coral community structure in ways not observed in the preceding 220 000 years' (Pandolfi and Jackson 2006).

[4] National Geographic. 'Earth's Systems.' https://www.nationalgeographic.org/encyclopedia/ecosystem/.

[5] The Sustainable Development Goals: UN Report: Nature's Dangerous Decline 'Unprecedented'; Species Extinction Rates 'Accelerating' https://www.un.org/sustainabledevelopment/blog/2019/05/nature-decline-unprecedented-report/.

[6] The Sustainable Development Goals: UN Report: Nature's Dangerous Decline 'Unprecedented'; Species Extinction Rates 'Accelerating' https://www.un.org/sustainabledevelopment/blog/2019/05/nature-decline-unprecedented-report/.

[7] The Sustainable Development Goals: UN Report: Nature's Dangerous Decline 'Unprecedented'; Species Extinction Rates 'Accelerating' https://www.un.org/sustainabledevelopment/blog/2019/05/nature-decline-unprecedented-report/.

current extinction level is 'tens to hundreds of times' higher than the average 'over the last 10 million years, and the rate is accelerating.'[8] Furthermore, 'since 1980, greenhouse gas emissions have doubled, raising average global temperatures by at least 0.7 degrees Celsius—with climate change already impacting nature from the level of ecosystems to that of genetics—impacts expected to increase over the coming decades, in some cases surpassing the impact of land and sea use change and other drivers.'[9]

Some of the specific factors caused by the activities of human beings that are adding to the destruction or imbalance of various ecosystems include air, water and soil pollution, deforestation, and the over-exploitation of natural resources. Despite many dire warnings from highly specialized scientists and environmental organizations, neo-liberal economists do not seem to take environmental issues, including the destruction of ecosystems, very seriously. This is not particularly surprising, given that the exploitation and extraction of the earth's natural resources are important factors in economic growth and development. For example, Becker (2017, 159) stated that:

> Although the physical size of the earth has been fixed and indestructible, the economic supply of land has been greatly changed by man's efforts. For example, much of the land in the Netherlands was under water a few hundred years ago and became available only through large-scale drainage programs. Similarly, irrigation programs have greatly increased the agricultural land in Israel and other dry parts of the world. Mankind has also cleared forests, drilled oil wells on the bottoms of seas, built tall buildings, and so forth. Economists now recognize these developments by treating land simply as a "produced" durable factor of production, that is, as one kind of capital.

Presently, many neo-liberal economists would not oppose Becker's views, which he expressed in 1971, despite the abundance of knowledge and scientific evidence that has emerged since then exposing the extent to

[8] The Sustainable Development Goals: UN Report: Nature's Dangerous Decline 'Unprecedented'; Species Extinction Rates 'Accelerating' https://www.un.org/sustainabledevelopment/blog/2019/05/nature-decline-unprecedented-report/.

[9] The Sustainable Development Goals: UN Report: Nature's Dangerous Decline 'Unprecedented;' Species Extinction Rates 'Accelerating' https://www.un.org/sustainabledevelopment/blog/2019/05/nature-decline-unprecedented-report/.

which capitalist activities are harming people, communities and the environment. This is because neo-liberal economists have consistently elevated and defended economic growth above all else, while regarding nature as little more than 'the chief storehouse of the standing energy reserve' to be exploited for capitalist gain (Heidegger (1889–1976) 1977, 21). This is indicative of the type of science supported by neo-liberals, termed capitalist science, which requires nature to satisfy the unreasonable, exploitive, and destructive demands of the corporate world.

This chapter begins by discussing neo-liberal environmental regulations during the Reagan Era. Since the rise of neo-liberalism, there has been widespread support for government policies and regulations that rely on free-market mechanisms to address environmental issues. Such regulations often take economic efficiency into consideration by utilizing cost-benefit analyses, which basically treat environmental damage as an economic activity, while seeking to determine the optimal levels of pollution and environmental destruction that should be permitted. This approach has been strongly promoted by neo-liberal economists, who are convinced that market mechanisms can be used to provide optimal solutions for pollution. Unfortunately, these kinds of solutions have been largely unsuccessful in terms of genuinely resolving environmental problems, because it is difficult to estimate a monetary value that accurately captures the immense intangible benefits that a healthy environment provides. Ultimately, it has become clear that the neo-liberal practice of employing market mechanisms to address environmental issues has been largely ineffective in terms solving environmental problems or reducing the polluting activities of corporations.

Subsequently, this chapter will illustrate the extent to which neo-liberal environmental regulations have failed by describing some of the destructive activities and irreversible environmental damage that can be attributed to a few major polluting industries, including mining, agriculture, livestock farming, and clothing. Other significant contributors to air, soil, and water pollution are not discussed, such as the transportation, construction, leather, rubber, paper, and tourism industries.

7.1 Neo-Liberal Environmental Regulations

The global environmental movement was born in 1960s and gained considerable momentum well into the 1970s, as evidenced by the number of mass protests that were organized to raise awareness about the destruction of the environment. At that time, their views were taken seriously by public officials in many countries, as it was fairly common for governments to institute environmental regulations before the influence of neo-liberalism began to reduce state involvement in safeguarding the environment. In particular, a number of federal programs and regulations adopted in the US during the 1970s 'to achieve broad social goals, reflected strong pressures from environmental and consumer organizations backed by a massive shift in public opinion favoring vigorous protection of public health, safety, and the environment' (Kraft and Vig 1984, 417). In fact, pressure applied on the government by the environmental movement led to the establishment of the Environmental Protection Agency (EPA) 1970 via presidential order. From the outset, neo-liberal economists have been highly critical of the regulatory powers granted to the EPA. For example, Friedman and Friedman (1990) harshly criticized the EPA for imposing large costs on industries, and argued that it became increasingly coercive as its authority, employees, and budget increased over time.

Since the emergence of the environmental movement, many scientists, thinkers, and pressure groups have accepted the premise that human activities are threatening the future of the environment, and have demanded that something be done about it. However, Friedman and Friedman (1990, 214) suggested that 'public discussion of the environmental issue is frequently characterized more by emotion than reason.' They were particularly frustrated that the environmental issue was often framed as 'pollution versus non pollution' (Friedman and Friedman 1990, 214). On this topic, they argued that zero pollution was neither possible nor desirable, and pointed out that 'the people responsible for pollution are consumers, not producers. They create, as it were, a demand for pollution' (Friedman and Friedman 1990, 215). Furthermore, Friedman and Friedman (1990, 215) believed that 'one person's pollution may be another's pleasure,' and that the elimination of pollution was not a rational idea. They also contended that, in reality, 'the air is in general far cleaner and the water safer today than one hundred years ago…Industrialization has raised new problems, but it has also provided the means solve prior problems' (Friedman and Friedman 1990, 218). However, contemporary knowledge and awareness about global environmental issues, particularly climate change, would dispute the claims made by Friedman and other neo-liberal economists about the present and future effects of pollution and environmental degradation.

Friedman 1982 [1962] advocated for using natural resources to the fullest extent possible in order to advance productivity and economic growth. He was of the opinion that property rights and freedom entitled people to use and exploit any land and resources they owned as they saw fit. In fact, placing any restrictions on how they could use their properties would violate their economic and individual freedom. Friedman was convinced that properties and natural resources could be used effectively under a system of voluntary cooperation. According to Samuelson (2010, XVI), when Hayek and Friedman warned against 'the road to serfdom,' they were basically 'arguing against social security, a minimum wage, national parks, progressive taxation, and government rules to clean up the environment or slow global warming.' Friedman and Hayek regarded these kinds of governmental services, programs and regulations as obstacles to the business activities of enterprises and people, meaning that they constituted threats to the preservation of a free society, even though many of those activities depleted natural resources and degraded the environment.

Neo-liberals do not consider the over-exploitation and eventual depletion of natural resources to be serious matters of concern. For example, Hayek (2011, 493) was confident that 'by the time the resource is exhausted, something new will have been discovered which will either satisfy the same need or at least compensate us for what we no longer have.' On this basis, he advised people and businesses to operate under 'the assumption' that the available supply of natural resources will continue to increase (Hayek 2011, 493). Meanwhile, he thought it best to simply ignore 'the conservationists' and their dire warnings about the exhaustion of natural resources, as listening to them would only delay economic development and progress (Hayek 2011, 493). Although Hayek (2011, 493) acknowledged that the physical facts and opinions presented by the experts are important, 'the result in most instances would have been very detrimental if they had had the power to enforce their views on policy.' He maintained that 'investment in the conservation of a particular natural resource to a point where the return is lower than the capital it uses would bring elsewhere would reduce future income below what it would otherwise be' (Hayek 2011, 497).

Free-market economists have been fiercely opposed to the centrally planned governmental regulations that were prevalent prior to the rise of neo-liberalism, whereby the state and its agencies were responsible for setting standards. Neo-liberal economists believe that, in addition to being wasteful, ineffective, and economic failures, government agencies are incapable of accurately determining who suffers or benefits from damages caused to the environment, which makes it difficult to find a solution that is satisfactory to all interested parties. In fact, they have maintained that when governments managed environmental problems, they typically turned out to do more harm than good. They argue that the free-market system would provide better solutions to environmental problems.

According to neo-liberals, the goal of environmental policy should be limited to determining the right amount of pollution that businesses should be permitted to release into the environment. More specifically, since neo-liberalism contends that reducing pollution to zero is impossible, because it would bring about an economic collapse, 'economists look to determine the socially efficient level of pollution by balancing social costs and benefits' (Samuelson and Nordhaus 2010, 273). The influence of neo-liberalism likely contributed to a striking transition in environmental policy that began in the Reagan era, as the approach to addressing environmental problems shifted away from centrally designed governmental regulations and towards market-based mechanisms. In particular, the notion of providing polluting industries with market-based incentives to reduce their environmentally destructive activities received strong support from neo-liberal economists and free-market thinktanks.

Reagan considered Friedman to be his most trusted advisor on economic and foreign policy matters, which may have contributed to the President adopting the view that, much like the economy, environmental policies should be guided by free-market principles. Accordingly, neo-liberal environmental regulations started to gain prominence during Reagan's presidency, whereby the free-market oriented regulations were regarded as the solution to environmental problems instead of centrally planned governmental regulations. Although Reagan's commitment to establishing a laissez-faire system to deal with environmental issues faced strong opposition from both the public and congress, his administration ultimately managed to obtain 'congressional approval for his economic policy, and the massive cut backs in environmental programs' (Kraft and Vig 1984, 424).

Reagan believed that protecting the environment conflicted with economic growth, productivity, efficiency, and prosperity. He was also of the opinion that many of the concerns surrounding environmental problems were exaggerated. For these reasons, his administration closely examined environmental regulations and revised them in order to minimize their impacts on the cost of doing business. Reagan supported the development of business-friendly environmental regulations that entailed: the 'extensive use of cost-benefit analysis;' a 'reliance as much as possible on the free-market to allocate resources; and decentralization or environmental federalism, shifting responsibilities for environmental protection to state and local governments whenever feasible' (Kraft and Vig 1984, 425). Furthermore, to ensure the emergence of conditions that would facilitate economic growth, productivity, efficiency, and prosperity, he advocated for a reduction in state environmental regulations that were established by previous governments, and even managed to reverse a number of them.

President Reagan thought that a greater emphasis needed to be placed on corporations policing themselves when it came to protecting the environment. Accordingly, he imposed major budget cuts that reduced the size, scope, and effectiveness of government environmental agencies. For example, he relieved all employees of the Council on Environmental Quality (CEQ) of their duties, some of whom had been with the organization since the Nixon and Ford administrations. Subsequently, new employees were hired for the CEQ from 'the president's campaign organization, but the overall size of the staff was reduced by more than half' (Kraft and Vig 1984, 429). Clearly, the CEQ would no longer have the resources needed to adequately perform many of its previous tasks, which ultimately did not matter since it no longer played any role in advising and assisting 'the President on both national and international environmental policy matters' or preparing 'the President's annual environmental quality report to Congress.'[10]

The CEQ was originally established as part of the National Environmental Policy Act (NEPA) that was signed into law by President Nixon in 1970.[11] The NEPA, which is recognized as the first major

[10] Federal Register. 'Council on Environmental Quality.' https://www.federalregister.gov/agencies/council-on-environmental-quality.

[11] National Environmental Policy Act. https://ceq.doe.gov/.

environmental law passed in the United States,[12] declared that the American congress:

> recognizes the profound impact of man's activity on the interrelations of all components of the natural environment, particularly the profound influences of population growth, high-density urbanization, industrial expansion, resource exploitation, and new and expanding technological advances and recognizes further the critical importance of restoring and maintaining environmental quality to the overall welfare and development of man, declares that it is the continuing policy of the Federal Government, in cooperation with State and local governments, and other concerned public and private organizations, to use all practicable means and measures, including financial and technical assistance, in a manner calculated to foster and promote the general welfare, to create and maintain conditions under which man and nature can exist in productive harmony, and fulfill the social economic, and other requirements of present and future generations of Americans.[13]

In addition to effectively neutering the CEQ, President Reagan was extremely critical of the EPA, describing it as too large and costly, and excessive when it came to using its independent authority to regulate business in order to protect human health and the environment. His administration began requiring the EPA to provide cost-benefit analyses in order to explain and justify its regulatory activities. Thus, it came as little surprise when the Reagan administration cut the budget of the EPA by 22% in 1981 (Davis 2019). The budget and staff cuts imposed on the EPA during the Reagan presidency made it extremely difficult for the agency to effectively perform its duties, which included protecting air and water quality, endangered and at-risk species, and biological diversity from toxic and hazardous waste and various other pollutants caused by the economic activities of corporations.[14]

[12] National Environmental Policy Act. https://ceq.doe.gov/.

[13] 'NATIONAL ENVIRONMENTAL POLICY ACT: public law 91-90 (42 USC 4321-4347) sec. 101.' https://www.fsa.usda.gov/Internet/FSA_File/nepa_statute.pdf.

[14] After the implementation of neo-liberal economic reforms in the United States, the governments of many developing countries followed suit and slashed the budget of their own environmental agencies or organisations. The reduction of public spending on environmental agencies has greatly diminished their role of enforcing environmental regulations.

After neo-liberalism became the leading school of economic thought and, as such, exerted considerable influence over the development of state policies, the US government showed little signs of commitment to environmental conservation. In fact, since the Reagan presidency, federal legislation has played a much smaller role in establishing and enforcing environmental standards in the US compared to the 1960s and 1970s. Instead, federal authorities have placed a greater emphasis on supporting free-market mechanisms in addressing environmental issues. Consequently, industry groups, industry-backed free-market think tanks, and lobby organizations have played an increasingly important role in steering the environmental agenda. These groups, organizations and institutions highly value the application of cost-benefit analyses in helping to resolve environmental problems, which is consistent with the views of neo-liberal economists, who argue that free-market processes can protect the natural environment more efficiently than governmental regulations. Some of the specific approaches that neo-liberals have proposed for protecting and managing the environment include charging marginal emission fees, issuing permits that allow for the release of certain volumes of pollution for a predetermined period of time, enacting taxes on pollution, voluntary negotiations[15] between polluters and affected parties, and rewarding environmentally-friendly practices with tax credits.

Environmental policies are designed in extremely politicized settings, where influential parties will attempt to steer decisions in ways benefit their interests at the expense of others. Since the rise of neo-liberalism, corporations have gained influential power over governments, which has led to the weakening or outright elimination of many regulations aimed at protecting the environment and natural resources. By spending vast sums of money on lobbying efforts and making financial contributions to election campaigns, corporation have been able to persuade governments to introduce market-oriented environmental regulations that effectively

[15] Another free-market approach to dealing with externalities, like environmental degradation, was developed by Ronald Coase (1910–2013) (1960), professor of economics at the University of Chicago who was awarded the Nobel prize in 1991 in economics. Coase (1960) showed that, in the case of externalities, the presence of well-defined property rights allowed for an efficient outcome to be reached through voluntary negotiations between the parties that created externalities and those affected by them. Neo-liberals have accepted that this approach can produce an efficient resolution in the presence of externalities.

allow them to continue their harmful business practices, while only paying a minimal amount for the damages they cause to the environment. In addition to influencing governments to introduce market friendly environmental regulations, corporations also influence the opinions of the masses by confusing the debate presented in the mass media, because a majority of consumers will do little research to inform themselves outside of reading and viewing mainstream sources. As a result, most people are not fully aware of the destructive consequences of their consumption patterns on the environment, which leaves them unmotivated when it comes to responding to the environmental crisis in a constructive manner. Consequently, the masses generally do not concern themselves with the development of high-level environmental policies, which is left in the hands of politicians whose decisions are susceptible to the influence of financial support and pressure by individuals and organizations that stand to incur significant losses from effective and properly enforced environmental regulations.

The Reagan Presidency was committed to the free-market capitalist goal of reducing the social responsibilities and costs faced by the corporate world. Subsequently, the rise of neo-liberalism significantly bridged the gap that existed between the Democratic and Republican parties when it came to environmental policy, to the point of both of them adopting similar market-oriented environmental regulations during their respective presidencies after Reagan left office. The unanimity of political support for market-oriented environmental regulations in recent decades, not only in the United States but also in many other countries, has played a significant role in leading the world towards the road to environmental apocalypse.

The fact that the destructive polluting activities of corporations have expanded so significantly since the rise of neo-liberalism is an indication that the practice of employing market mechanisms to solve environmental issues has failed. That means none of free-market oriented environmental regulations represent genuine solutions when it comes to effectively protecting the environment from the polluting activities of private businesses. This is because free-market environmental regulations need to strike a balance between addressing the externalities and the costs that businesses are willing to incur in order to do so, which ultimately dilutes their effectiveness. Decades of following the neo-liberal approach to environmental policy has revealed that the various free-market incentives that have been offered to businesses have not been able to prevent or reduce industrial pollution. For example, given the vast financial resources available to large corporations, the emissions fees prescribed by neo-liberals were too low to dissuade them from polluting, while the tax incentives were not significant enough to offset the cost of properly disposing of toxic, nuclear and hazardous wastes. Furthermore, corporations feel no sense of obligation to reduce the vast amounts of pollution and hazardous waste they generate and release into the environment through their business activities, because their cost-benefit analyses are almost exclusively concerned about economic efficiency. This leads them to try to squeeze as much as possible out of available natural resources in order to facilitate mass production, regardless of the environmental degradation that occurs as a result. More precisely, while factors like government deregulation, free-trade policies and the technological boom have greatly enhanced the ability of corporations to exploit the world's human and natural resources, thereby generating more waste, they have done little to remedy the harmful outcomes of their business practices on the environment. In fact, they are content with treating the planet as a limitless source of natural resources and a global waste repository.

Neo-liberal environmental regulations do not account for costs that cannot be expressed as a monetary value in economic calculations. That allows corporations to treat the damages that their business practices cause to the environment and the health of people as externalities that are not taken into consideration when completing their balance sheets or setting the price of their products. In other words, corporations can enrich themselves by damaging the environment without paying for the real cost of the harm that they have caused. Therefore, it should come as no surprise that corporations are not concerned about the present and future destructive outcomes of their capitalist business practices on the environment, and show little interest in advancing or improving the quality of life for people. If environmental regulations were actually intended to achieve the maximum benefit for the environment, then many enterprises would end up going out of business, because they could not afford pay penalties or fines that accurately reflected the real damages that their business practices were causing.

Practically speaking, it is difficult to accurately account for all of the damages caused to the environment by the production of commodities, because prices cannot include the harm instigated to 'the beauty and tranquillity of our surroundings,' and there is also no way to remedy 'the damage from its production or use' (Galbraith 2001, 148, 149). Neo-liberals maintain that the exclusion of accurate external costs from the price of the goods represents a minor defect of the price. However, if the harm that the activities of corporations caused to people, different species, future generations and the environment could be tangibly estimated and entered into their cost-benefit analyses, they would likely find that many of the activities that they typically engage in would no longer be profitable or feasible.

For many decades, an abundance of scientific research and evidence has shown that the release of toxic chemicals, nuclear waste and other hazardous materials into the environment are having devastating impacts on the earth's natural cycles, ecosystems and inhabitants. The scientific community has been particularly concerned about the adverse effects of such substances on important life-sustaining resources like clean air, agricultural land, drinkable water, and various food chains, especially with respect to their direct impacts on human health. Despite these severe consequences, corporations would still choose to simply dump and store their harmful waste and by-products in the environment if left to their own devices, because properly disposing of them would be very costly. In other words, corporations will not voluntarily reduce or clean up the toxic waste and other pollutants released into the environment by their production processes and business practices (e.g., agriculture, farming, manufacturing, construction, mining, etc.) if doing so harms their profitability, nor will they willingly assume responsibility for any costs associated with their environmentally destructive activities. Corporations prefer externalize such costs onto society and the environment, because internalizing them would significantly raise their costs of production, which would go against their mandates. For them, the most cost-effective methods of dealing with their waste and pollution include dumping them into rivers, lakes or other bodies of water, burying them underground, and releasing them into the air.

Dire predictions about the consequences of continuing on the current trajectory of ecological apocalypse have not been enough to dissuade corporations from obstinately adhering to neo-liberal economic principles and methods of production that are unsustainable and degrade the environment. They remain staunchly opposed to any regulations aimed at protecting the environment by instituting limits on their business practices and activities, because corporations are only interested in their short-term monetary gains. Meanwhile, corporations have 'shown outspoken antagonism toward those who think our planet is more important than their profiteering. So they defame environmentalists as eco-terrorists, EPA Gestapo, Earth Day alarmists, tree huggers, and purveyors of Green hysteria' (Parenti 2015, 135). Corporations regard this approach of attacking the reputations of climate scientists and environmentalists as more cost effective than paying the additional expense of adjusting their business practices to make them more sustainable, or restoring past damages caused by their production processes, both of which would affect their bottom line or reduce their competitive advantage. American political scientist and author, Michael John Parenti (2011) explained that:

> With their eye on the bottom line, big business leaders know that every dollar a company spends on oddball things like environmental protection is one less dollar in earnings. Moving away from fossil fuels and toward solar, wind, and tidal energy could help avert ecological disaster, but six of the world's ten top industrial corporations are involved primarily in the production of oil, gasoline, and motor vehicles. Fossil fuel pollution brings billions of dollars in returns. Ecologically sustainable forms of production threaten to compromise such profits, the big producers are convinced.

Prioritizing the safety, security, cleanliness, and sustainability of the environment, as advocated by various environmental groups, institutions and movements, is not supported by corporations, because these types of measures do not bring significant gains in productivity, economic efficiency and economic growth. Unfortunately, the narrow-mind neo-liberal principle of self-interest maximization has become so ingrained in western countries that corporations continue to exploit the planet at extreme levels, treating the earth as a source of endless resources, as well as a bottomless garbage bin for their dangerous pollutants and waste.

7.2 Wasteful Consumption, the Mining Industry and Electronic Waste

The mining industry is well known for causing long-term destruction to natural habitats, and for being among the largest emitters of various pollutants and toxins. It is also responsible for considerable societal harm in many developing countries by engaging in human rights violations, disregarding worker safety, and employing child labour.

Each year, the extraction, purification and refining of metals used by the mining industry causes serious ecological degradation by discharging millions of tons of industrial wastewater (i.e., water containing elevated concentrations of metals) and releasing over a billion cubic meters of industrial waste gas. This leads to the contaminating of the air and surrounding soil, as well as surface and ground water in the area, which eventually spreads the pollution to rivers, seas, lakes, and oceans. These wastes are eventually absorbed by plants, and ingested by animals and aquatic life, thereby entering into the food chains of many living organism and species, including human beings. In some cases, fruits, vegetables and livestock cultivated in the vicinity of the mining activity contain high concentrations of heavy metals, exceeding the maximum levels permitted by law. Studies have shown that these metals are extremely toxic to human health, having been linked to various forms of cancer, birth defects, neurological and pulmonary diseases, not only in the present, but also for future generations.

The negative environmental impacts of mining have been worsened by the consumption habits of individuals, who are not averse to throwing away functioning goods and devices that were produced using various metals. In particular, discarded electrical or electronic devices (e.g., appliances, toys, tools, and information and communications technology products, such as computers, mobile phones, tablets, printers, etc.) have been among the most rapidly-growing types of waste in recent years.[16] In 2016, '44.7 million metric tonnes of e-waste were generated. This is an equivalent of almost 4500 Eiffel towers' (Baldé et al. 2017, 38). Discarded electronic waste often contains heavy metals, non-biodegradable materials, and toxic substances like cadmium, lead and mercury, which end up in landfills. In fact, the global 'value of all raw materials present in e-waste is estimated at approximately 55 Billion Euros in 2016' (Baldé et al. 2017, 7). It should also be pointed out that, in that same year, 'the richest country in the world...generated an average of 19.6 kg/inhabitant, whereas the poorest generated only 0.6 kg/inhabitant' of e-waste (Baldé et al. 2017, 41). This is not particularly surprising, given that people have enthusiastically adopted a culture of consumerism in western countries,

[16] Solving the e-waste problem. 'What is e-waste?' http://www.step-initiative.org/e-waste-challenge.html.

which highly values gaining possession of the latest devices on the market, particularly when it comes to tech products and gadgets. However, it is also due to the fact that the global market for electrical and electronic equipment has been growing exponentially on a global scale, while the lifespans of these products have been getting shorter.

As previously mentioned, certain components used to produce electrical or electronic devices contain many toxic substances that do not biodegrade easily, if at all. In fact, 'more than 40 elements are used during the production of mobile phones' (Weiss et al. 2016, 106). To be more precise, the production of a single cellphone involves a number of heavy metals and metalloids, some of which are highly toxic.[17] After a cellphone ends up in a landfill, many of these harmful substances will eventually seep out and contaminate the surrounding environment, which should be very disconcerting when considering how often people discard their "out of date" cellphones, in addition to various other electric and electronic products. Eventually, these pollutants will spread out further where they will irreversibly damage the soil, water, and air, as well as various organisms and species when they eventually make their way into the food chain. As long as mass consumption and production continue unabated, more electronic waste will end up in landfills and gradually make their way into the surrounding environment and the food chain, especially given the rate at which technology products now become redundant.

Instead of finding sustainable solutions to the growing problem of e-waste via state regulation or social responsibility, corporations have adopted an 'out of sight' solution by exporting the problem to less developed countries. When advanced countries claim to recycle, it is suspected that hazardous electronic waste is being exported illegally from locations like 'Australia, Japan, Korea, North America, and Western Europe' to destinations like 'Brazil, China, Ghana, India, Nigeria, Mexico, Pakistan, Singapore, and Thailand' (Weiss et al. 2016, 119). Other suspected destinations include 'Argentina, Benin, Chile, Egypt, Eastern Europe, Haiti,

[17] These heavy metals and metalloids include 'a mixture of indium and tin oxides,' aluminosilicates, potassium ions, 'several rare earth elements, such as yittrium, lantharium, terbium, praseodymium, europium, dysprosium, and gadolinium,' 'lithium cobalt oxides or manganese and carbon,' copper, gold, silver, magnesium, platinum, 'nickel, praseo-dymium, gadolinium, neodymium, terbium,' arsenic, gallium, etc. (Weiss et al. 2006, 106).

Indonesia, Ivory Coast, Kenya, Malaysia, Philippines, Russia, Senegal, Tanzania, Ukraine, United Arab Emirates, Venezuela, and Vietnam' (Weiss et al. 2016, 119). The countries exporting hazardous electronic waste, which are typically developed, deliberately choose destinations where environmental regulations are lax or nonexistent, and working conditions are poor. Most of these importer countries do not have adequate infrastructure in place to ensure the safe disposal of such hazardous materials, meaning the toxic chemicals contained in e-waste will eventually be released into the environment. Also, 'there is the high risk that the pollutants are not taken care of properly, or they are taken care of by an informal sector and recycled without properly protecting' the health and safety of its workers (Baldé et al. 2017, 6). Therefore, electronic waste exporter countries are not actually addressing the problem of hazardous by-products damaging the environment and human health; they are merely exporting these issues to other regions of the world, so that their enlightened citizens cannot see them.

Even though recycling does reduce the amount of electronic waste in landfills, only a small percentage of it can actually be recycled, amounting to less than 20% of the total (Baldé et al. 2017, 2). When considering the exponential growth in the production and consumption of electronic goods and devices, as well as the rapid rate at which technology products are becoming redundant, it becomes abundantly clear that recycling does not represent a sustainable solution to the problem of mounting e-waste. Furthermore, imposing of fines to discourage the illegal dumping of electronic waste is also not a viable solution, because it would do nothing to address the overconsumption of electric goods on the part of consumers, nor would it slow the rapid technological innovation that is rendering so many products obsolete.

A truly sustainable solution to the electronic waste problem requires that societies be reorganized in major ways. In particular, people will need to be made to change their consumption habits and reduce their dependence on electronic gadgets, devices, tools, and appliances, even though it will entail a loss of convenience. There could be a role for education, as informing people about the destructive outcomes of their consumption patterns could encourage some of them to adopt more environmentally responsible behaviours that could mitigate the amount of e-waste they generate. However, there is no chance that corporations that manufacture electronic and electrical devices, as well as any of their inputs, would willingly curtail production for the benefit of society and incur the financial losses that would entail. Therefore, a realistic solution to the problem of mounting e-waste will likely require coercing consumers and businesses into changing their behaviours and practices in ways that move society away from the neo-liberal economic approach of facilitating mass consumption and mass production. Such an approach will need to involve the development of comprehensive regulations that are implemented, monitored, and enforced by a strong state authority across a broad array of countries, perhaps with the involvement of international organizations.

7.3 Oceans, Ice and Marine Life

According to a 2019 UN report, '66% of the marine environment have been significantly altered by human actions. On average these trends have been less severe or avoided in areas held or managed by Indigenous Peoples and Local Communities.'[18] Oceans are one of the earth's main life support systems, as they regulate the weather and climate by absorbing excess carbon dioxide from the atmosphere. Unfortunately, oceans appear to be among the natural resources that cannot escape the freedom of corporations to exploit, which does not bode well for combatting climate change. The business practices of corporations have had devastating outcomes for millions of species that live in or depend upon oceans, including fish, plants, birds, land and sea mammals, and even microscopic organisms that are the foundations of many food chains (e.g., plankton). Since the rise of neo-liberalism, oceans have been significantly impacted by a diverse mix of waste being discharged into them in large quantities, including metals, textiles, pesticides, agriculture runoff and waste, plastics, fishing gear, and biological, chemical and nuclear waste. In addition to pollution, the health of oceans and the species that depend on them are also being irreversibly damaged by a variety of business activities, including destructive fishing practices, mining, the extraction of sand, etc. This section focuses on: the environmental and climate implications of melting Arctic sea, as well as the potential impacts of the economic activities that rapidly changing conditions might bring to the region; and, the extensive damage

[18] The Sustainable Development Goals: UN Report: Nature's Dangerous Decline 'Unprecedented'; Species Extinction Rates 'Accelerating' https://www.un.org/sustainabledevelopment/blog/2019/05/nature-decline-unprecedented-report/.

that deep-sea mining could cause to the ocean floor and the various species that it supports. It also discusses the destructive environmental outcomes of sand and gravel mining, the growing problem of ocean acidification, and the dumping large quantities of physical garbage into the oceans, particularly plastics.

Petroleum and gas companies have spent decades lobbying the US government to have the entire coastal plain of the Arctic National Wildlife Refuge in northeastern Alaska opened for oil and gas exploitation. Many of these companies have been enthused by the fact that climate change has significantly melted the ice in that the region at an alarming rate in recent years, making the process of drilling and extracting its large gas and oil reserves far easier and much less expensive. Meanwhile, they are largely unconcerned about the fact that Arctic ice plays an important role in regulating global climate processes and balancing temperatures by reflecting heat back into space. As large ice sheets melt, more of that heat is being absorbed by exposed oceans, causing them to warm, thereby further accelerating the melting process and contributing to rising sea levels. Additionally, climate change has the potential to make extreme weather events more severe and frequent, including large snowfalls and rainfalls, tornados, hurricanes, and coastal flooding. The enthusiasm for easier exploration and drilling conditions displayed by oil and gas companies also ignores the seriousness of melting permafrost in the Arctic National Wildlife Refuge, as well as a number of other regions. Permafrost contains large deposits of methane, a powerful greenhouse gas that 'traps 84 times as much heat as carbon dioxide over a 20-year time frame,' and is 'responsible for 25 per cent of already observed changes to Earth's climate.'[19] While keeping the Arctic National Wildlife Refuge closed to oil and gas exploration will not be enough to stop climate change and avoid an impending environmental apocalypse, it would be a positive step in the right direction.

Oil and gas companies continue to push hard for permission to conduct drilling and exploration activities in the Arctic, despite the implications that it would have for the environment, including oceanic and atmospheric warming, higher coastal water levels, more extreme weather events, etc. Meanwhile, shipping companies and certain exporters are pleased that

[19] David Suzuki Foundation. 'Methane is a dangerous greenhouse gas.' https://davidsuzuki.org/project/methane-pollution/?gclid=EAIaIQobChMI7626hoj46QIVNwiICR07Xwf_EAAYASAAEgI7XPD_BwE.

climate change is permanently changing the composition of the Arctic region in ways that will create shorter trade routes between the Pacific and Atlantic oceans, thereby reducing transportation costs and making it cheaper to export and import various products. Proponents of free-market capitalism are truly thrilled about the economic prospects that climate change might bring to the Arctic, while being totally indifferent to the fact that drilling and other economic activities in the region would cause irreparable damage to its fragile ecosystem and disrupt the diverse wildlife that reside there, including polar bears, migratory birds, wolves, artic foxes, and various fish and marine mammals. In September 2019, many large resource corporations received encouragement from the Trump administration, which indicated that it might be in favour of opening up the entire coastal plain of the Arctic National Wildlife Refuge to gas and oil exploration, despite opposition from many scientists who contend that doing so would significantly contribute to climate change (Fountain 2019). More specifically, they suggest that drilling in the area, which is already experiencing the devastating effects of climate change more severely than anywhere else on the planet, could unleash a carbon bomb that would spray millions of tonnes of methane into the atmosphere, thereby accelerating global warming.

Another activity that poses a major threat to marine ecosystems is deep-sea mining. Although the deep-seabed is very expensive and difficult to mine, ambitious entrepreneurs have financed innovative technological projects that can allowed them to gain access to these regions and exploit their rich natural resources, including various minerals, precious metals like gold, and other metals, such as rare earth elements,[20] which are used in the production of rechargeable batteries, smartphones, solar generators and wind power plants.[21] These technological innovations mean that mining companies will be able to send large, noisy machines and equipment to deep seabeds, where they will use various chemicals to cut into the ocean floor in order to extract the desired metals and minerals. Although these techniques will cause immense irreversible damage to deep-sea ecosystems and the various creatures they support, large mining companies are not

[20] More precisely, the growing interest in deep-sea mining is largely due to 'depleting terrestrial deposits for metals such as copper, nickel, aluminium, manganese, zinc, lithium and cobalt.' The International Union for Conservation of Nature (IUCN). 'Deep-sea Mining.' https://www.iucn.org/resources/issues-briefs/deep-sea-mining.

[21] The Ocean Foundation. 'Seabed Mining.' https://oceanfdn.org/seabed-mining/.

particularly concerned given the potential financial windfalls associated with successful extraction. Therefore, their main priorities are further advancing technological innovation that will allow them to successfully access and mine the seabed, and obtaining legal permission to exploit as much of the seabed beneath international waters as possible.

Contrary to the enthusiasm displayed by mining corporations, many scientists, deep-sea biologists, conservationists, and geologists have expressed serious reservations about deep-seabed mining, because of its potential to cause irreversible harm to deep-sea ecosystems and the many organisms they host. They point out that the deep-sea includes 'underwater mountains that are oases for sea creatures, ancient coral reefs and sharks that can live for hundreds of years. These are among the longest living creatures on Earth, which makes them particularly vulnerable to physical disturbance because of their slow growth rates. Researchers estimate that harm to wildlife from mining "is likely to last forever on human timescales"' (Casson 2019). In particular, scientists have explained that 'noise generated by churning machinery risks harming and disturbing marine mammals like whales, while floodlighting areas of the dark deep ocean could cause permanent disruption to sea creatures adapted to very low levels of natural light' (Casson 2019). Since various ocean creatures rely on sonar to communicate,[22] the noise pollution generated by deep-sea mining activities would reduce their ability to communicate with each other, disturb their reproductive patterns, and force them to abandon their natural habitats.

On December 17, 1970, the General Assembly of the United Nations declared that 'the area of the seabed and ocean floor and the subsoil thereof, beyond the limits of national jurisdiction, as well as its resources, are the common heritage of mankind, the exploration and exploitation of which shall be carried out for the benefit of mankind as a whole.'[23] Subsequently, the International Seabed Authority (ISA) was established in 1994, under the UN Convention on the Law of the Sea (UNCLOS), to regulate deep seabed mining. The ISA is supposed to 'ensure the effective protection of the marine environment from harmful effects that may arise

[22] For example, 'marine mammals use sound as their primary method for communicating over large distances, fish do the same over shorter spatial scales. Marine invertebrates also produce sound both as a behavioral display and as a result of feeding or movement' (Weis 2020, 170).

[23] United Nations. 'Preamble.' https://www.un.org/depts/los/convention_agreements/texts/unclos/preamble.htm.

from deep-seabed related activities.'[24] Although the ISA includes 168 member countries and the European Union, its influential Legal and Technical Commission (LTC) consists of only 30 people who have been elected for a period of five years.[25] The LTC is tasked with a number of 'functions relating to activities in the Area [in the deep seabed area] including…the review of applications for plans of work, supervision of exploration or mining activities…assessment of the environmental implications of activities…and make recommendations to the Council on all matters relating to exploration and exploitation of non-living marine resources.'[26] The ISA's commitment to protecting deep-sea life is questionable, as its goals are mostly free-market-oriented. That is to say, instead of heeding the warnings put forth by scientists, deep-sea biologists, conservationists, and geologists, the ISA listens to the profit-oriented myopic opinions of the business classes. Furthermore, rather than prohibiting destructive mining practices and protecting the habitats and well-being of deep-sea life, the ISA is planning to issue exploitation permits, and charge fees and taxes on the extraction of valuable metals from the seabed.[27] In essence, the ISA supports market oriented environmental regulations.

Scientists, deep-sea biologists, conservationists, and geologists have called for the prohibition of deep-seabed mining, arguing that it will cause irreversible damage over tens of thousands of square kilometers of the ocean floor, including the destruction of extensive areas of hydrothermal vent habitat, many unique and unseen species, and the biodiversity of the ecosystems. However, mining companies have no regard for the preservation and protection of the marine environment, as they eagerly await their commercial mining licenses so that they can begin extracting the rare and valuable metals and minerals embedded in the deep-seabed and earn vast profits. Once these licences are awarded, no amount of the fees, penalties or taxation will be able to protect the marine environment from the harmful effects of exploration and exploitation. History has also shown that market oriented environmental regulations have been unable to confer

[24] ISA. 'About IS.' https://www.isa.org.jm/about-isa.

[25] ISA. 'The Legal and Technical Commission.' https://www.isa.org.jm/authority/legal-and-technical-commission.

[26] ISA. 'The Legal and Technical Commission.' https://www.isa.org.jm/authority/legal-and-technical-commission.

[27] Nature. 2019. 'Seabed mining is coming—bringing mineral riches and fears of epic extinctions.' https://www.nature.com/articles/d41586-019-02242-y.

even a modest degree of protection on the environment against the destructive business practices of corporations.

In addition to the extensive damage that deep sea mining would cause to the ocean floor, it would also contribute to altering the global climate by adding to atmospheric warming. This is because deep-sea mining will disrupt the natural carbon-capture process of the ocean seabed, which could release carbon dioxide that has been trapped in its sediment millions of years. Meanwhile, any significant disturbances to the natural habitats of deep-sea creatures could have adverse affects on their fragile ecosystems that persist for centuries. In all likelihood, mankind will only realize what has been lost long after the oceans have ceased to function properly and it is far too late to do anything in order to reverse the damage.

The deep-seabed and all of the wealth it contains should belong the to earth and all of its inhabitants, human and non-human alike, and as such, remain untouched by the pure profit-oriented intentions of mining activities. Unfortunately, as is the case with most other natural resources, the capitalist mindset holds the misguided notion that the wealth of the deep-sea is owned by human beings, who have the inherent right to exploit it. The unbridled desire to maximize profits has led people to forget that human beings are interconnected with all the species on earth in some way. They are not above or beyond the natural world and should not act independent of its well-being. Nonetheless, neo-liberals will always side with and support exploitation for monetary gain at the expense of the natural environment and the species it supports. Therefore, it is up to the scientific community, governments, international organizations and institutions, and the majority of the world's population to object to the exploitation of the oceans and their seabeds, and promote their conservation.

Ocean ecosystems around the world are also being destroyed by the growing problem of acidification, which occurs when 'carbon dioxide, emitted to the atmosphere by burning fossil fuels, dissolves in the ocean. Much of this CO_2 is absorbed by the ocean, where it is converted to carbonic acid, which releases hydrogen ions into the water, making it more acidic' (Weis 2020, 162). Additionally, 'pollution and fertilizers are another mechanism by which carbon dioxide can increase.'[28] The increase in the acidity of seawater causes a reduction in the abundance of carbonate ions, which play a crucial role in certain 'building block of structures such as sea shells and coral skeletons. Decreases in carbonate ions can make

[28] OAP. 'What is Ocean Acidification?' https://oceanacidification.noaa.gov/OurChangingOcean.aspx.

building and maintaining shells and other calcium carbonate structures difficult for calcifying organisms such as oysters, clams, sea urchins, shallow water corals, deep sea corals, and calcareous plankton.'[29]

Given that human activities and business practices are largely responsible for carbon dioxide (CO_2) emissions, there is little likelihood that oceans will be absorbing lower levels of CO_2 in the foreseeable future, meaning that their acidity levels will continue to rise. Based on current trends, some forecasts estimate that 'the surface waters of the ocean could have acidity levels nearly 150 percent higher' by the end of twenty-first century, 'resulting in a pH that the oceans haven't experienced for more than 20 million years.'[30] Since ocean acidification can inhibit or slow coral growth, and significantly 'impact the ability of coral reefs to recover from disturbance,'[31] such a change would likely endanger the survival of an 'estimated one million species that depend on coral reef habitat.'[32] Consequently, this could lead to a collapse of the food chains of many ocean creatures.

Ocean life is also being significantly impacted by the dumping of large quantities of physical garbage, including metals, plastics, and other types of solid waste, to the extent that they are forming into large garbage patches in some regions. Some estimates suggest that 'on average 8 million metric tons of plastic' is entering the ocean each year (Jambeck 2018). Furthermore, a majority of the plastic materials in the ocean originated from 'sources on land, often reaching the ocean as runoff that moves improperly discarded trash from land to river and finally, the ocean' (Jambeck 2018). Unfortunately, this will likely be a growing problem, as a 2019 UN report revealed that 'plastic pollution has increased tenfold

[29] National Ocean Service: National Oceanic and Atmospheric Administration, U.S. Department of Commerce. 'What is Ocean Acidification?' https://oceanservice.noaa.gov/facts/acidification.html.

[30] National Ocean Service: National Oceanic and Atmospheric Administration, U.S. Department of Commerce. 'What is Ocean Acidification?' https://www.pmel.noaa.gov/co2/story/What+is+Ocean+Acidification%3F.

[31] National Ocean Service: National Oceanic and Atmospheric Administration, U.S. Department of Commerce. 'What is Ocean Acidification?' https://www.pmel.noaa.gov/co2/story/What+is+Ocean+Acidification%3F.

[32] National Ocean Service: National Oceanic and Atmospheric Administration, U.S. Department of Commerce. 'What is Ocean Acidification?' https://www.pmel.noaa.gov/co2/story/What+is+Ocean+Acidification%3F.

since 1980.'[33] In 2016 alone, people produced approximately '335 million metric tons' of plastic globally, 50% of which were 'single-use plastics like water bottles and straws that are discarded immediately after use...Only about nine percent of plastic produced is recycled' (Jambeck 2018). Therefore, while people might believe that they are engaging in environmentally friendly habits and practices when they recycle, for the most part, 'recycling only delays the final disposal of an item, but does not avoid it' (Jambeck 2018).

On the sea surface, the Great Pacific Garbage Patch covers 'an estimated surface area of 1.6 million square kilometers, an area twice the size of Texas or three times the size of France.'[34] It includes an abundance of plastics, which eventually deteriorate and break down into smaller pieces due to the effects of sun light, harsh weather conditions, and marine life. Over time, this deterioration produces microplastics, which are very difficult to remove from the oceans. Another significant source of microplastics is microfibers, which are produced when a washing machine is used to clean 'clothes made with polyester, nylon, spandex and acrylic' (Jambeck 2018). A single wash can release around '100,000 fibers' that end up finding their way to the oceans through waterways and wastewater treatment systems (Jambeck 2018). According to recent studies, between '15 and 31% of the estimated 9.5 m tonnes of plastic released into the oceans each year could be primary microplastics, almost two-thirds of which come from the washing of synthetic textiles and the abrasion of tyres while driving.'[35]

Sea creatures often confuse microplastics with food and consume them, which means they are also ingesting the chemicals attached to the plastic. Digesting these microplastics and chemicals can be poisonous for sea creatures that ingest them, as well as the other animals that eat them. Undigested plastic in the stomach of sea creatures and animals are 'transferred from one predator to the next and can travel up to the top of the food web' (Jambeck 2018). Plastics can also clog the digestive systems of sea creatures, causing 'the animals die from blockage of their stomach or

[33] The Sustainable Development Goals: UN Report: Nature's Dangerous Decline 'Unprecedented'; Species Extinction Rates 'Accelerating' https://www.un.org/sustainabledevelopment/blog/2019/05/nature-decline-unprecedented-report/.

[34] https://theoceancleanup.com/great-pacific-garbage-patch/.

[35] IUCN. 2017. 'Invisible plastic particles from textiles and tyres a major source of ocean pollution – IUCN study.' https://www.iucn.org/news/secretariat/201702/invisible-plastic-particles-textiles-and-tyres-major-source-ocean-pollution-%E2%80%93-iucn-study.

intestines, sharp plastic shards can also pierce intestinal lining, and they can starve due to feeling falsely full from a stomach full of plastic' (Jambeck 2018). In fact, it has been found that 'sea turtles by-caught in fisheries operating within and around the patch can have up to 74% (by dry weight) of their diets composed of ocean plastics' (Jambeck 2018). Similarly, scientists have found plastics and microplastics in the stomach of dolphins, whales, fish, birds, and various other sea creatures.

Another practice that damages or destroys the habitats of various ocean creatures is the quasi-unregulated extraction of sand and gravel.[36] In fact, sand and gravel mining generates 'the largest volume of solid material extracted globally,'[37] accounting for between 68% and 85% of the total material mined annually (Krausmann et al. 2009). Each year, 'fifty billion tons of sand and gravel are used'[38] in the production of a number of different products and materials, many of which are used for construction. For example, sand is used to produce cement,[39] flooring, stucco, and shingles, as well as 'in the production of abrasives, absorbents, ceramics, chemicals, fracking fluid, electronics, filtration media, glass, paint, metal castings, pigments and synthetic fibers.'[40] It is also required for 'the filtration of drinking water, the processing of wastewater and the production of water from wells.'[41] Large quantities of sand are also used for land and beach reclamation projects, the building coastal cities or ports in places

[36] Sand is—after air and water—the third most used resource on the planet.' UN Environment Program. 2019. 'The search for sustainable sand extraction is beginning.' https://www.unenvironment.org/news-and-stories/story/search-sustainable-sand-extraction-beginning.

[37] UNEP IN EUROPE. 'UNEP Global Environmental Alert Service: Sand, rarer than one thinks.' http://unepineurope.org/index.php?option=com_content&view=article&id=86:unep-global-environmental-alert-service-sand-rarer-than-one-thinks&catid=15&Itemid=101.

[38] UN Environment Program. 2019. 'The search for sustainable sand extraction is beginning.' https://www.unenvironment.org/news-and-stories/story/search-sustainable-sand-extraction-beginning.

[39] Sand used in the production of cement for construction, and cement is 'a major source of greenhouse gases, and accounts for about eight per cent of carbon dioxide emissions.' UN Environment Program. 2019. 'The search for sustainable sand extraction is beginning.' https://www.unenvironment.org/news-and-stories/story/search-sustainable-sand-extraction-beginning.

[40] National Industrial Sand Association. 'Industrial Sand Products.' https://www.sand.org/page/Products.

[41] National Industrial Sand Association. 'Industrial Sand Products.' https://www.sand.org/page/Products.

like China, Malaysia, and Singapore, and the construction artificial islands such as the Palm Islands of Dubai.

Sand and gravel mining have destructive impacts on 'rivers, deltas and coastal and marine ecosystems,' as it 'results in loss of land through river or coastal erosion, lowering of the water table and decreases in the amount of sediment supply.'[42] More specifically, 'the removal of sand and gravel and agitation of fine sediments had negative effects on both mussels and the fish that play an important role in their life cycles' (Koehnken and Rintoul 2018, 58). Meanwhile, coastal[43] and offshore sand mining harms millions organisms that live 'buried in the sand,' such as 'clams and other shellfish, crustaceans, and numerous types of worms,'[44] which also impacts various other species that rely on them for food (Vazquez-Botello et al. 2020, 25, 26). Ocean sand mining causes fish populations to decline in the vicinity, not only by killing them directly, but also because the noise caused by sand extraction equipment frightens them into leaving the area, along with a variety of other marine creatures (Koehnken and Rintoul 2018, 57).

The process of sand extraction should be significantly curbed given its destructive impacts ocean and marine habitats, species, and 'the food-web structure' (Koehnken and Rintoul 2018, 5, 57). However, that is unlikely given the importance of sand and gravel in the production of material used for construction, particularly cement. As the global population continues to grows, so too will the cities and infrastructure required to house and support them, particularly the urban areas where the majority of the world population lives.[45] This is an important factor, because the expansion and maintenance of urban areas often involves construction projects that

[42] UNEP IN EUROPE. 'UNEP Global Environmental Alert Service: Sand, rarer than one thinks.' http://unepineurope.org/index.php?option=com_content&view=article&id=86:unep-global-environmental-alert-service-sand-rarer-than-one-thinks&catid=15&Itemid=101.

[43] 'Sand beaches provide multiple ecosystem functions including the regulation of biogeochemical cycles (e.g., nutrients, water, organic carbon), shoreline buffering, maintenance of genetic and biological diversity through the provision of habitat to many species, including vertebrate populations, many of which are of conservation concern, support of natural processes that promote energy flow among biological systems, and provision of several human-related services including recreation' (Vazquez-Botello et al. 2020, 25, 26).

[44] Oceana Protecting the World's Ocean. https://oceana.org/marine-life/marine-science-and-ecosystems/beach.

[45] 'Urban areas have more than doubled since 1992.' The Sustainable Development Goals: UN Report: Nature's Dangerous Decline 'Unprecedented'; Species Extinction Rates

require large quantities of cement, including the building of roads, high-rise buildings, and bridges.

In addition to the examples discussed in this section, a number of other human activities are also seriously damaging the oceans and the various species and organisms that inhabit them. For example, aquatic factory farms have been depleting wild fish stocks, which are used in great abundance to produce the fishmeal and fish oils that are fed to the farmed fish. Meanwhile, destructive fishing techniques like blast fishing using explosives and cyanide fishing inflict significant damage to coral reefs and other sea creatures in the vicinity. Marine life is also lost to ghost fishing, where fishing boats discard, lose, or abandon their fishing nets or traps, which continue to trap fish and other species that perish because they are unable to free themselves.

The freedom of corporations to exploit the world's human and natural resources has been expanded further since the rise of neo-liberalism. Oceans have not been spared from the profit-oriented activities of corporations, which have had devastating effects on the marine environment. Unfortunately, there is no reason to believe that consumers will voluntarily change their daily habits out of a sense of social responsibility in order to limit the extent of the damage that their consumption patterns are inflicting upon the world's oceans. It is even less likely that the business community will voluntarily limit their destructive business practices, because of their unbridled commitment to profit maximization. Therefore, unless government legislation and real international standards aimed at protecting the oceans are properly enforced, the destructive practices of mass production and consumption will continue unabated, thereby forsaking the oceans and the multitude of species they accommodate to continue on their precipitous decline, which will exacerbate global warming and other ecological crises.

7.4 Agri-Business and Chemicals

Friedman 1982 [1962] strongly opposed government intervention and protective trade measures in the agriculture sector. In discussing his aversion to protective trade measures, he explained that if a farmer cannot 'grow the amount of wheat he wants' on account of quotas or 'fair trade laws,' then

'Accelerating' https://www.un.org/sustainabledevelopment/blog/2019/05/nature-decline-unprecedented-report/.

both his economic freedom and 'total freedom' are being violated (Friedman 1982 [1962], 16). Meanwhile, he was also adamantly against the state 'control of output, such as through the farm program' (Friedman 1982 [1962], 37). Friedman was particularly critical of farm programs designed to 'help agricultural producers manage market risks, recover from disasters, and conserve and protect America's natural resources,'[46] for being discriminatory, because they were not 'designed to help people as people,' but as 'members of particular occupational groups' (Friedman 1982 [1962], 157). According to him, this represented 'a defect of farm programs,' similar to 'general old-age benefits, minimum-wage laws, pro-union legislation' (Friedman 1982 [1962], 159). Furthermore, he claimed that government agricultural programs intended to help impoverished farmers 'wasted public funds, distorted the use of resources, riveted increasingly heavy and detailed controls on farmers, interfered seriously with United States foreign policy, and withal has done little to help the impecunious farmer' (Friedman 1982 [1962], 162). Consequently, Friedman advocated for the elimination of protective trade measures and governmental agricultural programs, on the basis that both are ineffective and inefficient.

Hayek agreed with Friedman about abolishing protective trade measures and governmental agricultural programs. He was also very critical of traditional farming, and advocated for the elimination of small family farms in favour of adopting new advanced methods of cultivation that would reduce average production costs, while improving productivity and efficiency. Consequently, Hayek (2011, 487) was opposed to the protection of traditional farmer populations in Austria and Switzerland, criticizing such policies for facilitating the 'preservation of the mountain peasants' lifestyle, while discouraging farmers from adapting to new techniques and methods, which would make them increasingly dependent on public programs. Hayek (2011, 488) made his support for modernizing the farming industry at the expense of traditional practices very clear when he stated:

> It would certainly be the lesser evil if some remote homesteads disappeared and in some places pastures or even forests replaced what in different conditions had been arable land. Indeed, we should be showing more respect for the dignity of man if we allowed certain ways of life to disappear altogether instead of preserving them as specimens of a past age.

[46] United States Department of Agriculture Farm Service Agency. 'Farm Programs.' https://www.fsa.usda.gov/about-fsa/structure-and-organization/farm-programs/index.

Hayek (2011, 486–487) was convinced that greater freedom in farm practices would engender the necessary changes to move the farming industry in the right direction. According to him, the adoption of new farming technologies and methods, combined with the elimination of small family farms, would allow farmers to take advantage of new opportunities. Although many of the farm reforms proposed by Hayek and Friedman were implemented in a number of developing countries, their recommendations to eliminate farm subsidies were largely ignored in the US and European Union, which boast the largest farm subsidy programs in the world, mostly for the benefit of large multinational agribusiness corporations. The interests of US farmers have historically been protected by the American government, and the Reagan Administration was no exception, as state action in the agricultural sector was not reduced during his presidency. This situation clearly puts the double standards of the American government, as well as those of various European Union member countries, on display, as they incessantly call for free-trade when it works to their advantage by opening up new markets for their companies in poor countries, while supporting protectionist political measures when free-market conditions threaten the interests of their domestic agricultural sectors.

The US Farm Bill is a package of legislation that is renewed every five years, and has a significant impact on 'farming livelihoods, how food is grown, and what kinds of foods are grown.'[47] It covers a wide variety of 'programs ranging from crop insurance for farmers to healthy food access for low-income families.'[48] It also provides subsidies and financial assistance for American farmers through farm income support programs. Therefore, the Farm Bill violates free-trade principles, meaning that it is a clear example of a protectionist political measure. Although the Farm Bill is specific to US agriculture, it also exerts considerable influence over other important areas, including international trade, the environment, and water and wildlife conservation. In 2018, the Farm Bill allocated about $867 billion for the nation's agriculture sector over the subsequent five-year period.

Between 1995 and 2019, '$391 billion in farm subsidies from commodity, crop insurance, disaster programs and conservation payments'

[47] National Sustainable Agriculture Coalition. 'What is the Farm Bill?' https://sustainableagriculture.net/our-work/campaigns/fbcampaign/what-is-the-farm-bill/.

[48] National Sustainable Agriculture Coalition. 'What is the Farm Bill?' https://sustainableagriculture.net/our-work/campaigns/fbcampaign/what-is-the-farm-bill/.

were provided to farmers in the US.[49] According to the Environmental Working Group's (EWG) Farm Subsidy Database, 'the billionaires who received farm subsidies between 1995 and 2014 have a collective net worth of $331.4 billion' (Coleman 2016). EWG studies further revealed that 46 American billionaires 'grow corn, soybeans, sorghum, cotton, rice and barley—commodities that are eligible for both traditional farm subsidies and crop insurance subsidies' (Coleman 2016). It makes sense for state to be involved in supporting and protecting its agricultural and farming industries, given their importance in terms securing the food supply of the nation, particularly in the event of unfavourable weather conditions, economic crises, or imports that domestic farmers cannot compete with. However, providing generous subsidies to large and powerful agri-businesses, so that they can undercut prices and bankrupt farmers in developing countries has little to do with the national interest.

Contrary to the situations in the US and European Union, the rise of neo-liberalism brought substantial changes to the agricultural sectors in many poor and developing countries. More specifically, these countries were encouraged to adhere to free-market principles, which entailed the elimination of protective trade measures, lowering labour and environmental protection standards, the rapid removal of price controls, and the elimination of all subsidies for farmers. Proponents of neo-liberalism promised that such reforms would bring efficiency and productivity gains to the agricultural sectors of the countries that adopted them. In reality, they led to a greater concentration of wealth in the hands of a few large agri-business companies, which were then able to shape the national agricultural sector to suit their interests.

Neo-liberal reforms have put immense pressure on small and medium-sized farmers, while also altering the livelihoods of indigenous peoples around the world. For example, the devaluation of currencies combined with trade liberalization has led to large increases in prices for fuel, fertilizers and other farm inputs. Additionally, the imposition of austerity measures in many developing nations, as prescribed by IMF Structural Adjustment Programmes (SAP), significantly reduced government expenditures on agricultural development and protection programs. In some instances, the SAP prescribed the privatization of nationally-owned utilities, which put further pressure on farmers in the form of higher prices for

[49] Environmental Working Group (EWG). 'Farm Subsidies Education.' https://farm.ewg.org/index.php.

water and electricity. Therefore, the widespread implementation of free-market economic reforms has led to the impoverishment of farming communities in developing countries, as small-scale farmers suddenly faced greater difficulties accessing credit, subsidies, inputs, and technical expertise. This put them at a considerable disadvantage when it came to competing with agricultural imports from the US and Europe, where farmers continue to be heavily subsidized. Consequently, millions of small and medium-size family farmers in Asian, African and Latin American countries that used to be self-sufficient and produce surpluses, now found their farms to be unsustainable and unable compete with large transnational agri-business corporations. Therefore, far from delivering on their promises of greater efficiency and productivity, neo-liberal agricultural reforms forced many small-scale farmers in developing countries to declare bankruptcy and give up their farms, while domestic production was largely replaced by imported products.

Another significant change in structure of global agriculture attributable to the rise of neo-liberalism is that many poor countries have moved away from farming their traditional crops, in favour of cultivating cash crops and other products that are popular exports to developed countries, including sugar, tea, tobacco, cacao, bananas, flowers, and coffee. Consequently, an over-reliance on cash crops has made many small and medium-size farmers in developing countries extremely vulnerable to price fluctuations on the world market. Growing only cash crops also makes these farmers and their countries more food insecure, because most of these products cannot actually be eaten in case of a sudden emergency (e.g., natural disaster, war, economic crisis, etc.). This transition to an agricultural sector that focuses on the production of cash crops for exportation has also been detrimental to the environment in many poor countries, as it often leads to deforestation, and the excessive use of chemical fertilizers and pesticides that contaminate the soil, air, and water. Furthermore, many of the crops grown for exportation such as tomatoes, berries, broccoli, grapes, and flowers require large quantities of water, which is acquired by depriving local populations of this necessary good.

The spread of globalisation and the dominance of the free-market system has led to global agri-business being controlled by a few transnational corporations, namely, Monsanto (acquired by Bayer in 2018), DuPont, and Dow Chemical. These companies have facilitated the adoption of new practices in the global agriculture sector with the promise of attaining maximum yields at minimum expense, which involved the extensive use of their patented seeds and chemical inputs. However, it would appear that Bayer, DuPont and Dow Chemical were the main beneficiaries of these changes, as they managed to gain control over a combined 75% of the global market for farm inputs. These three companies also financed an abundance of scientific research and innovation projects focused on genetically modified organisms (GMOs), the creation of stronger pesticides and synthetic fertilizers, and defending the performance of these products.[50]

In 1982, the US FDA approved 'the first consumer GMO product developed through genetic engineering: human insulin to treat diabetes.'[51] Then, in the 1990s, 'the first wave of GMO produce created through genetic engineering becomes available to consumers: summer squash, soybeans, cotton, corn, papayas, tomatoes, potatoes, and canola. Not all are still available for sale.'[52] Subsequently, large agri-business corporations managed to gradually integrate GMOs into the local food systems of many countries. The significant power that these corporations wield over the global economy has allowed them to weaken and eliminate barriers that previously prevented the widespread cultivation and distribution of GMOs crops and products.

According to FDA reports, GMO crops are resistant to 'insect damage,' and 'plant viruses,' and tolerant to 'herbicides,'[53] as they were:

> developed to address the needs of farmers, but in turn they can help foods become more accessible and affordable for consumers. Some GMO crops were developed specifically to benefit consumers. For example, a GMO soybean that is used to create a healthier oil is commercially grown and available. GMO apples that do not brown when cut are now available for sale and may help reduce food waste.

[50] The term GMO refers to a 'plant, animal, or microorganism that has had its genetic material (DNA) changed using technology that generally involves the specific modification of DNA, including the transfer of specific DNA from one organism to another.' FDA. 'How GMO Crops Impact Our World.' https://www.fda.gov/food/agricultural-biotechnology/how-gmo-crops-impact-our-world.

[51] FDA. 'Science and History of GMOs and Other Food Modification Processes.' https://www.fda.gov/food/agricultural-biotechnology/science-and-history-gmos-and-other-food-modification-processes.

[52] FDA. 'Science and History of GMOs and Other Food Modification Processes.' https://www.fda.gov/food/agricultural-biotechnology/science-and-history-gmos-and-other-food-modification-processes.

[53] FDA. 'How GMO Crops Impact Our World.' https://www.fda.gov/food/agricultural-biotechnology/how-gmo-crops-impact-our-world.

In reality, GMO crops are not particularly effective when it comes to addressing hunger or eliminating food insecurity, because they were primarily created to help a few large agri-business corporations gain dominance over the world food market. Nonetheless, these companies consistently claim that their GMO crops are superior to their organic counterparts in terms of maintenance, nutritional value, and resistance to herbicides. However, the true intentions of these agribusinesses become very apparent when considering the example of Monsanto's genetically modified Roundup Ready (RR) seeds, which produce crops that are resistant to glyphosate, the main active ingredient in Roundup Ready brand herbicides.

Monsanto strongly promotes RR crop seeds for export, while claiming that RR does not harm human health, even though glyphosate has been linked to Alzheimer's Disease, asthma, autism, birth defects, multiple sclerosis, Parkinson's disease, various types of cancer, etc.[54] In fact, thousands of lawsuits have been filed in US and UK courts by people alleging that exposure to RR and other herbicides produced by Monsanto seriously affected their health. Prominent among them is a 2018 'wrongful death lawsuit filed by ClassAction.com Of Counsel attorney Robert F. Kennedy, Jr. alleges that Monsanto intentionally misinformed government agencies and the public about the safety of Roundup. Kennedy is part of a legal team representing plaintiffs in similar Roundup cases. More than 18,000 cases await trial in state and federal courts.'[55] According to Kennedy, 'mounting evidence suggests that Monsanto knew about the hazards posed by glyphosate exposure, but failed to disclose this information to the public' for decades.[56] In 2019, 'A jury in Oakland, California, has awarded a couple $2 billion in punitive damages after concluding that sustained exposure to Monsanto Co.'s popular Roundup weed killer led to their cancer diagnoses. The couple will receive an additional $55 million for pain and suffering and to cover medical expenses.'[57] However,

[54] Class Action.com. 'Roundup Weed Killer.' https://www.classaction.com/roundup-weed-killer/.

[55] Class Action.com. 'Roundup Weed Killer.' https://www.classaction.com/roundup-weed-killer/.

[56] Class Action.com. 'Roundup Weed Killer.' https://www.classaction.com/roundup-weed-killer/.

[57] CBS News. 'Jury awards couple $2 billion in Monsanto Roundup cancer lawsuit trial.' https://www.cbsnews.com/news/jury-awards-couple-2billion-monsanto-roundup-weed-killer-cancer-lawsuit-trial-today-2019-05-13/.

despite suffering such major setbacks in the courts, Monsanto continues to maintain that 'glyphosate is not a human carcinogen.'[58]

The rise of neo-liberalism has led the agricultural industry to use highly advanced biotechnology and chemistry to challenge the land and its capacity to produce crops, resulting in the widespread use of increasingly toxic chemicals with longer-lasting effects on the environment. This is because the cultivation of GMO crops involves the application of larger quantities of pesticides and synthetic fertilizers compared to traditional farming practices. Pesticides are basically chemicals that are designed to destroy organisms and creatures that are harmful to crops, including insects, rodents, unwanted plants, fungi, and micro-organisms. They come in three main forms: insecticides, which aim to kill insects; herbicides, which aim to destroy unwanted plants; and, fungicides, which aim to eradicate 'certain type of fungus' (Mirsal 2008, 139). Meanwhile, synthetic fertilizers are full of nutrients intended to help crops grow. However, unlike traditional fertilizers, they contain chemicals and inorganic ingredients such as calcium, phosphorus, potassium, and magnesium. Agri-businesses promote the use of both synthetic fertilizers and pesticides by claiming that they increase production yields and reduce costs.

Each year, contemporary agri-business practices that rely on the heavy use of synthetic fertilizers and pesticides result in large amounts of toxic chemicals entering into the soil and water. Nitrogen plays a particularly significant role in earning profit for the agricultural sector, because it is a key ingredient in many synthetic fertilisers on account of its importance as a nutrient in soil that is ideal for plant growth. However, the extensive application of synthetic fertilizers in industrial farming leads to nitrogen contaminating the soil, groundwater, rivers, lakes, and seas. Furthermore, it can lead to significant ecological imbalances when it eventually makes its way to non-agricultural ecosystems. For example, high levels of nitrogen in an aquatic system can accelerate the growth of thick algae on the surface water, which disturbs the normal photosynthesis processes of other plants that are situated deeper in the water by preventing sunlight from reaching them. Consequently, those particular plants could die off in large numbers, thereby disrupting the food chains that rely on them. Meanwhile, high levels of nitrogen in soil can also reduce biodiversity by facilitating the stronger growth of certain types of plants at the expense of others.

[58] Class Action.com. 'Roundup Weed Killer.' https://www.classaction.com/roundup-weed-killer/.

However, large agri-businesses deny the magnitude of the environmental damage caused by the extensive use of chemicals in farming.

Aside from nitrogen, synthetic fertilizers contain other hazardous chemicals that contaminate soil, groundwater, aquifers, rivers, lakes, and seas, along with pesticides. Many of these chemicals can also disrupt natural processes, disturb ecosystems, and kill various plants, animals, insects, birds and other species, including micro-organisms that serve as the foundations of food chains. However, many of the insects, weeds, fungi, and other undesirable plants targeted by pesticides have developed greater resistance to their effects over time, which has led agri-businesses to dump greater quantities or switch to stronger chemicals. This is causing further problems for the environment, including the loss of arable land and biodiversity.

In addition to the immediate damage they cause, toxic chemicals released into the environment through the extensive application of pesticides and synthetic fertilizers can reduce soil fertility over time, thereby lowering the yields of future agricultural harvests. These chemicals can change the quality and texture of the soil, and alter the balance of its components (e.g. minerals, organic and inorganic matter, etc.), which affects the amount of water and air that the soil can absorb and retain. They can also alter the pH level of the soil, thereby making it either more acidic or alkaline, which can affect the availability of minerals and nutrients for plants to absorb. If contemporary farming and agricultural practices are not modified to become more sustainable and less reliant on the extensive use toxic of chemicals, then large swaths of arable land will lose their fertility, setting the stage for increased desertification in the future. In 2015, Duncan Cameron, professor of plant and soil biology at the University of Sheffield, suggested that roughly 33% of 'the world's arable land has been lost to erosion or pollution' over the last four decades, an alarming rate when considering that the replacement of soil occurs 'over millennia and this represents one of the greatest global threats for agriculture.'[59] In the future, the combination of soil contamination and climate change are likely to contribute to the further reduction of arable land that can be used for agriculture, which means sustainability and food security could become major concerns for humanity.

[59] Grantham Centre for Sustainable Futures. 'Soil loss: an unfolding global disaster – Grantham Centre briefing note.' http://grantham.sheffield.ac.uk/soil-loss-an-unfolding-global-disaster/.

The widespread use of stronger chemicals on the part of agri-businesses has also contributed a rapid decline of insect populations. Over '40% of insect species are declining and a third are endangered,' while estimates suggest that the insect population is decreasing by approximately 2.5% per year.[60] In fact, some projections suggest that 50% of the total insect population will be gone in fifty years. Timothy D. Schowalter (2013, 13–14, 23), a specialist of insect ecology and ecosystem ecology, explained that there are three insect groups that play significant roles in ecosystems in a variety of ways:

> herbivores (including pollinators), detritivores, and blood-feeders—are particularly important. Herbivores and detritivores can affect ecosystem services directly by altering rates of growth, survival, and reproduction of plants or decomposition of dead material (Schowalter 2013), whereas blood-feeders are most important when famine, conflict, or persistent poverty increase human crowding and vulnerability to insect transmitted diseases.

Insects play vital roles in supporting biodiversity, protecting water resources, forming soil and maintaining its fertility, and pollinating plants. They are also instrumental in the food security of many species, as they represent the foundations of numerous food chains, not only as direct food sources, but also on account of their pollinating activities. Consequently, a significant collapse in insect populations would have devastating outcomes for the many ecosystems that provide 'food, fresh water, fiber, biofuels, and medical and industrial resources for humans' (Schowalter 2013, 4). Over the last five decades, human actions have changed 'ecosystems more rapidly and extensively than in any comparable period of time in human history, largely to meet rapidly growing demands for food, fresh water, timber, fiber and fuel. This has resulted in a substantial and largely irreversible loss in the diversity of life on Earth.'[61] Accordingly, appropriate human actions can also 'reverse the degradation of many ecosystem services over the next 50 years, but the changes in

[60] The Guardian. 'Plummeting insect numbers 'threaten collapse of nature'.' https://www.theguardian.com/environment/2019/feb/10/plummeting-insect-numbers-threaten-collapse-of-nature.

[61] World Health Organisation. 'Ecosystem goods and services for health.' https://www.who.int/globalchange/ecosystems/en/.

policy and practice required are substantial and not currently underway.'[62] Undoubtedly, one of the key changes that needs to be made is to move away from intensive farming practices, particularly the widespread use of strong toxic chemicals on the part of large agri-businesses.

Since the rise of neo-liberalism, intensive farming practices have been widely adopted in an effort to maximize agricultural production and yields, which has adversely affected the environment in many countries, particularly with respect to the quality of land. That is to say, soil quality has significantly deteriorated due to its exposure to many chemicals and other harmful substances, like pesticides, fertilizers, fuels, sewage wastewater, metal waste, and various other toxic substances, which are either intentionally applied to the soil and the plants it supports, or unintentionally spilled on it during agricultural processes. Eventually, these factors could contribute to reducing the fertility of the soil to the point of making it unfit for cultivation. Furthermore, depending on the intensity and levels of contamination, the fruits, vegetables and other crops grown in the soil could eventually begin lacking important nutrients, or even become toxic to the humans and the various other species that consume them.

Before the global food industry came to be dominated by a few large transnational corporations, due in large part to the prescriptions of neo-liberalism, agriculture was largely comprised of many small, family-owned farms. Since those farms were often kept in the same family for generations, sustainable farming practices were voluntarily used to maintain the fertility of the land and secure good growing conditions well into the future. This would include retaining seed stocks for the reproduction of crops in future harvests, using manure produced by livestock to fertilize crops, and using those crops to feed their animals. Simply put, it was not in the interests of farming families to exploit their natural resources to the fullest extent possible, because this would eventually hurt them over the longer term. Mises (1949, 653) explained that:

> In the central and western areas of continental Europe, where the institution of private property had been rigidly established for many centuries, things were different. There was no question of soil erosion of formerly cultivated land. There was no problem of forest devastation…The owners of the forests were impelled to conservation by their own selfish interests.

[62] World Health Organisation. 'Ecosystem goods and services for health.' https://www.who.int/globalchange/ecosystems/en/.

In the past, people believed that all living creatures were 'children of the soil,' which motivated them to establish close, harmonious relationships with the soil (George 2006, 163). Accordingly, they cherished all of the resources and opportunities that the land provided them with. In stark contrast, the agriculture practices of large agri-businesses in recent decades confirm Seneca's view that people who 'started to make a practice of desiring everything contrary to nature's habit, they finally end up by breaking off relations with her altogether,' a sentiment he expressed more than 2000 years ago (Seneca 1969, 223).

7.5 The Transformation of Livestock Farming

The rise of neo-liberalism has led to livestock farming undergoing a significant transformation, which has been accompanied by a substantial increase in the consumption of animal products. Essentially, there was a shift from small-scale, family owned and operated farms to large corporate industrial farms that occupy massive properties and house huge numbers of animals in overcrowded and unsanitary conditions. The small family farms that were the primary sources of meat and other animal products before the rise of neo-liberalism were actually far better-suited for more sustainable and environmentally-friendly practices, and allowed for some consideration to be paid to the well-being of the animals. However, the global implementation of neo-liberal policies and reforms has led to the prevalence of factory-farmed animal products that can be sold at lower prices, often with the assistance of subsidies, that many local producers cannot compete with.

Factory farms are designed to maximize profits, which has led to livestock farming becoming much more efficient with the introduction of new technologies and mechanical innovations. For example, 'larger and faster equipment allows a single producer to till, seed, fertilize, spray, or harvest more acres; to house and feed more livestock or poultry; or to milk more cows in a single day' (MacDonald and McBride 2009, IV). Innovative technologies and farming techniques have also been developed to grow animals as rapidly as possible at a minimum cost, which often entails inhumane[63] treatment and deplorable conditions. Moreover, modern factory

[63] Workers are also treated poorly at factory farms. They are also exposed to large amount of pesticides and chemicals and often work and live under inhumane, miserable and harsh conditions.

farms also rely on GMO feeds for their animals, as well as various chemicals and pharmaceutical products to mitigate the spread of diseases and facilitate the growth of their animals to unnatural sizes and proportions.

Large factory farms raise tens of thousands of birds, chickens, pigs, and cows in very high densities in order to efficiently produce maximum quantities of meat, milk, and eggs. To maximize output at a minimal cost, virtually all factory farms in the US employ substantial overcrowding, where the animals are confined to filthy barns, small cages, or tight pens that are too small for them to stretch or move around;[64] they also typically do not have access to natural light, nor do they have any opportunity to socialize or engage in behaviours that are natural to them.[65] Basically, each animal is regarded as a mere factor of production and a means to earning profits. As such, animals are bred frequently, and the offspring are often fed with specially formulated feeds developed to accelerate weight gain and fat production, which can limit their life expectancies to as little as a few months. When factory farm animals are ready for 'slaughter or their bodies have been worn out from producing milk or eggs, animals raised for food are crowded onto trucks and transported for miles through all weather extremes, typically without food or water. At the slaughterhouse, those who survived the transport will have their throats slit, often while they're still conscious. Many remain conscious when they're plunged into the scalding-hot water of the defeathering or hair-removal tanks or while their bodies are being skinned or hacked apart.'[66]

In the past, large-scale industrial livestock farming did not really exist in its present form. However, neo-liberal economists advocated for significantly increasing the size of farms, in order to take advantage of lower production costs. For example, a 2009 study by MacDonald and McBride (2009, III) estimated that a dairy farm with 1000 or more cows had 'average costs of $13.59 per hundredweight in 2005,' compared to $20.82 per hundredweight at a farm with between 100 and 199 cows. The prospects of lower production costs and higher returns motivated significant expansions in the size of livestock farms in this highly competitive industry.

[64] The fact that massive factory farms keep large numbers of animals cramped in small areas substantially increases risks of rapidly spreading diseases among the animals, while also increasing the pollution caused by manure to soil, water, and air.

[65] PETA. 'Factory Farming: Misery for Animals.' https://www.peta.org/issues/animals-used-for-food/factory-farming/.

[66] PETA. 'Factory Farming: Misery for Animals.' https://www.peta.org/issues/animals-used-for-food/factory-farming/.

From the late 1980s to the early 2000s, US livestock production shifted to factory farming, as 'the production locus (the farm size, in annual sales, at which one half of national production comes from larger farms and half from smaller) increased by 60 percent in broiler, 100 percent in fed-cattle, 240 percent in dairy, and 2000 percent in hog production. Recent surveys indicate that production has continued to shift to larger operations since 2002' (MacDonald and McBride 2009, III). Furthermore, annual broiler production in the US expanded from 11,996 million pounds on a ready-to-cook basis in 1982, to 43,435 million pounds in 2019.[67] Meanwhile, consumers have also benefitted from the shift to large-scale factory farming by enjoying lower retail food prices for meat, dairy products and eggs.

Presently, large-scale industrial livestock farming practices are major sources of environmental pollution. Worldwide, 'animal agriculture is responsible for more greenhouse gases than all the world's transportation systems combined.'[68] In particular, livestock manure is responsible for about '18% of greenhouse gas production' (Hribar 2010, 7). More specifically, it is one of the main 'contributors among the anthropogenic sources of the global warming gas methane' (Tauseef et al. 2013, 187). When manure is dumped into the environment, it releases methane emissions for two decades as it degrades. Research has shown that methane is '84 times more powerful than carbon dioxide at destabilizing the climate,'[69] because it absorbs heat so efficiently. 'Scientists say that methane could push the climate over a "tipping point" in the next 18–25 years, causing runaway global warming, and making a 100-year timeline obsolete.'[70]

Experts are also concerned that the methane released by animal waste is playing a significant role in the reduction of air quality. Poor air quality caused by animal farms can contribute to a number of health issues in people, including asthma, 'chronic bronchitis, chronic obstructive airways disease,' 'interstitial lung disease,' 'headaches, respiratory problems, eye irritation, nausea, weakness, and chest tightness' (Hribar 2010, 6, 7). Additionally, according to the scientific community, manure can harm

[67] National Chicken Council. 'U.S. Broiler Production.' https://www.nationalchicken-council.org/about-the-industry/statistics/u-s-broiler-production/.

[68] PETA. 'Meat and the Environment.' https://www.peta.org/issues/animals-used-for-food/meat-environment/.

[69] Greenpeace. 'Natural Gas: Methane's contributions to global warming.' https://www.greenpeace.org/usa/global-warming/issues/natural-gas/.

[70] Greenpeace. 'Natural Gas: Methane's contributions to global warming.' https://www.greenpeace.org/usa/global-warming/issues/natural-gas.

human health by contaminating water and food supplies with ‘E. coli, growth hormones, antibiotics, chemicals used as additives to the manure or to clean equipment, animal blood, silage leachate from corn feed, or copper sulfate used in footbaths for cows’ (Hribar 2010, 2).

Some estimates of the amount of organic animal waste generated by factory livestock farming in the US alone are staggering. For example, the EPA suggests that animal farms produce ‘between 3 and 20 times more manure than people’ (Hribar 2010, 2). To be more precise, the U.S. Department of Agriculture recently estimated that big livestock farming generates more than ‘335 million tons of dry’ manure per year, considerably more than the ‘7 million tons of fecal material per year, as measured in dry weight,’[71] generated by the human population. Additionally, ‘the Rachel Carson Council (RCC), a science-based, non-profit environmental group,’ pointed out that by factoring in ‘the liquid fraction and waste from smaller farms, food animals produce 2 billion tons of manure per year’.[72]

Properly treating and disposing of excess manure, which can be done by ‘pumping liquefied manure onto spray fields, trucking it off-site, or storing it until it can be used or treated,’ can be very costly for factory farms, given their size (Hribar 2010, 3. Some estimates suggest that the proper management of manure could raise production costs at large livestock farms by up to ‘5 percent in some regions’ of the US (MacDonald and McBride 2009, 31). Consequently, such establishments will often try to avoid incurring these costs by intentionally dumping large amounts of untreated manure into the surrounding soil and water, along with waste from other sources like feed, slurry, and dead animals, even though doing so is illegal in many countries. In fact, it is not uncommon for the manure to come into contact with surrounding water supplies ‘through a pipe that carries manure or wastewater to surface water, or by animal contact with surface water that runs through their confined area’ (Hribar 2010, 1). If large quantities of manure are frequently disposed in the same area, then the nutrients and toxins they contain can ‘overwhelm the absorptive capacity of the soil, and either run off or are leached into the groundwater’

[71] Newsweek. ‘Two Numbers: Animal Manure a Growing Headache in America.’ https://www.newsweek.com/2015/12/18/two-numbers-animal-manure-growing-headache-america-402205.html.

[72] Newsweek. ‘Two Numbers: Animal Manure a Growing Headache in America.’ https://www.newsweek.com/2015/12/18/two-numbers-animal-manure-growing-headache-america-402205.html.

(Hribar 2010, 3). Some countries address this issue by requiring farmers to obtain permits that set clear limits on the amount of manure they are allowed to discharge. However, while limiting the quantity of manure discharged by each farmer may be of some benefit, in the end, the pollution continues, which means an impending environmental apocalypse is really only being delayed, and not prevented.

In the past, small and medium sized family farms could use the manure produced by their livestock as organic fertilizers to grow crops, which in turn were often used as feed. However, the large industrial animal farms that are now prevalent following the rise of neo-liberalism no longer grow their own feed, which means they have no use for the excessive amounts of manure that their livestock produces. It is also too expensive to make it worthwhile to transport their manure so that it can be used as fertilizer at other locations. Additionally, the manure produced by the livestock at factory farms is generally of too low a quality to benefit soil and plants, because the animals are typically fed grain that is grown with synthetic fertilisers and toxic pesticides, as opposed to being organically grass fed.

Animal factories also significantly burden the environment on account of their energy-intensive practices and methods. For instance, large amounts of electricity and fossil fuels are required to grow the crops used to produce the abundant supplies of feed needed to sustain so many animals, particularly when factoring in the energy used to manufacture the synthetic fertilizers and pesticides that are applied to them. Additionally, intensive energy use is required for milking machines, heaters, ventilators, coolers, and storage, as well as the transport of various inputs (e.g., food, machines, etc.) and outputs (e.g., meat products, by-products, animal waste, etc.). Furthermore, animal farming also uses large quantities of water very inefficiently. It has been estimated that 15,000 litres of water is required to produce 1 kg of beef, compared to about 800 litres for the same quantity of wheat.[73] Specifically, water is needed 'to mix the animal feed, for maintaining the farm, and for drinking of the animals,' in addition to growing the considerable quantities of crops needed to produce feed, which also requires large areas of farm land (Gerbens-Leenes et al. 2013, 26). Some scientific studies have suggested that, all told, 'agriculture accounts for 92% of the global freshwater' usage (Gerbens-Leenes et al. 2013, 26).

[73] UNESCO. 'Good water, water to "eat". What is virtual water?' http://www.unesco.org/new/fileadmin/MULTIMEDIA/FIELD/Venice/pdf/special_events/bozza_scheda_DOW04_1.0.pdf.

Since the rise of neo-liberalism, livestock farming has undergone significant transformations in terms of the size and scale of production, specialization, and the intensive use of chemicals and pharmaceuticals, all of which contributed to lowering production costs, improving efficiency, and increasing profits, while also reducing prices for consumers. At the same time, highly-industrialized livestock farming has resulted in the animals being forced to endure increasingly inhumane treatment, while also generating large external costs in terms of polluting the air, soil and land, which ultimately damages human health. Modern livestock farming is also a significant contributor to global warming, which could eventually bring about an environmental apocalypse.

7.6 Environmental Impact of the Clothing Industry

Clothing is another industry that has undergone a significant transformation since the rise of neo-liberalism. Compared to the 1980s, the production of textiles has increased substantially, while clothing prices have dropped. In the US, for example, the quantity of textiles produced increased from only 253,000 tons in 1980 to around 1,689,000 tons in 2017.[74] Today, consumers in western countries frequently purchase large quantities of brand-name clothing, which are usually produced at a very low cost in developing countries. Large clothing companies have been able to considerably reduce the cost of the products they sell in western markets by shifting their manufacturing operations to developing countries, where there is an abundance of cheap labor, and a lack of effective worker rights and environmental protections. In fact, the clothing industry is well-known for its destructive social impacts in developing countries when it comes to violating worker rights by providing deplorable working conditions, imposing long work hours, paying low wages, employing child labour, and having poor health and safety standards in the workplace. However, this section mainly focuses on wasteful consumption patterns of clothing in western countries, and the destructive environmental impacts of clothing production, particularly in emerging and developing economies, which includes the depletion of natural resources and pollution in the form of toxic wastewater and other hazardous wastes.

[74] United States Environmental Protection Agency. 'Textiles: Material-Specific Data.' https://www.epa.gov/facts-and-figures-about-materials-waste-and-recycling/textiles-material-specific-data.

The fashion or clothing industry is 'the world's third-largest manufacturing sector after the automobile and technology industries.'[75] However, it is also among the industries whose production methods and business practices cause considerable damage to the environment. For example, the garment industry uses very high levels of energy and water in its manufacturing processes, which includes activities like preparing fibers, cleaning, bleaching, dyeing, and drying. The packaging, transportation, and distribution of its products also expends considerable amounts of energy. Meanwhile, 'every year the fashion industry uses 93 billion cubic meters of water—enough to meet the consumption needs of five million people.'[76] That makes it the second largest user of water among industries, behind only the agricultural sector. In fact, a study by the United Nations Environment Programme (UNEP) determined that 'it takes 3781 liters of water to make a pair of jeans, from the production of the cotton to the delivery of the final product to the store. That equates to the emission of around 33.4 kilograms of carbon equivalent.'[77] Although the global supply and quality of clean water is among the top environmental concerns, with predictions that around 5 billion people could suffer water shortages by 2050,[78] little progress has been made in terms of significantly reducing the high water usage in the clothing industry.

The clothing industry is also a significant source of greenhouse gas emissions. According to Greenpeace, the fashion industry 'emitted over a million tonnes of CO_2 and produced 92 million tonnes of waste' in 2015 (Campione 2017). Meanwhile, the World Bank reported that 'the fashion industry is responsible for 10% of annual global carbon emissions, more than all international flights and maritime shipping combined.'[79] That

[75] The World Bank. 2019. 'How Much Do Our Wardrobes Cost to the Environment?' https://www.worldbank.org/en/news/feature/2019/09/23/costo-moda-medio-ambiente.

[76] The World Bank. 2019. 'How Much Do Our Wardrobes Cost to the Environment?' https://www.worldbank.org/en/news/feature/2019/09/23/costo-moda-medio-ambiente.

[77] The World Bank. 2019. 'How Much Do Our Wardrobes Cost to the Environment?' https://www.worldbank.org/en/news/feature/2019/09/23/costo-moda-medio-ambiente.

[78] United Nations. 'Water Scarcity.' https://www.unwater.org/water-facts/scarcity/.

[79] The World Bank. 2019. 'How Much Do Our Wardrobes Cost to the Environment?' https://www.worldbank.org/en/news/feature/2019/09/23/costo-moda-medio-ambiente.

same report forecast that, 'at this pace, the fashion industry's greenhouse gas emissions will surge more than 50% by 2030.'[80]

In addition to depleting natural resources and emitting tonnes of CO_2 into the atmosphere, the clothing industry also impacts the environment on account of its large scale production of toxic pollutants and wastes. For example, it has been estimated that 25% of all chemicals produced globally are used by the textile and clothing industry (Niinimäki 2015, 272). In particular, the growth of cotton requires the application of huge amounts of synthetic fertilizers and pesticides to kills pests and weeds. To be more precise, a survey published by the National Agricultural Statistics Service on pesticide and fertilizer use revealed that, in 2011, 'cotton used 92% of nitrogen, 67% of phosphate, 52% of potash and 42% of sulphur…The United States Department of Agriculture; (USDA) report showed that more than 2.03 billion pounds of synthetic fertilizers were applied to conventional cotton, making it the fourth most fertilized crop after corn, winter wheat and soybeans' (Muthu 2014, 10). Toxic fertilizers and pesticides often runoff into surrounding rivers and other bodies of water, where they can contaminate ecosystems and inevitably enter the food chains of various animals, birds, fish and other creatures, which can contribute to the loss of biodiversity.

Even though some clothing is produced using natural fibers, including cotton, linen and silk, they are often subjected to techniques that involve the application of toxic chemicals, such as dyeing, printing and bleaching, which also require high volumes of water. Eventually, the toxic wastewater that is generated by these processes is released into the environment, thereby degrading the quality of the surrounding soil and water, and damaging ecosystems. In particular, the 'dyeing process adds many chemicals, such as heavy metals, salts, surfactants, sulfite, and formaldehyde, which can cause major pollution in the effluents' receiving waters' (Madhav et al. 2018, 37). Wastewater emitted by the clothing industry can also contain significant amounts of copper, cobalt, chromium, lead, nickel, manganese, and zinc. In addition to damaging the environment, clothing industry wastewater can directly impact the health of human beings by entering into their food chains or seeping into the groundwater that people in many countries rely on. According to World Health Organization

[80] The World Bank. 2019. 'How Much Do Our Wardrobes Cost to the Environment?' https://www.worldbank.org/en/news/feature/2019/09/23/costo-moda-medio-ambiente.

estimates, '20% of industrial water pollution globally is attributable to the dyeing and treatment of textiles.'[81]

Certain materials used to produce clothing are essentially plastics since they are made from petroleum, including polyester, nylon and acrylic. When synthetic and polyester clothes are put into washing machines, plastic fibres are washed off of them, which then end up at local wastewater treatment plants. Ultimately, around 40% of these fibres can find their way into rivers, lakes and oceans.[82] Furthermore, when clothes produced from petroleum are dumped on land, they will also eventually break down into non-biodegradable microplastics, which can still find their way into bodies of water, where they could be consumed by aquatic creatures and enter various food chains. Unfortunately, since polyester is such an affordable material, it is 'used in about 60% of our clothes' (Brodde 2017). It should also be noted that, due to 'the fossil fuels used in its production, CO_2 emissions for polyester clothing are nearly three times higher than for cotton!' (Brodde 2017).

Even though the clothing industry is among the largest polluters, the mass production and consumption of clothes has been an engine of economic growth and productivity. Currently, the industry's preferred business model is fast fashion, which involves the frequent release of new trends and fashions in order to encourage people to continuously consume its products. Before the rise of neo-liberalism, the fashion industry released new styles based on limited seasonal calendars, where it usually took around six months for the next collection to come out. This is no longer the case, as the industry now constantly produces large quantities of newly designed clothing at highly discounted prices to the extent that consumers can basically enjoy a new fashion season several times in a year. In fact, some of the larger companies in the industry release new lines of fashion almost every single week of the year, because their business models depend on the continuous mass consumption of fast-fashion products. Consequently, people enjoy their clothes for only a very short time before they feel compelled to replace them with new, more fashionable items. In recent years, technological innovation have been playing an increasingly

[81] Ellen MacArthur Foundation. 'A New Textiles Economy: Redesigning Fashion's Future.' https://www.ellenmacarthurfoundation.org/assets/downloads/A-New-Textiles-Economy_Full-Report_Updated_1-12-17.pdf.

[82] The Guardian. 'How your clothes are poisoning our oceans and food supply.' https://www.theguardian.com/environment/2016/jun/20/microfibers-plastic-pollution-oceans-patagonia-synthetic-clothes-microbeads.

significant role in the success of the fast fashion business model. For example, the advance of online shopping has provided consumers with the ability to shop 24/7, while social media influencers are frequently used to promote the latest fashion items on various platforms like Facebook, Instagram, Pinterest, and Snapchat.

Since the rise of neo-liberalism, people in the rich western countries have enjoyed large discounts in the price of clothing, which encourages them to make impulse purchases and engage in unsustainable consumption behavior. In fact, clothing consumption has reached record levels in recent years, as people stuff more clothes into their closets and consistently purchase the latest fashion items. However, when people overconsume large quantities of continuously changing fashion items at very low prices, the lifespan of these products becomes very short, as they are prematurely discarded and replaced. Although it appears as though people are becoming better informed about environmental issues, their consumptions patterns and wasteful use of commodities, especially when it comes to clothing, demonstrate that any concerns they may have about the environment are not enough to dissuade their desires for acquisitiveness.

When clothes are not sold in stores, online, or at outlets, they are simply dumped or destroyed by retailers, which releases toxic chemicals into the land, water, and air. For example, in 2017, the EPA estimates that, '11.2 million tons' of clothing were dumped in landfills in the US.[83] Worldwide, 'customers miss out on USD 460 billion of value each year by throwing away clothes that they could continue to wear, and some garments are estimated to be discarded after just seven to ten wears.'[84]

Even though people in western countries own so many clothes, they still feel a need to consume more of them, often in order to possess the latest fashion. In an effort to avoid throwing out perfectly good clothing, some of the more socially conscious consumers will donate them to charity organizations and second-hand stores. While some of these used clothes might be resold or make their way to people poor countries, the majority of them ultimately end up in landfills. In other words, recycling unwanted clothes does not represent a viable solution to the environmental

[83] United States Environmental Protection Agency. 'Textiles: Material-Specific Data.' https://www.epa.gov/facts-and-figures-about-materials-waste-and-recycling/textiles-material-specific-data.

[84] Ellen MacArthur Foundation. 'A New Textiles Economy: Redesigning Fashion's Future.' https://www.ellenmacarthurfoundation.org/assets/downloads/A-New-Textiles-Economy_Full-Report_Updated_1-12-17.pdf.

problems caused by clothing waste, as each year, 'less than 1% of material used to produce clothing is recycled into new clothing, representing a loss of more than USD 100 billion worth of materials.'[85]

On the supply side, the growth of clothing waste in western economies is directly related to mass production at a low cost, usually at factories that are located in developing countries. Meanwhile, on the demand side, it is attributed to mass consumption on the part of consumers, which is driven by lower prices, lower quality, and fast fashion. That is to say, when it comes to clothing, fashion and other apparel, both the business practices of producers and consumption patterns of consumers are responsible for the various forms of environmental damage and degradation that can be attributed to the industry. In order to reduce the environmental and social impacts of the textiles and fashion industries, research and efforts are largely focused on using innovation to develop more sustainable production processes that use less energy and water. There have also been suggestions about using more organic and recycled materials in production, and encouraging consumers to buy clothes made out of cotton, or more durable materials treated with longer-lasting dyes. Although these suggestions might be well intentioned, none of them represent long term solutions to the destructive outcomes of this industry. Ultimately, strong state regulations are required to mitigate the damaging aspects of the production processes and business strategies of apparel and clothing companies, while consumers need to re-evaluate their compulsive shopping habits when it comes to acquiring fashion, which can often resemble an addiction.

7.7 Conclusion

All things required for 'human subsistence have the power to multiply many fold, sometimes a million fold' if they are 'protected from their natural enemies' (George 2006, 69). That is to say, the earth is fully capable of providing all of its inhabitants with the necessities of life, such as food, water and shelter, in a sustainable manner, as long as there is a will among people to nurture and live in harmony with nature, the environment, and the various organisms and species that share the planet. However, the earth lacks the natural capacity to sustain the incessant demands of the

[85] Ellen MacArthur Foundation. 'A New Textiles Economy: Redesigning Fashion's Future.' https://www.ellenmacarthurfoundation.org/assets/downloads/A-New-Textiles-Economy_Full-Report_Updated_1-12-17.pdf.

capitalist system and its devotion to self-interest maximization and excessive acquisitiveness.

For decades, scientists have been warning that, if people do not change the direction of their social and economic lives, there will be no avoiding an ecological apocalypse in the foreseeable future. Additionally, many environmental movements, non-governmental organizations, and national and international agencies and institutions have been established with mandates to monitor and protect the environment. They have attempted to raise public awareness about key issues impacting various aspects of the environment, including water pollution, air pollution, deforestation, declining biodiversity, genetically modified organisms, the excessive use of pesticides and chemicals in agriculture, ocean acidification, ozone layer depletion, the destruction of ecosystems, the productive capacity of the earth, and climate change. Unfortunately, their noble efforts have been largely unsuccessful, because measures that effectively protect the environment are typically diametrically opposed to the principles and objectives of neo-liberal economics, which are fully-backed by corporations, individuals and organizations with considerable financial resources and influence. Neo-liberals are opposed to the idea of placing any significant limitations on business activities on the basis that doing so would represent a threat to the preservation of a free society. In fact, productivity, economic growth, and the notion of being free to choose have played important roles in the design of market-oriented environmental regulations. However, such regulations have been unable to confer even a modest degree of protection on the environment against the destructive business practices of enterprises and the wasteful consumption habits of people.

If there is any hope of avoiding an impending environmental apocalypse, people need to be made aware of the extent to which the system of mass production and mass consumption that governs neo-liberal societies challenges the environment. Only then will they understand that 'for those who follow nature everything is easy and straightforward, whereas for those who fight against her life is just like rowing against the stream' (Seneca 1969, 226).

References

Baldé, C.P., V. Forti, V. Gray, R. Kuehr, and P. Stegmann. 2017. *The Global E-Waste Monitor*. Bonn/Geneva/Vienna: United Nations University (UNU), International Telecommunication Union (ITU) & International Solid Waste Association (ISWA).

Becker, Gary Stanley. 2017 [1971]. *Economic Theory.* New York: Routledge.
Brodde, Kirsten. 2017. What Are Microfibers and Why Are Our Clothes Polluting the Oceans? *Greenpeace*, March 2. https://www.greenpeace.org/international/story/6956/what-are-microfibers-and-why-are-our-clothes-polluting-the-oceans/.
Campione, Chiara. 2017. Copenhagen Fashion Summit: How NOT to Make the Fashion Industry More Sustainable. *Greenpeace*, May 11. https://www.greenpeace.org/international/story/7575/copenhagen-fashion-summit-how-not-to-make-the-fashion-industry-more-sustainable/.
Casson, Louisa. 2019. 5 Reasons Why Deep Sea Mining Will Only Get Our Planet into Deep Trouble. *Greenpeace*, July 8. https://www.greenpeace.org/international/story/23164/5-reasons-to-stop-deep-sea-mining/.
Coase, Ronald. 1960. The Problem of Social Cost. *Journal of Law and Economics* 3 (October): 1–44. https://www.law.uchicago.edu/files/file/coase-problem.pdf.
Coleman, Robert. 2016. The Rich Get Richer: 50 Billionaires Got Federal Farm Subsidies. *Environmental Working Group.* https://www.ewg.org/agmag/2016/04/rich-get-richer-50-billionaires-got-federal-farm-subsidies.
Davis, Jonathan. 2019. *The Global 1980s: People, Power and Profit.* London: Routledge.
Fountain, Henry. 2019. Interior Dept. Takes Next Step Toward Sale of Drilling Leases in Arctic Refuge. *New York Times*, September 13. https://www.nytimes.com/2019/09/13/climate/anwr-oil-leases.html.
Friedman, Milton. 1982 [1962]. *Capitalism and Freedom.* Chicago: University of Chicago Press.
Friedman, M., and Friedman, R.D. 1990 [1980]. *Free to Choose: A Personal Statement.* New York: Harcourt Brace Jovanovich.
Galbraith, John Kenneth. 2001. *The Essential Galbraith.* Ed. Andrea D. Williams. Boston: Houghton Mifflin Company.
George, Henry. 2006. *Progress and Poverty: Why There Are Recessions and Poverty Amid Plenty – And What to Do About It!* Ed. Bob Drake. New York: Robert Schalkenbach Foundation.
Gerbens-Leenes, P.W., M.M. Mekonnen, and A.Y. Hoekstra. 2013. The Water Footprint of Poultry, Pork and Beef: A Comparative Study in Different Countries and Production Systems. *Water Resources and Industry* 1–2: 25–36.
Hayek, F.A. 2011 [1960]. *The Constitution of Liberty.* Chicago: The University of Chicago Press.
Heidegger, Martin. 1977. *The Question Concerning Technology and Other Essays.* Trans. William Lovitt. London: Garland Inc. Publishing.
Hribar, Carrie. 2010. *Understanding Concentrated Animal Feeding Operations and Their Impact on Communities.* Ed. Mark Schultz. Ohio: The National Association of Local Boards of Health. https://www.cdc.gov/nceh/ehs/docs/understanding_cafos_nalboh.pdf.

Jambeck, Jenna. 2018. Marine Plastics. *Ocean*, April. https://ocean.si.edu/conservation/pollution/marine-plastics.

Koehnken, L., and M. Rintoul. 2018. *Impacts of Sand Mining on Ecosystem Structure, Process and Biodiversity in Rivers.* WWF. ISBN: 978-2-940529-88-9.

Kraft, Michael E., and Norman J. Vig. 1984. Environmental Policy in the Reagan Presidency. *Political Science Quarterly* 99 (3): 415–439.

Krausmann, F., S. Gingrich, N. Eisenmenger, K.-H. Erb, H. Haber, and M. Fischer-Kowalski. 2009. Growth in Global Materials Use, GDP and Population During the 20th Century. *Ecological Economics* 68: 2696–2705.

MacDonald, James M., and William D. McBride. 2009. *The Transformation of U.S. Livestock Agriculture: Scale, Efficiency, and Risks.* A Report from the Economic Research Service. No. 43. United States Department of Agriculture.

Madhav, Sughosh Arif Ahamad, Pardeep Singh, and Pradeep Kumar Mishra. 2018. A Review of Textile Industry: Wet Processing, Environmental Impacts, and Effluent Treatment Methods. *Environmental Quality Management* 27: 31–41.

Mirsal, Ibrahim A. 2008. *Soil Pollution: Origin, Monitoring & Remediation.* Berlin: Springer.

Mises, Ludwig von. 1949. *Human Action: A Treatise on Economics.* Auburn: The Ludwig von Mises Institute.

Muthu, Subramanian Senthilkannan. 2014. *Assessing the Environmental Impact of Textiles and the Clothing Supply Chain.* Oxford: Woodhead Publishing Series in Textile.

Niinimäki, Kirsi. 2015. Consumer Behavior in the Fashion Field. In *Handbook of Sustainable Apparel Production*, ed. Subramanian Senthilkannan Muthu, 271–287. Boca Raton: Taylor & Francis Group.

Pandolfi, John M., and Jeremy B.C. Jackson. 2006. Ecological Persistence Interrupted in Caribbean Coral Reefs. *Wiley Online Library.* https://onlinelibrary.wiley.com/doi/abs/10.1111/j.1461-0248.2006.00933.x.

Parenti, Michael. 2011. Profit Pathology and Disposable Planet. *Global Research.* https://www.globalresearch.ca/profit-pathology-and-disposable-planet/23425.

———. 2015. *Profit Pathology and Other Indecencies.* New York: Routledge.

Samuelson, Paul. 2010. 'A Centrist Proclamation.' In Samuelson, Paul Anthon and William D. Nordhaus. 2010 [1948]. *Economics*, XVI-XVII. New York: The McGraw-Hill Companies, Inc.

Samuelson, Paul Anthon, and William D. Nordhaus. 2010 [1948]. *Economics.* New York: The McGraw-Hill Companies, Inc.

Schowalter, Timothy D. 2013. Insects and Sustainability of Ecosystem Services. In *Social-Environmental Sustainability Series*, ed. Chris Maser. New York: CRC Press Taylor & Francis Group.

Seneca. 1969 [65 AD]. *Letters from a Stoic.* London: Penguin Classics.

Tauseef, S.M., M. Premalatha, Tasneem Abbasi, and S.A. Abbasi. 2013. Methane Capture from Livestock Manure. *Journal of Environmental Management* 117 (15): 187–207.

Vazquez-Botello, Alfonso, Guadalupe Ponce-Velez, Luis A. Soto, and Susana Villanueva. 2020. Black Tides: Petroleum in the Ocean. In *Coastal and Deep Ocean Pollution*, ed. Andrés Hugo Arias and Sandra Elizabeth Botté, 3–40. Boca Raton: Taylor & Francis Group, LLC.

Weis, Judith S. 2020. Behavioral Responses of Marine Animals to Metals, Acidification, Hypoxia and Noise Pollution. In *Coastal and Deep Ocean Pollution*, ed. Andrés Hugo Arias and Sandra Elizabeth Botté, 153–183. Boca Raton: Taylor & Francis Group.

Weiss, Frederik T., Marianne Leuzinger, Christian Zurbrügg, and Rik I.L. Eggen. 2016. *Chemical Pollution in Low- and Middle-Income Countries*. Dübendorf: Swiss Federal Institute of Aquatic Science and Technology. https://www.eawag.ch/fileadmin/Domain1/Abteilungen/sandec/publikationen/Chemical_Pollution/ChemPoll-LAMICS_Chapter5.pdf.

CHAPTER 8

The Direction of Technological Innovation in the Public and Private Sectors

Throughout history, different societies had their own distinct goals and objectives for science that were largely determined by 'the political authority in power,' which resulted in the emergence of specific methods and approaches to conducting scientific research and achieving technological progress (Barber 1953, 4). In fact, 'there was a time when it was not technology alone that bore the name techne. Once that revealing that brings forth truth into the splendor of radiant appearing also was called techne. Once there was a time when the bringing-forth of the true into the beautiful was called techne. And the poiesis of the fine arts also was called techne' (Heidegger 1977, 34). In recent years, technological innovation has assumed a much more prominent role in people's lives, including in their daily habits, work, hobbies, and goals, as well as in their relationships with each other and with nature. It also plays a major role in helping corporations maximize their profits and attain greater market share.

Since the rise of neo-liberalism, corporations have played an increasingly significant role in funding scientific research and innovation projects. In fact, many scientists and engineers have been hired by corporations to conduct research and development in order to generate technological innovations for the direct benefit of their employers. This can include developing more effective methods for dominating and exploiting nature (i.e., resource extraction), uncovering process innovations to facilitate efficiency gains in production, and creating new and diverse products and services with novel features for people to consume.

B. Filip, *The Rise of Neo-liberalism and the Decline of Freedom*,
Palgrave Insights into Apocalypse Economics,
https://doi.org/10.1007/978-3-030-61623-6_8

Naturally, corporations place greater value on scientific research and innovation that can help them move to, or remain at, the forefront of global competition. Accordingly, significant resources and effort are devoted to rapidly increasing the quantity, and expanding the variety, of new and improved products available for consumption, which has mistakenly been interpreted as scientific progress. This has resulted in innumerable technological innovations being produced during the last four decades that have amounted to little more than slight upgrades or improvements over previous techniques and products for the purpose of facilitating mass consumption to earn capitalist gains.

Although innovation has contributed to unprecedented economic growth and improvements to living standards since the rise of neo-liberalism, with significant advances in areas like electronics, computation, and communications, the business-oriented direction of contemporary science has also entailed many destructive consequences for human health and the environment. This will likely continue going forward, as states have largely removed themselves from direct involvement in supporting and directing science and research in favour of increasingly enacting policies designed to foster and encourage private sector innovation and technological progress without properly addressing the negative outcomes of such activities.

This chapter explains how neo-liberalism has been playing a significant role in changing the course and direction of scientific research and technological progress. For decades, proponents of free-market economics have explained that economic growth, productivity, and living standards are positively correlated with technological innovation. Moreover, they have argued that the private sector can do a much better job of accelerating technological innovation than the public sector. Accordingly, neo-liberal reforms have helped the private sector gain considerable control over the direction and objectives of science and technological innovation since the 1980s, while limiting the role of governments in these areas. However, this expanded role for the private sector has restricted the freedom of scientists to choose their research areas and the projects they would like to work on. More precisely, scientists working in the private sector will only be able to conduct research with the potential to eventually bring tangible benefits for their employers. The influence of the private sector has also contributed to making society enormously dependent on technology and innovation, which in turn, has played an important role facilitating the onset of an impending environmental apocalypse.

8.1 Technological Innovation Under the Direction of the Public and Private Sectors

Governments, corporations and consumers have been highly supportive of accelerating technological innovation, which is associated with the advancement and progress of society. However, while scientific progress and technological innovations have undoubtedly improved people's lives in areas like health, communication, computation, and convenience, thereby raising living standards, the costs associated with rapid improvements to existing technologies and the development of new ones are very high. Covering these costs often requires large scale investments in research and innovation projects, which can be obtained from a variety of sources, including private businesses, governments, individual researchers, and various institutions and organizations.

Prior to the rise of neo-liberalism, the majority of scientific research and innovation projects were supported and funded by states. In fact, science played an important role in the public discourse in the first half of the twentieth century, as its goal was to broadly serve the public good or interest. In the United States, for example, before the 1950s, scientific research was almost exclusively performed by 'Government scientists,' and 'the achievements of Government science in both pure and applied fields have been of tremendous value to the American people "both in scientific advancement and in monetary terms"' (Barber 1953, 171). Under such circumstances, scientists were free from corporate influence, which meant they could engage in 'doing science to solve science's own questions, solving science's own unsolved puzzles. In this way science progressed, and was associated with the liberal "progressive" mindset' (Weintraub 2007, 272). Consequently, scientific advancement and progress became matters of public interest, and scientists were regarded as 'members of a public-policy priesthood who might offer expertise' in science and various other areas of life (Weintraub 2007, 270).

The state continued to play a vital role in directing and supporting scientific research and innovation in the US during the postwar period. The fact that the state was so important for the advancement of science meant that it was necessary to have 'a public sufficiently literate about science, and identified with science's own objectives, so that they would continue to provide scientists with access to public money for scientific research' (Weintraub 2007, 269, 270). The main impetus for 'these kinds of attempts to change the public mindset—to educate the public to the needs for public resources for scientific research—came from those who were connected to the scientific cum military establishment in WWII, and to the emergent Cold War anti-communist establishment' (Weintraub 2007, 269, 270). Samuelson and Nordhaus (2010, 311–312) underscored the important role that the state played in advancing technological progress in the past when they stated:

> Government support gave a powerful start to the electronics industries. The development of the transistor by Bell Labs, for example, was partially funded by the U.S. military, anxious for better radar and communications. Today's computer and airplane industries were boosted in their early years by strong government support. The Internet was developed by the Department of Defense to create a network that would continue to function in the event of nuclear war.

Despite the fact that the state played a major role in the advancement of science for many decades, neo-liberal economists have consistently argued that political factors and government authority represented threats to scientific progress. For example, Hayek (2011, 490) opposed extensive state involvement in scientific research on the basis that 'the government should not become the sole dispenser of knowledge, with the power of deciding what the individual should and should not know.' He believed that state control over the planning and spread of scientific research and knowledge would cause harm by 'preventing the growth of more effective forms of voluntary effort' (Hayek 2011, 490). Instead, he argued that only by ensuring freedom in the areas of knowledge and education would it be possible for 'countries to develop a viable civilization of their own, capable of making a distinct contribution to the needs of mankind' (Hayek 2011, 489).

Since the 1980s, neo-liberal economists have given considerable support to the idea of cutting publicly-funded scientific research projects, as they were of the view that states inhibited the capacity of innovation to flourish and stifled the freedom of scientists. Accordingly, they maintained that technological innovation and science belonged in the domain of the private sector. More specifically, neo-liberals were of the view that the goals and direction of scientific research and technological progress would be more reactive to market forces. As such, they strongly encouraged scientists to work for the commercial pursuits of private businesses.

In the UK, Margaret Thatcher's administration played a major role in changing the direction of scientific research and technological progress. Thatcherism considered 'science and technology to be central to economic performance, and that its new institutional structures and instruments should improve the effectiveness of the contribution of science and technology to economic performance' (Edgerton and Hughes 1989, 425). More precisely, the Thatcher administration was highly supportive of the idea of transferring control over technological innovation to the private sector while reducing the influence of the public sector. Although her government may have been opposed to an active state role in the development and advancement of science and technology, it had no issue with channeling public funds to support research and development within the private sector, or providing it with access to government laboratories and other facilities. In other words, the Thatcher government supported and funded various technological and innovation research projects within the private sector, in order to improve 'the efficiency, competitiveness and innovative capacity' of the nation (Edgerton and Hughes 1989, 425).

In the United States, Thatcher's ideological equivalent, President Ronald Reagan, also defended the practice of using state support to facilitate technological innovation conducted within the private sector. His administration strongly backed pure scientific research to 'strengthen national defense' and contribute to 'economic growth by making the nation more competitive in a high technology world.'[1] However, when it came to the social sciences, Reagan adhered to the view that 'federal support should be supplanted by greater private sector funding.'[2] Consequently, his 'administration took drastic budgetary measures in non defense areas to reduce the federal deficit while at the same time remove the government from activities it thought more appropriately belonged to other sectors.'[3] To be more precise, 'between 1980 and 1982 the National Science Foundation's budget for social and behavioral research dropped

[1] The National Science Foundation. 1994. A Brief History. https://www.nsf.gov/about/history/nsf50/nsf8816.jsp.

[2] The National Science Foundation. 1994. A Brief History. https://www.nsf.gov/about/history/nsf50/nsf8816.jsp.

[3] The National Science Foundation. 1994. A Brief History. https://www.nsf.gov/about/history/nsf50/nsf8816.jsp.

from $47.9 million to $28.9 million. Meanwhile, engineers, physicists, chemists and other "hard science" researchers are eagerly filling out the reams of forms that could get them a chunk of the $150 million that the Department of Defense will spend over the next five years to help universities buy equipment for scientific research' (Saiter 1982). These deep cuts in funding for the social sciences were attributed to the fact that 'the administration did not consider social science as an area that supported the long-term economic health of the nation' (Boyd 1987).

Friedman (1981) was highly supportive of President Reagan's cuts to National Science Foundation (NSF) grants for allocation within the social sciences. In fact, he even went so far as to call for the abolition of the NSF altogether, arguing that the agency has 'done harm to the progress' of science, because it obstructed the freedom of scientists (Friedman 1981, 99). More broadly, he was opposed to 'the ethical justification for extracting funds from the taxpayer to subsidize scientific research' in the public sector that was intended to achieve the common good of the nation (Friedman 1981, 99). Instead, he advocated for private funding, as it would to promote innovation and freedom in science.

During his presidency, Reagan stated that, in the past, '"roadblocks" existed between scientific research efforts in Government and those in the commercial world' (Boyd 1987). He promised to rectify this impasse between the public and private sectors in the US when it came to advancing science and innovation, which would include taking steps to 'encourage scientists working in Federal laboratories to patent, license and commercialize their research' (Boyd 1987). Eventually, both the Reagan and Thatcher administrations came to operate under the premise that the best approach to improving the economic performances and competitiveness of their respective nations was to advance technological innovation and scientific research through light regulation in combination with providing the private sector with greater access to state funding and government research facilities. However, that approach would necessitate that cuts be made to public scientific research. Furthermore, by channelling large sums of public funds to private sector R&D projects, both the Reagan and Thatcher administrations directly contributed to advancing the profits and interests of the corporations performing that research. Although, on the surface, publicly funding the private sector might appear to be a contradiction within the free-market economy, neo-liberals would argue that allocating significant portions of the government budget to technological innovation on the part of the private sector stimulates economic growth and productivity, which ultimately contributes to the proper functioning of the free-market system.

The changes to state science policy instituted during the Reagan-Thatcher Era led to corporations effectively gaining control over government funding for scientific research and the scientific community in general, which were extremely important factors in terms of altering the direction of scientific research and technological innovation in both countries. More specifically, since coming under the control of the private sector, technological innovation has become a highly market-oriented instrument for profit making. Consequently, the work of engineers and scientists has become increasingly focused on generating fast paced innovations and introducing new products and services to the market. Companies in a variety of industries recognized the importance of technological innovation and research and development for maximizing profits and attaining greater market share, and as such, have invested billions of dollars in recent decades to improve their existing products and services and create new ones. Prominent examples include e-commerce and digital streaming companies like Amazon, auto producers like Volkswagen, electronics companies such as Samsung, technology companies like Microsoft and Apple, and pharmaceutical companies like Johnson & Johnson.

Before the rise of neo-liberalism, 'publicly funded science operated' fairly independently (Weintraub 2007, 272). However, since neo-liberalism came to prominence, generating economic growth and productivity have become the driving factors of science. In other words, neo-liberalism has resulted in the work of talented scientists and researchers being motivated by business interests, which led to a greater focus on product and process innovations as opposed to genuine scientific progress and advancement. Even though private companies and enterprises might claim that they care about the advancement of science, this is only true when they stand to benefit them financially.

To maximize their profits, private businesses push the pace of innovation in order to release new products into the market as quickly and frequently as possible, particularly in the case of technology goods. However, by engaging in this process of rapid technological innovation, private businesses have induced 'the rational transformation of the human and natural environment,' in ways that could be described as aggressive and offensive, because their 'thoughts and actions were designed for mastering objects' (Marcuse 1998, 109). In other words, technological innovations have enabled the corporate world to achieve its capitals ends by gaining exploitive and aggressive destructive dominance over nature. To be more specific, many scientists working in the private sector have focused their efforts on developing technological innovations to help employers challenge, exploit and control nature, particularly its natural resources, in order to achieve continuous and boundless economic growth. This power achieved by the corporate world has provided the capitalist mindset with 'the pure concepts as well as the instrumentalities for the ever-more-effective domination of man by man through the domination of nature' (Marcuse 2007, 162).

Scientific research has clearly undergone profound changes on a global scale on account of the rise of neo-liberalism, which has put great emphasis on developing technological innovations, while largely ignoring science and research that could contribute to achieving genuine progress for humanity. Scientists and engineers who work for private enterprises have little opportunity to work on purely scientific research, nor are they able to significantly influence or disapprove of the direction of the innovation being conducted by their employers based on their own values, or a desire to serve the interests of humanity. In other words, private businesses rarely grant their scientists any autonomy in terms of selecting their areas of research, because they will not necessarily align with the goals of management. Accordingly, scientific research has mainly focused on developing commercial applications to benefit the interests of the private sector, whereas serving the common or public good has become largely irrelevant, particularly in instances where the endeavour will not yield a significant financial payoff. Today, technological innovation has essentially become a tool for companies to use in order to gain some kind of competitive advantage over their rivals, particularly when R&D leads to the acquisition of intellectual property rights (e.g., patents, copyrights, trademarks etc.). However, this situation harms the whole field of science by inhibiting its progress, because competition between enterprises often requires secrecy, especially in the case of intellectual property rights, which prevents scientists from sharing their work and openly consulting with their peers in the broader scientific community.

Given that contemporary technological innovation is largely driven by deliberate efforts to produce commodities at a lower cost, faster pace, and greater volume, business-oriented scientific research projects are unlikely to motivate the imaginations, creativity, and intellectual freedom of scientists. Additionally, scientists who do not support the ambitions of the corporate world could find themselves excluded from participating in technological innovation, given that they might face difficultly being recruited in the private sector where the majority of the opportunities to conduct scientific research are concentrated. That would suggest that the corporate world represents a real threat to the freedom of science and scientific research, as those scientists who resist or diverge from the scientific aspirations of the private sector are not free to pursue their own research interests, because they are unlikely to receive funding. To have real scientific progress, scientists must have some measure of control over the goals and direction of their own research.

In addition to significantly changing the direction of scientific research, the rise of neo-liberalism also brought with it higher levels of private sector funding for universities and their research agendas. This restricts the freedom and autonomy of university scientists and researchers, who may be forced to limit themselves to working on certain topics with the potential to attract financial support from the private sector. They are also likely to face pressure from the university and faculty administrations to orient their research to suit the needs of private sector donors that provide much needed funding. The advancement of science is endangered when scientific work is evaluated according to the economic ambitions of the corporate world, which will unabashedly leverage its financial support to influence or control the science and research being conducted at universities.

Before the rise of neo-liberalism, public funding for universities was rarely used to influence the research topics or agendas at the schools, because governments were committed to the common good and well-being of their citizens as opposed to commercial interests. Their priority was to provide students with a quality education, which is better served by an academic environment that encourages creativity, imagination and pure science. In the United States, the government provided most of the funding and facilities used for scientific research from the 1940s up until the 1980s. During that period, scientists and academics were not constrained by a dependency on private funding, and as such, enjoyed considerable freedom and autonomy in the research they conducted. In fact, many of the 'great achievements of numerous US university and government laboratories during and after World War II were conducted under conditions of central federal planning and public funding' (Parenti 2015, 141).

The direction that science has taken under the guidance of neo-liberalism raises considerable doubts about whether a free-market system is capable of providing the right conditions for scientific and technological progress. Despite the fact that scientists made significant contributions to the advancement of science with public support, people in western societies have been conditioned to believe that centrally designed systems, such as socialism and communism, were incapable of providing an environment that was conducive to stimulating scientific progress. In reality, history has shown that scientific progress has not been completely stifled in countries governed by central planning. For example, the development and advancement of science was a national priority for the Soviet Union, and the state provided considerable supported for scientific research, including 'the historical and social studies of science' (Werskey 2007, 404). In fact, the Soviet Union became 'the most enthusiastic supporter of science and technology of all contemporary governments' during Cold War Era (Werskey 2007, 404). The commitment of Soviet regime to scientific socialism 'extended far beyond massive increases in its technical—scientific workers, research facilities, and heavy industry. It was also the first country to institutionalize what we would now call STS [Science and Technology Studies] by establishing a dedicated research centre in the history of science and technology' (Werskey 2007, 404). As such, the country was able to achieve many advances in science for the well-being of humanity, while also developing a number of advanced technologies that rivaled those of the United States.

Regardless, neo-liberals constantly advocate for state controls and government regulations on technological innovation to be avoided as much as possible, because they handicap progress in a number of ways, including by raising costs of compliance and extending the approval process, which can lead to certain investments no longer being worthwhile. As a result, access to new technologies is delayed for both consumers and businesses, which ultimately hinders productivity and economic growth. On this basis, neo-liberals argue that state controls and regulations discourage technological innovation, which has the potential to trigger economic stagnation and lower living standards. In fact, Samuelson and Nordhaus (2010, 505) stated that:

> Many sectors of the Soviet Union under central planning saw technological stagnation because of the heavy hand of state regulation, lack of profit motivation, an inefficient pricing mechanism, and widespread corruption.

Even though Samuelson and Nordhaus (2010, 511) were critical of central planning in the Soviet Union, they recognized that, without 'government and not-for-profit support, basic research in mathematics, the natural sciences, and the social sciences would wither away.' To the contrary, many other neo-liberals are quick to criticize the role that the state played in directing science and scientific research under centrally planned systems without seemingly recognizing, or acknowledging, that corporations and the business classes essentially do the same thing in capitalist societies on account of the changes brought forth by neo-liberalism. That is to say, scientific research conducted in the free-market system is the domain of the business classes, which deliberately determine and control the goals and objectives innovation and technological development. However, instead of trying to benefit society as whole, they seek to advance their commercial interests by focusing scientific research on the development of more efficient production methods and the creation of new and improved products and services. These rich and powerful business classes fund the research of 'elite scientists,' while 'the rest of the world safely ensconced in bone ignorance' with respect to all disciplines of the sciences (Mirowski 2011, 326). In other words, the masses are kept in the dark about the direction of scientific research by 'corporations, think tanks, and other market actors' (Mirowski 2011, 327). As a result, science serves the interests of the business classes, as they earn profits 'from the knowledge' that the masses do not possess (Mirowski 2011, 327).

By exerting so much influence over the direction of science and research agendas, large corporations have limited the freedom of scientists and prevented the scientific spirit from flourishing. For example, by restricting their financial support to research aimed at market-oriented technological innovations, corporations have effectively suppressed the freedom of science by inhibiting creativity, imagination and inquisitiveness, which are important factors in the organic advancement of any discipline of science. Unfortunately, that means the influence of the corporate world and neo-liberalism have led to the prevalence of scientific research and technological innovations that are not conducive to addressing real-world problems that could genuinely benefit humanity. In order to effectively address many of the contemporary challenges facing societies, the environment, and humanity, the direction of science will need to be freed from its focus on commercial ends and interests. That means many of the changes to science facilitated by decades of neo-liberalism will need to be undone and reversed to a great extent.

8.2 Technological Innovation and Economic Growth

The origins of neo-liberal growth theory, which states that the achievement of economic growth requires technological innovation, can be traced back to American economist Robert Solow (1924–), who published two key papers on the topic: 'A contribution to the theory of economic growth,' (1956) and 'Technical change and the aggregate production function' (1957). In particular, he developed the Solow Growth Model, which shows that technological innovation increases economic growth over time by facilitating the growth of a number of economic variables, including output per worker and capital stock per worker. In other words, technological innovation increases the productivity of both capital and labor in long run, which raises the national income. Solow's contributions to the theory of economic growth led to him being awarded the Nobel Prize in Economic Sciences in 1987.

Samuelson and Nordhaus (2010, 508) stated that Solow's growth model 'serves as the basic tool for understanding the growth process in advanced countries and has been applied in empirical studies of the sources of economic growth.' Based on this neoclassical model of growth, if there no technological change, then within time 'the capital-labor ratio will stop rising. In the long run, the economy will enter a steady state in which capital deepening ceases, real wages stop growing, and capital returns and real interest rates are constant' (Samuelson and Nordhaus 2010, 510). Eventually, a lack of technological innovation would cause the standard of living to stop improving.

Similarly, Simon Smith Kuznets (1901–1985) (1973, 247), an American economist and statistician who was awarded the 1971 Nobel Memorial Prize in Economic Science, underscored the point that a nation's economic growth was based on 'advancing technology' and 'institutional and ideological adjustments.' He also emphasized that the 'mass application of technological innovations' was 'closely connected with the further progress of science, in its turn the basis for additional advance in technology' (Kuznets 1973, 250). Furthermore, 'mass-uses of technical innovations' also had a positive effect on economic growth (Kuznets 1973, 250). However, contrary to Solow, Kuznets (1955, 28) believed that understanding economic growth required getting more 'familiar with findings in those related social disciplines that can help us understand population growth patterns, the nature and forces in technological change, the factors that determine the characteristics and trends in political institutions, and generally patterns of behavior of human beings-partly as a biological species, partly as social animals.' He also proposed 'a shift from market economics to political and social economy' in order to gain a better comprehension of economic growth (Kuznets 1955, 28). Despite the fact that Kuznets' views on the technological innovation and economic growth was ground breaking, he is mainly known for the Kuznets curve.

Solow's theoretical model had a significant impact on economic policy, as both Thatcherism and Reaganism adopted his view that technological innovation was the engine of long-term economic growth and productivity. Accordingly, both administrations instituted reforms to reduce the state role in technological innovation, and make it largely fall within the purview of private industry. This has resulted in many specialists, free-market thinktanks, and various institutions and organisations conducting an abundance of research to determine how to advance technological innovation in a way that facilitates rapid economic and productivity growth for the nation.

Since the rise of neo-liberalism, enterprises have also been thoroughly convinced that technological innovation is the motor of productivity and economic growth. Consequently, many companies have allocated significant funds to research and development in order to facilitate novel product and process innovations. More specifically, corporations attempt to enhance their competitiveness by developing technological innovations that will allow them to offer lower prices or better quality products and services. Alternatively, they can also become more competitive relative to their peers by developing innovations that enable them to produce lower quality products at lower prices in much greater numbers, thereby increasing total productivity. The faster the introduction of a new commodity with the latest technologies into the market, the greater the possibility of gaining a significant advantage over competitors. Since commercial interests motivate the rapid pace of innovation for mass production and consumption, the latest versions of technological products or gadgets are rarely vastly superior to their previous iterations; rather, they are marketed based on new features that represent relatively minor improvements over the last model, which are often meaningless to the overall operation of the product. Galbraith (2001, 149) was of the view that rapid technological innovation was intended to satisfy the capitalistic tendencies of corporations, as he explained:

> Products are changed not to make them better but to take advantage of the belief that what is different is better. There is a high failure rate in engineering because its preoccupation is not with what is good but with what can be sold.

That means science and scientific research have essentially become mechanisms that corporations can employ in order to satisfy their capitalist ends and objectives. Furthermore, rapid technological innovation has played a crucial role in the prevalence of mass consumption by expanding the range of people's desires and wants for the new products they provide, leading to western homes and workplaces becoming completely inundated with gadgets and devices that boasted the latest features at some point in time. It is now the norm for people to buy the latest version of a particular device and discard the previous model even though it is still in good working condition, and the actual improvements or upgrades are relatively inconsequential. This kind of turnover is particularly rapid in the case of electronic products and devices, such as mobile phones, computers, tablets, and cameras, which have a tendency to become obsolete in a relatively short time span.

Since the rise of neo-liberalism, cycles of technological innovation, production, and consumption have all been considerably accelerated in the free-market system. However, while the rapid development and creation of new and more advanced goods might increase economic growth, they make limited contributions to advancing science or civilisation. They also entail high environmental costs, as mass production and wasteful consumption plays a major role in polluting the environment and depleting natural resources. In order to maximize profits, the corporate world has been operating as though all of the world's resources need to be discovered and exploited to the fullest extent possible in order to provide the goods required to meet the ever-expanding demands of mass consumption. Accordingly, new technologies have facilitated the more thorough and rapid exploitation of certain resources, while enabling access to others that were previously unobtainable.

To satisfy mass consumption, producers focus on introducing new and better goods that are infused with the latest technologies. Meanwhile, people have come to believe that the freedom to choose and consume these kinds of goods has provided them with *Eudaemonia* and brought meaning to their lives. Today, this union of the freedom to choose and servitude to mass consumption has become a vehicle for technological innovation. People need to be made to understand that while their latest technological gadget has 'a value in use' and 'is capable of satisfying human wants,' it is ultimately a 'product of human labour,' which 'changes the forms of the materials furnished by Nature' (Marx 2015, 47). When people attach so much value and devote so much attention to possessing the latest technology products, they completely ignore or neglect the negative consequences associated with producing them in their final form, including environmental damages and the poor working conditions faced by miners and manufacturing employees in developing countries. Marx labelled this relationship between people and their consumption products as 'fetishism of commodities' (Marx 2015, 47, 48). Similarly, it could be argued that corporations have a form of 'fetishism' of technological innovation, while consumers are suffering from a 'fetishism' of technological devices, as both neglect the destructive outcomes of the technological innovation of commodities. In the end, it appears that the entire planet has become a victim of 'fetishism' of technological innovation.

Instead of focusing on scientific advancement and progress for the well-being of humanity, such as combatting climate change or restoring the ecological balance of the planet, a great deal of investment is devoted to technological innovation for the development and creation of better weapons and war capabilities in order to kill more efficiently. In the United States, the defense industry accounted for more than 44% of total federal research and development expenditures in 2017 (National Science Board: Science & Engineering Indicators, 2020, 49). This devotion to research and technological innovation has helped keep American companies among to top weapons manufacturers and exporters in the world. 'With 42 companies listed in 2017, companies based in the United States continued to dominate the Top 100 in 2017. Taken together, the arms sales of US companies grew by 2.0 per cent in 2017, to $226.6 billion, which accounted for 57 per cent of total Top 100 arms sales' ($398.2 billion).[4] Parenti (2015, 141) pointed out that 'the entire defense industry and Pentagon arsenal is publicly funded and directed,' and that the government manages to find billions in 'public funds for killing people but not enough for housing and feeding people.'

[4] Stockholm International Peace Research Institute. 2018. 'Global arms industry: US companies dominate the Top 100; Russian arms industry moves to second place.' https://www.sipri.org/media/press-release/2018/global-arms-industry-us-companies-dominate-top-100-russian-arms-industry-moves-second-place.

Corporations would willingly support any technological innovations with the potential to earn them a profit, regardless of their adverse impacts on human health, other species, or the environment. If economics had the capacity to appreciate and value the well-being of humanity and the future of the earth, then the cost of these adverse impacts would have been included among the costs of production. That is to say, the costs of these destructive impacts should be internalized by the producers and taken into consideration before production begins, as is often the case with any project where investors calculate all of the expenses before making an investment decision. Already in 1973, Karl Gunnar Myrdal (1898–1987), a left-wing socialist economist from Sweden who was awarded a co–Nobel Prize in Economic Sciences in 1974 (in addition to Hayek), was expressing concerns about the destructive outcomes of fast innovation on human health and nature. In particular, he was hoping that there would be 'more effective controls of all sorts of novel chemical and biotic concoctions that for some time have increasingly gone into the supplies offered by pharmacies and been used in food production, as cosmetics or to improve taste,' even though only 'a minor fraction' of these new products were 'reliably tested for possible toxicity' (Myrdal 1973, 109). He emphasized the point that 'restrictive controls do not cause many real sacrifices and costs on the part of the consumers, who might even soon learn that they are better off with a less variegated supply of drugs, fancy foods,' etc. (Myrdal 1973, 109). The growing likelihood of an environmental apocalypse is testimony to the fact that that Myrdal's important advice from almost half a century ago have not been taken seriously by governments, business classes, or the general population.

Myrdal was not the first prominent figure to express his concerns and try to warn people about the adverse impacts of technological innovation. In the first half of the twentieth century, there was growing awareness of the destructive outcomes associated with technological innovations, and 'nowhere has this increased concern been more manifest than among the scientists themselves' (Barber 1953, 225). Before and after the Second World War, a number of scientists advocated for 'social responsibility for the consequences of their discoveries and inventions' (Barber 1953, 225). They wanted scientists and researchers to assume 'total responsibility for the social consequences of science' and make efforts to 'prevent some of the most abhorred ones' (Barber 1953, 225). For example, Norbert Wiener (1894–1964), 'the famous mathematician of M.I.T.' who published many books on the subjects of mathematics and engineering, 'publicly announced his intention not to publish any future work "which may do damage in the hands of irresponsible militarists"' (Barber 1953, 226). Wiener (1989, XXVII) strongly believed that 'the interchange of ideas which is one of the great traditions of science must of course receive certain limitations when the scientist becomes an arbiter of life and death.' His goal was to minimize the possibility that some kind of special interest groups could exploit the work of scientists to harm civilization. Wiener's (1989, XXVII) motivations were clearly evident when he stated:

> The experience of the scientists who have worked on the atomic bomb has indicated that in any investigation of this kind the scientist ends by putting unlimited powers in the hands of the people whom he is least inclined to trust with their use.

Unfortunately, many of the scientists who refused to serve as instruments for the destructive outcomes of the military and corporate activities were criticized for their principled stances. In the case of Wiener, a number of his scientific colleagues were 'offended or embarrassed' by his views, 'especially by his open refusal to engage in any more work related to the military' (Heims 1989, XII). Consequently, they regarded him as 'an eccentric at best and certainly not to be taken seriously except in his undeniably brilliant, strictly mathematical, researches' (Heims 1989, XII). Apparently, they preferred the views of Cambridge mathematician and 'author of A Mathematician's Apology,' G.H. Hardy (1877–1947), who suggested that mathematics is a 'harmless and innocent occupation,' and 'real mathematics has no effects on war' (Heims 1989, XI). Conversely, Albert Einstein viewed Wiener's 'attitude towards the military as exemplary' (Heims 1989, XII).

8.3 Conclusion

According to Rousseau (1921, 23), 'the science which instructs and the medicine which heals' are 'excellent, but the science which misleads' is 'evil.' Unfortunately, corporations and proponents of neo-liberalism have been using their considerable influence to direct scientific research and innovation towards goals and objectives that Rousseau would categorize under the latter. In other words, many contemporary technological innovations do not address the pressing social, economic, health and environmental issues of our time. In fact, scientific research has become an instrument by which corporations attempt to exert dominance over nature, particularly its various resources, which has generated considerable irreversible damage, or evils. This obsession with domination has separated science from its original purpose of understanding of natural phenomena, healing humanity and helping it to progress. Moreover, this divergence could be described as a folly of contemporary innovation, which has facilitated the prevalence of unfreedom in scientific research.

Neo-liberals have been operating under the false premise that the rapid pace of technological innovation would eventually enable people to gain extensive control over nature. This way of thinking has led corporations to function and conduct their business activities as though they were somehow separate or independent from the natural environment, which dramatically altered the way that the world's resources were being exploited. More specifically, corporations have used technological advances to accelerate their exploitation of natural resources to the point of raising concerns about depletion. This is not particularly surprising, given that neo-liberals argue that the failures and damages associated with technological progress are simply part of the learning experience, which can be corrected later. Furthermore, they claim that attempting to curtail or prevent scientific research on account of its negative impacts would constitute an infringement upon freedom.

Technological innovation has resulted in 'the great rationalization of the unfreedom of man' (Marcuse 2007, 162). One of the main outcomes of the private sector gaining considerable influence over the direction of scientific research and innovation was that corporations focused much of their R&D efforts on the wasteful and destructive practice of regularly flooding the market with large quantities of slightly improved items or gadgets to satisfy mass consumption. In other words, any upgrades or new features were largely intended to differentiate these commodities from the previous version/model in order to sell them, not to genuinely enhance their quality so that they last longer, or tangibly improve people's lives. With so much reliance on technological gadgets, devices, and various other advanced goods and services in everyday social and economic life, it is impossible to be free when living one's own life. This unfreedom is not an outcome of political oppression or coercion; rather, it is the product of 'submission to the technical apparatus which enlarges the comforts of life and increases the productivity of labor' (Marcuse 2007, 162). Contemporary technological innovation promotes and maintains the legitimacy of domination, as opposed to enabling people to be free. In a sense, technological innovation has been directing humanity towards the 'road to serfdom.'

Instead of helping to find solutions for the foremost challenges facing nature and humanity, sciences in the era of neo-liberalism has been largely focused on advancing the financial interests of the private sector by developing product and process innovations. This has included discovering more effective ways of exploiting natural resources, developing more efficient methods of production, and generating rapid product innovations to capture and retain the interest of consumers, particularly in the case of technological products and gadgets. Consequently, science and innovation have become extremely detrimental to the environment, not only by directly challenging nature to better exploit its natural resources, but also by facilitating the mass consumption of technological innovations, which has led to cell phones, laptops, tablets, televisions, and various other tech products piling up in landfills, where toxic chemicals eventually leach out of them, enter the surrounding environment, and gradually make their way to various ecosystems. In effect, scientific research under the direction of corporations has allowed human actions to become more destructive than at any other point in history. That would mean the most thorough destruction of the earth has been committed by mankind at its highest peak of technological innovation.

Science is far too important to be left up to corporations to control and manage for the benefit of their narrow and short-sighted objectives. More specifically, given that it may take a major scientific breakthrough to save the planet from the potentially devastating impacts of climate change, the focus and direction of scientific research cannot be limited by corporate interests or neo-liberal ideology, or any other ideology for that matter. Present circumstances suggest that there is an urgency to change the direction of scientific research going forward, so that it has greater orientation towards addressing the pressing needs of humanity and the planet, which will likely require more openness and collaboration on the part of scientists, and some level of central planning, interference, and support on the part of the state.

References

Barber, Bernard. 1953. *Science and the Social Order*. London: George Allen & Unwin Ltd.

Boyd, Gerald M. 1987. Reagan Hails U.S. Technology's Role. *New York Times*.

Edgerton, D.E.H., and K.S. Hughes. 1989. The Poverty of Science: A Critical Analysis of Scientific and Industrial Policy Under Mrs Thatcher. *Public Administration* 67: 419–433.

Friedman, Milton. 1981. An Open Letter on Grants. *The Newsweek/Daily Beast Company LLC*, 18 May. No. 99.

Galbraith, John Kenneth. 2001. *The Essential Galbraith*. Edited by Andrea D. Williams. Boston: Houghton Mifflin Company.

Hayek, F.A. 2011 [1960]. *The Constitution of Liberty*. Chicago: University of Chicago Press.

Heidegger, Martin. 1977. *The Question Concerning Technology and Other Essays*. Trans. William Lovitt. London: Garland Inc. Publishing.

Heims, Steve J. 1989 [1950]. Introduction. Ed. Norbert Wiener. *The Human Use of Human Beings: Cybernetics and Society*. London: Free Association Books.

Kuznets, Simon. 1955. Economic Growth and Income Inequality. *The American Economic Review* 45 (1): 1–28.

———. 1973. Modern Economic Growth: Findings and Reflections. *The American Economic Review* 63 (3): 247–258.

Marcuse, Herbert. 1998 [1956]. *Eros and Civilisation: A Philosophical Inquiry into Freud*. Abingdon: Roudledge.

Marcuse, H. 2007. *The One-Dimensional Man: Studies in the Ideology of Advanced Industrial Society*. London: Routledge.

Marx, Karl. 2015 [1867]. *Capital. A Critique of Political Economy. Volume I. Book One: The Process of Production of Capital*. Moscow: Progress Publishers. https://www.marxists.org/archive/marx/works/download/pdf/Capital-Volume-I.pdf.

Mirowski, Philip. 2011. *Science-Mart: Privatizing American Science*. Harvard University Press.

Myrdal, Karl Gunnar. 1973. Economics of an Improved Environment. *World Development* 1 (1–2): 102–114.

National Science Board: Science & Engineering Indicators. 2020. *Research and Development: U.S. Trends and International Comparisons*. NSB-2020-3, January 15, 2020

Parenti, Michael. 2015. *Profit Pathology and Other Indecencies*. New York: Routledge.

Rousseau, Jean-Jacques. 1921 [1762]. *Emile, or Education*. Trans. Barbara Foxley. London and Toronto: J.M.Dent and Sons. http://oll.libertyfund.org/title/2256.

Saiter, Susan. 1982. The Reagan Effect: Natural Scientists Gain, Social Scientists Lose. *The New York Times*. https://www.nytimes.com/1982/11/14/education/the-reagan-effect-natural-scientists-gain-social-scientists-lose.html.

Samuelson, Paul Anthon, and William D. Nordhaus. 2010 [1948]. *Economics*. New York: The McGraw-Hill Companies, Inc.

Solow, Robert. 1956. A Contribution to the theory of economic growth. *Quarterly Journal of Economics*. 70: 65–94

———. 1957. Technical Change and the Aggregate Production Function. *Review of Economics and Statistics*. 39: 312–320.

Weintraub, E.Roy. 2007. Economic Science Wars. *Journal of the History of Economic Thought* 29 (3): 267–282.

Werskey, Gary. 2007. The Marxist Critique of Capitalist Science: A History in Three Movements? *Science as Culture*. 16 (4): 397–461.

Wiener, Norbert. 1989 [1950]. *The Human Use of Human Beings: Cybernetics and Society*. London: Free Association Books.

CHAPTER 9

The Decline of Labor Unions and Protection of Employees Under Neo-Liberalism

Labour movements emerged during the Industrial Revolution (1760–1840), when rapid economic expansion was guided by laissez-faire capitalism. During this period, there were virtually no state regulations in place to protect workers against unbridled capitalist exploitation on the part by their employers. Accordingly, labour unions stepped in to offer workers some modicum of protection against mistreatment and terrible conditions at their places of employment, and they have continued to look after the well-being of their members ever since. However, they faced considerable obstacles in their quest for legitimacy as, in the beginning of the nineteenth century, union members were 'convicted by courts, fined, jailed, and harassed by various injunctive procedures' (Samuelson and Nordhaus 2010, 258). In the US, 'the Supreme Court repeatedly struck down acts designed to improve working conditions for women and children and other reform legislation on hours and wages' (Samuelson and Nordhaus 2010, 258). Subsequently, unions gradually became stronger due to the immense struggles and sacrifices of workers to the point of playing a considerable role in the economy by providing workers with legal protections, improving workplace conditions, and helping to raise living standards. The main instrument employed by unions to improve the working conditions and lifestyles of their members is collective bargaining, whereby a leadership group negotiates labour contracts with employers on behalf of all employees, which gives them tremendous leverage compared

B. Filip, *The Rise of Neo-liberalism and the Decline of Freedom*,
Palgrave Insights into Apocalypse Economics,
https://doi.org/10.1007/978-3-030-61623-6_9

to having each employee negotiate individually. Through collective bargaining, unions have been able to raise wages and provide their members with a variety of non-wage benefits like reduced work hours, unemployment benefits, safe and heathy workplaces, paid annual vacation, parental benefits, sick leave, life insurance, health and dental insurance, and pensions.

This chapter examines the rise and decline of labour unions. In doing so, it explains that prominent neo-liberal economists consistently targeted labour unions with selective arguments intended to create hostility towards them. Foremost among them were Friedman, Hayek and Mises, all of whom criticized unions for violating economic and individual freedom, relying on coercive powers to achieve their objectives, and causing unemployment and inflation. In fact, the influence of neo-liberal principles may have contributed to the dramatic decline in union membership that transpired during the Reagan presidency. This chapter contends that labor movements and the battles they waged should be associated with struggles for freedom and equality, as they sought to eliminate class privileges and establish social justice and freedom for society.

9.1 The Rise and Decline of Unions in the United States

In the United States, labor unions expanded significantly during World War I, supported by the passing of the Clayton Antitrust Act[1] in 1914. This act permitted the formation of labour unions, and gave workers the legal right to strike and boycott their employers under federal law. Subsequently, labour movements and unions experienced some setbacks during the 1920s right up until the Great Depression. During that time, union membership and activities declined significantly, as strong economic growth made it relatively easy for people to find work at higher wage rates, thereby eliminating the incentive for employees to become union members, while anti-union sentiment became widespread among employers and the government.[2] However, circumstances changed shortly after the Great Depression, as the unemployment rate rose to around 25 percent

[1] History, Art & Archives: United States House of Representatives. The Clayton Antitrust Act. https://history.house.gov/HistoricalHighlight/Detail/15032424979.

[2] National Labor Relations Board. Chapter 2: The 1920s and the Start of the Depression 1921–1933. https://www.dol.gov/general/aboutdol/history/dolchp02.

and people became impoverished, which led to many large protests and marches taking place across the US, many of which were organized by communist and socialist groups. Accordingly, unions came back strong, as membership increased significantly while the New Deal was being implemented, and during and after World War II. Also, in 1935, another important piece of labour legislation was passed in the form of the Wagner Act, which was also known as the National Labor Relations Act (NLRA).[3] The NLRA aimed to establish and protect the legal rights of employees against oppression and exploitation by their employers, which included forbidding the latter from engaging in unfair labour practices.[4] Based on the NLRA, employees in the private sector now had the right to organize into trade unions, engage in collective bargaining, and exercise collective actions. It also sought to strengthen the influence of unions by requiring employees to pay union dues to stay employed, and prohibiting employers from firing or discriminating against workers who organized or joined unions. Then, in 1938, the US government passed the Fair Labor Standards Act (FLSA),[5] which eliminated sweatshops, imposed limitations on child labour,[6] and improved wages by enforcing minimum wage requirements, and eliminated intolerable work hours. More specifically, weekly work hours in the US decreased to '42 hours on the eve of World War II,' well below the approximately '75 hours per week in 1870' (Leontief 1983, 406).

President Franklin Roosevelt (1882–1945) had a reputation of supporting better labor standards and legal protections for American workers, as evidenced by the fact that the New Deal, NLRA, and FLSA were all implemented during his administration (1933 to 1945), in addition to other laws and regulations pertaining to labour. The business community and Republicans were adamantly opposed to these and other pieces of legislation that supported labour rights. Consequently, 'the Wagner Act was challenged in court as a violation of the "freedom of contract" of employers and employees, and as an unconstitutional intrusion by the

[3] National Labor Relations Board. Our History. https://www.nlrb.gov/about-nlrb/who-we-are/our-history.

[4] Encyclopaedia Britannica. Wagner Act: United States [1935]. https://www.britannica.com/topic/Wagner-Act.

[5] U.S. Department of Labor. Fair Labor Standards Act of 1938: Maximum Struggle for a Minimum Wage. https://www.dol.gov/general/aboutdol/history/flsa1938.

[6] U.S. Department of Labor. Fair Labor Standards Act of 1938: Maximum Struggle for a Minimum Wage. https://www.dol.gov/general/aboutdol/history/flsa1938.

federal government in industries that were not directly engaged in interstate commerce, which Congress was empowered to regulate under the commerce clause (Article I, section 8). The U.S. Supreme Court eventually upheld (5–4) the constitutionality of the Wagner Act in National Labor Relations Board v. Jones & Laughlin Steel Corp. (1937).'[7] As a result, unions continued to 'consolidated their gains during and after World War II' (Friedman 1982, 106).

From the early decades of the twentieth century until the beginning of the Cold War (1947–1991), communist and socialist groups played major roles in the organisation and activities of labour unions in the US. This contributed to the rapid expansion of union membership. However, that changed during the Cold War Era, as business classes and republicans were able to successfully propagate their long-held anti-communist sentiments among much of the general population. Consequently, after consistently making gains since 1910, union membership began to gradually decline beginning in the 1950s. According to Friedman (1982, 163–164), by 'the 1950's, "labor union" was almost a dirty word; it was no longer synonymous with "labor," no longer automatically to be taken for granted as on the side of the angels.' However, Americans witnessed a much more dramatic decrease in union membership, as well as a significantly diminished role for unions, since the rise of neo-liberalism. In particular, many unions were weakened during Reagan's presidency, because they faced greater opposition on the part of employers, and received less public support.

In much of the twentieth century, unions were instrumental in enabling workers in the United States to effectively fight back against actions and measures that were detrimental to their interests, including anti-labor laws, union busting, contract violations, safety infractions, harassment at workplaces, and wage cuts. In response, unions could target the governments and businesses engaging in such practices with organized strikes, boycotts, and public protests and demonstrations. In the 1970s, U.S. labor unions averaged around '300 strikes per year' (Samuelson and Nordhaus 2010, 260).

Subsequently, strikes became much more rare occurrences beginning in the Reagan Era. 'The reason for the decline is that strikes have often backfired on workers. In 1981, the striking air-traffic controllers were all fired by President Reagan. When the professional football players went on strike

[7] Encyclopaedia Britannica. Wagner Act: United States [1935] https://www.britannica.com/topic/Wagner-Act.

in 1987, they were forced back to work when the football owners put on the games with replacement players. In 1992, workers striking at Caterpillar Inc., a huge maker of heavy equipment, had to end their 6-month strike when Caterpillar threatened to fill their jobs with permanent replacements' (Samuelson and Nordhaus 2010, 260). Consequently, the actions of the Reagan administration seriously stifled the ability of unions to benefit the interests of their members. This crisis of credibility may have precipitated their decline. In 1983, 'the union membership rate was 20.1 percent and there were 17.7 million union workers'[8] in the United States; by 2019, those figures had fallen to '10.3 percent' and '16.4 million' workers, respectively.[9] If fact, the rise of neo-liberalism not only put an end to the expansion of unions in the US, but it also managed to reverse many of the gains that workers had previously fought hard and struggled for decades to attain.

Similar patterns also emerged in a number of other developed countries, as only about 8 percent of the workers in France and around 16 percent of those in Germany were union members in 2018. However, this has not been a universal trend globally. For example, in 2018, over 90 percent[10] of workers in Iceland were union members, while that figures was over 81 percent[11] in Cuba, and over 60 percent in Sweden, Denmark, and Finland.[12] It should also be noted that, even though union membership is relatively low in some Western European countries, the majority of their workers are covered by collective bargaining agreements.[13]

Labour unions fought to establish many of the rights and benefits that workers enjoy today. In addition to workers, governments also benefitted from union activities that successfully achieved certain non-wage benefits for their members, because many of those were previously provided by the state. By alleviating the government of its responsibilities in these areas, state budgets were freed up to be allocated elsewhere. However, neoliberal economists have always been highly critical of unions for

[8] U.S. Bureau of Labour Statistics. 'Economic News Release: Union Members Summary.' https://www.bls.gov/news.release/union2.nr0.htm.

[9] U.S. Bureau of Labour Statistics. 'Economic News Release: Union Members Summary.' https://www.bls.gov/news.release/union2.nr0.htm.

[10] OECD. Trade Union. https://stats.oecd.org/Index.aspx?DataSetCode=TUD.

[11] International Labour Organisation. Statistics on union membership. https://ilostat.ilo.org/topics/union-membership/.

[12] OECD. Trade Union. https://stats.oecd.org/Index.aspx?DataSetCode=TUD.

[13] OECD. Trade Union. https://stats.oecd.org/Index.aspx?DataSetCode=TUD.

contributing to artificially high wages and restricting the ability of businesses to run their operations freely and efficiently.

9.2 A Neo-liberal Claim: Unions are Coercive and Destructive

The emergence of unions was a response to the unfair, unjust and oppressive treatment of employees at the hands of large companies in many industries, as workers sought protection, better working conditions, and some balance of power in the market. Through collective bargaining,[14] which appoints a leadership group to negotiate labour contracts with employers on behalf of all employees, union members attained tremendous leverage compared to the practice of having each employee negotiate on their own. In the event of a breakdown in negotiations, unions can put pressure on management to return to the bargaining table by exercising their right to organize a strike, where its membership engages in collective actions designed to slow or stop output at their place of work.

During the Cold War Era, liberal economists were concerned about the rising popularity of unions, and the influence they were able to exert on the development of economic policies in many countries. In fact, they were opposed to virtually every single protection or benefit that workers were able to attain through unions, such as work safety requirements, paid vacations, minimum wage, health insurance, and paid sick leave, on the basis that such measures were expensive and left less money for the business classes. However, Hayek believed that, in reality, it was a 'myth' that unions improved worker rights and working conditions. Instead, he contended that it was because of the workers' own personal 'efforts that the standard of living of the working class has risen as fast as it has done and that only through their continued efforts will wages continue to increase as fast as possible' (Hayek 2011, 392). That is to say, Hayek claimed that unions falsely took credit for fighting against the exploitation of employers, and improving working conditions when, in fact, it was the efforts of the workers themselves that brought about any changes in these areas.

Mises (1962, 478) completely agreed with Hayek's view that unions are falsely credited with improving the working conditions and living standards of employees. More specifically, he claimed that the masses were

[14] United Nations, Right to Organise and Collective Bargaining Convention, 1949 (No. 98), https://www.ohchr.org/EN/ProfessionalInterest/Pages/RightToOrganise.aspx.

mistaken to believe that it was 'the efficiency of trade unionism to improve the conditions of labour, because the standard of living of the masses has been steadily rising in the last hundred years' (Mises 1962, 478). Furthermore, Mises (1962, 478) pointed out that numerous economic studies demonstrated that 'this improvement is due to the progress of capitalism, to the progressive accumulation of capital and to its corollary, the increase of the marginal productivity of labour.' Consequently, he claimed that workers and 'eminent philanthropists who have advocated trade unionism as the corner stone of future society' had completely 'misunderstood' the role of that free-market capitalism played in improving their working conditions and raising their living standards.

Hayek was critical of the means used by unions to exert influence. He claimed that unions acted as if all of the coercive measures they employed in their efforts to raise wages and improve non-wage benefits were legitimate. For example, he pointed out that 'striking has been accepted as a legitimate weapon of unions, it has come to be believed that they must be allowed to do whatever seems necessary to make a strike successful' (Hayek 2011, 393). However, he highlighted that 'it is the techniques of coercion that unions have developed for the purpose of making membership in effect compulsory, what they call their "organizational activities" (or, in the United States, "union security"—a curious euphemism) that give them real power' (Hayek 2011, 392). In other words, Hayek contended that unions used their coercive power, including intimidation and violent means, to 'keep non-members out of employment,' while using the threat of job losses to force 'unwilling workers' to become members (Hayek 2011, 385). In fact, he claimed that a 'labor dispute' is not solely 'a disagreement about remuneration and the conditions of employment;' it is often the case that its only aim is to force workers that are unwilling to join the labour union to do so (Hayek 2011, 385). Similar to Hayek, Mises (1962, 481) believed that 'unionism is compulsory membership,' as any workers who do not want to join the union are 'sometimes compelled to do so by rough handling.' Both Hayek and Mises maintained that unions acted independently of the wills of the individual workers. They argued that the power and influence held by unions, whereby they could legitimately exercise coercion over their fellow workers, threatened freedom, which they regarded as the very foundation of free societies. They believed that if the decision to join a union was voluntary and free of coercion, membership would be very limited. Furthermore, Hayek (2011, 388) suggested that 'any union effectively controlling all potential workers of a firm or industry can exercise almost unlimited pressure on the employer and that, particularly where a great amount of capital has been invested in specialized equipment, such a union can practically expropriate the owner and command nearly the whole return of his enterprise.'

Even though neo-liberalism accepts the market as a place where buyers and sellers can engage in bargaining, Mises (1998 [1949]) did not support the notion of collective bargaining to negotiate how much workers will be paid, and establish the details of their working conditions. He was critical of the influential power that collective bargaining bestowed upon unions, given that they did not respect the conditions and principles of the free-market system. In fact, he went so far as to describe collective bargaining as 'bargaining at the point of a gun,' because negotiations were taking place 'between an armed party, ready to use its weapons, and an unarmed party under duress' (Mises 1998 [1949], 772). Mises (1962, 480) also suggested that 'the philosophy of violence, which replaced the conciliatory teaching of liberalism and democracy, started as a philosophy of trade unionism.' He was especially critical that labor unions appear to have free reign when it comes to employing forceful measures and organizing violent actions to respond to challenges to their demands for higher wage rates and changes to their work environment. According to Mises (1962, 480), 'the glorification of violence which characterizes the policy of Russian Sovietism, of Italian Fascism and of German Nazism, and which today seriously threatens all democratic governments, sprang from the teachings of revolutionary' trade unions. In fact, he was of the opinion that trade unions were fighting against the free-market capitalist order on many frontiers before the emergence of fascism, socialism, communism and Nazism (Mises 1962).

Friedman shared similar views with Mises with respect to labour unions having the freedom to act with impunity during labour stoppages, which included harming strike-breakers and damaging the property of the businesses that employ them. Friedman (1982, 110) was particularly frustrated that coercive activities and physical violence conducted by unions are treated differently than the average citizen engaging in similar activities, with 'law enforcement applying different standards to actions taken in the course of a labor dispute than to the same actions under other circumstances.' That is to say, unions had incomparable privileges when it came to violence and coercion, as police forces, state attorneys and other members of the legal system would not react unless the actions were particularly severe or egregious. For example, he pointed out that, if people 'turn cars over, or destroy property, out of sheer wickedness or in the course of exacting private vengeance, not a hand will be lifted to protect them from the legal consequences' (Friedman 1982, 110). However, if these same people are members of union who 'commit the same acts in the course of labor dispute, they may well get off scot free' (Friedman 1982, 111). Meanwhile, Mises (1998 [1949], 773) stated:

> When the unions invoke the right to strike in justification of such intimidation and deeds of violence, they are on no better ground than a religious group would be in invoking the right of freedom of conscience as a justification of persecuting dissenters.

Mises (1962, 483) argued that 'there are only two classes in the country: members of the trade unions for the branches of production essential to life, and the remainder of the people, who are slaves without rights.' Consequently, he was convinced that every single strike inevitably 'becomes, even in the short run and not only in the long run, a strike against the rest of the people' (Mises 1998 [1949], 854). He further claimed that union members are able to 'dominate the remaining classes by the rule of violence' (Mises 1962, 483). Therefore, Mises (1962, 481) argued that 'every strike is an act of coercion, a form of extortion, a measure of violence directed against all who might act in opposition to the strikers' intentions.' He also explained that employers often suffer the greatest consequences after a strike has been settled, because the coercive measures of unions increase their costs in the form of higher wages and better social benefits for their employees, whereas the prices of the products they produce and sell remain unchanged or go down (Mises 1998 [1949]). Consequently, the coercive measures available to unions seriously handicap capitalist enterprises.

Hayek (1998b, 57) suggested that the 'government is the most helpless of employers, the labour unions in public employments have achieved an increasing power to blackmail all and sundry by paralysing public life.' He was frustrated that, when it came to unions, governments completely failed in 'their prime function,' which is 'the prevention of coercion and violence' by any entity, group or organisation within society (Hayek 2011, 384). Furthermore, he also explained that labour unions had the ability to exercise coercive power over society as a whole by refusing to supply 'an essential service' as a bargaining chip (Hayek 1998b, 81). In fact, Hayek (1998b, 32) went so far as to suggest that it was 'the spectacular legal privileges granted' to the unions that became 'the chief cause of the progressive decline of the British economy.' Such factors led Hayek to conclude that the coercive methods and powers of labour unions are: destructive to individual and economic freedom; and, irreconcilable with the preservation of a free society.

9.3 Social Justice and the Wage Rate

Throughout history, labor movements and the battles they waged for worker rights were associated with struggles for freedom and equality, because they sought to eliminate class privileges and establish social justice. However, neo-liberals did not believe that unions genuinely wanted to achieve freedom and criticized their efforts to achieve social justice. For example, Hayek was adamant that the fact that unions resorted to coercive means in order to achieve their goals violated freedom. In fact, he was frustrated that the government permitted trade unions to 'use coercion' in order to attain 'social justice' (Hayek 1998a, 141).

Neo-liberals point out that supporters of social and distributive justice seek to raise wages through government intervention, or via well-organized and coordinated actions on the part of labor unions. They argue that, in a free society, free-market principles are supposed to dictate the wage rate according to the balance that is established between the available supply of labor and the demand for it, irrespective of issues like justice, morals, or ethical standards. As such, there is no reason for an employer to raise wage rates if there is an abundance of unemployed people available to work for them. Mises (1998 [1949], 764) explained that, in a free-market system, the wage rate has a tendency to move towards 'a height at which all those eager to earn wages get jobs and all those eager to employ workers can hire as many as they want.' Consequently, the wage rate has a propensity to achieve full employment based on voluntary interactions between employees and employers. Mises (1998 [1949], 764) believed that the ideal scenario for the labour market was when 'there is only voluntary or catallactic unemployment,' meaning that there is no external intervention in matters of employment or wages. However, he argued that when the wage rate is set at an artificially high level due to the activities of governments and unions, it makes the free-market system un-free and very inefficient, which is detrimental to both the economy and society.

Friedman (1982, 105) explained that labour unions played a significant role in increasing the wage rates of their members above the free-market level. In particular, he called attention to the fact that unions had the ability to force employers to increase wages by using their coercive ability to withhold labour in order to limit or completely stop output. Friedman (1982, 105) made:

> a rough estimate that because of unions something like 10 to 15 per cent of the working population has had its wage rates raised by something like 10 to 15 per cent. This means that something like 85 or 90 per cent of the working population has had its wage rates reduced by some 4 per cent.

He noted that since he made 'these estimates, much more detailed studies have been done by others,' and his 'impression is that they yield results of much the same order of magnitude' (Friedman 1982, 105). Samuelson and Nordhaus (2010, 259) agreed with Friedman's view that labour unions possessed the capability to artificially elevate wages, as 'union workers receive on average a 10 to 15 percent wage differential over non-union workers.'

That said, Friedman (1982, 105) suggested that while unions had the power to affect the wages of their members, 'even the strong and powerful unions have only a limited effect on the wage structure' of the country. This would likely come as surprise to the general public, who believe that unions exert consider influence over labour market conditions and have been instrumental in raising wages for all workers over the years. Friedman (1982, 105) further elaborated that:

> Given a labor union, any wage increase will come through the union, even though it may not be a consequence of the union organization. The wages of domestic servants have risen very greatly in recent years. Had there been a union of domestic servants, the increase would have come through the union and would have been attributed to it.

However, Friedman did not regard unions as completely inconsequential, as he stated that, similar to an 'enterprise monopoly, they play a significant and meaningful role making many wage rates different from what the market alone would establish. It would be as much a mistake to underestimate as to overestimate their importance' (Friedman 1982, 105). That said, Friedman argued that 'unions have generally been strongest among groups that would have been high-paid anyway, their effect has been to make high-paid workers higher paid at the expense of lower paid workers'

(Friedman 1982, 105). In other words, he believed that unions significantly harm the wages of low-paid workers and reduce 'the opportunities available to the most disadvantaged workers' (Friedman 1982, 105). Friedman (1982, 105) explained that 'if unions raise wage rates in a particular occupation or industry, they necessarily make the amount of employment available in that occupation or industry less than it otherwise would be just as any higher price cuts down the amount purchased.' This is because setting the wage rate above the free-market level causes labour demand to fall below labour supply, due to the profits of enterprises being adversely affected by their costs of production being raised. Ultimately, the consequence usually ends up being an increase in the number of people looking for other jobs (Friedman 1982, 105). According to Mises (1998 [1949], 770):

> real wage rates can rise only to the extent that, other things being equal, capital becomes more plentiful. If the government or the unions succeed in enforcing wage rates which are higher than those the unhampered labor market would have determined, the supply of labor exceeds the demand for labor. Institutional unemployment emerges.

Mises (1962, 486) argued that supporters of unions do not realize that their efforts to increase the wage rate above the free-market level must 'lead to unemployment, and that in the long run unemployment doles can have no other effect than the perpetuation of unemployment.' He believed that institutional unemployment cannot be eliminated as long as the state and unions are able to set wage rates at artificially high levels. Hayek also stressed that institutional unemployment would persists if real wages were too high. He was frustrated with the fact that unions can cause institutional unemployment by raising wage rates above the flexible rates without taking any responsibility for the consequences of their actions. It would then be left to the state to take care of the people who lost their jobs on account of the actions of unions by providing them with unemployment assistance, and using monetary and fiscal policies to preserve or re-establish full employment. In other words, since the government would step in to ensure full employment whenever permanent institutional unemployment materialized, the state would effectively 'relieve the unions of the responsibility for any unemployment' that they may have contributed to (Hayek 2011, 399). That said, Hayek explained that public policy cannot resolve the issue of institutional unemployment by lowering the wage rate directly. He believed that the real solution could be found in lowering the value of money, which could be attained by easing credit conditions or increasing the money supply. According to him, using state mechanisms to remedy institutional unemployment by expanding the supply of money and the availability of credit causes the prices of all goods and services to increase, thereby raising the cost of living. Therefore, it could be argued that 'the aggregate effort of the unions' aimed at setting the wage rate at a higher level than the one that would naturally emerge under the free-market system will eventually result in 'progressive inflation' (Hayek 2011, 399). Hayek (2011, 399) concluded that the best available option for the state to 'prevent union policy from producing unemployment is...to counter through inflation whatever excessive rises in real wages unions tend to cause.' Nevertheless, he was concerned that unions could eventually 'destroy the whole market order' by exercising their power to increase wages rates above the free-market level (Hayek 1998b, 144).

Neo-liberals often pointed to the threat of institutional unemployment to justify their opposition to the power of labour unions. They argued that the ability of unions to influence the wage rate had damaging economic implications, not only for employees and employers, but also for the nation in general. This is because 'union wage increases "spill over" into the non-union sector' by increasing the unemployment rate and inflation in the whole country (Ashenfelter 1978, 38). In reality, however, history has shown that labour unions cannot significantly affect aggregate wages. For example, while the aggregate wage level in the US increased by 44 percent between 1967 and 1973, the influence of labour unions is estimated to have accounted for only one to two percent of that gain (Ashenfelter 1978, 40). Samuelson and Nordhaus (2010, 259) also contended that even though unions can increase 'the wages of their members above competitive levels,' they cannot raise 'the average wage of the entire economy.' They also suggested that 'if unions succeed in raising their wages above competitive levels, their gains come at the expense of the wages of non-union workers' (Samuelson and Nordhaus 2010, 259).

Mises was concerned that state support for full employment policies and unions would eventually lead to the emergence of a centrally planned system, as evidenced by his view that, practically speaking, 'all these devices of an alleged full employment policy finally lead to the establishment of socialism of the German pattern' (Mises 1998 [1949], 771). He also explained that the general public falsely believed that 'permanent mass unemployment' was testimony that free-market capitalism is unable to solve economic issues and problems on its own; 'therefore government interference, totalitarian planning and Socialism are necessary' (Mises 1962, 485). He further added that this type of argument was 'irrefutable when people realize that the only big country which does not suffer from the evils of unemployment is communist Russia' (Mises 1962, 485). That said, he countered that 'the logic of this argument however, is very weak' (Mises 1962, 485, 486). He also claimed that unemployment in the free-market system was the result of 'the policy both of the government and of the trade unions aims at maintaining a level of wages which is out of harmony with the existing productivity of labour' (Mises 1962, 485, 486). In *Socialism* (1962, 484), Mises went so far as to suggest that 'it is certain that a society which aims at preserving trade unionism on its present lines is in a fair way towards destroying itself.'

Similarly, Hayek (2011, 392) claimed that unionism had a tendency to lead towards 'socialist planning,' which was in everyone's 'best interest to avoid.' He was adamant that 'the basic principles of the rule of law have nowhere in recent times been so generally violated and with such serious consequences as in the case of labor unions' (Hayek 2011, 383). He further claimed that 'the whole basis of our free society is gravely threatened by the powers arrogated by the unions' (Hayek 2011, 386). As such, he was frustrated that society largely supported unions on the basis that they contributed the public good, despite the fact that they had coercive and violent power at their disposal. However, while Hayek argued that many of the coercive techniques used by unions to achieve their objectives needed to be limited or banned outright, he was not in favor of prohibiting unions, as he recognized that this would violate the fundamental principles of a free society (Hayek 2011, 394). Accordingly, he believed that an ideal solution could be found in 'curbing union power' (Hayek 2011, 400), based on his contention that unions could play a 'useful and important role even in the process of wage determination' without resorting to coercive means (Hayek 2011, 395). He made it clear that the 'freedom of organization' for labourers should not exceed the 'freedom of contract,' while their 'action of organizations should not be restricted by rules which do not apply to individuals' (Hayek 1998b, 89).

9.4 Conclusion

In an ideal world where all men are equal, it would be the case that 'each person belongs to himself or herself, so labor belongs to the individual' (George 2006, 182–183). People would also agree that 'what someone makes or produces belongs to that person—even against the claim of the whole world. It is that person's property, to use or enjoy, give or exchange, or even destroy. No one else can rightfully claim it. And this right to the exclusive possession and enjoyment wrongs no one else' (George 2006, 182–183). Although such ideals might not be feasible in the real world, labour unions have been striving to achieve just, fair and ethical results for workers through various means. Historically, labour unions have always had close relationships with left-wing groups and socialist democratic political parties, which posed a threat to the success of the free-market system. This raised concerns among economists during the rise of neo-liberalism, who consistently targeted labour union with selective arguments in order to create hostile sentiments towards them. In particular, they claimed that unions relied on coercive powers to achieve their objectives, violated individual and economic freedom, and caused unemployment and inflation. In reality, however, their main motivations for opposing and weakening labour unions and collective bargaining were mainly related to union efforts to achieve freedom, economic equality, and social justice.

Since the rise of neo-liberalism, the increasingly global orientation of economies significantly expanded the pool of workers that corporations could choose from by essentially removing national borders as a barrier to employing people. As a result, enterprises started outsourcing production to poor countries with an abundance of natural and human resources, as well as weak environmental and labour standards. The workers in these countries were willing to accept much lower wages, very few benefits, if any, and hazardous working conditions.[15] These factors allowed

[15] Allowing corporations to move some of their operations to developing countries in order to take advantage of lower wages, weak labour laws and poor environmental standards raises a number of moral and ethical concerns with respect to forms of exploitation that would elicit outrage among the general populations of western countries. For example, child labour is common in many Asian countries, where children work long hours under hazardous conditions for wages that amount to little more than a pittance, sometimes being forced to do so. However, poor working conditions and outright exploitation matter little for corpora-

enterprises to downsize or close down some operations in their home countries and move them abroad to take advantage of lower production costs.

Under global free-market capitalism, unions are not afforded legal protections in many poor countries, which means any attempts by workers to better their conditions can be put down swiftly, often with the assistance of local governments and security forces. In the event that workers in one of these countries realize some success in organizing for better wages and working conditions, then the corporations operating there can simply pack up and relocate to another country where workers can still be easily exploited. Unfortunately, unions and collective bargaining have not managed to expand and thrive in underdeveloped and developing countries where they could play a significant role in combatting and raising awareness of important labour issues that are prevalent in these regions, such as child labour, unfair labour practices, unhealthy and unsafe workplaces, and long working hours. Although strengthening and expanding unions in poor countries is unlikely to stop corporations from offshoring some of their operations in search of lower costs, it would contribute to slowing the rampant expansion of global inequality.

As corporations have increasingly offshored their production in an effort to expand their market shares, workers in western capitalist countries were adversely affected, as they could not compete with the low wages being paid to their counterparts in developing and underdeveloped countries. As a result, unions lost considerable leverage and there was a shift in the balance of power in favour of employers. In other words, the prevalence of international free trade agreements has been harmful to unions in the US and other western countries.

The rise of neo-liberalism significantly contributed to undoing much of the success that labour unions managed to achieve in the US in the first half of the twentieth century, as it coincided with dramatic declines in union density, union membership, and strike frequency, which negatively impacted the working conditions, earnings, benefits, and living standards of workers. In fact, many employees who lost well paid unionized jobs were forced to accept low paying or minimum wage jobs, with little job security, few benefits, and often of the part-time variety. Presently, labour unions in many western countries are not strong enough to fight against

tions if they can contribute to accelerating growth, raising productivity, and attracting investment.

the detrimental impacts that free-market capitalism is having on workers and society. That is very unfortunate, because the presence of influential labour unions that are able to collectively bargain effectively can play an important role in achieving just, fair and ethical outcomes for workers, as well as society as a whole.

References

Ashenfelter, Orley. 1978. *Union Relative Wage Effects: New Evidence and a Survey of Their Implications for Wage Inflation.* Ed. Richard Stone and William Peterson. Econometric Contributions to Public Policy: proceedings of a conference held by the International Economic Association, Urbino, Italy. International Economic Association. New York: Palgrave Macmillan, 31–60.

Friedman, Milton. 1982 [1962]. *Capitalism and Freedom.* Chicago: University of Chicago Press.

George, Henry. 2006 [1879]. *Progress and Poverty: Why There are Recessions and Poverty Amid Plenty—And What to Do about It!* Edited by Bob Drake. New York: Robert Schalkenbach Foundation.

Hayek, F.A. 1998a [1976]. *Law, Legislation and Liberty Volume 2: The Mirage of Social Justice.* London: Routledge & Kegan Paul.

———. 1998b [1979]. *Law, Legislation and Liberty Volume 3: The Political Order of a Free People.* London: Routledge & Kegan Paul.

———. 2011 [1960]. *The Constitution of Liberty.* Chicago: University of Chicago Press.

Leontief, Wassily. 1983. Technological Advance, Economic Growth, and the Distribution of Income. *Population and Development Review* 9 (3): 403–410.

Mises, Ludwig von. 1962 [1951]. *Socialism: An Economic and Sociological Analysis.* New Haven: Yale University Press.

———. 1998 [1949]. *Human Action: A Treatise on Economics.* Auburn: The Ludwig von Mises Institute.

Samuelson, Paul Anthon and William D. Nordhaus. 2010 [1948]. *Economics.* New York: The McGraw-Hill Companies, Inc.

CHAPTER 10

The Expansion of Global Inequality Under Free-Market Capitalism

After the collapse of the Soviet Union, many declared capitalism to be the outright winner of the final ideological battle against communism, and without a valid rival. Some believed that this marked the end of history, meaning that there would be no more fighting over large ideological issues going forward. Neo-liberals also suggested that people would enjoy higher living standards, because most of the world would be governed by free-market capitalism, which is superior to any other system of societal organization in terms of meeting the needs of human beings. However, while the spread of free-market capitalism may have contributed to gains in economic growth, productivity, technological progress, and efficiency since the collapse of the Soviet Union, it also brought unprecedented economic and social inequality and injustice to much of the world.

Since the 1980s, the Bretton Woods Institutions, which consist of the International Monetary Fund (IMF) and the World Bank (WB), have played major roles in the implementation of neo-liberal economic policies and reforms around the world. Subsequently, the World Trade Organisation (WTO) also significantly contributed to the global spread of neo-liberal economic reforms since it was established in 1995. These international institutions and organizations used their considerable influence to facilitate the adoption of free-market economic reforms in countries on all continents, which has allowed transnational corporations to gain significant control over the world economy. In other words, the actions of the IMF,

B. Filip, *The Rise of Neo-liberalism and the Decline of Freedom*,
Palgrave Insights into Apocalypse Economics,
https://doi.org/10.1007/978-3-030-61623-6_10

WB and WTO have essentially allowed 'transnational companies to do whatever they wish without any regulations placed on them by any country' (Parenti 2011, 60).

One of the main roles of the Bretton Woods Institutions has been to ensure that countries seeking financial assistance implemented the neo-liberal reforms that they prescribed before any loans were provided. Since the 1980s, the required reforms have been presented as Structural Adjustment Programs (SAPs), which mandate economic restructuring and austerity measures. The SAPs typically consist of some combination of cutting deficits, liberalizing trade, currency devaluation, the dollarization and liberalization of domestic prices, privatizing land and state-owned enterprises, raising interest rates, and reforming key sectors of the economy like agriculture, transportation, and banking and finance. Although the stated objectives of SAPs include restoring fiscal balance, promoting economic growth and alleviating poverty, their reforms are actually intended to ensure that the borrowing countries are able to repay their international creditors in a timely manner. By removing controls on foreign exchange and weakening financial protection barriers, SAPs opened economies up for free trade and facilitated the influx of large quantities of foreign direct investment (FDI).

SAPs have been implemented in developing countries in all regions of the world, including Latin America, Africa, and the transitional economies of former communist countries. However, a close examination of the SAPs reveals that they are virtually identical even though the countries they were applied to varied considerably in terms of their economic structures and levels of development. That means, rather than carefully considering the specific needs, characteristics and circumstances of each country when designing the programs, the reform process is driven by the interests of the countries and other stakeholders that are providing the funds for the loans. For this reason, it should not be surprising that SAPs have achieved very similar results in most of the countries that implemented them. That is to say, they have been largely unsuccessful in attaining their stated objectives and, instead, have exacerbated economic problems by increasing poverty, causing widespread unemployment, raising utility prices, displacing farmers, increasing bankruptcies, causing a collapse in domestic production, advancing malnourishment, etc. Despite the important roles played by the WB, IMF, and WTO in the spread of neo-liberalism, this chapter does not discuss their involvement in great detail given the abundance of literature already published on this subject.

The free-market economic reforms advanced since the rise of neo-liberalism promised to put countries on the road to development, higher productivity, and accelerated economic growth, which would eventually lead to higher living standards and economic prosperity. However, neo-liberal economic reforms failed to deliver on these promises; instead, they have resulted in unfair global economic outcomes, as some have profited disproportionately at the expense of others. In particular, people in Western countries have seen their living standards improve considerably during this period, including some of the richest and most elite individuals, families and groups, who experienced unprecedented increases in their wealth and incomes even though they were already living lavish lifestyles. Conversely, large numbers of people living in developing countries in Latin America, Asia and Africa became landless, homeless, jobless, hopeless, and unfree. This chapter mainly focuses on the nature of the inequalities that emerged as a result of the implementation of neo-liberal economic reforms, the relationship between freedom and equality, and some of the views expressed by neo-liberal economists on the topic of inequality.

10.1 Some Are More Equal Than Others

The rise of neo-liberalism has largely delivered on its promises of higher productivity and economic growth rates. In fact, both indicators reached unprecedented levels, which would lead one to believe that the living standards and material conditions would have been elevated for all of society, including the poorest of people. However, neo-liberalism also engendered previously unseen levels of social and economic inequality, both within and between countries. More specifically, neo-liberal economic reforms did not bring poor people or developing countries the economic prosperity that was promised prior to their implementation. While the world's largest corporations have realized unprecedented growth and expanded their share of the global economy, billions of people experienced a contraction of their purchasing power, while the population 'living in poverty is growing at a faster rate than the world's population' (Parenti 2015, 106). It has been estimated that around '80 percent of all humanity live on less than $10 a day,' and that 'the poorest 50 percent [of the world population] live from hand to mouth, maintaining only 7.2 percent of the world's private consumption' (Parenti 2015, 102). Furthermore, Oxfam

International recently reported that 'in 2019, the world's billionaires, only 2,153 people, had more wealth than 4.6 billion people.'[1]

Contrary to billions of poor people around the world, the mega-rich are experiencing unparalleled improvements to their already-lavish living standards. They will own a number of multi-million dollar properties where they divide their time, including: luxurious mansions the size of hotels or resorts, that are often staffed full-time by butlers, cleaners, cooks, gardeners, drivers, etc.; penthouse apartments in some of the world's most bustling cities, with amazing skyline views; and, ranches or tropical getaways, including private islands, where they can enjoy pristine nature. Their safety is assured by advanced security systems, bodyguards and security teams, often comprised of former law enforcement and military personnel, as well as the fact that they live in safe neighbourhoods, far away from areas where crime is rampant, where poor people tend to reside. In addition to being safe, these locations and neighbourhoods are also clean, as they are not situated anywhere near polluting industries or unsightly garbage dumps, where it is not uncommon to see poor people scavenging for food or anything that can be salvaged or sold in many countries. In terms of mobility, the mega-rich get around via chauffeured limousines, fleets of luxury, classic and sports cars that they have the means to collect, and even massive yachts, private jets and helicopters. In addition to living lives of extreme luxury, these people can leverage their wealth to their advantage when it comes to obtaining services that are supposed to be publicly-available in many countries. For example, in the case of education, they can send their children to elite private schools with stellar reputations that give them an edge when it comes to applying to post-secondary institutions, even over their peers with superior academic results. Furthermore, their wealth means they have the freedom to study at any college or university that accepts them, including elite Ivy League schools where the tuition fees and other expenses are prohibitive for most students in the absence of a significant scholarship or financial assistance. When it comes to their health, the mega-rich do not have to worry about the costs of expensive treatments in countries with private health care systems, like the U.S., where healthcare expenditures are among the leading causes of bankruptcy. Even in countries with public health care, rich people can use

[1] Oxfam. 'Time to Care: Unpaid and underpaid care work and the global inequality crisis.' https://www.oxfam.ca/publication/35449/?gclid=EAIaIQobChMIh46BzcLU6AIVjYCfCh2tuAqjEAAYASAAEgIFIPD_BwE

their wealth to their advantage. In some developing countries where officials can be more easily corrupted, they can receive faster treatment while gaining access to the best doctors and facilities. Alternatively, if they reside in a country where they cannot bribe their way to better or faster service, they can simply hop onto their private jets and jump the queue by seeing specialists in other countries. Still on the topic of health, rich people also have the means to eat healthier than most people by consuming foods that are organic, fruits and vegetables that are free of pesticides and chemicals, or meat from animals that are grass fed and free range. In fact, there have been cases where members of the elite classes have employed scores of workers to run their own private farms and gardens to produce organic food, which has become a profitable endeavour for some of them. Worst of all, it appears that the mega-rich are likely the best prepared to withstand an eventual environmental apocalypse and societal collapse, having purchased specialized bunkers in remote locations, which is highly unfair, given that it is the economic activities of these people and the companies they own and invest in that are contributing most to the emergence of these developments.

In addition to controlling most of the world's wealth, the richest people on the planet also own a majority of the means of production, such as factories, land, natural resources, and farms. They are able to leverage these assets in order to make huge profits, largely at the expense of the environment and natural resources, and often in violation of human rights. Despite their immense wealth and power, as well as the freedom they enjoy in their luxurious lifestyles, the mega-rich seem to have an insatiable appetite to accumulate even more. However, they cannot be 'rich without the poor who labor to produce vastly more value than they are paid. The few cannot live in splendor if the many do not labor hard for them. Those at the very top understand that they have lives of preferred quality. And most of them want to keep it that way. They have a lot; they can get more; and they want it all' (Parenti 2015, 113).

In 2015, Habitat for Humanity estimated that '1.6 billion people live in inadequate shelter around the world,' and 'more than 100 million people worldwide are homeless.'[2] As a result, these individuals are frequently exposed to the elements, which means their health is particularly at risk during extreme temperatures in both the summer and winter. They are

[2] Habitat for Humanity. World Habitat Day. https://www.comalhabitat.org/events/world-habitat-day

also easy targets for physical violence and sexual assault, particularly in the case of women and girls, as well as trafficking at the hands of violent criminal gangs. In fact, their low standing in society facilitates their victimization, because they are not afforded the same protections by the state that their peers receive. That is to say, cases of homeless people being assaulted, murdered, or otherwise abused are often given a low priority by the police and the legal apparatus, if they are investigated at all. Homeless people are also disadvantaged in terms of their access to healthcare compared to their societal counterparts, particularly in countries without a public system, where they can receive little to no service at all. As a result, they live their lives while enduring injuries, illnesses and diseases that can often be easily treated.

In addition to adequate shelter, a large segment of the world population also lacks access to another basic need: water. Insufficient supplies of potable water has led to millions of people becoming dependent on trucks for the regular delivery of drinkable water. According to the United Nations World Water Development Report, in 2019, more than '2 billion people live in countries experiencing high water stress, and about 4 billion people experience severe water scarcity during at least one month of the year. Stress levels will continue to increase as demand for water grows and the effects of climate change intensify.'[3] All told, the UN estimated that '40% of the global population lacks access to clean and safe drinking water.'[4] In some poor countries, it is not only the people that are suffering from limited access to water and food insecurity[5], as cattle and other livestock are dying from dehydration and starvation. Along with climate change, water shortages in some developing and underdeveloped

[3] United Nations. 2019. 'World Water Development Report 2019: Leaving no one behind.' https://www.unwater.org/publications/world-water-development-report-2019/

[4] The Sustainable Development Goals: UN Report: Nature's Dangerous Decline 'Unprecedented'; Species Extinction Rates 'Accelerating' https://www.un.org/sustainabledevelopment/blog/2019/05/nature-decline-unprecedented-report/

[5] Food insecurity and malnutrition are experienced by hundreds of millions of people daily, including in rich countries where some people rely on foodbanks. The distribution of food is an important aspect of global social and economic inequality. According to the Food and Agriculture Organization (FAO) of the United Nations, each year, 'one third of food produce for human consumption is lost or wasted globally,' which amounts to approximately 1.3 billion tonnes of food (http://www.fao.org/food-loss-and-food-waste/en/). While some of this waste occurs at the household level, a significant amount is attributed to farmers. In Western countries, when farmers have more crops than they can sell, or if their crops do not meet the standards demanded by retailers, they end up discarding it.

countries can also be attributed to the privatization of water resources, resulting in water becoming a very lucrative and profitable commodity for the corporations that acquired those utilities. In some places, corporations have gone as far as 'prohibiting local residents from using barrels to collect their own rainwater. The companies claim to own the water that comes from deep within the earth and from the rivers and streams, and now from the heavens too' (Parenti 2011, 63).

Many poor people around the world also suffer from hunger and food insecurity on a daily basis. The United Nations estimated that, in 2018, about '821 million people in the world suffered from hunger.'[6] In many countries, it is not uncommon to see poor people picking through 'garbage dumps' in search of food, in addition to anything else that could be of use to them (Parenti 2015, 104). Food insecurity is also among the main reasons why poor families often require their children to 'work in grim, soul-destroying sweatshops or to be trafficked in sex houses or preyed upon as domestics in affluent homes' (Parenti 2015, 104). In 2016, the International Labour Organization (ILO) reported that '152 million children are victims of child labour; 73 million of them work in hazardous child labour. Almost half of all 152 million children victims of child labour are aged 5-11 years.'[7] The ILO also estimated that '40.3 million people are in modern slavery,' and that '1 in 4 victims of modern slavery are children.'[8]

The rise of neo-liberalism led to the emergence of large pools of unskilled workers in poor and developing countries, who were left with little choice other than to sell their labour at extremely low wages, given that their skillsets are easily replaced. Transnational corporations take advantage of these circumstances by employing people in these countries under sweatshop conditions, where they can work a 'twelve to fourteen-hour shift' per day, with only a 'few bathroom breaks and restricted access to water' (Bakan 2004, 67). Sweatshops in developing countries usually hire female employees whenever possible, because they are less likely to complain about poor working conditions or make demands about their

[6] United Nations. 'Food.' https://www.un.org/en/sections/issues-depth/food/index.html

[7] https://www.ilo.org/global/about-the-ilo/how-the-ilo-works/departments-and-offices/governance/fprw/lang—en/index.htm

[8] International Labour Organisation (ILO). 'Fundamental Principles and Rights at Work Branch (FUNDAMENTALS).' https://www.ilo.org/global/about-the-ilo/how-the-ilo-works/departments-and-offices/governance/fprw/lang—en/index.htm

rights. Many of them are also regularly subjected to physical and sexual abuse, exploitation, and harassment in their places of work. It is common for workers in sweatshops to be constantly 'supervised by guards who beat and humiliate them on the slightest pretext and who fire them if a forced pregnancy test comes back positive' (Bakan 2004, 66). Similarly, transnational corporations will often employ underage workers at their facilities, including children if they can get away with it, because they are unlikely to complain about their terrible working conditions, or the fact that they are being paid wages that are even lower than those of their peers. Improving the deplorable working conditions at their factories situated in developing countries is not a priority for the large transnational corporations that employ these people, because they regard them as little more than affordable factors of production. According to Henry George (1839-1897) (2006 [1879], 194), an American political economist and writer who was widely regarded as 'the third most famous man in the United States' during his lifetime, 'only surpassed in public acclaim by Thomas Edison and Mark Twain' (George de Mille 2006, 305), the conditions faced by many workers in third world countries could be described as slavery, since:

> The essence of slavery is that everything workers produce is taken from them, except enough to support a bare existence. Under existing conditions, the lowest wages of free labor invariably tend toward this same state. No matter how much productivity increases…the condition of the masses in every civilized country is tending toward virtual slavery.

By establishing sweatshops in underdeveloped countries, transnational corporations can significantly lower their costs of production by avoiding minimum-wage requirements in the countries that they are based in or headquartered. In many 'Third World countries, workers are paid pennies per hour by corporate giants such as Nike, Disney, Walmart, and J.C. Penney' (Parenti 2011, 54). Employers also save money by not compensating their worker for overtime, which is often mandatory in sweatshops. They also benefit from higher productivity in their offshored facilities, because they place high production quotas on their employees, who can be fired or subject to physical abuse if they fail to meet them. These factories often have a 'barbed-wire fence, locked gates and armed security guards,' not only to prevent their employees from leaving freely, but also to keep their poor working conditions hidden from the public (Parenti 2011, 77). In fact, corporations conceal the locations of their 'factories and sweatshops all over the world,' and rarely respond to 'requests for the factories' names and addresses' (Bakan 2004, 66).

In addition to benefitting from an abundance of natural resources and cheap labour in poor countries, transnational corporations also take advantage of lower taxes, ineffective labour laws, deregulation, and weak environmental protection when they offshore production to these locations. That is to say, offshoring production to poor countries benefits corporations by freeing them from their obligation to respect the stringent regulations in place in their home countries, which can be costly and time consuming. It could be argued that the presence of sweatshops in many parts of the world serves as testimony that the free-market system has facilitated the emergence of exploitative work environments, where workers are regularly subjected to physical and psychological abuse, while also being forced to endure unhealthy and unsafe work conditions. For example, employees in sweatshop factories risk serious injury because proper procedures are often not followed when operating heavy machinery or handling dangerous tools and equipment. Furthermore, many of these workers will come into direct contact with hazardous pesticides, chemicals, and a variety of toxic substances without adequate protection, particularly those working in the agriculture, mining and manufacturing industries. Many of these chemicals have been linked with numerous ailments and diseases in human beings, including various forms of cancer, respiratory diseases, and neurological disorders. Contrary to the prescriptions of neo-liberals, most of these poor workers do not have the option of quitting their jobs and seeking out better pay and working conditions elsewhere. Simply put, no alternatives are available to them, because sweatshops could not exist without the large pool of desperate labour that the free-market system provides them with.

There is little likelihood that labourers in poor countries could receive any gratification or satisfaction from their work. They endure unsafe, deplorable and dehumanizing work conditions for the sole purpose of providing their families with their basic physical and biological needs, such as food, clothing, shelter, and safety. That is to say, their work is compulsory on account of their low living standards and the absence of better employment opportunities. If these people had genuine freedom, they would not willingly accept working under such hazardous and exploitative working conditions. That means the unfettered market economy has essentially forced the masses in poor and underdeveloped countries to 'act in order to live,' and not 'live in order to act' (Knight 1922, 463). Knight

(1922, 463) was of the opinion that if all people were forced to devote their lives to struggling to obtain their basic needs, then a significant 'proportion of civilized mankind would certainly commit suicide rather than accept life on such terms, the prospect for improvement being excluded.'

Since neo-liberalism sets no legal limits on the extent of one's wealth, billions of people around the world have had any hope of living a decent life ruined, because mega-rich people and corporations need to exploit them in order to accumulate even more wealth and assets. In other words, the luxurious lifestyles of the rich are 'founded merely on the inconveniences acquired by the labour' of poor people (Montesquieu 1977v1, 132). As a result, those people whose lives are dedicated to the struggle to obtain their basic necessities under extreme circumstances have essentially been deprived of the freedom of choice that is so strongly advocated by proponents of neo-liberalism. Meanwhile, the transnational corporations that employ them possess an abundance freedom, including the freedom to choose between expanding numbers of desperate workers in many different countries that they are able to hire and fire at will. The rich and powerful people that run these companies and own many resources and factors of production around the world elect to shut their eyes to the large and growing number of poor and miserable people, because they are fully aware that this situation helps preserve the social order they need in order to safeguard their lavish lifestyles. Many of the people permanently trapped in poverty will never experience even a small fraction of the freedom and self-indulgent consumption that common people in Western capitalist countries can enjoy on a daily basis. The extent of the contrast between the extravagant lifestyles of the wealthiest classes, who also enjoy strong political and economic connections, and the misery endured by billions of economically and politically marginalized poor people, who often live in ghettoes and slums, shows just how deeply ingrained social and economic divisions, as well as conflicts of interest, are in the free-market capitalist system.

10.2 Neo-liberal Economic Reforms and the Rise of Global Inequality

According to Rousseau (2002), there are two type of inequality between individuals. The first is 'natural, or physical inequality, because it is established by nature, and consists in the difference of age, health, bodily strength, and the qualities of the mind, or of the soul;' the second is economic and political inequality (Rousseau 2002, 87). The latter form of inequality involves 'different privileges, which some men enjoy...such as that of being richer, more honored, more powerful' (Rousseau 2002, 87). Throughout history, social, political and economic inequalities have been outcomes of the appropriation of natural opportunities by a minority, which in turn, are denied to the masses, who endure a life of servitude instead of freedom (George 2006).

Friedman and Hayek wanted to convince their audiences that the adoption of a free-market economy would liberate people from servitude, and help them avoid the road to serfdom. However, much like many of the successful liberation movements of the past against feudalism, colonialism, military occupation, and imperialism, neo-liberalism simply freed people from their servitude to one set of rulers only to make them submit to new overlords: the corporate world. In other words, the doctrine of neo-liberalism established laws and conditions that favoured corporations and enabled them to expand their power, wealth and influence at the expense of the masses. People around the world did not accept neo-liberalism because it possessed some kind of intrinsic values that made it superior to other forms of societal organization; rather, it was imposed on them. This situation has disrupted the subtle adjustments that communities were making to adapt to changing social, political and economic conditions, which took place before the widespread implementation of neo-liberal economic reforms.

Proponents of neo-liberalism highly valued the idea of reducing government functions to a bare minimum. They argued that natural resources and many publicly-owned enterprises and institutions could be managed more efficiently and effectively by the private sector. Accordingly, they promoted the notion that competitiveness, economic growth, and productivity could all be boosted in underdeveloped countries by transferring the ownership of public goods from the government to private foreign and local companies via purchase or joint ventures. In the 1980s, many governments started to deregulate their economies, which meant state-owned 'industries were privatized, income-tax rates were lowered, and the generosity of many welfare programs was reduced' (Samuelson and Nordhaus 2010, 41). More precisely, the free-market economic reforms that accompanied the rise of neo-liberalism included a wave of privatizations that curtailed government involvement in the operation and ownership of properties and resources like water, oil, natural gas, electricity, telecommunications, farmlands, forests, fisheries, transportation systems, hospitals, schools, banks, airlines, railways, highways, and factories. However, widespread privatization combined with trade liberalization resulted in valuable national properties and resources becoming concentrated in the hands of a minority of rich owners in many developing countries. Additionally, many of the small and medium-sized enterprises in those countries were pushed into bankruptcy, because they could not compete with large transnational corporations in the absence of government support (e.g., subsidies, tax breaks, etc.). Eventually, many of these enterprises were acquired by transnational corporations, while others were absorbed by large local companies. That means neo-liberal economic reforms allowed transnational corporations to effectively gain control over entrepreneurship in many poor countries.

The privatization of social services and programs that were previously publicly-funded caused considerable hardships for the citizens of the underdeveloped countries that broadly applied neo-liberalism to their economies, particularly the poor segments of their populations. For example, the privatisation of education systems led to school closures, teachers being laid off, and larger class sizes, depriving millions of children of their right to a quality education. Meanwhile, the privatisation of health care has led to people being denied access to hospital services and medicines due to a lack of money, while any public hospitals and clinics that may have remained open began to consistently lack personnel, medical equipment and supplies. Additionally, neo-liberal economic reforms also led to reductions in public funds allocated to finance the maintenance and construction of important infrastructure, like roads, highways, bridges, ports, factories, and refineries. When the governments in developing countries actually do invest in infrastructure in the age of neo-liberalism, the funding will usually be directed towards projects that directly benefit foreign investors and transnational corporations, such as better roads to allow for the quicker transport of natural resources to ports or processing plants.

Neo-liberal economists also strongly promoted trade liberalization, which stipulates the elimination, or unification, of tariff barriers in order to encourage the development of exports and make domestic industry more competitive. In reality, the implementation of these kinds of reforms in developing countries often leads to domestic goods and commodities being replacing by imports, because domestic producers are unable to compete with foreign companies whose products can be highly subsidized. For example, in the case of agriculture, the elimination of protectionist tariffs and other trade restrictions in poor countries has resulted in a concentration of wealth in the hands of a few transnational agri-business companies, which have been able to shape the production processes and consumption patterns in those nations. In particular, under its Agreement on Agriculture (AoA), the WTO requires all developing countries to open their markets to imported food, while allowing the United States and European countries to retain their barriers on imports of agricultural products coming back the other way. This has had devastating impacts on rural communities in many developing countries, as they lack the state programs and services needed to adequately protect themselves and counteract the negative effects of trade liberalization.

Before the implementation of neo-liberal economic reforms, when agricultural policies fell within the purview of national governments, states could intervene to correct market failures by implementing price controls, providing farm and food subsidies, or taking measures to protect certain agricultural products that a majority of the population relied upon. However, the deregulated environment that emerged following the widespread adoption of neo-liberal reforms effectively led states in the developing world to abandon their farm and rural policies. Consequently, millions of small and medium-sized family farms around the world, which were once self-sufficient and produced surpluses, found themselves coerced into participating in an extremely unequal and unfair system of trade that forced them to compete with large transnational agri-business corporations. In many African, Asian, and Central and South American countries, the broad implementation of free-market economic reforms led to the impoverishment of farming communities, as farmers were hit by a sudden decrease in their incomes, forcing many of them into bankruptcy, because they could not compete with cheap imports of poultry, vegetables and dairy products from heavily subsidized American and European factory farms. Similarly, many local small businesses in these regions were completely wiped out by cheap imports of various goods from transnational corporations. However, the devastation of rural communities and small scale farmers in poor countries was not a negative outcome for everyone, as transnational corporations benefitted from the expansion of the pools of desperate unemployed people that they could choose from to work in their overseas operations.

The rise of neo-liberalism and the restructuring of the global system of agriculture that accompanied it led to domestic agricultural production in poor countries moving away from farming traditional crops in favour of a narrow range of crop varieties. Basically, developing countries have focused on cultivating cash crops for export to developed countries, including sugar, tea, tobacco, cacao, bananas, flowers, and coffee. However, farmers that grow only cash crops become dependent upon foreign demand and prices set on international markets for their incomes and livelihoods, as do the national economies of many developing countries that are highly reliant on agriculture. Cultivating cash crops can also make farmers and countries more food insecure, because many of them cannot actually be eaten in the event of an emergency. That means the 'type of export from underdeveloped countries which deprives them of primary products from land and sea that they would very badly need themselves for feeding their largely undernourished and malnourished population…the fact must be spelled out that the small minority of people in developed countries appropriate and use for their own production and consumption an entirely disproportionate and steadily increasing part of the world's resources' (Myrdal 1973, 108). Ultimately, neo-liberal economic reforms not only failed to deliver on their promises to bring economic prosperity to the developing world, they also left poor farmers in these regions more vulnerable than ever before on many fronts, thereby contributing to elevated risks of food insecurity for entire countries.

Cultivating mostly cash crops not only reduces biodiversity to agro-industrial monocultures, it also requires the intensive use of water. Since cash crops are primarily cultivated for exportation, it could be argued that free-trade measures have indirectly led to massive transfers of water from developing countries to advanced capitalist nations. Mass-produced cash crops also have a very large ecological footprint on account of the significant energy usage needed to grow them and then transport them over vast distances through agri-food chains. Therefore, wealthy Western countries have managed to externalize a segment of their environmental footprint by importing many water and energy intensive goods from poor countries, such as agricultural products (and textiles).

Since the rise of neo-liberalism, free-market capitalism has made people accept the idea that it is legitimate for the most acquisitive individuals and entities (e.g., corporations) to legally engage in socially irresponsible and environmentally destructive activities in unfettered and deregulated markets in pursuit of self-interest maximization. Not only that, they were also led to believe that this would somehow produce beneficial outcomes for society as a whole in the form of productivity gains, economic growth and technological innovation. However, it is not always the case that free-market capitalism has a positive influence on the economic outcomes of a country. In fact, the implementation of free-market economic reforms and uninhibited international trade have actually delayed long-run economic growth and engendered poverty in many developing countries. For example, Stiglitz (2003, 6) pointed out that the introduction of free-market economics was unable to attract foreign investment to African countries or bring them sustained growth, nor did it lead to economic prosperity in Latin America, East Asia, Russia, or the other former communist countries. To the contrary, he stressed that the introduction and application of a standard set of free-market reforms has created 'unprecedented poverty' in many nations (Stiglitz 2003, 6). Stiglitz (2003) did acknowledge that there were some instances where countries were able to attain some degree of success after reforming their economic and financial systems, including Poland, Uganda, Ethiopia, Botswana, India, Malaysia, and China. However, he suggested that many of these countries were able to improve their economic situations because their governments selected and applied policies and reforms that were appropriate for their specific set of circumstances, as opposed to reforming their whole economies (Stiglitz 2003, 88, 126).

The widespread implementation of neo-liberal economic reforms has essentially allowed the stakeholders of transnational corporations to gain control over every aspect of the domestic economy in many countries with relative ease. This includes a wide array of activities involved in the extraction of natural resources, the production and distribution of goods and other products, and the provision of services across a broad range of industries and sectors, including agriculture, mining, oil and gas extraction, manufacturing, utilities, transportation, banking, finance and insurance, as well as the public sector (i.e., education, health care, etc.). Furthermore, consumer goods and products imported from developed nations have effectively replaced the entire system of domestic production in numerous underdeveloped countries, which does not bode well for the economy, because it exacerbates a balance of payments crisis and increases external debt. Ultimately, free trade, privatization, and the dismantling of state institutions have greatly expanded the economic power and influence of a limited number of already wealthy individuals and corporations at the expense of billions of people around the world, who have seen their livelihoods destroyed. Basically, the interests of the citizens of many poor countries have taken a back seat to those of corporate shareholders.

Neo-liberal economic reforms have significantly weakened or eliminated the public welfare function of governments worldwide. That does not mean the role of the state has been reduced; rather, states have modified their 'raison d'être'. In essence, free-market economic reforms have dramatically altered the prevailing relationship between the state, its citizens and the market, whereby the main role of the state has become facilitating global flows of private capital, goods and services. In particular, states have shifted their energies away from providing social services and programs intended to achieve the common good, in favour of supporting the welfare of large corporations, so that they can be successful and contribute to realising better efficiency, productivity and economic growth for the entire country. Over time, the state has become very proficient at protecting the wealth and property of the rich from an invasion by the poor.

Prior to the extensive implementation of free-trade reforms, proponents of neo-liberalism claimed that removing barriers to trade would generate economic growth, higher productivity, more employment opportunities, lower production costs, and a much larger variety of goods to consume. While the eventual elimination of many protective trade barriers did in fact bring many of these benefits, it also allowed large corporations in highly developed capitalist countries to relocate many of their economic activities to poor nations, where they were able exploit rich natural resources and an abundance of cheap labour. Corporations do not hesitate to over-exploit the natural resources and pollute the surrounding environment to the extent that these places become 'disfigured, stripped of whatever offerings it once had,' at which point they will move their operations elsewhere (Parenti 2015, 31). Furthermore, since these natural and human resources are mainly used to produce commodities for consumption in Western markets, it would appear that free-trade measures have enabled transnational corporations to over-exploit the resources in poor countries and then transfer the resulting value to their developed capitalist counterparts. In fact, while only about 17 percent of the world's population resides in developed countries, they are responsible for consuming about 80 percent of the world's natural resources, a significant portion of which was imported to them from under-developed nations. Presently, it could be argued that a vast number of people live under poverty and experience unprecedented social and economic inequality, not because they 'suffer from underdevelopment but from overexploitation' (Parenti 2015, 31).

The free-market economic reforms that accompanied the rise of neo-liberalism not only generated inequality between advanced and developing countries in terms of income, living standards, and wealth creation, but also when it came to pollution. It is the rich countries, and the richest people within them, that are the main producers and beneficiaries of pollution. However, poor people are primarily the ones that suffer from the direct consequences of the pollution, as they live in the areas closest to where production actually takes place, and are regularly exposed to hazardous chemicals and fumes in their places of work, often without adequate protection. As it turns out, the poor are also disproportionately targeted by the destructive impacts of climate change. This is because poor countries are generally situated in 'the tropical and sub-tropical zones, while all industrialized countries are to be found in the temperate zones' (Myrdal 1973, 106). As a result, the former are more 'defenceless' against the 'direct and indirect effects' of climate change 'on human beings, animals, soil and various materials' (Myrdal 1973, 106).

10.3 Equality and Distributive Justice

The rise of neo-liberalism has engendered a dramatic increase in social and economic inequality by bringing poverty and misery to billions of people, while further expanding the already massive fortunes of powerful corporations. Large inequalities in wealth and income also generate disparities in the power to influence the affairs of governments. By spending vast sums of money on lobbying political parties and making generous financial contributions to election campaigns, powerful economic agents gain the ability to influence government policies. These wealthy individuals or companies then use this influence to shape the economic policies and regulations of governments and agencies in ways that advance their own personal interests, which can ultimately impact the livelihoods of billions of people around the world.

Neo-liberals have not been particularly concerned about the unprecedented levels of inequality that have emerged in terms of wealth, income, living standards, power and influence. They generally claim that inequality is a natural product of free-market systems, whereas poverty is not caused by capitalism, but rather, by its absence. In fact, neo-liberals are strongly opposed to any state interventions intended to bring about the equality of income and wealth, because they believe that these outcomes cannot be achieved in a free society. However, they maintain that even though people have many differences and inequalities between them, they should nonetheless be treated alike before the law. Based on the principle of equality under the law, everybody must be treated equally by the same general abstract rules, regardless of their particular economic, political or social circumstances. That means equality under the law does not seek to eliminate the natural inequalities that exist between people by birth, nor does it 'aim to achieve particular results' (Filip 2018, 356). Basically, the law does not impose 'positive duties or a particular kind of actions on anyone (i.e. implementing social policies to achieve an equal distribution of wealth and income)' (Filip 2018, 356).

In his arguments against using the legal system to impose particular laws that are intended to achieve social justice, Hayek explained that equality before the law and economic equality are totally different concepts. In fact, the two are in conflict with one another, as 'the equality before the law which freedom requires leads to material inequality' (Hayek 2011, 150). In other words, both equality before the law and economic equality cannot be achieved at the same time. Hayek (2011, 150) maintained that, in a free society, the state should treat 'all people alike,' even if 'the result must be inequality in their actual position.' Thus, he was completely opposed to any state efforts designed to make people more 'alike in their condition,' which would require the 'discriminatory coercion' of citizens (Hayek 2011, 150). Hayek (1998bv2, 81) was insistent that no government should possess the authority 'to determine the shares of the different members of society' based on discriminatory rules, which would be required to achieve social or distributive justice. He explained that 'treating all citizens according to the same rules,' and treating all citizens differently in order to make people equal in terms of their material possessions were two very different goals that were completely in conflict with each other (Hayek 1998bv2, 82). In other words, the achievement of distributive justice for the purpose of lessening inequality requires the government to treat disadvantaged people and their rich counterparts unequally. More specifically, state policies would need to benefit socially and economically disadvantaged people at the expense of rich people. Hayek (1998bv2, 82) further stated that:

> to assure the same material position to people who differ greatly in strength, intelligence, skill, knowledge and perseverance as well as in their physical and social environment, government would clearly have to treat them very differently to compensate for those disadvantages and deficiencies it could not directly alter. Strict equality of those benefits which government could

provide for all, on the other hand, would clearly lead to inequality of the material positions.

Hayek (2011, 163) was convinced that using state authority to provide equality in terms of social and economic conditions must 'lead to inequality of results.' He believed that a majority of people would be opposed 'not to the bare fact of inequality but to the fact that the differences in reward do not correspond to any recognizable differences in the merits of those who receive them' (Hayek 2011, 156). He emphasized the point that 'neither the equal provision of particular public facilities nor the equal treatment of different' people can 'secure reward that is proportional to merit' (Hayek 2011, 163).

Hayek (2011, 150) criticized distributive justice for imposing 'a preconceived pattern of distribution' within society. For example, he considered progressive taxation to be among the coercive measures used by states to achieve distributive justice. Hayek (2011, 448) claimed that while progressive taxation might aim to reduce inequality, 'it in fact helps to perpetuate existing inequalities.' Furthermore, he believed that allocating state expenditures towards the achievement of income equality would increase public debt, which would eventually engender higher poverty instead of greater equality. He also emphasised that, over the long-run, the noble goal of achieving equality not only leads to more inequality, it also generates public deficits, unfreedom, and serfdom. Thus, Hayek concluded that implementing measures and expending efforts to achieve a more egalitarian society ultimately worsens the ills that the state is targeting.

Issues like inequality and a lack of economic resources due to the unjust distribution of wealth and income in a free-market economy did not concern Hayek. In fact, he did not accept the premise that the emergence of economic inequality within a society was an outcome of social and economic injustice; rather, he considered it to be a product of 'misfortune' (Plant 1994, 165). That means there is nothing to prevent anyone from prospering and becoming wealthy under a system of free-market capitalism, including a poor and miserable person (Hayek 2011, 448). Similarly, Friedman (1982, 139) argued that people often make the mistake of blaming capitalism and free enterprise for producing 'wider inequality than alternative systems.' He argued that, contrary to popular belief and misinterpretation, in reality, 'capitalism leads to less inequality than alternative systems of organization and that the development of capitalism has greatly lessened the extent of inequality' (Friedman 1982, 140). He also suggested that when a country is 'highly capitalist,' 'inequality appears to be less, in any meaningful sense' (Friedman 1982, 140). Conversely, he claimed that 'non-capitalist societies tend to have wider inequality than capitalist' countries (Friedman 1982, 140).

Hayek (2011, 148) argued that free-market societies have 'nothing to do with any other sort of equality, but it is even bound to produce inequality in many respects.' He associated the desire and sense of moral duty to achieve a more egalitarian society with the 'primitive conditions' of tribal societies (or closed societies) (Hayek 1998bv2, 88). He was basically referring to societies that were 'simple and small, and individuals knew each other intimately and were bound to one another through kinship. As a result, members of the tribe supported each another in times of need' (Filip 2012, 78). He explained that a tribe is an 'end-connected' society, where people try to achieve moral and ethical ends for the welfare of their small community (Hayek 1998bv2, 110). With that in mind, he described any efforts to achieve social justice in free societies as a revival of tribal sentiments. More specifically, Hayek (1998bv2, 144) argued that 'the demand for "social justice" is indeed an expression of revolt of the tribal spirit against the abstract requirements of the coherence of the Great Society with no such visible common purpose.' He further suggested that 'socialism is simply a re-assertion of that tribal ethics whose gradual weakening had made an approach to the Great Society[9] possible' (Hayek 1998bv2, 113-114).

Contrary to tribal societies, Hayek explained that, under free-market capitalism, populations are large, and relationships are impersonal, individualistic, formal, and instrumental, meaning that people 'do not have complete knowledge of the needs, welfare, and interests of their fellow citizens' (Filip 2012, 78). In other words, societies operating under a free-market system are comprised of a vast number of people with diverging and conflicting goals and ends, suggesting that a lack of common moral and ethical values could form the basis upon which to achieve a more egalitarian society.

Hayek (1998bv2, 83) argued that 'while an equality of rights under a limited government is possible and an essential condition of individual freedom, a claim for equality of material position can be met only by a

[9] Hayek interchangeably used the terms the Great society, open society, and free-market capitalism.

government with totalitarian powers.' He stressed that there is a significant difference 'between treating people equally and attempting to make them equal,' explaining that 'the first is the condition of a free society,' whereas the latter represents 'a new form of servitude' (Hayek 1958, 16). He was particularly worried that, in their efforts to achieve a more egalitarian society, states would progressively alter the legal system that coordinates individual activities in a free society.

Hayek (1998bv1, 142) emphasized that movements 'towards a 'socialization' of the law have been taking place in most Western countries for several generations and have already gone far to destroy the characteristic attribute of universal rules of conduct, the equality of all under the same rules.' Similarly, Friedman (1982 [1962], 134) claimed that 'a central element in the development of a collectivist sentiment in this century, at least in Western countries,' has been the misguided belief that state intervention could be employed to achieve the equality of income. Both Hayek and Friedman disapproved of states attempting to achieve social justice by supporting disadvantaged groups of individuals through methods like income redistribution and the provision of public programs and services (e.g., universal health care, free education, affordable public housing etc.).

Hayek (1998bv2, 83) warned people that they needed to exercise caution when making demands for the equal distribution of income and material possessions, because the state response has the potential to transform a free-society into a totalitarian state. In other words, satisfying demands for the equality of opportunity requires a central planning authority to control 'the whole physical and human environment of all persons,' which will eventually lead to the government gaining control over every aspect of people's lives (Hayek 1998bv2, 85). Hayek was concerned that this transition would eventually provide states with unlimited powers of coercion. Consequently, the free-market system would cease to exist, being effectively replaced by the commands of the directing authority. Furthermore, since this transition from a free-market system to a command economy would be performed in the name of achieving a more egalitarian society, the central planning authority will likely impose new duties and burdens on individuals so as to realise the collective good. Accordingly, he concluded that even though goals like social justice and equality of opportunity sound very 'attractive,' when a government actually attempts to achieve them, such goals become a 'wholly illusory ideal, and any attempt concretely to realize' them is 'apt to produce a nightmare' (Hayek 1998bv2, 85).

Similarly, Mises (1962, 78) argued that 'equality of income through equal distribution of commodities is unjustified.' He suggested that if this was actually accepted as a societal goal, then people would be guided towards 'self-sufficient agriculturists, leaving room for at most a few artisans,' which would obstruct progress (Mises 1962, 51). He argued that Western civilization was founded 'on the fact that men have always succeeded in beating off the attack of the re-distributors' (Mises 1962, 51). Thus, he was convinced that if supporters of the redistribution of wealth and income were to succeed, as they did in former communist countries, they would eventually destroy Western civilisation. Mises (1962, 77) was of the opinion that proponents of the ideal of equality 'sought to justify' its attainment based on 'religious, psychological, and philosophical arguments; but all these proved to be untenable.' This is because redistribution 'according to needs' is 'an old slogan of the unsophisticated communist. It is occasionally backed up by referring to the fact that the Early Christians shared all goods in common' (Mises 1962, 156). He concluded that 'the principle of equal distribution derives from the old doctrine of natural law of the equality of all human beings. Rigidly applied it would prove absurd' (Mises 1962, 155).

Hayek maintained that achieving distributive justice and equality has nothing to do with 'an innocent expression of good will towards the less fortunate, but that it has become a dishonest insinuation that one ought to agree to a demand of some special interest which can give no real reason for it' (Hayek 1998av1, 97). In fact, he believed that people who want to achieve a more egalitarian society are guided by 'envy' as opposed to humanitarian ends. Practically speaking, he was convinced that 'equality of the general rules of law and conduct' was 'the only kind of equality conducive to liberty and the only equality which we can secure without destroying liberty' (Hayek 2011, 148). That said, he believed that it was an inevitability that a free-market system would eventually produce inequality in society. This is evidenced by the fact that neo-liberal economic reforms have generated higher productivity, economic growth, and capital accumulation for the benefit of a very small number of privileged people to the exclusion of the mass majority. This has led to the emergence of extreme levels of social and economic inequality globally.

Unlike Friedman, Hayek, and Mises who were not concerned with growing social and economic inequality, Stigler did express reservations about 'the policy of ignoring inequalities of resources' and not 'battling vigorously against inequalities of income' (Stigler 1949, 10). To the contrary, he specifically stated that 'our concern should be much more with the ownership of resources that leads to the wide differences in income. We should seek to make labour incomes more equal by enlarged educational systems, improvements of labour mobility, elimination of labour monopolies, provision of medical care for poor children, and the like. We should seek to make property incomes more equal (and smaller) by elimination of monopoly and by extremely heavy taxation of inheritances' (Stigler 1949, 10). Knight (1929) also did not share the views of Friedman, Hayek, and Mises when it came to social justice, as he believed that social and economic inequalities were inclined to 'overwhelmingly' reduce the level of 'total satisfaction' in a society. According to him, 'the distribution of economic resources atomistic motivation tends powerfully toward cumulatively increasing inequality' (Knight 1951, 20). He also underscored the point that social and economic inequalities are worsened by the inheritance of significant amounts wealth by some people, who in turn are provided with a greater capacity to attain prosperity relative to their poor counterparts. They are 'always in a better position to acquire still more, with the same effort and sacrifice' (Knight 1951, 20). By making this point, he was highlighting that social and economic inequality was not limited to just one generation, as it continues to persist 'from generation to generation, through the family and transmission of advantages' (Knight 1951, 20). According to Knight (1948, 53), wealth and individual abilities are:

> largely historical creations—neither given by nature nor produced by individual effort—there is a tendency for inequality to increase cumulatively. Those who at any time have more are in that much better position to acquire still more. Through the family, and other institutions, this goes on beyond the individual life. And it should be stressed—because it is generally ignored—that this tendency applies not only to personal capacities but to taste and appreciation, to all culture, which is humanly more important than means of gratification.

He believed that the fact that poor people had very little opportunity to escape misery and poverty was unjust and unfair. Knight (1951, 20) suggested that social and economic inequality between people was 'a gross injustice' that could be attributed to the very nature of free-market capitalism, specifically caused 'by one of several conflicting norms of justice generally accepted in liberal society.' Despite the concerns expressed by Stigler and Knights with respect to the inequality of resources, neo-classicals and neo-liberals have generally been opposed to any form of income and wealth redistribution, as well as the public provision of social services and programs, in order to achieve a more egalitarian society.

Neo-liberals regard the achievement of social justice via state intervention as evil. This contrasts with the view that justice is 'the chief of the virtues,' which has been put forth by many prominent philosophers, theologists and political theorists since the times of the Ancient Greeks (Aristotle, 1893 [1999], 139). In fact, it was accepted as 'the complete virtue, with the addition that it is displayed towards others' (Aristotle, 1893 [1999], 139). Basically, it could be said that 'justice sums up all virtues in itself' (Aristotle, 1893 [1999], 139).

10.3.1 Freedom and Equality

A 'primitive tribe may not produce much wealth, but all members are capable of an independent life…They can make their own shelter, clothing, and weapons…they are all capable of supplying their own wants. The independence of all of the members makes them free contracting parties in their relations with the community' (George 2006, 156). In the event of misery and poverty, there was also a moral and ethical obligation between family members, relatives, friends and neighbours to help each other. Although primitive tribal societies lacked many of the comforts and advances associated with Western civilization and free-market capitalism, land and wealth were equally distributed, and people enjoyed more freedom. However, the complexity of contemporary social and economic systems does not mean that humanity has to distance itself from the true human values that prevailed in tribal societies, where it could be argued that people had a better understanding of the concepts of justice and freedom.

Contrary to tribal societies, people living under a system of free-market capitalism do not start their lives on equal footing or with equal rights. Furthermore, social and economic inequalities are exacerbated when there are gains in productivity, efficiency, and economic growth in a free-market society, because most of the benefits associated with these developments are monopolized by large corporations. That means the presence of inequality in terms of income, wealth, and power are not outcomes of natural causes; they are created by human actions and activities.

Knight (1997 [1935]) warned that economic freedom in the 'sense of extreme individual laissez-faire' is destructive, because of the fact that rich people can use their wealth to get richer. He explained that 'the more of it anyone has, the more advantage he has in the struggle to get still more' (Knight 1997, 183). Consequently, according to the free-market concept of freedom, which considers human beings to be self-interest oriented and acquisitive, 'a cumulative growth of inequality' is inevitable (Knight 1997, 183). Knight (1997, 183) further explained that, under a free-market system, 'with "gross" inequality in the distribution of wealth among individuals, all ethical defences of freedom lose their validity' (Knight 1997, 183).

Neo-liberals often claim that the free-market system provides better economic, political and social arrangements for everybody involved compared to any other economic system. This is because it allows individuals to voluntarily exchange goods and services in ways that do not interfere with the goals, decisions and actions of others. Furthermore, according to neo-liberals, people in a free-market system are protected from coercion by any particular producer, seller, or employer, on account of the availability of many other such economic agents with whom they can deal. However, over last four decades, the free-market system has proven that in the absence of a commitment to social and economic equality on the part of the government, there is nothing to prevent an economic agent from taking advantage of weak and powerless people so as to acquire material gains. That is to say, many of the conditions of positive, negative and economic freedom are satisfied for rich people under a free-market system, because they are permitted to increase their wealth and privileges at the expense of billions of other people. Meanwhile, the masses are largely excluded from the benefits provided by free-market economic reforms, which ultimately end up restricting both their economic freedom and positive freedom.

Neo-liberals oppose using state interventions to establish the conditions of positive freedom, as they regard such actions as violations of economic and negative freedom. That means they are against all government efforts to create more just and equal societies by redistributing income and wealth in order to achieve the conditions of self-development. Although Hayek (2011, 150) recognized that some people might enjoy an egalitarian society, where 'there are no extreme contrasts between rich and poor,' he was nonetheless opposed to states resorting to coercive measures in order to achieve this kind of scenario. He maintained that 'the desirability of a particular object is not sufficient justification' for employing state coercive power (Hayek 2011, 150). He further stated that 'many of those who demand an extension of equality do not really demand equality but a distribution that conforms more closely to human conceptions of individual merit and that their desires are as irreconcilable with freedom' (Hayek 2011, 150). He suggested that, to achieve distributive justice, the state will intentionally control the lives and actions of individuals by imposing patterns of distribution instead of leaving people to be guided by their own wills and goals. Basically, Hayek was arguing that people who demanded distributive justice and equality did not realized the extent to which the government would need to be involved in their lives in order to achieve such a state of affairs. He further contended that people would only realize that they had sacrificed their freedom in order to attain distributive justice and equality after the government began to interfere in their private spheres.

According to Hayek, achieving a more egalitarian society means that individuals have no choice other than to obey the rules of just conduct imposed on them by the state. He was convinced that all efforts to attain an objective standard in order to have equality would end up destroying freedom. As such, he argued that if people wanted to preserve their freedom, they needed to oppose any attempts to achieve equality by imposing deliberately chosen patterns of distribution on society. Similarly, Friedman insisted that the achievement of equality was an ethical belief that did not justify the distribution of income in a free-market society. In fact, he claimed that any state program or policy of paternalism intended to achieve the equality of outcome was antithetical to liberty. According to Friedman, 'this includes the collection of taxes in the name of security and equality because, despite the fact that these funds are used to provide citizens with social programs like public assistance, education, health care, unemployment insurance, housing subsidies, and infrastructure, individual freedom is reduced when people are forced to involuntarily hand over their money in order to finance programs for the benefit of others' (Filip 2018, 348).

While neo-liberals consider state interference aimed at ensuring the conditions of equality to be an infringement upon freedom, they do not regard social and economic inequality as violations of the freedom of the disadvantaged segments of the population. This is not particularly surprising, given that the negative freedom defended by neo-liberals does not require that people are provided with opportunities for their own self-development. In free-market societies, opportunities are generally available for powerful and privileged people to the exclusion of all others. Conversely, positive freedom, which is not recognized by neo-liberals, seeks to provide opportunities for everybody, while striving to achieve common ends by harmonizing the goals of individuals with those of society.

It is hypocritical to suggest that the most miserable, poor and disadvantaged segments of the population are perfectly free to choose in a free-market system. In fact, since freedom and equality are complementary, freedom could be rendered 'virtually useless' under a system of free-market capitalism, given the prevalence of extreme inequalities (Berlin 2002, 46). For example, the opportunity to exercise freedom of choice is denied when people are unable to secure adequate access to their basic needs. That is to say, when people perpetually struggle to satisfy their minimum basic necessities, their lives cannot be free expressions of their own individualities. More precisely, if people are homeless, jobless, or penniless, they often face food insecurity, which takes precedence over all other needs and desires, meaning they do not have the freedom to achieve their highest development of individuality. This is consistent with the views held by defenders of positive freedom, who argue that the development of individuality is hindered when social and economic inequalities are prevalent. Certain conditions need to be in place in order to provide individuals with the opportunity to achieve their highest development and unveil their creative faculties. Foremost among them are that an individual must earn an adequate income, work limited hours in a safe and healthy work environment, possess a safe and secure shelter, and have access to education, health care services, and training opportunities. In general, human beings need to be free from constraints in order to have freedom. A constant preoccupation with a lack of a safe and secure shelter, health problems, and food insecurity are destructive to the human mind and the development of capacities. Without some sort of social and economic security, freedom is meaningless, because people are unable to realize their own goals, or make free choices based on their own wills.

Although equality might prevent certain citizens from receiving special privileges, it does not seek to make everybody absolutely equal in all aspects while eliminating the possibility of diversity. That is to say, equality does not attempt to make individuals identical in the sense of the products they consume, the meals they eat, the clothes they wear, their educational attainment, the houses they live in, or their goals, desires, and needs. Rather, it entails providing the same treatment to different people who can be distinct from one another in a variety of ways, including their backgrounds, particular histories, personalities, capacities and interests. Equality means everyone has access to adequate opportunities to develop their individual capacities and abilities to the fullest extent possible. More precisely, equality is supposed to help individuals unveil their differences in character, and discover and develop their individualities, thereby contributing to the achievement of their highest self-development.

In fact, establishing equality via state interference can promote freedom by preventing anyone from leveraging their coercive power over others for their own personal gain. To attain positive freedom, it is necessary that the state provides all citizens with adequate opportunities that make it possible to achieve self-development, which adds to collective good of the whole society. Only under such conditions can differences in the social and economic situations of people be tolerated. Any disparities in social and economic status between people should be outcomes of their highest development of individuality and personal efforts, as opposed to the reckless exploitation of natural resources and other people's labour.

According to Aristotle (1999), inequality is bound to deny freedom, which can only be secured when all are able to rule equally without privileges. The more equal that people are in terms of economic and political power, the greater use they can make of their freedom. Across history, inequality has been 'a cause of revolution,' as 'the desire of equality' has led to 'rebellion' (Aristotle 1999, 109). In other words, Aristotle realised that the desire for equality is one of the most profound catalysts of revolution. Similarly, any attempt to achieve the conditions of self-development is also a revolt against the inequality upon which society rests.

10.4 Conclusion

After four decades of dominating almost every aspect of people's lives, it has become evident that free-market capitalism and its unwavering commitment to efficiency, competitiveness, productivity, technological innovation, and economic growth have allowed a handful of very powerful economic agents to gain possession of an abundance of the earth's natural resources and various other means of production, while also enjoying many privileges that are not available to the masses. This exclusive collection of people and corporations have essentially monopolized 'opportunities nature freely offers to all,' whereas labourers have been 'robbed' of their 'earnings, while greed rolls in wealth' (George 2006, 295, 298).

That would suggest that some of the most important objectives advocated by neo-liberalism have become instruments of widespread control, and catalysts of unprecedented inequality and unfreedom around the world.

The broad implementation of free-market economic reforms on a global scale has led to billions of people being coerced into significantly altering their lifestyles. Unfortunately, these changes have not been for the better, as free-market capitalism has brought them misery, unfreedom, poverty, bankruptcy, unemployment, hunger, health problems, pollution, environmental degradation, etc. In other words, people have been experiencing inequality 'in a thousand shapes according to their passions, their talents, and circumstances' (Rousseau 2002, 133). The emergence of various forms of inequality is not an 'inexplicable' phenomenon (George 2006, 187). Some people have not chosen to live in poverty, because they think that it is somehow preferable to enjoying material well-being (George 2006, 187). Furthermore, 'it is not that nature has produced children it has failed to provide for. It is not that the Creator has left injustice in natural laws, such that material progress should bring such bitter fruits. It is not due to any lack of nature—but to human injustice. Vice and misery, poverty and pauperism, are…the direct and necessary result of violating the supreme law of justice— giving to the exclusive possession of a few, what nature has provided for all.' (George 2006, 187).

Freedom is not afforded to people in a society when they lack political, social and economic equality, and cannot obtain adequate material security, health and knowledge. Even if an abundance of choices are available to these people in the market, they are not free to choose, because they do not possess the means by which to use this freedom due to the lack of money, health, education, training, etc. Furthermore, neo-liberals are fervently opposed to state interventions aimed at achieving the conditions of equality, because they associate them with coercion, even though such measures can play a major role in achieving freedom. At the same time, they do not criticize free-market capitalism for creating unprecedented levels of social and economic inequality, which actually facilitate coercion. When people live under constant threats of hunger, starvation and homelessness, they are not really free to choose, as they have to devote their lives to working in order to obtain their basic needs. Moreover, while they are working, their actions, thoughts, imaginations, and feelings are shaped and controlled by the rules set out by their employers. In a way, they end up becoming 'slaves, machines, commodities. In some respects, they are lower than animals' (George 2006, 157). These people do not 'live their own lives but perform pre-established functions. While they work, they do not fulfill their own needs and faculties but work in alienation' (Marcuse 1998, 45).

References

Aristotle. 1999. *Politics*. Trans. Benjamin Jowett. Kitchener: Batoche Book.

Bakan, Joel. 2004. *The Corporation: The Pathological Pursuit of Profit and Power*. Simon & Schuster Inc.

Berlin, Isaiah. 2002 [1969]. In *Incorporating Four Essays on Liberty*, ed. Henry Hardy. Oxford: Oxford University Press.

Filip, Birsen. 2012. Polanyi and Hayek on Freedom, the State, and Economics. *International Journal of Political Economy* 41 (4): 69–87. https://doi.org/10.2753/IJP0891-1916410405.

Filip, B. 2018. Friedman and Hayek's Converging Ideas on Freedom and the State. In *Hayek: A Collaborative Biography Part XV: The Chicago School of Economics, Hayek's 'Luck' and the 1974 Nobel Prize for Economic Science*, ed. Robert Leeson, 327–372. Cham: Palgrave Macmillan.

Friedman, Milton. 1982 [1962]. *Capitalism and Freedom*. Chicago: University of Chicago Press.

George, Henry. 2006 [1879]. In *Progress and Poverty: Why There Are Recessions and Poverty Amid Plenty—and What To Do About It!* ed. Bob Drake. New York: Robert Schalkenbach Foundation.

George de Mille, Agnes. 2006. Who Was Henry George? In Henry George. 2006 [1879]. *Progress and Poverty: Why There Are Recessions and Poverty Amid Plenty—and What To Do About It!* Ed. Bob Drake. New York: Robert Schalkenbach Foundation. 304–310.

Hayek, F.A. 1958 [1948]. *Individualism and Economic Order*. Chicago: University of Chicago Press.

———. 1998a [1973]. *Law, Legislation and Liberty: Rules and Order, Volume 1*. London: Routledge & Kegan Paul.

———. 1998b [1976]. *Law, Legislation and Liberty Volume 2: The Mirage of Social Justice*. London: Routledge & Kegan Paul.

———. 2011 [1960]. *The Constitution of Liberty*. Chicago: University of Chicago Press.

Knight, Frank H. 1922. Ethics and the Economic Interpretation. *The Quarterly Journal of Economics. Oxford: Oxford University Press* 36 (3): 454–481. https://www.jstor.org/stable/1886033.

———. 1929. Freedom as Fact and Criterion. *International Journal of Ethics. Chicago: The University of Chicago Press* 39 (2): 129–147. https://www.jstor.org/stable/2377742.

———. 1997 [1935]. *The Ethics of Competition*. New Brunswick: Transactions.
———. 1948. Free Society: Its Basic Nature and Problem. *Philosophical Review* 57 (January): 39–58. https://www.jstor.org/stable/2181733.
———. 1951. The Role of Principles in Economics and Politics. *The American Economic Review. American Economic Association* 41 (1): 1–29. https://www.jstor.org/stable/1815957.
Marcuse, Herbert. 1998 [1956]. *Eros and Civilisation: A Philosophical Inquiry into Freud*. Abingdon: Routledge.
von Mises, Ludwig. 1962 [1951]. *Socialism: An Economic and Sociological Analysis*. New Haven: Yale University Press.
Montesquieu, Charles Louis de Secondat. 1977. *The Complete Works of M. de Montesquieu*. London: T. Evans. https://oll.libertyfund.org/titles/837.
Myrdal, Karl Gunnar. 1973. Economics of an Improved Environment. *World Development. Stockholm: Institute for International Economic Studies* 1 (1,2): 102–114.
Parenti, Michael. 2011. *The Face of Imperialism*. New York: Routledge.
———. 2015. *Profit Pathology and Other Indecencies*. New York: Routledge.
Plant, R. 1994. Hayek on Social Justice: A Critique. In *Hayek, Co-ordination and Evolution: His Legacy in Philosophy, Politics, Economics and the History of Ideas*, ed. J. Birner and R. Van Zijp, 164–177. London: Routledge.
Rousseau, Jean-Jacques. 2002. *The Social Contract and The First and Second Discourses. Intro. Susan Dunn*. London: Yale University Press.
Samuelson, Paul Anthon, and William D. Nordhaus. 2010 [1948]. *Economics*. New York: The McGraw-Hill Companies, Inc.
Stigler, George J. 1949. *Five Lectures on Economic Problems*. London: Longmans, Green and Co.
Stiglitz, Joseph. 2003. *Globalization and Its Discontents*. New York: W.W. Norton & Company.

CHAPTER 11

The Rise of Neo-liberalism and the Decline of Moral and Ethical Values

The attainment of methodological monism, which refers to having faith in a single paradigm, has proven to be a deep source of satisfaction for practitioners of neo-liberal economics, who contend that they belong to a paradigm that is superior to all others that have existed in the history of economics. Their absolute belief in the superiority of neo-liberalism compared to any other school of economic thought is largely premised on their adoption and application of the methodology, procedures, language, and presentation of mathematics in their economic research. As a result, economists falsely claim that economics is a branch of physical science, which would make it a value-free discipline, meaning there is no relationship between economics and moral and ethical values. Therefore, economic decisions, actions and policies are immune from any moral and ethical judgements. These views are not particularly surprising, given that it is extremely rare to see neo-liberal economists criticize the free-market system for producing outcomes that are unjust, unfair, immoral, unethical, etc. Furthermore, they do not feel that it is necessary to adjust their paradigm so as to address or correct these features and outcomes by integrating moral and ethical judgements.

Instead of allowing ethical and moral judgements to guide the actions and decisions of people, mainstream economists have advised for the integration of neo-liberal economic principles and reasoning into every aspect of life. Consequently, people have been encouraged to adopt

B. Filip, *The Rise of Neo-liberalism and the Decline of Freedom*,
Palgrave Insights into Apocalypse Economics,
https://doi.org/10.1007/978-3-030-61623-6_11

self-interested, rational, impersonal, and individualistic behaviors in their daily actions and decisions, which is supposed to make them feel as though they are free to choose. By imposing a meticulously designed set of principles and ideas, neo-liberalism has been largely successful in terms of shaping the vision, perspectives and goals of the masses, governments, private enterprises, and public institutions and organizations. That means neo-liberals have not only managed to make economics into a discipline of the natural sciences, they also became ideologues whose principles replaced religion and moral philosophy as the sources of people's core beliefs, views, practices, and values. In other words, neo-liberalism has been providing people with guidance in their daily lives, much like Christian theology and moral philosophy did in the past.

The widespread adoption of neo-liberal economic views and values around the world has led to the disengagement of moral and ethical judgements from people's decisions and actions. Very few countries and societies have been immune from the penetration of the standards and principles prescribed by neo-liberalism. As a result, neo-liberalism has led to the emergence and global spread of societal diseases, like moral failure, which is one of the main causes of social and economic inequality, and a key factor in the potential onset of an environmental apocalypse. This chapter focuses on the rise of neo-liberalism and the decline of moral and ethical values in society. It also discusses some of the arguments put forth by neo-liberals against ethical and moral philosophy.

11.1 Moral and Ethical Values in Economics

For many decades, neo-liberals have claimed that economics is a value-free science, and that the principles and goals of neo-liberalism are applicable to all areas of life, including those not considered parts of traditional economic analysis, such as daily activities, education, family, hobbies, crime, marriage, fertility, politics, law, healthcare, illness, pollution, etc. That means these areas of political, personal and social life can be treated as though they are business transactions that do not take moral and ethical judgements into consideration. This is not surprising, given that neo-liberals believe that moral and ethical values have no place in the free-market system, because good intentions and virtuous actions are not required for the achievement of capitalist ends. Ultimately, the consistent elevation and application of neo-liberal principles, as well as an unwavering commitment to the achievement of capitalist ends, have yielded societies where individuals are primarily recognized and treated as economic agents instead of human beings.

Throughout history, people sought to achieve freedom and happiness through their decisions and actions, which have been guided by a variety of different factors, including 'by the climate, by the religion, by the laws, by the maxims of government, by precedents, morals, and customs,' as well as compassion, culture, and traditional values (Montesquieu 1977a, 187). When ethical and moral values served as the foundations of judgment, people were opposed to the purely individualistic and egoistical motivations advocated by classical *homo economicus*. However, the advance of neo-liberalism radically altered this state of affairs, as it facilitated a general movement away from the practice of moral and ethical values. Meanwhile, the increasing importance attributed to productivity, economic growth, and efficiency 'involved growing degeneration of the life instincts,' and a decline of moral and ethical practices (Marcuse 1998, 121). To be more precise, since the rise of neo-liberalism, freedom and happiness were no longer sought out through virtue in the Ancient Greek or Aristotelian sense, nor were they granted by the heavens as advocated by Aquinas and Augustine; rather, they were to be found in individual self-interest maximization, an unrestrained desire for power, and acquisitiveness.

Contrary to neo-liberalism, the history of political thought and philosophy often regarded individual self-interest maximization, the desire for power, and acquisitiveness as root causes of some of the most serious forms of injustice, destruction, and misery known to humanity (Rousseau 1967). According to Ancient Greek philosophy, acting in accordance with virtue over the duration of one's lifetime brings freedom and happiness, whereas pleasure and self-interested behaviors were regarded as poor and petty (Aristotle 1893). Meanwhile, adherents of Aristotelian ethics and Stoicism, a school of Hellenistic philosophy, would advise that no values should be based on selfish, individualistic and intemperate goals.

For centuries, moral philosophy and various religions regarded the dedication of one's life to the achievement of external ends, such as wealth, power, and physical pleasure, with contempt, and advised doing everything possible to become an ethical and moral human being instead of a vicious one. For example, the Ancient Greeks believed that the goal of society was to create good citizens, and contended that every social, political and economic issue or problem that arose needed to be 'studied primarily from the ethical and educational point of view' (Ingram 1915, 19).

Each citizen of the Ancient Greek city-states was not 'regarded as a producer, but only as a possessor, of material wealth; and this wealth is not esteemed for its own sake or for the enjoyments it procures, but for the higher moral and public aims to which it may be made subservient' (Ingram 1915, 19). In fact, Aristotle (1893, 8) explained that 'money-making life' is 'contrary to nature; and wealth evidently is not the good of which we are in search, for it is merely useful as a means to something else.'

Across history, many philosophers, theologists, and political theorists were preoccupied with people's obsessions with selfish goals, power, and acquisitiveness, which they believed would transform people into vicious, corrupt, manipulative, and destructive beings. This is because they were fully conscious of the fact that, contrary to animals, the wants and desires of human beings are neither fixed nor limited. More precisely, they suggested that human beings are unique as 'the only animals whose desires increase as they are fed—the only animal that is never satisfied' (George 2006, 72). They are always 'moving to higher forms of desire,' which 'awaken to other things' (George 2006, 72). For example, since the very poor people are at the lowest levels of wants and desires, they largely focus their efforts on satisfying their necessary needs, not unlike animals. However, once those basic needs are satisfied, they demand more quantity; then, once this desire for more quantity has been satisfied, they want better quality. Subsequently, once people's wants and desires for better quality have been satisfied, their 'aspirations grow' (George 2006, 72).

Many social scientists believed that such incremental improvements in human wants and desires, from necessity goods to much higher aspirations, would inevitably lead individuals to make choices that are destructive and damaging to other people and their surroundings if moral and ethical judgments are not taken into consideration when evaluating their decisions and actions. Accordingly, Jean-Jacques Rousseau (1712–1778) (1921, 247) explained that the physical needs, wants and desires of people grow naturally; however, they cannot make 'the same progress' in their 'moral being,' as 'the soul is still frail and delicate, and whatever can be done by human art, the body is always ahead of the mind.' He advised people to restrain their physical wants and desires and, instead, strive to become moral beings, 'so that the man might be as far as possible at one with himself' (1921, 247). Rousseau believed that the development of individuality would drive people towards becoming moral and ethical beings.

Many philosophers and political theorists throughout human history, beginning with the Ancient Greeks, adhered to the view that becoming a moral and ethical being required limiting one's own freedom. Therefore, people who are committed to moral and ethical judgements are mindful that freedom requires restrictions. More precisely, the freedom of each individual should be restricted by the freedom of other people. According to Johann Gottlieb Fichte (1762–1814) (2000, 9), who is well known as one of the main contributors of the *German Idealism*, one should not 'ascribe' to oneself all of the freedom that is perceived to exist, because there are 'other free beings as well, and must ascribe to them a part of this freedom.' In other words, one must limit what is allocated to oneself when 'appropriating freedom' for the purpose of 'leaving some freedom for others as well' (Fichte 2000, 9). Basically, self-limitation is an important condition for the achievement of freedom and becoming a moral and ethical being.

Since the times of Ancient Greece, numerous philosophers, thinkers and theorists have sought to eliminate people's obsession with selfish goals, power, and acquisitiveness. In doing so, they contended that excellence of moral character required temperance, a virtue that is well-known for playing a major role in Aristotle's ethics, along with justice, and courage. Temperance needs to be 'preserved by moderation' of pleasures, and cannot exist in an environment of excess and defect (Aristotle 1893, 38). That means 'the pleasures of the body and the pleasures of the soul, such as the pleasures of gratified ambition,' all have to be moderated (Aristotle 1893, 91). According to Aristotle (1893, 94, 96), an ethical individual is temperate and gains no satisfaction from 'profligacy,' unmoderated excess in pleasures, acquisitiveness, and intemperance. he term 'profligacy' is associated with 'childish faults,' as children are motivated by an irrational need to satisfy 'their appetites, and the desire for pleasant things,' and as such, are not 'submissive and obedient to the governing principle' (Aristotle 1893, 97). Similar to children, 'for in an irrational being the desire for pleasant things is insatiable and ready to gratify itself in any way, and the gratification of the appetite increases the natural tendency, and if the gratifications are great and intense they even thrust out reason altogether' (Aristotle 1893, 97). To be a virtuous being, the desire to satisfy appetites needs to be moderated, so that it is in harmony with reason (Aristotle 1893, 98). Aristotle (1893, 99) labelled intemperate people that wasted their money on living luxurious and lavish lifestyles 'prodigals,' who he considered to be destructive, egoistic, and 'very worthless individuals, as they combine a number of vices.' He argued that the worst person 'displays vice both in his own affairs and in his dealings with his friends, the best man is not he who displays virtue in his own affairs merely, but he who displays virtue towards others' (Aristotle 1893, 140).

According to Aristotle, if individuals have ethical commitments, and view themselves as members of society, then they can discard egoistic desires and wants that might require the use of unethical means or produce unethical outcomes. Individuals can still pursue their particular desires, wants and goals if they are committed to moral and ethical judgements, provided that their aspirations are not 'egoistic' (Neuhouser 2000, 91). In other words, if individuals view themselves as 'members of social' world instead of 'self-sufficient' and egoistical entities, then they cannot act purely based on their private interests and personal benefits (Neuhouser 2000, 91). Even if individuals make decisions as members of a community, and not as isolated selfish entities, they are still free and self-determining agents who make ethical and moral decisions based on their own free individual wills. While it is also possible for people to achieve morally good ends by being influenced by an 'authority' instead of following their personal principles and beliefs, such people cannot be described as 'free or self-determining' (Patten 1999, 67). For people to be moral self-determining agents, they cannot be coerced into accepting morally and ethically good actions by an authority; rather, they need to be able to rationally evaluate, recognize and accept moral and ethical behaviours based on their own wills and interpretations of what it means to be good and bad (Patten 1999, 67).

For decades, neo-liberal ideology has taught people that self-interest maximization, individualism, exploitation, intemperance, and acquisitiveness are virtues. In fact, theorists, contributors and practitioners of neo-liberalism have consistently advocated for these core values and principles of their paradigm to be adopted in the daily lives of individuals at every opportunity. They were largely successful in accomplishing this objective. Integrating these values and principles into people's thoughts, minds, and behaviours has involved inundating them with persuasive propaganda designed to promote the virtues of neo-liberalism through various mediums, including newspapers, books, advertisements and programs transmitted via television, the radio and the internet, movies, the education systems, and the discourses of well-known public figures like politicians, academics, experts, celebrities and athletes. That said, neo-liberals can also attribute much of their success in terms of integrating free-market economic principles and values into people's daily lives to the financial, technical and ideological support they consistently receive from democratically-elected politicians, powerful corporations, free-market think thanks, and various international institutions and organizations. Their success was also aided by the fact that these principles and values nourish vices, and promote the satisfaction of the intemperate and egoistic appetites and desires of individuals, thereby appealing to the primitive, uncultivated, unpolished, and under-developed nature of man.

In only a few decades, neo-liberals were able to integrate their values and principles into society to the extent that they now exert considerable influence over people's daily habits, choices and actions. During that same period, they also managed to eliminate nearly all remnants of the valuable work accentuating the importance of moral and ethical values produced by scores of prominent philosophers, theologists, and political theorists since the times of the Ancient Greeks.

Now that free-market capitalist values are so ingrained among the masses to the point of becoming second nature, it will be extremely difficult for any moral and ethical philosophy, or economic school of thought, to factor into people's decisions and behaviours in short-term. In all likelihood, the first step would require somehow weakening or dislodging the deep roots that neo-liberal values and principles have established over the last four decades. Much like 'a state cannot change its religion, manners and customs, in an instant,' the world will need some time to re-accustom itself to the prospect of having ethical and moral values play a significant role in every aspect of people's daily lives (Montesquieu 1977b, 187). This is because a majority of the customs, traditions and cultural values that people practice are not established by the legal system; rather, they are 'trained faculties,' meaning they are outcomes of repetition and practice, which leads to the formation of habits (Aristotle 1893, 20). Nobody is virtuous by accident, and moral and ethical values are not 'implanted in us by nature,' nor can they be imposed as rules via the coercive powers of the state (Aristotle 1893, 34). To the contrary, entrenching ethical and moral values into people's lives requires that they be cultivated and acquired through the practice of good habits (Aristotle 1893, 34).

Many of the destructive outcomes caused by free-market economics could be avoided if society somehow managed to free itself from the principles, reasoning and values of neo-liberalism. However, that would require replacing the selfish, egoistical and individualistic principles that have been carefully ingrained into society via neo-liberal propaganda with new values, habits, ways of thinking, and lifestyles. Generally speaking, when 'manners and customs are to be changed, it ought not to be done by laws; this would have too much the air of tyranny: it would be better to change them by introducing other manners and other customs' (Montesquieu 1977a, 412). Normally, when a ruler seeks to make significant changes in the country, 'he should reform by law what is established by law, and change by custom what is settled by custom; for it is very bad policy to change by law what ought to be changed by custom' (Montesquieu 1977a, 412). Unfortunately, the process of integrating moral and ethical judgements into the daily lives and routines of the majority of people around the world could take many decades, which may not be feasible, since humanity could be on the brink of an environmental apocalypse at that point. That is to say, the gravity of the current situation means it might be necessary to impose new laws and rules on society mandating people to behave and act in accordance with ethical and moral judgements for a transitional period. This manner of making significant changes to customs by establishing new rules that value the universality of thought was discussed in Georg Wilhelm Friedrich Hegel's (1770–1831) *Philosophy of Right* (2008).

Hegel (2008, 199) was adamant that customs are subjective and known in 'a contingent way,' because they are created by human beings for the purpose of guiding them in their lives. He also argued that the 'universality of thought is less clear in' customs compared to laws, which are objective and definitive, and intended to guide individuals to the achievement of a defined purpose (Hegel 2008, 199). That said, Hegel (2008, 199) was of the opinion that man has 'law as custom.' He believed that the idea that a custom 'possesses the privilege of having become part of life is a delusion, since the valid laws of a nation do not cease to be its customs by being written and codified' (Hegel 2008, 199). Therefore, based on Hegel's views, it would be legitimate for a state to pass a set of entirely universal laws for the purpose of achieving an absolutely universal end that is based on ethical values. Accordingly, since the world appears to be in an extreme situation in the form of an impending environmental apocalypse, it will likely be necessary to impose new laws and rules intended to drastically change the lifestyles of people, including their daily habits and customs.

11.2 Neo-liberal Economists on Ethical Values

The discipline of economics continues to defend the pursuit of self-interests, individualism, rationalism, and the notion of a laissez-faire economy, all of which were fundamental principles of Adam Smith's (1723–1790) original framework of classical economics. However, it would be difficult to argue that Smith considered economics to be a 'value neutral' science, when considering the importance he attributed to the ethical and moral values in guiding people's actions and decisions in his book *Theory of Moral Sentiments* (1759 [1982]). To the contrary, he envisaged economics as a moral science rather than natural science. Although Smith is widely regarded as the father of modern economics, this particular viewpoint, which was also shared by many of his contemporaries at that time, has been largely ignored by neo-liberal economists, who consider their discipline to be a branch of the natural sciences, thereby negating any role for ethical and moral values and judgements.

Smith's perception of economics as a moral science could likely be attributed to the influence of Christian ethics, as well as the works of many philosophers since the times of the Ancient Greeks. In fact, his work was particularly influenced by Stoicism, a philosophical movement of the Hellenistic period that highly valued virtues, though he did disagree with some Stoic views. In *Theory of Moral Sentiments*, Smith referred to the views and ideas of two main contributors to Stoicism who underscored the importance of virtues like prudence, temperance and justice in the achievement of *eudaemonia*: Seneca (4 BC–AD 65) and Epictetus (50–135 AD). He also emphasized the importance of moderation between excess and deficits in people's decisions and actions. In discussing virtues, Smith (1982, 137) stressed that:

> It is not the love of our neighbour, it is not the love of mankind, which upon many occasions prompts us to the practice of those divine virtues. It is a stronger love, a more powerful affection, which generally takes place upon such occasions; the love of what is honourable and noble, of the grandeur, and dignity, and superiority of our own characters.

Smith (1982) did not really support the pursuit of purely individualist, self-interested, and egoistical goals. He stated that a person 'must never prefer himself so much even to any other individual, as to hurt or injure that other, in order to benefit himself, though the benefit to the one should be much greater than the hurt or injury to the other' (Smith 1982, 138). In addition to discussing Stoic philosophy at length in *Theory of Moral Sentiments*, Smith (1982) specifically referred to the views expressed by Roman emperor Marcus Aurelius Antoninus Augustus (121–180), who was a well-known adherent of Stoicism. Smith's (1982, 140) appreciation for Stoicism and his support of moral and ethical values are clearly evident in the following passage, among many others, from *Theory of Moral Sentiments*:

> Among the moralists who endeavour to correct the natural inequality of our passive feelings by diminishing our sensibility to what peculiarly concerns ourselves, we may count all the ancient sects of philosophers, but particularly the ancient Stoics. Man, according to the Stoics, ought to regard himself, not as something separated and detached, but as a citizen of the world, a member of the vast commonwealth of nature. To the interest of this great community, he ought at all times to be willing that his own little interest should be sacrificed. Whatever concerns himself, ought to affect him no more than whatever concerns any other equally important part of this immense system. We should view ourselves, not in the light in which our own selfish passions are apt to place us, but in the light in which any other citizen of the world would view us.

Like the Stoics, Smith supported justice, prudence, temperance and benevolence as virtues to be practices and promoted. In defending justice and prudence in particular, Smith (1982, 149) stated that a person who pursues 'extravagant passions:'

> is not only miserable in his actual situation, but is often disposed to disturb the peace of society, in order to arrive at that which he so foolishly admires…Some of those situations may, no doubt, deserve to be preferred to others: but none of them can deserve to be pursued with that passionate ardour which drives us to violate the rules either of prudence or of justice; or to corrupt the future tranquillity of our minds, either by shame from the remembrance of our own folly, or by remorse from the horror of our own injustice.

The fact that Smith valued Stoic ethics and often referred to them in his writings meant that he did not believe that economics is a value-free science. Of note, Smith's (1982, 184–185) theory of the invisible hand, as presented in *Theory of Moral Sentiments*, meant that rich people, 'in spite of their natural selfishness,' are:

> led by an invisible hand to make nearly the same distribution of the necessaries of life, which would have been made, had the earth been divided into equal portions among all its inhabitants, and thus without intending it, without knowing it, advance the interest of the society, and afford means to the multiplication of the species

Smith (1982, 184) suggested that rich people should share with 'the poor the produce of all their improvements.' Furthermore, he maintained that 'when Providence divided the earth among a few lordly masters, it neither forgot nor abandoned those who seemed to have been left out in the partition. These last too enjoy their share of all that it produces' (Smith 1982, 185). Smith also discussed 'the invisible hand' in *the Wealth of Nations* (1776), which was received with enthusiasm by classical, neo-classical and neo-liberal economists, none of whom were particularly familiar with the thoughts he expressed on moral philosophy in *Theory of Moral Sentiments*. Economists continue to use the concept of the invisible hand as a tool to defend the outcomes of the free-market system. However, their understanding and application of this concept has little to do with the original conception of the invisible hand as described by Smith in *Theory of Moral Sentiments*. In fact, they have completely dismissed the relevance of this book, which highlighted the importance of moral and ethical values in every aspect of human life.

By proclaiming that economics is a discipline of the natural sciences, economists have shown that they have little regard for moral and ethical values, despite the important roles that they played in directing human decisions and actions since the times of the Ancient Greeks, who are widely credited with establishing the ethical norms and standards that are required to achieve the highest human good. Neo-liberals consider ethical norms and standards to be archaic, outdated, and entirely beyond the scope of reason. In particular, Mises (1962, 437) stated that ethical philosophers romanticise about the past, and the weakness of their arguments forces them to appeal to 'the feelings rather than to the mind' (Mises 1962, 437). He was especially critical of the ethical judgements in socialism, which he labelled 'the philosophic product of a period of decay' (Mises 1962, 439). Hayek was also strongly opposed to the notion of imposing moral and ethical values on society. In fact, he criticized some of the most renowned moral and ethical philosophers, including Plato, St Augustine, Rousseau and Marx, for being prophets, as well as moralists and 'reactionaries, defending the old against the new principles' (Hayek 1979, 165, 166). He explained that these philosophers had 'no conception that the system of competitive prices and remunerations signalling to the individual what to do, had made possible that extensive specialization by informing the individuals how best to serve others of whose existence they might not know' (Hayek 1979, 166). He further claimed that 'in most parts of the world the development of an open market economy has long been prevented by those very morals preached by prophets and philosophers, even before governmental measures did the same' (Hayek 1979, 165). Moreover, Hayek (1979, 166) argued that 'modern civilization has become largely possible by the disregard of the injunctions of those indignant moralists.'

Hayek associated moral and ethical values with the tribal society. That said, he was concerned that tribal ethics were being reasserted through the interventionist policies of the welfare state, whose proponents wanted to achieve social justice 'in a manner which gratifies natural emotions' (Hayek 1998, 147). In particular, Hayek was strongly opposed to what he perceived to be a revival of tribal ethical and moral values in many of the public programs and projects associated with the New Deal. He claimed that if these kinds of moral and ethical values were to triumph in free societies, they would 'not only destroy the Great Society but would also greatly threaten the survival of the large numbers to which some three hundred years of a market order have enabled mankind to grow' (Hayek 1998, 147).

Hayek also opposed centrally planned systems that aim to achieve the conditions of positive freedom, arguing that every step away from economic freedom and towards positive freedom will provide moral and ethical justifications for the achievement distributive justice, which, in turn, would warrant a more extensive state role in society in the name of attaining the conditions of freedom. In other words, he believed that if the definition of freedom were to include the development of individual capacities and abilities as components, moral and ethical judgements would play decisive roles in state policies, as well as the decisions and actions of individuals. Hayek (2011) was strongly opposed to any state interference in society based on some preconceived notion of moral judgements that aim to achieve justice. According to him, the achievement of justice in accordance with moral and ethical values does not provide any justification for state interventions designed to realize the common good. In fact, he associated the integration of moral and ethical judgements into economic decisions with socialist regimes, which he accused of imposing uniform ethical and moral views on everybody for the purpose of achieving the collective good (Hayek 2006, 117). In *The Road to Serfdom*, Hayek argued that totalitarian regimes in Germany, Italy and Russia used various forms of collective, rational, and conscious control over society to provide their citizens with positive welfare, which is guided by a single common ethical code or ethical value. He was convinced that a totalitarian state that imposes moral and ethical values on society will probably cause more harm than good, as doing so would violate people's freedom by indoctrinating them with a definite set of values (Hayek 2006, 141).

Hayek (2006, 140) also opposed the imposition of moral judgements on the basis that 'the ruling moral views will depend partly on the qualities that will lead individuals to success in a collectivist or totalitarian system, and partly on the requirements of the totalitarian machinery.' That is to say, he believed that it would not be particularly challenging for the socialist ruling class to impose its ethical and moral values on the masses, because none of the socialist leaders would have been able to rise through the ranks of their party without possessing moral values that coincided those held by the majority of the population. With that in mind, Hayek (2006, 142) further explained that:

> the largest group of people whose values are very similar are the people with low standards. It is, as it were, the lowest common denominator which unites the largest number of people. If a numerous group is needed, strong enough to impose their views on the values of life on all the rest, it will never be those with highly differentiated and developed tastes it will be those who form the "mass" in the derogatory sense of the term, the least original and independent, who will be able to put the weight of their numbers behind their particular ideals.

Hayek (2006, 142) believed that socialist regimes supported moral values of a lower standard, which do not appeal to people of free-societies, because they possess 'highly differentiated and developed tastes.' In fact, he argued that the types of moral commitments that prevailed in socialist regimes are destructive to the values of free societies. In addition to socialist states, Hayek was also critical of welfare state policies and programs, which are guided by ethical and moral values to achieve distributive justice. For example, he believed that the imposition of taxation and the provision social services and programs by the state in the name of some kind of ethical commitment actually distract economic agents from the principles necessary to preserve an efficient free-market mechanism. Furthermore, he suggested that when states acted in accordance with ethical commitments by securing a moderate or just income for the weak and poor, they violated the conditions of a free society. In *The Mirage of Social Justice* (1998 [1976]), Hayek made it clear that he believed social justice was an empty concept, and there was no need to adjust or correct social and economic inequality through state intervention based on moral and ethical principles.

Although Hayek recognized the importance of ethical concerns and moral obligations for the welfare of families, neighbors and friends, he rejected the idea of having a state authority to use coercion and persuasion to instill individuals with a sense of ethical and moral obligation for their respective communities. Similarly, while he acknowledged that the outcomes of a free-market system are 'often in conflict with ethical views,' he opposed having the state intervene in order to correct any unjust outcomes based on ethical and moral values (Hayek 2011, 144). He pointed out that an 'agreement' on a 'complete ethical code,' according to which all social activity is directed, does not 'exist in a free society' (Hayek 2006, 160). Hayek (2011, 161) suggested that this would lead to the emergence of a society:

> in which people were rewarded for duty performed instead of for success, in which every move of every individual was guided by what other people thought he ought to do, and in which the individual was thus relieved of the responsibility and the risk of decision.

Hayek was adamant that moral and ethical values are personal in nature, and as such, people living in a free-market system are free to choose their own moral and ethical conduct according to their 'own conscience' in their private spheres (Hayek 2006, 217). That means moral values can exist in the private spheres of individuals, and only free individuals can voluntarily decide 'to sacrifice personal advantage to the observance of a moral rule' (Hayek 2006, 216). Hayek (2006, 216) contended that:

> outside the sphere of individual responsibility there is neither goodness nor badness, neither opportunity for moral merit nor the chance of proving

> one's conviction by sacrificing one's desires to what one thinks right. Only where we ourselves are responsible for our own interests and are free to sacrifice them.

Hayek accepted that the state needed to play a role in enforcing general and abstract rules of conduct in public places, which are value-free. However, he viewed the imposition and enforcement of particular rules, based on moral and ethical values, as a completely different matter, describing it as a perfect example of the state exercising coercive control over society (Hayek 2011, 213).

Mises (1962, 439) was also critical of coercive regimes using ethical judgements, claiming that 'ethical Socialism' had an 'imperfect understanding of human social co-operation.' He maintained that making commitments to 'ethical ideas of duty and conscience' required 'the blindest submission' (Mises 1962, 397). Mises (1998 [1949], 243) explained that:

> to call something fair or unfair is always a subjective value judgment and as such purely personal and not liable to any verification or falsification. Economics is not intent upon pronouncing value judgments. It aims at a cognition of the consequences of certain modes of acting.

Basically, Mises argued that economics is a theoretical science, and as such, should abstain from making any judgments of value. According to him, ethical values aim to protect social goals, while being opposed to economic ends (Mises 1962). Mises (1962, 396) further argued that 'the conception of absolute ethical values, which might be opposed to economic values, cannot therefore be maintained.' Ultimately, he believed that it was not the role of economists to tell people what ends they should aim for or how they should live their lives (Mises 1998 [1949], 10).

Mises also believed that state interventions designed to achieve ethical ends would require a centrally-planned economy, a system that he strongly opposed in *Socialism* (1962). Still, despite his opposition to the idea of having an external superior authority, such as a state, impose moral and ethical values on people, Mises recognized that individual actions alone could not be trusted to make free and harmonious lives possible within society as a whole. However, instead of imposing moral and ethical values, he supported an effective legal framework to ensure the conditions of a free society. When discussing the true interests of society, Mises (1962, 398) specifically stated:

> If it left everyone to judge of his own it would expose itself to the caprice of every foolish, sick, and weak-willed person, leaving him free to put its very existence into question, thus imperilling the continuity of development. This is what led to the creation of powers of social coercion which, vis-à-vis the individual, appear as external constraints because they demand imperative obedience. And here we see the social significance of the State and the Law.

The law lies at the heart of Mises' views of a free society, as well as those of many of his neo-liberal counterparts. For them, the best way to ensure the conditions of a free-society is to avoid coercion by limiting the free actions of individuals, as well as the coercive powers of the state, through abstract and general rules, instead of relying on the specific and concrete rules and commandments prescribed by ethical and moral judgements.

Friedman shared similar views with Hayek and Mises, as he argued that moral indifference defines the economic world. He contended that ethical values are individual matters in a free-market society, meaning that nobody has the authority to say anything about what kind of ethical values an individual should adhere to. Indeed, he stated that 'a major aim of the believer in freedom is to leave the ethical problem for the individual to wrestle with' (Friedman 1982 [1962], 22). According to Friedman and Friedman (1990 [1980]), the free-market is an impersonal mechanism that separates the economic activities of individuals from their personal characteristics. For instance, that means it is irrelevant for consumers to know whether or not the social, economic and working conditions of the labour that produces the goods they consume are unfair, unjust, unethical, etc. He was also opposed the redistribution of income, which is inherently motivated by ethical judgements, on the basis that there are 'no value judgments in economics' (Friedman 1967, 85). Friedman (1967, 85) maintained that economics is a science that is only concerned with 'the consequences of changes in circumstances on the course of events, with prediction and analysis, not with evaluation.' It has nothing to say about whether goals and ends are good, bad, just, unjust, etc. Therefore, while there might be some disagreements between economists about certain aspects of monetary or fiscal policy, these kinds of differences are largely scientific and do not reflect any value judgements. Friedman (1966) actually played a prominent role in establishing economics as a positive science that is only concerned about empirical facts, while ignoring ethical and moral values.

Friedman was highly critical of members of the business classes who defended moral and ethical commitments in the marketplace. According to him, achieving social ethical and moral ends, 'eliminating discrimination, avoiding pollution' are 'the catchwords of the contemporary crop of reformers' (Friedman 1970). He believed that 'there is one and only one social responsibility of business-to use its resources and engage in activities designed to increase its profits so long as it stays within the rules of the game, which is to say, engages in open and free competition' (Friedman's 1970). Consequently, he attributed any ethical and moral practices by members of the business classes to 'the schizophrenic character of businessmen' (Friedman 1970). He maintained that moral judgements belonged purely in the private spheres of individuals and had nothing to do with economics.

Friedman (1970) regarded people who defended social responsibility in the economic arena as 'incredibly short-sighted and muddle-headed in matters that are outside their businesses'. He also claimed that they were 'unwitting puppets of the intellectual forces that have been undermining the basis of a free society' (Friedman 1970). Friedman (1970) elaborated by suggesting that adhering to the premise of social responsibility in the marketplace, based on moral and ethical values, could be interpreted as 'the acceptance of the socialist view that political mechanisms, not market mechanisms, are the appropriate way to determine the allocation of scarce resources to alternative uses.' He further claimed that if social responsibility is taken seriously, it would 'extend the scope of the political mechanism to every human activity' and destroy the foundations of a free society, much like in a centrally planned system (Friedman 1970).

Buchanan and Tullock (1962) also held views that were similar to those of Friedman, Hayek, and Mises on the subject of morals and ethics, as they argued that voluntary cooperation among individuals in a free-market system does not require any specific moral and ethical values in their behaviors. Furthermore, they believed that one of the most important features of the free-market economy was that it separated the economic activities of individual agents from their ethical, moral, and political views, ideas or activities. Buchanan and Tullock (1962, 195) explained that, in the marketplace, even if one person thinks that others are:

> morally wrong, the individual, in effect, says: "I think that they are doing themselves harm by such actions; but, since I value freedom of individual

> choice and since there is no harm imposed on me by their actions, I do not interfere by placing constraints on their behavior."

They claimed that economics does not make value judgments, and ethical values should have no role in the development of public policies and business strategies. They were completely opposed to the idea that bureaucrats could dedicate their work to the achievement of common or collective goals for the nation based on moral and ethical judgements. They suggested that defenders of the collective good were little more than moral crusaders, who believe that they are above the law and can impose single-minded values on the whole society, via bureaucratic coercion if necessary, in order to achieve teleological goals. According to Buchanan and Tullock (1962, 195), in most cases, 'moral standards would become significantly weaker than they initially appear if those who hold them were asked to contribute positive sums toward the elimination of that behavior in others which they condemn as immoral.' Meanwhile, Buchanan (1975, 148) specifically argued that, in liberal societies, it is 'impossible to give meaning to an ethical obligation on the part of the individual to improve society.'

Contrary to neo-liberal economists, Alfred Marshall (1842–1924) (2013 [1890], XIX), who was one of the main founders of neoclassical economics, stressed the importance of ethics in economics in his *Principles of Economics* (1890), where he stated:

> ethical forces are among those of which the economist has to take account. Attempts have indeed been made to construct an abstract science with regard to the actions of an "economic man," who is under no ethical influences and who pursues pecuniary gain warily and energetically, but mechanically and selfishly. But they have not been successful, nor even thoroughly carried out.

Marshall (2013) accentuated the necessity of ethics in economic studies, decisions and actions. In particular, he underlined the importance of the ethical quality of the individual motives by which people make a choice of action.

Frank H. Knight (1885–1972) (1922, 454) was an economist and a moral philosopher, who was among the founders of the Chicago School of Economics, and actually taught Friedman, Stigler and Buchanan when he was a professor there; however, despite possessing some impressive neo-liberal credentials, he argued that 'economics and ethics naturally come into rather intimate relations with each other since both recognizably deal with the problem of value.' Christian ethics was the basis of Knight's (2017 [1935]) advocacy for the use of ethical judgements in the free-market capitalist system. He believed that individuals are not isolated entities; to the contrary, they are social by nature, and as such, belong to a cultural and traditional system that practices ethical and moral values. Instead of eliminating moral and ethical judgements from the discipline of economics, as advocated by neo-liberal economists, Knight suggested that people 'learn to think in terms of "value-standards" which have validity of a more subtle kind. It is the higher goal of conduct to test and try these values, to define and improve them, rather than to accept and "satisfy" them' (Knight 1922, 480). These value-standards are based on moral and ethical judgements, and cannot be determined by the principles and goals of free-market capitalism.

Knight (1951, 20, 9) was critical of free-market capitalism because it 'tended to see the whole problem of life in terms of the acquisition of power and efficiency in its use' (Knight 1972, 9). Accordingly, its theorists and practitioners ignored the role of moral and ethical values in economic decisions. Contrary to neo-liberals, who uncritically accepted the free-market system, Knight recognized that it had flaws and errors. He believed that ethical and moral judgements would not defend many of the outcomes of free-market capitalism (Knight 2017). In fact, he went so far as to suggest that an ethical evaluation based on Ancient Greek philosophy, Christian theology or Biblical studies would conclude that competitive markets are indefensible (Knight 2017). Knight (2017, 66) elaborated that:

> we appear to search in vain for any really ethical basis of approval for competition as a basis for an ideal type of human relations, or as a motive to action. It fails to harmonize either with the Pagan ideal of society as a community of friends or the Christian ideal of spiritual fellowship. Its only justification is that it is effective in getting things done; but any candid answer to the question, "what things," compels the admission that they leave much to be desired. Whether for good or bad, its aesthetic ideals are not such as command the approval of the most competent judges, and as for spirituality, commercialism is in a fair way to make that term incomprehensible to living men. The motive itself has been generally condemned by the best spirits of the race.

Knight (1929, 144) did not defend the same concept of freedom that was promoted by neo-liberals. According to him, 'freedom means freedom to use power, and the only possible limitation on the use of power is intrinsically ethical' (Knight 1929, 144). He explained that if one's freedom to use power is inhibited by anything other than ethical judgments, that 'amounts to saying that he does not really have the power, that it is cancelled by some opposing force' (Knight 1929, 144). Furthermore, he claimed freedom and economic freedom in the free-market system cannot be explained or justified on the basis of science alone, they need to have some moral and ethical content as well.

Knight (1929, 144) was worried about potential conflicts of interest and destructive results associated with the free-market system, as he believed that the free use of political and economic power to 'exploit the rest of society' would result in vices and evil outcomes. He further argued that liberal thinkers failed to understand that 'the social problem is not at bottom intellectual, but moral, and it utterly misconceived the genuinely intellectual element involved. Individual intelligence in the instrumentalist sense, so far from being a solution of the problem, is a perfect formula for the war of each against all' (Knight 1934, 423). Accordingly, Knight supported a more prominent role for moral and ethical judgements in social and economic life, as this would contribute to creating a society where the decisions and actions of individuals are virtuous. He believed distinguishing between right and wrong acts and behaviours necessitated 'some basis for discrimination between right and wrong motives' (Knight 1929, 141). In other words, evaluations to determine whether certain acts and behaviours are right or wrong should be performed in accordance with moral and ethical judgements, and not be based on individual self-interest maximization, as advocated by proponents of neo-liberal economics.

Contrary to the opposition expressed by neo-liberal economists with respect to the integration of an ethical orientation into the economics, a study of the history of economic though reveals that the German Historical School of Economics (GHSE) was highly supportive of a role for ethical values in economics. For instance, Gustav von Schmoller (1838–1917), leader of the younger GHSE who was accepted as the best and 'most authoritative spokesman of that branch of historical economics,' while his *Grundriß der Allgemeinen Volkswirtschaftslehre* (1900) was recognized as 'an event of the first importance in economic literature' (Veblen 1901, 69, 72), argued that 'the strategic problems of economic life cannot be overcome unless people act, in virtue of their common ends, as members' of moral or ethical communities (Haller 2004, 15). Schmoller believed that ethical values are the true basis of political economy, as did many other theorists of and contributors to the GHSE (Filip 2018, 116).

The theorists of the GHSE rejected the individualism, self-interest maximization and rational acquisitiveness assumptions of classical economics, regarding them as unethical and abstract. Schmoller (1894, 723) argued that the 'masses tend to destroy each other' on account of the selfish wants and desires promoted by both classical economics and the Austrian School of Economics. He also claimed that 'if in the economic order we could recognize only the ruling of blind forces, of selfish interests, natural masses and mechanical processes, it would be a constant battle, a chaotic anarchy' (Schmoller 1894, 722). Schmoller (1894, 733) further contended that:

> There is no worse delusion than that of the older English economists that...all progress of civilization and wealth is simply an individual or technical one; that this is simply a question of increased production or consumption which will and can be accomplished on the basis of the same legal institutions. This faith in the stability of economic institutions was the result of the naive overweening confidence of the older economists in the omnipotence of the individual and of the individual life.

Wilhelm Georg Friedrich Roscher (1817–1894) (1882, 73), one of the founders of the GHSE who was accepted as 'the incarnation of professorial learning, mainly of a philosophico-historical nature...and a leading figure on the stage of academic economics' (Schumpeter 1986, 817), had similar views to those of Schmoller with respect to the classical *homo economicus* abstract assumption, arguing that the pursuit of individual self-interest maximization eventually degenerates into 'egoism' and 'covetousness.' According to Roscher (1882, 73), misery, poverty and deplorable working conditions, are all outcomes of individual self-interest maximization.

The GHSE was generally of the view that self-interest maximization represented the moral and ethical decline of people, which can produce great harms within society. As such, adherents of this economic school of thought advocated for state reforms based on ethical values. They highlighted the role that the state could play in establishing institutions that could work towards the achievement of ethical outcomes within society, such as social and distributive justice. According to theorists of the GHSE, institutions of society play important roles in the development of ethical relationships and responsibility in the social lives of individuals. As such, these institutions, which include churches, the press, cooperatives, trade unions, and various other establishments, institutions and associations, should be designed or reformed in a way that makes them into ethical entities, which act and make decisions based on a higher moral-ethical standard. Subsequently, citizens of that society can learn to practice the ethical values and norms promoted by those institutions in their everyday practical reasoning, which could unite individuals into a community, and achieve social justice. Theorists of the GHSE were convinced that life in an ethical community could ultimately lead to the achievement of social *eudaemonia*. Furthermore, they believed that crises, as well as various unjust, unfair and destructive outcomes associated with economic life, could be overcome if individuals, as members of ethical communities, cultivated, worshipped and practiced virtues and ethical and moral habits in their daily lives and actions.

For many decades, neo-liberal economists made the dangerous mistake of looking at the world through their own narrow window, towards the same direction, by not studying and learning from the achievements and errors of their predecessors from different schools of economic thought, as well as philosophers. This is not surprising, given that neo-liberals believe that other paths and destinations that came before them are inferior compared to the ones generated by their own paradigm. They have been so infatuated by the road that they have been rapidly advancing on that they could not see the world beyond the boundaries of their horizons.

11.3 Conclusion

In addition to playing prominent roles in people's lives over the course of history, moral and ethical values were also important aspects of economics in the past. In fact, a few centuries ago, the discipline of economics was recognized as a 'moral science…but [it] is now mostly forgotten' (Myrdal 1973, 113). Neo-liberal economists typically reject traditional forms of thinking, living, and societal organization, on the basis that they were archaic, outdated, inflexible and would not accommodate the values of the free-market system. As a result, they have basically ignored an abundance of valuable and meticulous work explaining the importance of moral and ethical values in guiding people's actions, so that they can achieve freedom and happiness, since the times of Ancient Greece. Instead, they proclaimed that their paradigm, which has only existed for a little more than half a century, is free from moral and ethical values. This is consistent with their view that ethical and moral responsibility is an individual matter, which means people possess their own set of moral and ethical values as part of their private spheres.

Many neo-liberals firmly believe that economics should not involve moral and ethical norms and standards, which are purely arbitrary and subjective judgements. Rather, economics should be about free human choices and actions, which are rational and self-interest oriented. Accordingly, an economic action should be evaluated based on a cost and benefit analysis, which ignores factors like fairness, equality, justice, and virtues, because they are irrelevant from the perspective of economic analysis. As neo-liberalism spread around the world, so did the fixation with pursuing self-interest maximization and acquisitiveness, which essentially led to many human wants, motives and goals becoming primarily economic in nature. That is to say, people have disassociated themselves from their moral and ethical values and responsibilities in order to focus their activities and actions on maximizing their personal interests.

By associating freedom with the maximization of individual self-interests and materialistic ends, while disregarding the importance of moral and ethical judgments in limiting one's own freedom, the neo-liberal economic paradigm has contributed to human beings becoming apathetic about the consequences of their decisions and actions on the lives of others, and on their surroundings. This is not surprising, given that neo-liberals do not value the capacity to set aside one's own self-interests in order to take ethically good actions for the benefit of others or society as a whole. When it comes to maximizing profits, neo-liberal economists maintain that all actions are legitimate and should be taken without accepting any responsibility or expressing remorse for them, even if they destroy the environment, endanger the future of the planet, or ruin the dreams and lives of other people. By promoting this kind of thinking, neo-liberalism has significantly contributed to the destruction of communities, shared common values, and societal goals, which has delivered unfreedom, isolation, loneliness, vulnerability, and powerlessness to the majority of the world's population, and brought the planet to the brink of an environmental apocalypse.

References

Aristotle. 1893. *The Nicomachean Ethics of Aristotle.* Trans. F.H. Peters. London: Kegan Paul, Trench, Trübner & Co. Ltd.

Buchanan, James. 1975. *The Limits of Liberty.* Chicago: University of Chicago Press.

Buchanan, J.M., and G. Tullock. 1962. *The Calculus of Consent: Logical Foundations of a Constitutional Democracy.* Ann Arbor: University of Michigan Press.

Fichte, Johann Gottlieb. 2000. *Foundations of Natural Right.* Ed. Frederick Neuhouser. Cambridge: Cambridge University Press.

Filip, Birsen. 2018. The German Historical School of Economics and the Foundations and Development of the Austrian School of Economics. In *Hayek: A Collaborative Biography: Part XIII: 'Fascism' and Liberalism in the (Austrian) Classical Tradition*, ed. Robert Leeson, 79–128. Cham: Palgrave Macmillan.

Friedman, Milton. 1966. The Methodology of Positive Economics. *Essays in Positive Economics* 3 (16): 30–43.

———. 1967. Value Judgments in Economics. In *Human Values and Economic Policy, A Symposium*, ed. Sidney Hook, 85–93. New York: New York University Press.

———. 1970. The Social Responsibility of Business is to Increase its Profits. *The New York Times Magazine*, September 13. https://www.nytimes.com/1970/09/13/archives/a-friedman-doctrine-the-social-responsibility-of-business-is-to.html.

———. 1982 [1962]. *Capitalism and Freedom.* Chicago: University of Chicago Press.

Friedman, Milton, and Friedman, R.D. 1990 [1980]. *Free to Choose: A Personal Statement.* New York: Harcourt Brace Jovanovich.

George, Henry. 2006 [1879]. *Progress and Poverty: Why There Are Recessions and Poverty Amid Plenty—and What to Do About It!* Ed. Bob Drake. New York: Robert Schalkenbach Foundation.

Haller, Markus. 2004. Mixing Economics and Ethics: Carl Menger vs Gustav von Schmoller. *Social Science Information* 43 (1): 5–33.

Hayek, F.A. 1979. *Law, Legislation and Liberty Volume 3: The Political Order of a Free People.* London: Routledge & Kegan Paul.

———. 1998 [1976]. *Law, Legislation and Liberty Volume 2: The Mirage of Social Justice.* London: Routledge & Kegan Paul.

———. 2006 [1991]. *The Collected Works of Friedrich August Hayek Volume 3: The Trend of Economic Thinking: Essays on Political Economists and Economic History.* Ed. W.W. Bartley and Stephen Kresge. London: Routledge.

———. 2011 [1960]. *The Constitution of Liberty.* Chicago: University of Chicago Press.

Hegel, G.W.F. 2008. *Outlines of the Philosophy of Right*. Ed. Stephen Houlgate, Trans. T.M. Knox. Oxford: Oxford University Press.

Ingram, John Kells. 1915 [1888]. *A History of Political Economy*. London: A. and C. Black.

Knight, Frank H. 1922. Ethics and the Economic Interpretation. *The Quarterly Journal of Economics* 36 (3): 454–481. https://www.jstor.org/stable/1886033.

———. 1929. Freedom as Fact and Criterion. *International Journal of Ethics* 39 (2): 129–147. https://www.jstor.org/stable/2377742.

———. 1934. Social Science and Political Trend. *University of Toronto Quarterly* 3 (4): 407–427.

———. 1951. The Role of Principles in Economics and Politics. *The American Economic Review* 41 (1): 1–29. https://www.jstor.org/stable/1815957.

———. 1972. Social Science. *Ethics* 83 (1): 1–12.

———. 2017 [1935]. *The Ethics of Competition*. New York: Routledge.

Marcuse, Herbert. 1998 [1956]. *Eros and Civilisation: A Philosophical Inquiry into Freud*. Abingdon: Routledge.

Marshall, Alfred. 2013 [1890]. *Principles of Economics*. New York: Palgrave Macmillan.

Mises, Ludwig von. 1962 [1951]. *Socialism: An Economic and Sociological Analysis*. New Haven: Yale University Press.

———. 1998 [1949]. *Human Action: A Treatise on Economics*. Auburn, Alabam: The Ludwig von Mises Institute.

Montesquieu, Charles Louis de Secondat. 1977a [1748]. *The Complete Works of M. de Montesquieu*. Vol. 1. London: T. Evans. https://oll.libertyfund.org/titles/837.

———. 1977b [1748]. *The Complete Works of M. de Montesquieu*. Vol. 2. London: T. Evans. https://oll.libertyfund.org/titles/837.

Myrdal, Karl Gunnar. 1973. Economics of an Improved Environment. *World Development* 1 (2): 102–114.

Neuhouser, F. 2000. *Foundations of Hegel's Social Theory. Actualizing Freedom*. Cambridge, MA: Harvard University Press.

Patten, A. 1999. *Hegel's Idea of Freedom*. Oxford: Oxford University Press.

Roscher, Wilhelm Georg Friedrich. 1882 [1877]. *Principles of Political Economy*. Vol. 1. Chicago: Callagilan and Company.

Rousseau, Jean-Jacques. 1921 [1762]. *Emile, or Education*. Trans. Barbara Foxley. London & Toronto: J.M. Dent and Sons. http://oll.libertyfund.org/title/2256.

———. 1967 [1762]. *The Social Contract and Discourse on the Origin of Inequality*. New York: Washington Square Press.

Schmoller, G. 1894 [1881]. The Idea of Justice in Political Economy. *The Annals of the American Academy of Political and Social Science* 4: 697–737.

———. 1900. *Grundriß der Allgemeinen Volkswirtschaftslehre.* Leipzig: Erster Teil, Duncker & Humblot.

Schumpeter, Joseph A. 1986 [1954]. *History of Economic Analysis.* New York: Routledge.

Smith, Adam. 1982 [1759]. *The Theory of Moral Sentiments.* Ed. A.I. Macfie and D.D. Raphael. Indianapolis: Liberty Fund.

Veblen, Thornstein. 1901. Gustav Schmoller's Economics. *The Quarterly Journal of Economics* 16 (1): 69–93.

CHAPTER 12

The Poverty of Neo-liberalism: The Rise of Mathematical Economics and the Decline of the History of Economic Thought

Adam Smith, who is widely considered to be the founding father of modern economics, included almost no mathematics in his work, including his seminal book *Wealth of Nations* (1776). That said, the direction of economics has been significantly altered since the time of Smith, with one of the major changes being the mathematization of the discipline in an attempt to turn it into a branch of the natural sciences. Neo-liberal attempts to make economics into a discipline of the natural sciences has meant that studying and conducting research in the field of economics requires a strong understanding of mathematics. The mathematization of economics involves the extensive use and application of mathematical concepts, language, presentations, formulae, and techniques to economic theory. As a result, having a proficiency with mathematical tools has become more important for contemporary economists than understanding economic issues and realities, whereas the inability to master mathematical tools is regarded as a sign of weakness and incompetence within their discipline. Consequently, over the last few decades, students of economics have been immersed in mathematical economics, beginning in the early years of their undergrad studies. As they progress, they are expected to master economic theories presented via sophisticated mathematical modelling in their more advanced classes. By the time they have completed their education, graduates of economics have been conditioned to believe that the methods of mathematical modelling need to be employed

B. Filip, *The Rise of Neo-liberalism and the Decline of Freedom*,
Palgrave Insights into Apocalypse Economics,
https://doi.org/10.1007/978-3-030-61623-6_12

in much of their research and work for it to be scientifically respected by their peers.

For many decades, the language, formulas, and methodologies of mathematics and the natural sciences have become widely used and uncritically accepted by mainstream economists, who have come to regard themselves as scientific authorities within their discipline. In fact, mathematical economists appear to have an unwavering faith in mathematical modelling. This chapter focuses on efforts to make economics into a branch of the natural sciences, which has significantly contributed to the mathematization of economics. It also briefly discusses the diminished importance of the history of economic thought within the discipline of economics since the post war era.

12.1 The Economic 'Science Wars' and the Downfall of the History of Economic Thought

The dominant position of neo-liberalism as the leading program of economic research has led to many mainstream economists ignoring its limitations, while also being unaware of, or disinterested in, other economic schools of thought that existed throughout the history of economics. Before the 1930s, economics highly valued the history of economic thought, and it was not uncommon for articles and books to be published on the subject. However, in the post war period, the widespread acceptance that scientific thought and progress were vital for advancing national interests and the public good led to natural sciences becoming an important part of the public discourse and the development of government policies. Consequently, scientific research received considerable public funding and support, while 'science education became part of the general education programs in the liberal arts' (Weintraub 2007, 270).

At the same time, there was an existential crisis within the discipline of economics, in that its practitioners wanted demonstrate their relevance, value and importance to the national interest. As such, economists started to intensely focus on mastering the techniques, methods and goals of the natural sciences, which ultimately became more important within the discipline of economics than gaining a solid understanding of the history of economic thought. In fact, it could be said that 'economics refashioned itself as economic science' shortly after WWII (Weintraub 2007, 272).

Despite the fact that mathematical economics was still in its infancy as a subject within the discipline economics at that time, economists already started to have a diminutive opinion of the history of economic thought. Eventually, some would say that the history of economic thought became openly unwelcome in the discipline of economics, as well-known neo-liberal economists like Stigler, Lionel Robbins, Samuelson, Friedman, Hayek, Mises, and Becker made it quite clear that they did not value it, as did a number of their contemporaries.

As economics became increasingly oriented towards mathematics, it became almost impossible to reference the work of economists specialized in the history of economic thought when teaching economics. Economics professors required 'graduate students to master statistics, mathematics, and econometrics' instead of gaining a solid understanding of the history of economic thought (Weintraub 2007, 273). Similarly, work and research in the history of economic thought became largely irrelevant to the discipline of economics. In particular, proponents of mathematical economics did not believe that the history of economic thought made any important contributions to the progress and advancement of the discipline of economics. In fact, 'doing the history and methodology of economics came to be seen as doing no economics at all' at the economics departments of most American universities (Weintraub 2007, 277). Moreover, economists who focused on 'doing history and methodology of economics were generally seen as critics, often hostile critics, of mainstream economics' (Weintraub 2007, 277).

Shortly after WWII, economics departments around the world started to significantly reduce the resources and funding allocated for the research and teaching of the history of economic thought. In fact, 'the slow starvation of resources for history and methodology of economics...is an exact manifestation of economic science wars' (Weintraub 2007, 277). Anyone that failed to recognize this war between mathematical economics and the history of economic thought suffered from 'a curious blindness' (Weintraub 2007, 277). Ultimately, it appears that mathematical economists won this war outright, as they have been the ones to obtain large funding to finance their research from both the public and private sectors. Meanwhile, the history of economic thought has gradually become irrelevant following its defeat in the 'economic science wars.' Since then, historians of economics and specialists in the history of economic thought have encountered adversity when attempting to obtain a post at universities or publish their work in leading economics journals. Stigler (1965, V) was among the prominent neo-liberal economists who argued that economics is a branch of the natural sciences, and as such, the history of economic thought was becoming largely irrelevant within the discipline:

> The study of the history of economics has escaped all the forces that have transformed the character of economic research in the twentieth century. Neither foundation nor government is at all interested in intellectual history, so it is perhaps the last unsubsidized research area in economics.

In the 1970s, the history of economic thought began to officially be abandoned as a mandatory class in most graduate economic programs in the United States. That led to the 'involuntary removal of historians and philosophers of economics from the Economics Department,' to be replaced by mathematical economists (Weintraub 2007, 278). In other words, the 'economic science war had already rendered historians of economics hors de combat on the university battlefield' (Weintraub 2007, 279). Subsequently, many economics departments at universities around the world followed suit. As a result, there is currently a generation of economists who are not familiar with the origins or development of the ideas, methodologies, models and theories that they study and work with in the discipline of economics. Moreover, most of them have no interest in learning about these aspects of their discipline, because they regard the study of the history of economic thought as a mere hobby that is of little practical use. They believe that since mainstream economics is the latest and best program of research, there is no reason to study the history of economic thought or any of the other failed economic programs of research that came before neo-liberalism.

In the past, the history of economic thought was considered to be an important element in the education and training of economics students; however, as neo-liberalism rose to prominence, and its principles were widely adopted, many renowned economists from this school of thought openly revolted against the history of economic thought. Among them was Stigler (1982, 57), who argued that 'the history of economics…is strewn with costly errors: of ideas, so to speak, that wouldn't run far or carry many passengers.' According to him, learning about the history of economic thought is a time consuming process, which ultimately is not worth the effort given that it does not address the questions, issues, and concerns of the modern time. In particular, he noted that while the work of economists from previous centuries might be important for certain special interests, they are of little value for mathematical economics (Stigler 1982, 58). In fact, he did not hesitate to support the notion of eliminating the history of economic thought as a mandatory class for economics students. Instead of properly appreciating the history of economic thought and learning from it, neo-liberal economists have essentially chosen to reject the historical origins and development of their own discipline. Furthermore, by focusing their efforts on making economics into a branch of the natural sciences, largely by placing more emphasis on mathematical economics, they have managed to avoid addressing some of the real problems affecting their discipline. Ultimately, by turning their backs on the history of economic thought, contemporary economists have made mathematics and statistics the main purposes of economics, maybe even the only reasons for its existence. This would be to the liking of neo-liberal economists, since 'the influence of mathematics is now so deeply ingrained within our culture, indeed, that many people (especially non-professional scientists) appear to suppose that anything stated in mathematics must be correct, whilst for things to be correct, reliable, insightful or scientific (or at least conferring of scientific status), they must be stated in mathematics' (Lawson 2015, 159).

Neo-liberal economists are of the view that anything stated in mathematics must not only be correct, it must also be universal. This corresponds with their adherence to the universality principle of the natural sciences, which would suggest that their economic program of research is valid regardless of time or geographical location. In other words, based on the principle of universality, the truths of neo-liberalism are objective truths that are valid across history and geographical regions. Solow (1985, 330) confirmed that neo-liberal economists treated their discipline as though it were a branch of the natural sciences and adhered to the universality principle when he stated:

> the best and brightest in the profession proceed as if economics is the physics of society. There is a single universally valid model of the world. It only needs to be applied. You could drop a modern economist from a time machine—a helicopter, maybe, like the one that drops the money-at any time, in any place, along with his or her personal computer; he or she could set up in business without even bothering to ask what time and which place.

Solow believed that his exaggerated impression of mathematical economists was not far from reality, as neo-liberals have consistently claimed that economics is a branch of the natural sciences, along with physics, classical mechanics, and biology, where the universality principle actually does apply.

Since neo-liberalism became the leading paradigm in the discipline of economics, previous theories, methodologies, procedures, explanations, preoccupations, and goals attributed to other economic schools of thought have been largely neglected and treated as though they are inferior. Furthermore, given that neo-liberal economists consider their paradigm to be the best one available, they devote significant time to defending their ideas, principles, goals, and outcomes against all criticisms emanating from any of the other schools of economic thought. In fact, the tenacity and vigour with which they defend neo-liberalism often gives the impression that they have been personally offended, or believe that the critiques put forth by their peers from other schools of economic thought are ill-intentioned. This hostile attitude exhibited by neo-liberal economists towards other economic programs of research and non-mathematical economics is extremely destructive to the free and independent development of the discipline of economics. To be more precise, by 'snubbing, disparaging, excommunicating, or prohibiting the working habits of' other schools of thought, and 'preaching a methodology that implies that they are inferior in scientific workmanship,' neo-liberal economists have inhibited the progress of their discipline by obstructing diversity in views, methods, theories, models, solutions, etc. (Machlup 1956, 172). That is to say, the aggressiveness and inflexibility of mathematical economists when it comes to the views of alternative schools of economic thought have resulted in the emergence of methodological monism in the discipline of economics. This methodological monism has led to unfreedom in terms of the areas and subjects deemed acceptable for economic research and analysis, which has seriously hindered progress and caused poverty in the discipline of economics. More specifically, the poverty of neo-liberalism lies in the restrictions and limitations that it places on the horizons of the discipline of economics by narrowly and obsessively focusing on mathematical modelling, which can say nothing about the true nature of human behaviour or the realities of the world. In doing so, it neglects the importance of the history of economic thought, moral philosophy, heterodox economics, and multidisciplinary research.

12.2 The Rise of Mathematical Economics: Going Down the Wrong Path

In the beginning of the twentieth century, there was a reaction against mathematical economics, as among 'scientists and mathematicians in particular, there was an enduring belief that mathematical methods were unlikely to be of relevance to the analysis of society' (Lawson 2013, 973). In fact, economic journals devoted little 'more than 5 percent of their pages to mathematical discourse' between 1887 and 1924 (Mirowski 1991, 151). Around that time, political economists were not convinced that the simple fact that 'price and quantity are expressed as numbers in the quotidian operation of markets' was 'sufficient' to accept that 'mathematical discourse would be regarded as uniquely correct or appropriate in discussions of the economy' (Mirowski 1991, 153).

In the post war period, scientific progress was regarded as a national interest in the United States, and as such, scientific research received considerable amounts of public funding. This also led to economists that were 'doing scientific economics' following World War II receiving significant 'public funds' and 'grants and contracts' from various departments of the government, including defence, health, agriculture, and commerce (Weintraub 2007, 273). Consequently, efforts to make economics into a more respectable, rigorous, true, and exact science, by incorporating the mathematical formalisms of physics, intensified in the second half of the twentieth century. However, many of the important contributions to the development of mathematical economics were made well before World War II. In fact, mathematical economics had already started to be used in the development of modern theories of 'the consumer, the producer, oligopoly, and general equilibrium' between 1838 and 1947 (Arrow and Intriligator 1981, 1). Meanwhile, the 'first systematically formulated mathematical theory of general Economic Equilibrium' was developed by French economist Léon Walras[1] (1834–1910) in the late nineteenth century (Leontief 1985, 23). Walras (2010, 47) emphasised that 'in any case, the establishment sooner or later of economics as an exact science is no longer in our hands and need not concern us. It is already perfectly clear that economics, like astronomy and mechanics, is both an empirical and a rational science.' It was evident that Walras (2010, 47–48) was pleased

[1] The origins of neo-classical economics are often traced back to the Marginalist Revolution, which finds its own origins in the works of Walras, Jevons, and Menger.

with the rapid pace at which economics was being transformed into a branch of the natural sciences when he stated:

> It took from a hundred to a hundred and fifty or two hundred years for the astronomy of Kepler to become the astronomy of Newton and Laplace, and for the mechanics of Galileo to become the mechanics of d'Alembert and Lagrange. On the other hand, less than a century has elapsed between the publication of Adam Smith's work and the contributions of Cournot, Gossen, Jevons, and myself. We were, therefore, at our post, and have performed our duty.

In addition to Walras, some of the main contributors to the early development of mathematical economics included William Stanley Jevons, Francis Ysidro Edgeworth, Irving Fisher, and Vilfredo Pareto, who 'copied the physical mathematics literally term for term and dubbed the result mathematical economics' (Mirowski 1991, 157). In its early stages, Cournot, Wicksteed, Wicksell, Marshall, Hotelling, Georgescu-Roegen, Hicks, and Hahn were also among the many other economists that contributed to the development mathematical economics (Arrow and Intriligator 1981, 3). Subsequently, from 1948 to 1960, 'the set-theoretic/linear models' were developed. A number of mathematical economists played significant roles in this process, including Arrow, Debreu, McKenzie, Leontief, Koopmans, Morgenstern, Kantorovich, Nash, and Samuelson (Arrow and Intriligator 1981, 6). Since 1961, mathematics have been used in 'virtually all areas of economics,' such as 'uncertainty and information,' 'global analysis,' 'duality theory,' 'aggregate demand functions,' 'core of an economy and markets with a continuum of traders,' 'temporary equilibrium,' 'computation of equilibrium prices,' 'social choice theory,' 'optimal taxation,' 'optimal growth theory,' and 'organization theory,' just to name a few (Arrow and Intriligator 1981, 8–9).

In the 1940s, economists thought that they needed to gain a 'mastery' over mathematics, so as to 'decrease its mastery' over them (Stigler 1949, 44). Since then, a lack of proficiency with mathematical techniques has come to be regarded as a sign of weakness and ignorance within the discipline of economics. Many neo-liberal economists now believe that sophisticated mathematical modelling is the only suitable method for dealing with economic problems, meaning that any competent economist must have this ability within their skillset. Accordingly, garnering a reputation as a respected and skilled economist since the rise of neo-liberalism has required a strong understanding of both econometrics and mathematics, which are important tools for the development of new models and theories. Furthermore, econometrics and mathematical models are extensively used by neo-liberal economists to empirically evaluate policies, strategies, reforms, and programs prior to their implementation in both the public and private sectors.

Expressing economic concepts and ideas in the form of increasingly complicated and intricate mathematical language, formulas, and presentations, as well as econometric models, has become the norm in economic textbooks, articles, and books, as well as at academic conferences and seminars, and in classrooms, lectures and presentations. Presently, economists have to master mathematical economics in order to obtain an academic position, receive funding for their research projects, or publish in the main academic journals. This is not particularly surprising, given that neo-liberal economics is currently the leading paradigm, which means its practitioners have significant influence over what is taught in economics classrooms, the content that is published in economic journals, and the kinds of projects that receive financial support. In other words, neo-liberalism has been shaping the minds and choices of economics students, professionals and academics at different stages of their development and careers for decades. However, teaching, studying and supporting only neo-liberal (i.e., mainstream) economics would suggest that neo-liberals object to plurality within the discipline of economics. In all likelihood, they do not even realize that this methodological monism has resulted in the poverty of their program of research, as their efforts to safeguard the dominant status of neo-liberalism have made economics into a one-dimensional discipline that focuses on imitating the methods, language, and presentation of the natural sciences, while preventing a diversity of views, and ignoring or rejecting its own origins, evolution, and historical background.

Mastering mathematical economics has not only been a requirement for obtaining academic employment, funding for research projects, and publications in most academic journals, it has also been an important criteria for awarding the Nobel Prize in economics. A significant number of economists have been awarded the Nobel Prize for their work in the area of mathematical economics, including: Ragnar Frisch and Jan Tinbergen in 1969, 'for having developed and applied dynamic models for the analysis of economic processes;' Paul Samuelson in 1970, 'for the scientific work through which he has developed static and dynamic economic theory and actively contributed to raising the level of analysis in economic science;' Sir John R. Hicks and Kenneth J. Arrow in 1972, 'for their pioneering contributions to general economic equilibrium theory and welfare theory;' Leonid Kantorovich and Tjalling Koopmans in 1975, 'for their contributions to the theory of optimum allocation of resources;' Milton Friedman in 1976, 'for his achievements in the fields of consumption analysis, monetary history and theory and for his demonstration of the complexity of stabilization policy;' Lawrence Klein in 1980, 'for the creation of econometric models and the application to the analysis of economic fluctuations and economic policies;' James Tobin in 1981, 'for his analysis of financial markets and their relations to expenditure decisions, employment, production and prices;' Gerard Debreu in 1983, 'for having incorporated new analytical methods into economic theory and for his rigorous reformulation of the theory of general equilibrium;' Trygve Haavelmo in 1989, 'for his clarification of the probability theory foundations of econometrics and his analyses of simultaneous economic structures;' Ronald H. Coase in 1991, 'for his discovery and clarification of the significance of transaction costs and property rights for the institutional structure and functioning of the economy;' Gary Becker in 1992, 'for having extended the domain of microeconomic analysis to a wide range of human behaviour and interaction, including nonmarket behaviour;' and, Robert W. Fogel in 1993, 'for having renewed research in economic history by applying economic theory and quantitative methods in order to explain economic and institutional change,' in addition to Douglass C. North 'for having renewed research in economic history by applying economic theory and quantitative methods in order to explain economic and institutional change.'[2] According to Hayek (2008, 29), the 'establishment of the Nobel Memorial Prize in Economic Science marks a significant step in the process by which, in the opinion of the general public, economics has been conceded some of the dignity and prestige of the physical sciences.'

Neo-liberal economists have been using methodologies of the physical sciences and mathematics to develop formal theories in economics aimed at attaining exact calculability. Much like the natural sciences, contemporary economics focuses on quantitative methods involving the collection, interpretation and analysis of vast amounts of data in order to objectively measure, explain and forecast various phenomena and events. Neo-liberals now claim that the laws of economic transactions and interactions are

[2] The Nobel Prize. 'All Prizes in Economic Sciences.' https://www.nobelprize.org/prizes/lists/all-prizes-in-economic-sciences.

analogous to the laws of physics. This is very important for them, because neo-liberal economists are of the opinion that 'anything stated in mathematics must be correct, whilst for things to be correct, reliable, insightful or scientific (or at least conferring of scientific status), they must be stated in mathematics' (Lawson 2015, 230). In fact, they believe that applying the ideas, tools and methodologies of natural science to economics distinguishes it from other social sciences due to the refined techniques used to perform various calculations. On this basis, they contend that economics is a rigorous, theoretically consistent, respected and solid discipline.

Stigler (1982, 60) contended that economics is an empirical science, with an objective to 'provide general understanding of events in the real world.' At the same time, however, he emphasized that this does not mean 'it must be responsive to the contemporaneous conditions and problems of the society in which it is situated' (Stigler 1982, 60). That is to say, 'there could not be a science of economics' if economists were constantly altering the way they conducted their research in order to adapt to and accommodate the frequent changes in the conditions and problems faced by society (Stigler 1982, 61). He emphasised that 'an essential element of a science is the cumulative growth of knowledge, and that cumulative character could not arise if each generation of economists faced fundamentally new problems calling for entirely new methods of analysis. The change of problems and methods would also undermine the training of economists: if the young studied under the old, the young could be confident that they were learning things that were rapidly becoming obsolete. A science requires for its very existence a set of fundamental and durable problems' (Stigler 1982, 61). Therefore, much like any other discipline within the natural sciences, economics cannot be concerned with actual real world changes, and 'new circumstances which call for more than a routine application of standard knowledge' (Stigler 1982, 61). For example, Stigler (1982, 61) pointed out that the oil crisis of the 1970s 'provided much employment to economists, but it has not called for important changes in economic science.'

Stigler also explained that economics, as a rigorous and respectable science, necessitates 'the persistent and almost timeless theories that naturally ignore the changing conditions of their society and the unsettled theories that encounter much difficulty in attempting to explain current events' (Stigler 1982, 62). Since economists are not concerned with the emergence of new circumstances, economics at its highest level has essentially disconnected itself from the practical realities of not only economics, but other disciplines as well. That means mathematical economics has essentially isolated itself from the true social and economic context that establishes the facts on the ground faced by regular people. In other words, practitioners of mathematical economics and econometrics are more interested in developing and working with mathematical formulas and complex models than properly understanding and addressing the economic realities confronting the world.

Friedman (1966) pointed out that, in the past, most economic theories were preoccupied with realism, or the realities of the prevailing social and economic context, which did not contribute to the progress of economics. Instead, he suggested that the main purpose of economics should be to make solid predictions and forecasts based on abstract mathematical modelling. Accordingly, Friedman (1966) maintained that a theory should not be evaluated based on how realistic its assumptions are, but rather, according to the accuracy of its predictions. In fact, he believed that empirical realism had little or no importance when compared with the capacity of theories to make empirical predictions. This was evident when Friedman (1966, 14) stated:

> Truly important and significant hypotheses will be found to have "assumptions" that are wildly inaccurate descriptive representations of reality, and, in general, the more significant the theory, the more unrealistic the assumptions.

In his essay 'The Methodology of Positive Economics,'[3] Friedman (1966) provided rationale for using unrealistic assumptions in economic theories in order to make correct predictions. He explained that the main goal of economics, as a positive science, should be to develop theories, hypothesis and models that make accurate predictions 'about phenomena not yet observed' (Friedman 1966, 7). He believed that science does not exist without an accurate predictive capacity. Friedman even went so far as to suggest that the correctness of a theory, hypothesis or model can be determined by the accuracy and precision of its predictions. According to Friedman, even though a model is constructed by eliminating the realities of social and economic life, an econometric model with an accurate predictive capacity will still allow specialists to recommend appropriate

[3]Friedman's (1966) essay 'The Methodology of Positive Economics' is 'sometimes referred to as the most cited paper in economic method—and sometimes in method generally—in the social sciences' (Ebenstein 2007, 63).

policies for economic agents. Basically, he was of the view that constructing a better theory with a better model requires highly advanced mathematical modelling and assumptions that oversimplify real-life events and features.

Contrary to Friedman, Knight (2017 [1935], 102) argued that it was not possible to have a scientific worldview in the discipline of economics, because the world is not always the same; rather, there are always changes, which means 'the world is knowable only historically, the future is unpredictable.' Accordingly, he was opposed to prophecy in economics, as he specifically stated that 'if the world is always the same there is no problem of prediction, while if it is not always the same prediction is impossible' (Knight 2017 [1935], 102).

To achieve abstraction, mathematical economists remove 'all features of social reality that prove inconvenient' (Lawson 1997, 235). To be more precise, mathematical economists will often include assumptions that oversimplify reality when constructing a model based on mathematical language, presentation, and form, in order to ensure that they obtain a desirable outcome (e.g., find an important correlation between key economic variables). This can involve oversimplifying reality to the extent of supposing that individuals are atomistic, independent, self-sufficient and isolated, like Robinson Crusoe. Such a 'fiction of atomistic, quasi omniscient, infallible ('economically rational') agents acting in the closed, isolated conditions described in contemporary modelling, does indeed constitute such a different world' (Lawson 1997, 236). Practically speaking, assuming that everybody acts as if they are isolated agents in an oversimplified world provides little insight into the real life issues, problems and preoccupations facing complex contemporary societies.

Abstraction can be a very useful tool in scientific research, as it can allow people to 'access and understand a structured, dynamic and holistic reality' (Lawson 1997, 236). However, it is important to recognize that the goal of 'abstraction is not to mask (or legitimate) a pretence that the aspect in question exists in isolation,' as mathematical economists often do (Lawson 1997, 236). In other words, the achievement of abstraction should not involve the elimination of all the inconvenient features of a variable, while also treating that variable as though it exists in isolation from other variables and outside the realm of social reality. That said, since many of the mathematical models used in economics are constructed based on a useless form of abstraction, characterized by unrealistic assumptions, they do not provide solid foundations for the conclusions they arrive at. Therefore, anyone who is genuinely interested in understanding the real world and how it works should not look towards mathematical economics as a reliable and rigorous source of answers. Similarly, mathematical models based on oversimplified abstract assumptions, so as to achieve a particular result, should never be relied upon as the basis for providing policy advice.

Since the rise of neo-liberalism, mathematical modelling has garnered an unmerited reputation for being scientifically sound due to 'the cultural belief that a reliance on mathematical technique in science is somehow so normal or neutral or natural that any questioning of this emphasis can be ignored or swiftly dismissed' (Lawson 2015, 162). However, a number of well-known neo-classical and neo-liberal economists, who played major roles in the development of contemporary economics, were critical of the extensive use of the methodology, presentation, formulas, and language of mathematics in economics. In fact, the same could be said of the practitioners of mathematical economics in its early years, as they were less careless and more selective in their application of mathematics to economics. Even Stigler (1949, 37) had reservations about mathematical economics despite the fact that he believed that 'mathematics is a powerful and a beautiful method of reasoning—it is the poetry of logic. Its flexibility and versatility are extraordinary…Mathematics is indeed the queen of the sciences.' More precisely, while Stigler (1949, 39) recognized that mathematics is 'the suitable language for communication among economists,' he was nonetheless concerned about its overuse within the discipline. Stigler (1949, 43) suggested that it was precisely:

> Because the mathematical method is so powerful and beautiful, and its possession still sufficiently rare to command distinction, the mathematical economist is under constant temptation to use it just for the sake of using it.

Although Stigler (1949, 38, 42) accepted that mathematics was a useful tool that could contribute to 'good economic theory,' he was very clear that he did not consider it to be 'indispensable.' He also emphasized the point that 'mathematical training will not turn a mediocre economist into a great economist—a statement most mathematical economists will immodestly accept' (Stigler 1949, 38, 39).

Samuelson (1952, 65) shared similar views with Stigler, as he maintained that 'mathematics is neither a necessary nor a sufficient condition for a fruitful career in economic theory.' Although he acknowledged that the methodology, presentation, formulas, and language of mathematics can be useful in the field of economics, he also suggested that 'it can certainly be a hindrance, since it is only too easy to convert a good literary economist into a mediocre mathematical economist' (Samuelson 1952, 65). Nevertheless, Samuelson (1952, 65) stated that economists without a proficiency in mathematical economics:

> run grave psychological risks. As you grow older, you are sure to resent the method increasingly. Either you will get an inferiority complex and retire from the field of theory or you will get an inferiority complex and become aggressive about your dislike of it.

Prominent neo-classical economist Alfred Marshall (1842–1924) (2013 [1890], 71), who played a significant role in the original application of 'mathematical language and mathematical habits of thought' to economics, did not share the views held by many of neo-liberal theorists with respect to the use of mathematics in economics. Marshall (2013, 71) was very selective with his own application of mathematics in economics, as he did not want 'mathematical language' and 'mathematical reasoning' to come to dominate the discipline of economics. He also strongly objected to the frequency of 'mathematical formulae' in economic studies. In fact, stated that it is 'doubtful whether much has been gained by the use of complex mathematical formulae' (Marshall 2013, 71).

Carl Menger (1841–1921) (1985, 86), founding father of the Austrian School of Economics, explained that mathematics 'do not deal with the world of real phenomena in its totality, but only with a single side of it...they are therefore, in contrast to 'full empirical reality,' arbitrary and unempirical.' Menger (1985, 38) further argued that mathematical modelling did not make people 'aware' of economic phenomena or people's goals, 'either from the historical point of view or from the theoretical; they do not teach us at all what is.'

Hayek also opposed the extensive use of mathematics in economic modelling that was so enthusiastically supported by most neo-liberals. Although Hayek believed that some level of mathematical modelling could be useful as a tool for economists, he argued that economics is ultimately a branch of the social sciences; as such, he criticized the tendencies of some of his peers to make economics into a branch of the natural sciences. Hayek labelled this 'slavish imitation' and application 'of the method and language of Science' to the social sciences as 'scientism,' which included efforts to transform economics into a branch of the natural sciences (Hayek 1952, 15). When discussing mathematical economists, Hayek (2008, 42–44) stated:

> I must confess that I still doubt whether their search for measurable magnitudes has made significant contributions to our theoretical understanding of economic phenomena…I confess that I prefer true but imperfect knowledge, even if it leaves much indetermined and unpredictable, to a pretense of exact knowledge that is likely to be false. The credit which the apparent conformity with recognized scientific standards can gain for seemingly simple but false theories may, as the present instance shows, have grave consequences.

Hayek (1952, 16) was strongly opposed to the 'mechanical and uncritical application of habits of thought' of natural sciences to economics. He pointed out that economists 'make constant use of formulas, symbols, and rules' that they do not properly understand (Hayek 1958, 88). In fact, he believed that the practice of imitating 'as closely as possible the procedures of the brilliantly successful physical sciences' constituted a 'failure of the economists' (Hayek 2008, 31). Hayek (2008, 54) was clearly worried about the long run implications of mathematical economics for society when he stated the:

> danger of which I want to warn is precisely the belief that in order to have a claim to be accepted as scientific it is necessary to achieve more. This way lies charlatanism and worse. To act on the belief that we possess the knowledge and the power which enable us to shape the processes of society entirely to our liking, knowledge which in fact we do not possess, is likely to make us do much harm.

Furthermore, Hayek (1958, 73) explained 'the theories of the social sciences do not consist of "laws" in the sense of empirical rules about the behavior of objects definable in physical terms.' He was of the opinion that mathematical economists had a tendency to ignore or neglect the differences between economics and the natural sciences. According to him, the scientific method is experimental, and economics is not an experimental science; it can never deliver the type of knowledge that a scientist conveys from a laboratory experiment. That means, contrary to the theories and models of the natural sciences, those associated with economics cannot be 'verified or falsified by reference to facts' (Hayek 1958, 73).

In the natural sciences, scientists are often able to establish ideal conditions in their laboratories, allowing them to test their theories and hypotheses in controlled experiments that provide knowledge and insights about the physical world. Since it is possible to organize and control variables in a way that allows for predicted results to emerge when conducting research in the natural sciences, the results are generally precise and accurate, in addition to being considerably similar to the outcomes that would emerge in the real world. For a theory to be accepted as valid in the natural sciences, different scientists must be able to replicate the results of an experiment if they establish the same conditions. Conversely, it is highly unlikely that two different economists would be able to obtain identical results when conducting the same experiment via economic modeling, because external phenomena will not only affect different individuals in different ways, they will also affect the same individual in different ways at different points in time. Therefore, contrary to the natural sciences, economic theories and models can never be realistically tested and verified with any degree of certainty.

Hayek explained that, unlike the natural sciences, there are no regularities in 'complex phenomena' that could be 'observed twice under identical conditions' in economics (Hayek 1958, 127). In other words, he believed that it was impossible to recreate the same phenomena when conducting experiments in economics, even under identical or sufficiently similar conditions. Factors like imperfect information, dispersed knowledge, spontaneous individual action, and spontaneous changes in social and economic conditions, among others, prevent sophisticated mathematical modelling from capturing the realistic economic conditions and behaviours needed to achieve exact and precise results, like those generated by scientific experiments. That means economic theories and models cannot be verified on account of the complexity of social phenomena, as well as a lack of the same kinds of certainties that characterize the natural sciences (Hayek 1989, 126). As such, Hayek (1958, 127) warned against forcing the empirical methods of the natural sciences 'on the social sciences which was bound to lead to disaster.' Through econometrics and highly sophisticated mathematical modelling, 'numerous diagnoses have been made and various solutions have been suggested. In the event, however, the remedies proposed, if in the context sometimes remarkable, have failed to make any headway in terms of facilitating a project that is seemingly capable of illuminating social reality' (Lawson 1997, 86). That is to say, even when mathematical economists manage to identify problems, they do not 'fully represent the real nature of the relevant disorder' (Lawson 1997, 86).

According to Fritz Machlup (1902–1983) (1956, 172), a well-known Austrian-American economist, 'the aggressiveness and restrictiveness' expressed by mathematical economists, which have been 'developed-in subconscious attempts to compensate for their feelings of inferiority vis-a-vis the alleged "true scientist"—are deplorable'. Machlup (1956, 166) had similar views with Hayek with respect to differences between economics and the natural sciences, as he stated:

> In its narrowest sense, scientific method is supposed to mean experimental method, or the demand that every proposition be "verified" by repeated laboratory experiments with strict controls of all conditions. In a wider sense, scientific method is supposed to mean statistical method, or the demand that every proposition be "verified" by numerous sets of statistical data relating to sufficiently comparable situations. If no wider extension of the definition is conceded and if no proposition is deemed "scientifically" acceptable unless it is confirmed by such scientific method-alas, only a minute fraction of all propositions about human action in society would be acceptable, and only the most insignificant propositions at that.

Machlup (1956, 166) stressed that 'this largess in the meaning of scientific method is not widely accepted' by mathematical economists, who 'continue to labor under' their 'restrictive definitions' of the natural sciences, which means society will continue to 'bear the consequences of the inferiority complex' of neo-liberalism.

Much like Hayek and Machlup, Mises (1949, 350–351) was also very concerned about the transformation of economics to extensively incorporate mathematical language, equations, charts and curves that pretend to depict reality, even though they are just hypothetical and unrealistic representations of it. According to him, 'the equations formulated by mathematical economics remain a useless piece of mental gymnastics and would remain so even if they were to express much more than they really do' (Mises 1949, 351). Mises (1978, 39) further elaborated that:

> All of mathematical economics with its beautiful equations and curves is nothing but useless doodling...setting up equations does not enhance our knowledge. Because there are no constant relations in the field of human action, the equations of mathematical catallactics cannot be made to serve practical problems in the same way the equations of mechanics solve practical

> problems through the use of data and constants that have been ascertained empirically.

Mises (1978, 89) also argued against efforts to make economics into a branch of the natural sciences, stating that:

> Logic and the epistemology of the sciences of human action cannot learn anything from physics and mathematics…The gap between the natural sciences and those of human action will not be bridged thereby.

Mises (1978, 77) questioned the use of mathematical equations in economics when he asked, 'How can economic action that always consists of preferring and setting aside, that is, of making unequal valuations, be transformed into equal valuations, and the use of equations?' For him, 'mathematics deal with an ideal system of thought,' meaning it is not particularly useful for the comprehension of reality (Mises 1949, 99). He suggested that an observant 'housewife knows much more about price changes as far as they affect her own household than the statistical averages can tell…she is no less "scientific" and no more arbitrary than the sophisticated mathematicians in choosing their methods for the manipulation of the data of the market' (Mises 1949, 224). In other words, he was arguing that, in the case of economics, individual value judgments were worth more than sophisticated mathematical language and equations when it came to expressing changes in economic life, or making a choice in the market. Basically, according to Mises, mathematical language, modelling and representations do not affect the essence of people's interpretations, nor do they contribute to human understanding or insights.

Mises was highly critical of the time and effort that mathematical economists devoted to describing economic life and phenomena via mathematical symbols. In particular, he objected to: the way they 'deal with equilibrium as if it were a real entity and not a limiting notion, a mere mental tool;' and, how 'they stress exclusively the imaginary state of equilibrium which the whole complex of all such actions would attain in the absence of any further change in the data' (Mises 1949, 251). Mises (1949, 251) went so far as to suggest that these mathematical economists were being 'vain playing with mathematical symbols, a pastime not suited to convey any knowledge.' This is because he was of the opinion that they basically devoted their time to working with imaginary constructions based on mathematical modelling, which are not well-suited for representing the people that live in society, whose actions, experiences, and decisions change spontaneously. In fact, Mises (1949, 347) strongly advised for the exclusion of the mathematical method from economics 'on account of its barrenness.' More specifically, he argued that it needed to be rejected, because it was 'an entirely vicious method, starting from fake assumptions and leading to fallacious inferences. Its syllogisms are not only sterile; they divert the mind from the study of the real problems and distort the relations between the various phenomena' (Mises 1949, 347).

Contrary to many of the other economists from the Chicago School, Knight (1947, 547) did not view the extensive application of the methods of the natural sciences to economics in a positive light. In fact, he described mathematical economics as a new form of religion that promised 'salvation' by applying the methods of the natural sciences within economics (Knight, 1947). Accordingly, he was critical of mathematical economists for trying to use the scientific method to solve social problems, which he referred to as 'propaganda for science' (Knight 1947, 547).

Knight (2017, 139) explained that, in the natural sciences, 'the exact methods of science have carried understanding and control enormously farther than common sense could go,' because of the fact that 'the data are relatively stable, reducible to classes of manageable number, and especially classes with recognizable and measurable indices' (Knight 2017, 139). However, these fundamental features of the natural sciences do not hold for 'human data' (Knight 2017, 139). In other words, understanding the social and economic behaviours of human beings requires a method that is 'very different from the technique of natural science' (Knight 2017, 139). Ultimately, Knight (2017, 139) was of the opinion that 'economics must be branches of literature as much as of science.'

According to Knight (1922, 479), in economics, 'the main argument for the validity and necessity of a real, non-scientific, transcendental ethics comes out of the limitations of scientific explanation.' Since abstraction eliminates many of the inconvenient features of social reality in mathematical economics, its models cannot explain the true nature of human motives, or the real social and economic problems that human beings face. In fact, Knight was of the opinion that it was dangerous to believe that human behaviors could be rationally explained through the formulas, languages, representations and laws of the natural sciences. He argued that 'any attempt at use of the unqualified procedures of natural science in solving problems of human relations is just another name for a struggle for power, ultimately a completely lawless one' (Knight 1948, 57).

Philip Mirowski (2011, 330), a well-known economist and professor of history of economic thought at the University of Notre Dame, also has little faith in mathematical economics. This is due in part to his low opinion of mathematical economists, as Mirowski (2011, 330) stated that they:

> regard themselves as intellectuals and lovers of knowledge, by and large. Many in the profession think economists are the true heirs of the Enlightenment (that is, in the eventuality they have some notion of what the Enlightenment was). Most of them really do love physics, even if they flunked out or otherwise bailed out of physics programs elsewhere earlier in their careers. Nonetheless, I want to explore the proposition that recent trends have enrolled them into practical complicity with the new production of ignorance, and therefore, by implication, economists may be among the last people on earth to whom you should voluntarily entrust your science base.

Galbraith was of the opinion that since economics affects the daily lives of every human being, it should not focus on mathematical modelling; rather, it should concentrate on real issues affecting people's lives, society, and the planet. He argued that a 'prolonged commitment to mathematical exercises in economics can be damaging' (Galbraith 1971, 41, nn.10). More specifically, he suggested that the extensive use and over-valuation of mathematics in economics leads to 'the atrophy of judgment and intuition which are indispensable for real solutions and, on occasion, leads also to the habit of mind which simply excludes the mathematically inconvenient factors from consideration' (Galbraith 1971, 41, nn.10).

Furthermore, Wassily Leontief (1906–1999), a Russian-American economist who was awarded the Nobel Prize in 1973, was also worried about the extensive use of mathematics in economics. He explained that many mathematical economists 'entered the field after specializing in pure or applied mathematics. Page after page of professional economic journals are filled with mathematical formulas leading the reader from sets of more or less plausible but entirely arbitrary assumptions to precisely stated but irrelevant theoretical conclusions' (Leontief 1982, 104). Leontief (1982, 107) also criticized mathematical economics for not contributing to the understanding of real economic life and phenomena, stating that:

> year after year economic theorists continue to produce scores of mathematical models and to explore in great detail their formal properties; and the econometricians fit algebraic functions of all possible shapes to essentially

> the same sets of data without being able to advance, in any perceptible way, a systematic understanding of the structure and the operations of a real economic system.

Although neo-liberal economists like to claim that economics is a rigorous and exact science, their discipline lacks the continuous self-correction that characterizes the natural sciences. This self-correction mechanism has enabled the natural sciences to progressively obtain better approximations of reality. To the contrary, neo-liberal economics has shown no signs of correcting itself, as all of the flaws and errors contained in its fundamental principles continue to persist. That would suggest that mathematical economists are not committed to obtaining a better understanding of the real world. They disregard the realities of social and economic life by reducing nature and social phenomena into mathematical formulas, symbols, presentation, and language for the purpose of oversimplification and quantification. In other words, by focusing their attention on combining highly sophisticated mathematical modelling with unrealistic assumptions in their theories and hypotheses, the minds of economists have become distracted from studying and understanding real economic problems and issues. Consequently, economics has 'increasingly become an intellectual game played for its own sake and not for its practical consequences for understanding the economic world' (Blaug 1997, 3). More precisely, mathematical economists have 'converted the subject into a sort of social mathematics in which analytical rigour is everything and practical relevance is nothing' (Blaug 1997, 3).

Myrdal (2007 [1953], XIV) underscored the point that 'the history of science is a history of scientific controversy.' In other words, there are conflicting ideas within the natural sciences and scientists frequently disagree with each other on a wide range of issues, including methodology, procedures, explanations, and goals. However, this 'warfare of ideas usually leads to some definite result,' as 'theories are refuted, hypotheses become obsolete, the frontiers of knowledge are pushed forward' (Myrdal 2007, XIV). To the contrary, adherents of neo-liberalism act as though the entire existence of economics is limited to a single paradigm since their school of thought achieved dominance in the discipline. Consequently, divergent views, ideas and perspectives, which are crucial for the progress and evolution of society, have been harshly criticized, strongly rejected, or roundly ignored.

During the time that a paradigm is dominant in the natural sciences, there is an accumulation of knowledge where new ideas are added to a pre-existing knowledge base; Thomas Kuhn (1922–1996)[4] (1970) referred this period between two paradigm shifts as 'normal science.' He explained that normal science is not intended to produce new fundamental principles, different perspective, or novel theories. Instead, competing scientific schools and communities work with actual paradigms in an attempt to resolve any unanswered questions that scientists may have. Furthermore, past scientific achievements are still valued and studied during periods of normal science, meaning that old theories are never completely replaced by new ones (Kuhn 1970, 10). However, Kuhn (1970) explained that when the leading paradigm is challenged, the normal rules for 'solving a puzzle' will no longer be capable of providing answers to prevailing anomalies, thereby making the contradictions within that paradigm apparent.

Anomalies pose a threat to the dominant paradigm in the natural sciences, because they are signs that it is not working effectively. Scientists will react to the presence of anomalies by changing 'the nature of their research problems,' which eventually leads to the emergence of a new paradigm (Kuhn 1970, 25). Once the paradigm shift occurs, theories, concepts, and hypotheses are refuted and replaced with new ones. Consequently, the successor and predecessor paradigms are incompatible with one another. However, a paradigm shift does not necessarily mean that the former paradigm has been replaced with a superior one. All that is certain is that the current paradigm is superior to its predecessor when it comes to resolving a specific set of anomalies.

Throughout history, scientific progress has revealed that many of the theories, concepts and ideas that were once part of the dominant paradigm in the natural sciences were not, in fact, universal. Natural scientists tend to see their 'discipline's past developing linearly toward its present vantage' (Kuhn 1970 [1962], 138). Contrary to the natural sciences, neoliberal economists treat old views, ideas and theories, as well as former schools of economic thought, as though they never existed. This is because adherents of neo-liberalism are so convinced of the superiority of their paradigm over all others that came before it that they believe there is no

[4] Thomas Kuhn was an American philosopher of science who is well known for writing *The Structure of Scientific Revolutions* (1962), one of the most influential works in the history of the philosophy of science in the twentieth century.

possibility of gaining any knowledge or insights from earlier economic school of thoughts, theories and methods. Moreover, they act as though neo-liberalism will endure as the leading paradigm in the discipline of economics indefinitely.

In reality, economics can never experience a true paradigm shift in the sense of how the term is understood in the natural sciences. Since economics is not really a branch of the natural sciences, despite the insistence of neo-liberals, Kuhn's definitions of scientific revolution and paradigm shift face many limitations in the discipline of economics, which prevents them from being properly applied. One important issue in this regard is that an economic school of thought is rarely able to completely replace a former one. For example, although there is no disputing that neo-liberalism has clearly been the dominant school of economic thought for decades, the movement away from Keynesian economics to neo-liberalism could not be accurately called a paradigm shift in the sense of the natural sciences. First of all, a key factor that enabled neo-liberalism to achieve its dominant position in the discipline of economics was the financial, technical and ideological support that was consistently provided by academics, democratically-elected politicians, powerful corporations, free-market think thanks, and international institutions, among others. Therefore, what we are witnessing in the discipline of economics is the deliberate and well-planned imposition of the neo-liberal doctrine, which has not emerged as a result of a paradigm shift. A second important factor suggesting that neo-liberalism did not come to prominence through a true paradigm shift is that economists have never been anywhere near a consensus that neo-liberalism is, in fact, the leading paradigm. When a paradigm shift takes place in the natural sciences, the entire scientific community recognizes that it has occurred and starts working with the new paradigm. However, since neo-liberalism has been the leading of program of research in the discipline of economics, many economists affiliated with other schools of economic thought (i.e., heterodox economists) persisted in working with their own diverse methodologies, models, theories, perspectives, and goals, even though their voices have been largely silenced by neo-liberals. Instead of contributing to the progress of economics, neo-liberals have been obstructing its development by systematically and deliberately opposing alternative views and opinions that do not conform with their own values, ideas, objectives, methods, and fundamental principles.

Neo-liberals have consistently endorsed and advocated for the further development and application of mathematical modelling within economics, while rarely critiquing mathematical economics or acknowledging any of its weaknesses. However, while proponents of mathematical economics are often the ones that establish the frontiers of the minds, perspectives, knowledge, practices and work of future economists, their own minds have lost the creativity to imagine a world that is fundamentally different from the one they work in. That is to say, it has become impossible for them to escape mathematical economics. While mathematic techniques and formulas can be useful tools for the analysis of various economic variables, economics cannot be limited to pure mathematics or abstract science. Economic theory should deal with real world issues, which might enable economists to make more meaningful contributions to society. In other words, since mathematical economists so fully immerse themselves in the development of sophisticated mathematical models, they overlook many of the real problems affecting people's lives such as environmental degradation, and social and economic inequality. Nonetheless, they are sought out to provide expert advice to corporations and governments on issues that concern the masses, other species and the future of the earth.

Consequently, the overreliance on mathematical modelling in the development of public policy recommendations that typifies contemporary economics, on the premise that the results are scientific, has been very destructive for humanity and the environment. That is not to say economists should abandon mathematics altogether, just that it should be used primarily as a tool for the advancement of analysis, explanation, presentation and reasoning. Ultimately, mastering sophisticated mathematical modelling and becoming proficient with equations and symbols is of little worth to economists if they do not understand the political economy, are not familiar with the history of economic thought, do not value multidisciplinary research, and fail to realize the importance of moral and ethical values in economics. In particular multidisciplinary research and a pluralism of methodology could enrich economics and make it into a more coherent and comprehensive discipline that is capable of addressing real world issues.

12.3 Conclusion

In an effort to be accepted as respectable researchers and academics, neo-liberal economists have placed great emphasis on applying the tools and methodologies of the natural sciences to economics, with a particular focus on the development of forecasting models that are able to accurately predict future shocks, events, and states of affairs, so that they can assist with a wide array of key policy decisions. As neo-liberalism rose to prominence, non-mathematical economics have been gradually pushed aside for being unscientific, based on the perception that they were incapable of generating rigorous and reliable results. Consequently, economists specialized in such areas have faced great adversity when it came to obtaining funding and support for their research, acquiring academic posts, or finding employment. The extent of the hostility that neo-liberals have exhibited in their suppression of alternative viewpoints and methodologies within the discipline of economics is somewhat ironic given how vigorously they criticized centrally planned systems for imposing patterns of individual behaviour and eliminating diversity in views and opinions. Although diverse views, ideas and concepts are supposed to flourish in a free society, free-market capitalism has shown itself to be more conducive to methodological monism. Methodological monism within the discipline of economics has coercive elements to it, as it demands uniformity in thoughts and opinions, and keeps the profession mobilized in support of mathematical economics. In a genuinely free society, no coercive or superior power should have the ability to impose a particular view, idea, concept, or theory on people or within a discipline.

Methodological monism has not only resulted in the loss of knowledge by limiting the tools that economists have at their disposal to help them understand and interpret human behaviour, it has also created unfreedom within their discipline by restricting areas of research, objectives, methodology, etc. In fact, many of the changes and developments that transpired in the discipline of economics since the rise of neo-liberalism have revolved around the application of econometric, technical and mathematical tools, instead of making profound changes to methodology, ideas, goals and principles of economic research. Therefore, by supporting methodological monism, neo-liberalism has caused poverty in the discipline of economics. However, neo-liberal economists appear to be ignorant of this poverty, as they have been conducting themselves as though their proficiency with mathematical modelling has made them into savants that can foresee the future with clairvoyance on account of the scientifically rigorous and reliable results generated by their sophisticated models, equations and graphs. In fact, they have come to believe that they should be given the authority to influence and contribute to policy decisions that affect all aspects of people's lives. In reality, these economists are far from savants, as they know very little about many of the subjects they provide policy advice on, including within their own discipline. This is why they have been providing distorted advice and recommendations for many decades.

Despite their unwavering commitment to applying the methods of the natural sciences to economics, mainstream economists have not managed to develop models that successfully emulate the real world or accurately predict future shocks and crises. For example, they failed to anticipate the stagflation of the 1970s, the cyclical trends of the 1980s, and the financial crisis of 2008. These and many other flagrant failures to obtain accurate forecasts demonstrate that economics cannot be treated as a reliable, respectable and rigorous discipline of the natural sciences. Nevertheless, arguments or criticisms against the extensive use and application of mathematics in economics are often inaccurately portrayed as attacks on mainstream economics, unless they are ignored altogether. Additionally, critics of neo-liberal models, theories, views and principles have often been dismissed for being unfamiliar with mathematical economics and economics in general.

Economics cannot be a rigorous and exact discipline in the same vein as the natural sciences, because it deals with highly complex situations formed by social interrelationships between human beings that cannot be understood through mathematical formulas and expressions. Mathematical economics attempts to quantify real life events, actions and decisions into numbers that can then be plugged into equations, formulas and graphs. However, mathematical modelling in economics relies on unrealistic assumptions and hypotheses that grossly over-simplify the real world, ignore human content, and do not account for intangible value. In reality, human lives and personal decisions, actions, and events are affected by a multitude of factors, including emotions, customs, traditions, personal beliefs, and moral and ethical values, none of which can be effectively translated into numbers and formulas or interpreted through mathematical modelling. Since mathematical tools and methods are incapable of helping economists understand and interpret the true nature of human relationships and motives, or the issues that people are preoccupied with in their daily lives, they cannot be expected to provide appropriate solutions to the real problems that humanity is facing. As such, sophisticated mathematical modelling does not really enlighten society or bring value to the lives of the masses, because it tends to ignore or underestimate many of the important problems facing society, like inequality, injustice, unfairness, extinction, over-production, over-consumption, waste, pollution, and the destruction of nature.

References

Arrow, Kenneth J., and Michael D. Intriligator. 1981. Historical Introduction. In *Handbook of Mathematical Economics*, ed. Kenneth J. Arrow and Michael D. Intriligator, 1–14. New York: Sole Distributors.

Blaug, M. 1997. Ugly Currents in Modern Economics. *Options Politiques* September: 3–8.

Ebenstein, Lanny. 2007. *Milton Friedman: A Biography*. New York: Palgrave Macmillan Ltd.

Friedman, Milton. 1966. The Methodology of Positive Economics. In *Essays in Positive Economics*, 3–16, 30–43. Chicago: The University of Chicago Press.

Galbraith, John Kenneth. 1971. *A Contemporary Guide to Economics Peace and Laughter*. London: Andre Deutsch Limited.

Hayek, F.A. 1952. *The Counter-Revolution of Science: Studies on the Abuse of Reason*. London: Free Press of Glencoe.

———. 1958 [1948]. *Individualism and Economic Order*. Chicago: University of Chicago Press.

———. 1989. *Hayek on Hayek: An Autobiographical Dialogue*. Edited by Stephen Kresge and Leif Wenar. Chicago: University of Chicago Press.

———. 2008 [1974]. 'The Pretense of Knowledge.' In *A Free-Market Monetary System*. Auburn: Ludwig von Mises Institute. ISBN: 978-1-933550-37-4.

Knight, Frank H. 1922. Ethics and the Economic Interpretation. *The Quarterly Journal of Economics* 36 (3): 454–481. https://www.jstor.org/stable/1886033.

———. 1947. 'Salvation by Science: The Gospel According to Professor Lundberg. *Journal of Political Economy* 55 (Dec.): 537–552.

———. 1948. Free Society: Its Basic Nature and Problem. *Philosophical Review* 57 (Jan.): 39–58. https://www.jstor.org/stable/2181733.

———. 2017 [1935]. *The Ethics of Competition*. New York: Routledge.

Kuhn, Thomas S. 1970 [1962]. *The Structure of Scientific Revolutions*. Chicago: The University of Chicago Press.

Lawson, Tony. 1997. *Economics and Reality*. London: Routledge.

———. 2013. What Is This 'School' Called Neoclassical Economics? *Cambridge Journal of Economics* 37: 947–983.

———. 2015. *The Nature and State of Modern Economics*. New York: Routledge.

Leontief, Wassily. 1982. Letters. *Science* 217: 104–107.

———. 1985. *Essays in Economics: Theories, Theorizing, Facts, and Policies*. New York: Routledge.

Machlup, Fritz. 1956. The Inferiority Complex of the Social Sciences. In *On Freedom and Free Enterprise: Essays in Honor of Ludwig von Mises*, ed. Mary Sennholz, 161–172. Toronto: D. Van Nostrand Company.

Marshall, Alfred. 2013 [1890]. *Principles of Economics*. New York: Palgrave Macmillan.

Menger, C. 1985 [1883]. *Investigations into The Method of the Social Sciences with Special Reference to Economics*. Edited by Louis Schneider. Translated by Francis J. Nock. New York: New York University Press.

Mirowski, Philip. 1991. The When, the How and the Why of Mathematical Expression in the History of Economics Analysis. *The Journal of Economic Perspectives* 5 (1): 145–157. https://www.jstor.org/stable/1942707.

———. 2011. *Science-Mart: Privatizing American Science*. Cambridge, MA: Harvard University Press.

Mises, Ludwig von. 1978. *Notes and Recollection*. Edited by Bettina Bien Greaves. Translated by Hans F. Sennholz. Indianapolis: Liberty Fund Inc.

———. 1998 [1949]. *Human Action: A Treatise on Economics*. Auburn, Alabam: The Ludwig von Mises Institute.

Myrdal, Karl Gunnar. 2007 [1953]. *The Political Element in the Development of Economic Thought*. Abingdon: Routledge.

Samuelson, Paul A. 1952. Economic Theory and Mathematics: An Appraisal. *American Economic Association: The American Economic Review* 42 (2, May): 56–66. https://www.jstor.org/stable/1910585.

Solow, Robert M. 1985. Economic History and Economics. *The American Economic Review* 75 (2): 328–331. http://www.jstor.com/stable/1805620.

Stigler, George J. 1949. *Five Lectures on Economic Problems*. London: Longmans, Green and Co.

———. 1965. *Essays in the History of Economics*. Chicago: University of Chicago Press.

———. 1982. The Process and Progress of Economics. Nobel Memorial Lecture. Graduate School of Business, University of Chicago.

Walras, Léon. 2010 [1954]. *Elements of Pure Economics: The Theory of Social Wealth*. New York: Routledge.

Weintraub, E.Roy. 2007. Economic Science Wars. *Journal of the History of Economic Thought* 29 (3): 267–282.

CHAPTER 13

Conclusion: Corporations and the Hobbesian Right to Nature under Free-Market Capitalism

Neo-liberal economists have demonstrated an unwavering commitment to the notion that economics is a rigorous, exact and respected discipline of the natural sciences, which has given them a sense of superiority and prestige over their peers working in the other 'unscientific' social sciences. Their elevated sense of self-worth is also supported by the fact that they play a significant role in shaping the development of economic reforms and policies for all economic agents, and because their expert advice is sought out during periods of adversity and economic crisis. Furthermore, the application of the language, formulas, and methodologies of the natural sciences to modern economics has led neo-liberal economists to claim that their paradigm is superior to all others that have ever existed in the field of economics. In fact, they are devoted to maintaining the status quo by defending the validity of their fundamental principles and theories, as well as the extensive application of mathematical modelling to economics, so as to ensure that neo-liberalism remains the leading program of research within the discipline. Consequently, neo-liberal economists have played a significant role in the emergence of methodological monism within economics, as they have also gone to great lengths to prevent other schools of economic thought from flourishing. However, methodological monism has resulted in the poverty of economics, and delayed the progress of the entire discipline.

B. Filip, *The Rise of Neo-liberalism and the Decline of Freedom*,
Palgrave Insights into Apocalypse Economics,
https://doi.org/10.1007/978-3-030-61623-6_13

Although neo-liberals claim to champion freedom, methodological monism is incompatible with a genuinely free society. If a society is truly free, then neo-liberalism would be treated as a single economic school of thought among many others, rather than the standard that other schools of economic thought must adhere to. That is to say, a genuinely free society is supposed to objectively provide equal opportunities for diverse views, ideas, and ideologies to flourish, instead of facilitating the dominance of a particular paradigm. In reality, methodological monism impedes fair competition and violates the rights of other schools of economic thought by preventing them from reaching a wider public, as heterodox economists often face challenges obtaining academic employment, securing funding for their research projects, and publishing in prominent academic journals. Therefore, the freedom that neo-liberals defend so adamantly is only granted to economists who adhere to their specific paradigm.

Methodological monism has essentially helped neo-liberals maintain their dominant status in the field of economics by eliminating all possible threats and rivals. The opposition to plurality exhibited by neo-liberal economists over the last four decades has demonstrated that, when it comes to tolerance, freedom and fairness, they lag well behind totalitarian regimes, which Hayek considered to be the successors of tribal societies. Inhibiting the diversity and plurality of views not only violates the fundamental principles of a free society, it also stifles alternative ideas, goals, and theories that could prove to be useful in solving problems in the economic, social and political arenas.

Neo-liberal economists disregard ethical and moral values on the basis that virtuous intentions and actions are wholly irrelevant to disciplines of the natural sciences, as well as the achievement of capitalist ends in a free-market system. In fact, Hayek (1979, 165) claimed that the work and ideas of moral 'prophets and philosophers' has prevented or delayed the development of free-market capitalism in many countries. He further argued that free-market capitalism could only be realized through 'the disregard of the injunctions of those indignant moralists' (Hayek 1979, 166). In other words, economic decisions, actions and policies have to be immune from moral and ethical judgements in a free-market system, which entails the complete absence of concern about anyone else's social and economic situations, or their moral and ethical values. Mises (1998 [1949], 270) explained that people, in 'their capacity as buyers and consumers they are hard-hearted and callous, without consideration for other people.' This is because they have been indoctrinated into adopting self-interested, rational, impersonal, instrumental, and individualistic behaviors to guide their economic decisions in the marketplace, without any ethical and moral considerations. This corresponds with the views of Friedman (2002, 24) who claimed that, 'the wider the range of activities covered by the market, the fewer are the issues on which explicitly political decisions are required.' Accordingly, adherents of neo-liberalism have consistently advocated for its core values and principles to be adopted in every aspects of people's lives, including those that are not considered to be parts of traditional economic analysis, such as daily activities, education, family, hobbies, crime, marriage, fertility, politics, law, criminology, health-care, illness, etc. That would mean these areas of personal and social life could be treated as though they are business transactions in the market-place, free from the influence of politics, and moral and ethical values.

Integrating neo-liberal values and principles into people's thoughts, decisions and actions has involved inundating them with propaganda via various mediums, including newspapers, books, movies, advertisements and programs transmitted via television, the radio and the internet, education systems, and through the discourses of well-known public figures like politicians, academics, experts, celebrities and athletes. The largely successful application of free-market economic principles and values into the daily lives of individuals can also be attributed to the financial, technical and ideological support consistently provided by democratically-elected politicians, powerful corporations, free-market think thanks, academics, and various international institutions and organizations. In the end, very few countries and societies have managed to resist the broad implementation of neo-liberal standards, policies and reforms in their economies, as well as their social and political arenas. Consequently, the widespread acceptance of neo-liberalism on a global scale has facilitated a general movement away from the practice of moral and ethical values. In fact, it could be argued that the values and principles of neo-liberalism have largely replaced religion and moral philosophy as sources of the core beliefs, views, practices, and standards that guide people in their decisions and actions. More specifically, four decades of being constantly exposed to the values and principles of neo-liberalism has led to the masses understanding and viewing the world, including their physical, spiritual and emotional lives, through a framework that has been provided to them by neo-liberal economists. Unfortunately, the integration of free-market economic principles and values into the daily lives of individuals has led to the emergence of mediocre, weak, and narrow-minded people who think and act according to the capitalist spirit, which has resulted in the prevalence of many forms of social and economic inequality, unfreedom, the over-exploitation of natural resources, pollution, climate change, and the real risk of an environmental apocalypse.

Contrary to modern neo-liberals, many economists, philosophers, theologists, and political theorists throughout history have regarded individual self-interest maximization, the desire for power, and acquisitiveness as root causes of some of the most serious forms of destruction and misery known to humanity. More precisely, they have warned that selfish wants and desires would inevitably lead people to make choices that are detrimental to other people and damaging to their surroundings, both in the present and future. Sadly, in only four decades, neo-liberals have managed to effectively eliminate virtually all remnants of the valuable work accentuating the importance of moral and ethical values produced by scores of prominent historical figures and thinkers from many different disciplines since the times of the Ancient Greeks.

Although neo-liberals like to claim that economics is a value-free science, the discipline was originally conceived as a moral science, and past economists were very familiar with the work of moral philosophers throughout history. In fact, they valued the work and ideas of virtue ethics and moral philosophy, and applied them to economics order to help them understand the issues and problems of their own time. However, since neo-liberals consider the study of the history of economic thought to be little more than a mere hobby that does not offer very much in the way of practical use, they have forgotten the history and *raison d'être* of their own discipline. By rejecting virtue ethics, moral philosophy and the history of economic thought, neo-liberal economists undervalue the importance of studying 'the writings of wise men, to learn the truths that have emerged from their researches, and carry on the search ourselves for the answers that have not yet been discovered' (Seneca 1969, 189). Contrary to the views expressed by neo-liberals, understanding and learning from moral science and past economists is 'the way to liberate the spirit that still needs to be rescued from its miserable state of slavery' (Seneca 1969, 189).

In addition to transforming economics into an ahistorical and value-free science, neo-liberals have also managed to successfully spread their distorted and misleading concept of freedom on a global scale. The neo-liberal concept of freedom and the notion that economics is a value-free science played significant roles in justifying the limitation of state actions designed to achieve the common good. Before the rise of neo-liberalism, efforts to define the concept of freedom, identify its components, and determine the ideal conditions to achieve it spanned centuries. However, neo-liberal economists have rejected much of the work and many of the ideas put forth on the subject of freedom by countless renowned philosophers and political thinkers since the times of Ancient Greece. To be more precise, they elected to ignore, criticize, and suppress the various conceptions of freedom developed over the course of human history, in favour of formulating their own version derived from the principles and values of neo-liberal economics. However, if economics is in fact a branch of the natural sciences, as neo-liberals like to claim, then its theorists and practitioners should not be accepted social scientists, which would suggest that they do not possess the knowledge, experience, or credentials required to define a political and philosophical concept like freedom, or advise on what the role of the state should be in order to secure its conditions. The achievement of the conditions of freedom and the formation of states were based on historical, political and philosophical movements. Consequently, they cannot be defined or understood according to the language, formulas, presentations and methodologies of mathematics that neo-liberal economists insist on using so as to be regarded as respected natural scientists.

Even though neo-liberal economists do not possess the knowledge, understanding, or credentials required to define a political and philosophical concept like freedom, they have convinced themselves that their version of freedom is superior to all other formulations or definitions of the concept. They explain that, contrary to artificially organized societies, the free-market system allows individuals to choose their own ends and pursue them in their own way, spontaneously and voluntarily, without coercive intervention on the part of the state aimed at achieving predetermined teleological ends. In fact, neo-liberals argue that such state interventions would eventually guide societies towards the 'road to serfdom.' To be more precise, they believe that imposing moral and ethical values on society so as to achieve the collective good brings more harm than benefit, because doing so violates freedom, disrupts the conditions of a free society, and eventually leads to the emergence of a totalitarian regime. Moreover, neo-liberal economists have managed to successfully use influential marketing and propaganda techniques to persuade the masses that positive state actions aimed at achieving the collective good are evil, coercive, and oppressive to economic freedom and freedom in general. After being exposed to sophisticated techniques of persuasion for decades, the masses are now convinced that such state interventions will eventually lead society to descend into totalitarianism, even though positive state actions are actually designed to advance the specific interests of common people, as they include public services and programs like state-funded housing, public transportation, free universal education and health care, welfare, and environmental protection. In other words, by limiting the role of the state in the achievement of the common good, the masses are largely prevented from realizing freedom in the sense of self-development and self-realisation. More specifically, when people lack certain necessary goods and services, such as adequate education, training, healthcare, housing, income, food, and information, they are unable to achieve self-development, which means they are not free. Nevertheless, neo-liberals have managed to convince the masses to defend and worship the neo-liberal concept of freedom, despite the fact that it does not provide them with genuine freedom. Therefore, when the masses defend freedom, they do not really understand what they are defending. Similarly, when they attack the paternalist state that aims to achieve the common good, they do not realize that their support for minimal state action undermines their own freedom. In reality, the neo-liberal ideology has managed to suppress genuine freedom by transforming the masses into homogenous, well-trained and narrow-minded consumers who are slaves to their self-interests.

Neo-liberals were concerned that moral and ethical judgements might have decisive roles in state policies if the definition of freedom were to include self-development, or the development of individual capacities and abilities, as a component. In other words, they were fully aware that supporting positive freedom would necessitate state intervention in order to help the masses achieve their highest development of individuality. Consequently, neo-liberals oppose all government efforts to create more just, fair and equal societies through the provision of social services and programs, which they claim are coercive because they violate individual and economic freedom. Accordingly, their definition of freedom, which is basically being free from coercion (or *negative freedom*), has been used as a tool to prevent governments from imposing policies and reforms intended to achieve the common good based on ethical or moral judgements. The widespread commitment to economic freedom and negative freedom over the last four decades has significantly weakened or eliminated the public welfare function of governments worldwide.

Despite their professed dedication to freedom, neo-liberals have never really cared about providing and maintaining the conditions of genuine freedom. Instead, they deliberately utilized the concepts of economic freedom and negative freedom to convince the general public that the free-market system was superior to any other form of societal organization. In other words, they merely used their over-simplified concept of freedom as a powerful tool to diminish support for alternative ideas of freedom, and promote the widespread implementation of free-market capitalism around the world, all in the absence of a strong and well-organized opposition.

Neo-liberals often argue that free-market capitalism results in the highest form of freedom, because it works spontaneously, without resorting to central deliberate planning in order to control people's decisions and actions. In reality, there is nothing spontaneous about free-market capitalism, as its conditions are centrally designed. Furthermore, the role of the state has not been reduced since the rise of neo-liberalism; rather, governments have modified their *raison d'être*. To be more precise, states no longer exist to protect the welfare of their citizens by providing them with social services and programs aimed at achieving the common good; instead, their main priority has become safeguarding the welfare of the corporate world, which is an important development, since the wealth and power of corporations are actually heavily dependent upon deregulation, public subsidies, and the occasional bailout. In fact, the voices of the masses are largely ignored when high level decisions that could significantly impact their lives for years to come are made by democratically elected leaders behind closed doors, whereas the privileged access granted to the corporate world ensures that its voice is heard loud and clear. Even though neo-liberals strongly advocate for limited state action and the elimination of many publicly-funded services and programs, they are actually quite tolerant of increases in government expenditures and public sector employment, provided that they are intended to help establish and sustain the conditions of a free-market system.

Given the major role that corporations play in important areas like investment, employment, productivity, economic growth, and technological innovation in the free-market system, states have become very proficient at protecting the power, wealth, property and rights of the corporate world. Over the last four decades, states have moved away from their traditional role of trying to achieve the common good for their citizens by providing them with services and programs designed to protect their interests, freedom, and rights. In fact, they have become largely impotent in terms of exercising their sovereign authority due to the widespread implementation of neo-liberal economic reforms and policies during that period. Meanwhile, corporations have amassed unprecedented levels of power, freedom and influence within society, to the extent that they have become leading actors in the social, political and economic lives of people. In addition to controlling many aspects of the global production and distribution of goods and services, corporations also fabricate the wants and desires of consumers, control and shape the direction of scientific research and technological innovation, exploit natural and human resources to the maximum extent possible, and influence the policies and reforms of states. The vastly expanded role of the corporate world in society, combined with the placement of greater limitations on the ability of states to intervene, has not only engendered poverty, misery, and social and economic inequality, it has also left countries ill-prepared for major crises, natural disasters, and the approaching environmental apocalypse.

Although corporations have a penchant for corrupting politicians, including by contributing to political campaigns in order to influence the legal framework, regulations, and policies for the benefit of their own interests, they have largely managed to avoid serious punishment for their socially irresponsible and destructive actions. As amoral entities with a mandate to maximize the profits of their shareholders, corporations feel no obligation to serve the interests of society, nor are they inclined to alter any of their business practices that have detrimental impacts on people and the environment. More accurately, they are fully prepared to undertake any actions that serve to maximize the profits of their shareholders, regardless of whether they are destructive, unethical, immoral, or even illegal. Much like mainstream economists, states have often sided with corporations since the rise of neo-liberalism, defending their business practices by firmly opposing genuine environmental regulations, labour rights, and protective trade measures that could limit the profit-making potential of the private sector, even though states were originally founded to protect the interests, safety, and security of their people. Presently, corporations rule societies with more influence and authority than most democratically-elected politicians, despite the fact that people fought for centuries to win their freedom and the right to be governed by elected representatives.

It could be argued that the unrestrained appetite for power, freedom, and destruction displayed by modern corporations is reminiscent of the Hobbesian State of Nature. According to Thomas Hobbes (1588–1679), the evil and purely self-interested nature of man in all his decisions and actions under all circumstances makes him prone to quarrel. Moreover, the purely self-interested nature of man meant the State of Nature was characterized by disorder and violence, where people lived in 'continual fear, and danger of violent death,' and 'the life of man' was 'solitary, poor, nasty, brutish, and short' (Hobbes 1998, 84). If two men living in the State of Nature wanted something that could not be simultaneously enjoyed by both of them, they became enemies. Furthermore, since these men had the 'Right of Nature,' (natural right) or the 'right to all things,' they were in unending combat with one another in search of power and individual self-interests, with death being the only possible outcome (Hobbes 1998, 96). In other words, there was 'a perpetual war of every man against his neighbour; and therefore everything is his that getteth it, and keepeth it by force' (Hobbes 1998, 164).

The powers and freedoms accumulated by corporations under the system of free-market capitalism has led them to conduct themselves as though they possess the 'Right of Nature' that governed the actions and decisions of primitive man prior to the formation of governments and the institutions of civil society. In the State of Nature, primitive man would create weapons and specific tools so that he could kill and destroy anybody that interfered with the advancement of his interests. Similarly, modern corporations also possess the will, incentive, and power, as well as a variety of tools and instruments, to overcome any obstacles to the achievement of their self-interests, including nature, competing firms, popular opposition, ideological antagonists, and government rules and regulations.

According to Hobbes, there were no moral and ethical responsibilities or legal boundaries in place to restrict what one could do in the State of Nature, as man had an unlimited right to all. That means people had unrestricted rights to freely pursue their desires, emotions, impulses, and compulsions. Similarly, there is no role for moral and ethical judgments, or social responsibility, in free-market capitalism. Moreover, the power and wealth possessed by corporations allows them to avoid having their freedom restrained by the legal system, meaning they do not experience many of the inconveniences faced by most members of civil society. Since corporations are amoral entities with no social responsibilities that face no legal repercussions when they break the law, they can act as though they have the 'Right of Nature,' which is why they do not hesitate to engage in destructive activities if it suits their interests. Consequently, the selfishness and destructiveness exhibited by contemporary corporations in the pursuit of ever-expanding profits resembles the actions of men in the State of

Nature, where nothing can be evaluated based on moral and ethical judgements (Hobbes 1998, 96). This is not particularly surprising given that the notions of right and wrong, and justice and injustice, are meaningless in free-market capitalism.

Hobbes (1998) argued the State of Nature was the worst possible situation that people could find themselves in, because they were locked in a perpetual violent and destructive conflict of all against all. Given the option, everybody would choose to escape the State of Nature and enter into civil society. Hobbesian civil society was formed through a social contract, where people gave up their freedom to all ('Right of Nature') and, instead, allowed a sovereign (an individual or a group of people) to act on their behalf so that they could live in a world of morality, law, and peace. Essentially, the fear of death combined with the desire to live a satisfactory life motivated people living in the State of Nature to mutually renounce their unlimited rights in favour of entering into a social contract. In doing so, people submitted themselves the absolute authority of the government, which would enforce the social contract through a legal system and sovereign power that were legitimized by the consent of the people. Consequently, when people disobey or breach the 'covenants' of civil society, thereby causing 'injuries to the person of the commonwealth,'[1] they have to be punished (Hobbes 1998, 99, 138).

According to Hobbes, even though living in a civil society means the state is granted coercive powers and authority, it is nonetheless preferable to living under the chaotic and intolerable conditions of the State of Nature. That said, he warned that every civil society would inevitably include some people who believe that the sovereign has too much power to be in the interests of the people, and take actions to try to mitigate its authority. However, he underscored the point that while some people might experience some inconveniences by submitting to a social contract, as that would mean they have given up their freedom to all, any setbacks would be relatively minor compared to the challenges they would face in the State of Nature.

Neo-liberals clearly do not share Hobbes' view that the state should play a positive role in securing and protecting the interests of its citizens,

[1] Hobbes (1998, 123) discussed three types of commonwealth: 'when the representative is one man, then is the commonwealth a MONARCHY: when an assembly of all that will come together, then it is a DEMOCRACY, or popular commonwealth: when an assembly of a part only, then it is called an ARISTOCRACY'.

given their extensive efforts to limit the role of the state, which has resulted in the corporate world gaining excessive power and influence over society. In fact, the business practices of corporations violate the terms of the Hobbesian Social Contract. More precisely, corporations operate as though they have an unlimited right to all, similar to the primitive man in the State of Nature, because they are amoral entities, face few legal restrictions on their activities, and are guided by what Hobbes would describe as 'a perpetual and restless desire of power after power' (Hobbes 1998, 66). Consequently, corporations have caused tremendous damage to the environment and adversely impacted the lives of billions of people across the planet. Hobbes (1998, 138) would likely not be overly surprised by these results, as he warned that 'many evil consequences' might emerge whenever an economic agent obtains too much power.

In the Hobbesian State of Nature, people were faced with perpetual war, as they were more or less equal to one another in terms of their wants, freedom and power, meaning that even the weakest man could kill the strongest one. To the contrary, there is no possibility of continuous and violent conflict between the corporate world and the masses under a system of free-market capitalism, as the latter does not have power, freedom, or 'the Right of Nature' possessed by the former. That is to say, free-market capitalism does not provide the masses with adequate means by which to defend their interests, lives and security against the actions of corporations. Furthermore, it has become abundantly clear that state interventions, the legal system, and moral and ethical values, which are associated with civil society, are largely ineffective when it comes to defending the rights of citizens against the needs and activities of modern corporations. Since the rise of neo-liberalism has essentially rendered the masses powerless when it comes to protecting their interests, corporations are not burdened by the fear of 'death and wounds' faced by the primitive man in the State of Nature, nor are they worried about being punished for disobeying the state's authority or breaching the law in a civil society. In other words, the destructive activities of modern corporations cannot be stopped through deadly force initiated by the masses, state authority, or the legal system. In fact, since corporations do not fear violence, death, or serious legal repercussions, their actions are far more destructive in terms of scale, longevity and intensity compared to those of any man in the State of Nature.

Under free-market capitalism, the legal system protects the interests of the corporate world at the expense of those of the masses. It has become abundantly evident that law enforcement applies different standards to the criminal activities of corporations compared to those of ordinary people. To be more precise, corporations have incomparable privileges when it comes to destroying the environment and depleting its natural sources, violating human and worker rights, and adversely impacting the health of people. For example, if an ordinary person were to physically harm others by poisoning their source of water, they would be punished accordingly by the legal system. However, when similar crimes are committed by corporations on a much larger scale, they rarely receive adequate punishment, particularly when considering the financial resources they have at their disposal. Moreover, many of their damaging and destructive activities are legitimized by free-market oriented reforms and regulations, which rarely hold corporations fully accountable for the negative impacts of their business practices.

There has been an abundance of literature throughout human history, explaining the necessity of state authority in achieving the conditions of the common good, which include freedom, security, safety, and peace. However, the dominance of neo-liberalism has largely eliminated state authority and its ability to safeguard the common good for its citizens in only a few short decades. It is unlikely that most people would have given up the extensive freedom and the rights to all that they possessed in the State of Nature unless they were certain that their freedom, safety, interests, and security would be safeguarded after entering into civil society. More specifically, primitive man may not have agreed to willingly forego his 'Right of Nature' and escape the State of Nature just to submit to the authority of a powerful and destructive entity, like a corporation, that possesses the ability to threaten the peace, freedom, safety, and security of the masses. Presently, the social contract leaves people completely disarmed against the power and influence of corporations, as a handful of these dominant and self-interested economic agents have managed to gain control over an abundance of the earth's natural resources and other means of production, while also enjoying many privileges that are not available to the masses. However, given that free-market capitalism has allowed the state, corporations and other powerful entities to break the terms of the social contract, the masses should be under no obligation to respect its terms either.

The significant expansion of corporate power, to the extent that corporations behave as though they possess the 'Right of Nature,' combined with the elimination of the paternalistic state, has contributed to greatly increasing social and economic inequality, poverty, and misery around the world, while also raising the likelihood of an impending environmental catastrophe. Unfortunately, even though it is now widely recognized that it may not be possible to recover from the unthinkable consequences of climate change and the destruction of the environment, there is little indication that corporations, consumers and governments are willing to undertake the drastic measures required to stave off such an outcome.

One might be tempted to blame Friedman, Hayek, and a few of their neo-liberal colleagues, as well as politicians like Reagan and Thatcher, for being the architects of the present situation, where the survival of humanity is threatened. The original mandate, values and principles of neo-liberalism were largely designed by Friedman and Hayek, who are often regarded as some kind of sages or spiritual leaders of free-market capitalism. The framework they provided was very attractive for the masses, because it appealed to the untrained, uncultivated, raw, unpolished, undeveloped and most primitive nature of human beings, by promoting individualism, selfishness, and the freedom to choose. At the same time, Reagan and Thatcher played considerable roles in establishing the most fertile environment in which neo-liberal reforms and policies could flourish and spread. Subsequently, a majority of world leaders of all ideological orientations followed suit and implemented neo-liberal reforms in their own countries, with some going much further Reagan and Thatcher could have foreseen, encouraged by armies of neo-liberal economists. In fact, it is entirely possible that Friedman and Hayek would have been opposed to many of the policies and reforms advocated by neo-liberal economists during the last two decades. They also might have objected to the extensive and destructive power accumulated by corporations. It must be remembered that their work and ideas were addressing the specific problems and issues of their time, which witnessed the destructive outcomes of the Great Depression, two world wars and the Cold War Era. Meanwhile, instead of addressing or resolving the issues and problems of their own time, most mainstream economists have focused on preserving and maintaining this outdated, amoral, and ahistorical ideology, even though many of them are not particularly familiar with the issues, problems, worries, and conditions of the Great Depression and Cold War Era. In doing so, they act as though the neo-liberal economic program of research is universal and applicable to any time and place.

For decades, neo-liberalism has served as an ideology, providing a worldview that has been widely adopted and adhered to on a global scale in order to achieve productivity, economic growth, and efficiency. During that time, neo-liberals have undertaken extensive efforts to ensure that critical, opposing and alternative views were ignored or silenced, even though the discipline of economics has been in need of significant changes for a long time. They have been largely successful in convincing the world that non-conformity with the ideas, principles, values, and policies of the free-market system is destructive and counterproductive. However, while the rise and dominance of neo-liberalism did bring unprecedented levels of technological innovation, productivity, wealth and economic growth, it did not reduce wars, poverty, hunger, inequality, or environmental problems. Instead, it has exacerbated global misery, pollution, climate change, environmental degradation, and the over-exploitation of natural resources. These and many of the other negative outcomes associated with the rise of neo-liberalism suggest that people, governments and businesses should not have been so inclined to trust and adopt neo-liberal economic reforms and policies without reservation. Nevertheless, neo-liberals have complete faith in their program of research and claim that problems only emerge when the conditions of a free-market economy are lacking. Furthermore, since mainstream economists do not have the humility to recognise the limits of their knowledge, they have been advancing on the same path towards the same destination, without taking a moment to engage in critical thinking. They have been persistent and relentlessly pushed for the implementation of the fundamental values, principles, means and strategies of free-market capitalism to economies around the world, in addition to all aspects of human life. Their considerable success in doing so means the neo-liberal economist may have become 'the destroyer of a civilization' that has not been designed by a single mind, but rather, was 'grown from the free efforts of millions of individuals' across history (Hayek 2008, 56).

Humanity has experienced many destructive man-made and natural catastrophes since the times of Ancient Greece, from which it has always managed to recover. However, things might be different this time, as the damage that neo-liberalism has inflicted upon the environment in less than half a century is so extensive that there are concerns about an existential threat to people and many of the other species they share the planet with. The real risk of an impending environmental apocalypse requires radical, but realistic, reforms in all areas of life. However, neo-liberalism cannot be radically reformed in a way that would allow it to retain its status as the leading economic school of thought, as one cannot remove the foundation from a building without demolishing the entire structure. Basically, societies will need to be significantly reorganized and restructured, with urgent changes to production processes, the distribution of goods and services, and the consumption habits of people, regardless of the inconveniences, economic losses, and reductions in material well-being and living standards that will be incurred. In all likelihood, such extensive changes will not be possible without relying upon considerable central planning designed to achieve the collective good, based on moral and ethical values. This level of planning would require highly moral and intellectual leaders who cannot be corrupted and rule wisely with the sole objective of achieving the common good, much like the philosopher-kings of Plato's Ideal State. Given the dire situation that humanity presently finds itself in, with the possibility of an approaching environmental apocalypse, there should be almost no limits as to what centrally planned governments are permitted to regulate in order to secure the collective good and avoid disaster. Ultimately, opponents of central planning will need to realize that it is 'where the public and private interest are most closely united, there is the public most advanced' (Hobbes 1998, 124).

References

Friedman, Milton. 2002 [1962]. *Capitalism and Freedom*. Chicago: The University of Chicago Press.

Hayek, F.A. 1979. *Law, Legislation and Liberty Volume 3: The Political Order of a Free People*. London: Routledge and Kegan Paul.

———. 2008 [1974]. The Pretense of Knowledge. In *A Free-Market Monetary System*. Auburn: Ludwig von Mises Institute. ISBN: 978-1-933550-37-4.

Hobbes, Thomas. 1998 [1996]. *Leviathan*. Edited by J.C.A. Gaskin. Oxford: Oxford University Press.

Mises, Ludwig von. 1998 [1949]. *Human Action: A Treatise on Economics*. Auburn: The Ludwig von Mises Institute.

Seneca. 1969 [65 AD]. *Letters from a Stoic*. London: Penguin Classics.

Index[1]

[1] Note: Page numbers followed by 'n' refer to notes.

B. Filip, *The Rise of Neo-liberalism and the Decline of Freedom*, Palgrave Insights into Apocalypse Economics,
https://doi.org/10.1007/978-3-030-61623-6

C

G

H

J

K

L

N

T

U

The manufacturer's authorised representative in the EU is Springer Nature Customer Service Centre GmbH, Europaplatz 3, 69115 Heidelberg, Germany. If you have any concerns regarding our products, please contact ProductSafety@springernature.com

Printed and bound by CPI Group (UK) Ltd, Croydon, CR0 4YY
30/09/2026
02225696-0005